Free Stuff For Seniors

by

Matthew Lesko

with

Mary Ann Martello

Contributing Editor
Andrew Naprawa

Senior Copy Editor
Martha Hess

Researchers
Caroline Pharmer, Julie Paul, Lynda Burns
Laurie Orr, Diann Turner

Production
Meserve Associates, Inc.

Production Designer
Beth Meserve

Production Staff
Peggy Yates; Caroline Fields

Cover Design
Jim Hammar

FREE STUFF FOR SENIORS, Copyright 1995 by Matthew Lesko with Mary Ann Martello. All rights reserved. Printed in the United States of America. Published by Information USA, Inc., P.O. Box E, Kensington, MD 20895.

Clip art used in this publication © New Vision Technologies, Inc.; Dynamic Graphics, Inc.; Totem Graphics; One Mile Up; Tech Pool; Image Club Graphics, Inc., and Corel Corp.

FIRST EDITION

Library of Congress Cataloging-in-Publication Date
    Lesko, Matthew
    Martello, Mary Ann

Free Stuff for Seniors

ISBN # 1-878346-30-X (paperback)

The information in this book is continually updated online through the CompuServe Information Service. For subscription information, call 800-524-3388 and ask for Representative 168.

Other books written by Matthew Lesko:

Getting Yours: The Complete Guide to Government Money

How to Get Free Tax Help

Information USA

The Computer Data and Database Source Book

The Maternity Sourcebook

Lesko's New Tech Sourcebook

The Investor's Information Sourcebook

The State Database Finder

The Federal Data Base Finder

Government Giveaways for Entrepreneurs II

The Great American Gripe Book II

What To Do When You Can't Afford Health Care

Lesko's Info-Power II

IRS Secrets, Shortcuts, and Savings

1001 Free Goodies and Cheapies

Free College Money, Termpapers & Sex(ed)

Table of Contents

Help With Diet and Exercise 119

Free Legal Help and Consumer Advice 135

Information USA, Inc.

Information USA, Inc.

Travel Cheap   257

Money, Help, and Cheap Tickets for Art Lovers 367

Directory of State Information   573

Introduction

I recently turned 50 and I wanted to celebrate. So, as an author of dozens of reference books on government information, I decided to write this book that shows people my age and older that Uncle Sam has over 2,500 places you can turn to for free money, services, discounts, videos, help, publications, and more freebies.

All this stuff is one of the best kept secrets. Why? Because the government doesn't advertise. You'll never see signs in Washington, or anywhere else for that matter, saying **"Seniors can get $5,000 to fix up their home"**, or **"Seniors can get free videos on financial planning"**, or **"Take free college courses"**, or **"Travel free overseas."**

The government has hundreds of millions of dollars of goodies like these that it's giving away to seniors, but Uncle Sam doesn't spend a nickel telling people where to get them. With this book, you'll now know where to go to tap into all these goodies.

There's lots of free stuff in this book that seniors can use to solve serious problems like, how to **get free prescription drugs**, or how to get **free dentures**, or where to go to find the **latest treatment for Alzheimers**. But the book also has a whole lot of fun, neat stuff such as where to get **free tickets to the symphony, free sewing classes, free fishing videos, free speakers for your group**, and even a **Smithsonian exhibit for your next fundraiser**.

No matter what subject you may be interested in during your golden years...travel, gardening, or even sex, Uncle Sam has a free source that can make a difference in your life. So why not use it, you've already paid for it.

☆ ☆ ☆

Warning: This Book is Out of Date

Everything in our country is out of date the moment it is published. Your phone book is out of date as soon as you get it. Your newspaper is even out of date when it hits the streets.

We live in a fast changing world, and there is no way any of us in publishing can always have only the latest information in print. So please be patient. Although we updated and verified each listing right before printing, you may contact one of the offices in this book and find that the telephone number or program has changed.

For a wrong number you can always call the information operator in the city where the office is located and get a new listing. And, if you happen to contact an agency where the program has changed, be sure to ask that office if they know of any additional programs that may also satisfy your request. New programs are always being added or changed, or transferred to a local level.

☆ ☆ ☆

Dealing with Bureaucrats: Ten Basic Telephone Tips

An important part of your success in using this book is the careful handling of bureaucrats. Whether you are dealing with your local power company or with the government, you will be speaking to another human being. If you deal with them pleasantly and patiently, you will get quicker service and more of the publications and information that you are interested n.

Here are a few important tips to follow when you attempt to get information of any kind from a government agency over the telephone. Above all, remember that patience is often rewarded — even by weary government bureaucrats!

- **Introduce Yourself Cheerfully**
  Starting the conversation with a cordial and upbeat attitude will set the tone for the entire interview. Let the official know that this is not going to be just another mundane telephone call, but a pleasant interlude in an otherwise hectic day.

- **Be Open and Candid**
  Be as candid as possible with your source. If you are evasive or deceitful in explaining your needs or motives, your source will be reluctant to provide you with anything but the most basic information.

- **Be Optimistic**
  Relay a sense of confidence
  throughout the conversation. If you
  call and say "You probably aren't
  the right person" or "You don't have
  any information, do you?" it's easy
  for the person to respond, "You're
  right, I can't help you." A positive
  attitude encourages your source to
  dig deeper for an answer to your
  question.

- **Be Courteous**
  You can be optimistic and still be
  courteous. Remember the old adage
  that you can catch more flies with
  honey than you can with vinegar?
  Government officials love to tell
  others what they know, as long as
  their position of authority is not
  questioned or threatened.

- **Be Concise**
  State your problem simply. Be
  direct. A long-winded explanation
  may bore your contact and reduce
  your chances for getting a thorough
  response.

- **Don't Be A "Gimme"**
  A "gimme" is someone who expects
  instant answers and displays a "give

me that" attitude. Be considerate and sensitive to your contact's time, feelings, and eccentricities. Although, as a taxpayer, you may feel you have the right to put this government worker through the mill, that kind of attitude will only cause the contact to give you minimal assistance.

- **Be Complimentary**
  This goes hand in hand with being courteous. A well-placed compliment ("Everyone I spoke to said you are the person I need to ask.") about your source's expertise or insight will serve you well. We all like to feel like an "expert" when it comes to doing our job.

- **Be Conversational**
  Briefly mention a few irrelevant topics such as the weather or the latest political campaign. The more conversational you are without being too chatty, the more likely your source will be to open up and want to help you.

- **Return the Favor**
  You might share with your source information or even gossip you have

picked up elsewhere. However, be
certain not to betray the trust of
either your client or another source.
If you do not have any relevant
information to share at that moment,
call back when you are farther along
in your research.

- **Send Thank You Notes**
A short note, typed or handwritten,
will help ensure that a government
official source will be just as
cooperative in answering future
questions.

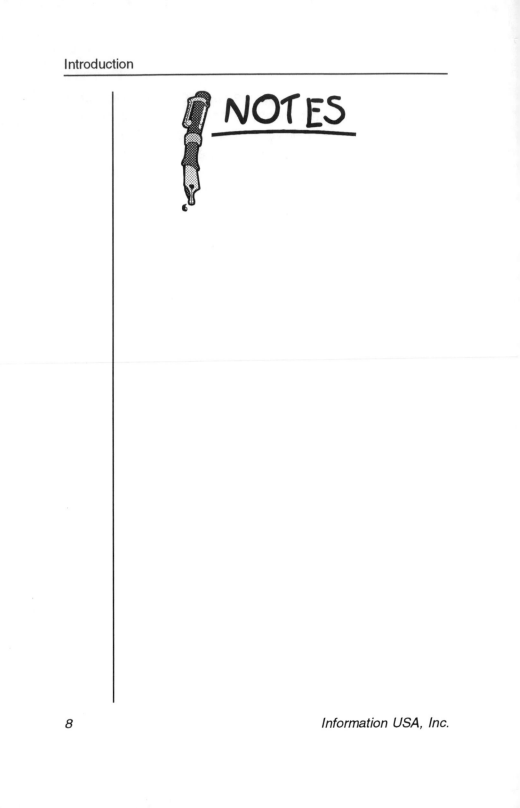

Free Help To Get A Job

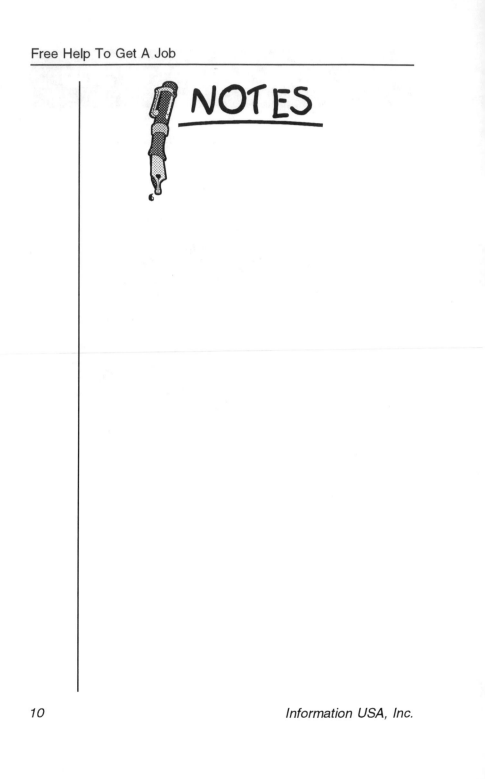

America's population is aging. In fact, by the year 2000 the number of Americans over the age of 65 will exceed the entire population of Canada. The problem is — when they retire, many will discover that their Social Security and pension income just isn't enough to make ends meet. That could very well mean a short retirement for many.

If you find that you do need a job but don't have the skills, there's plenty of free help. All across the country there are free job training programs set up just for seniors who need help getting the job skills they need even if you:

- haven't worked in a long time

- never worked outside the home

- have limitations on your ability to work

- live in a small town or in the country

- receive Social Security income

- do not have a high school education

Free Job Training and Part-Time Jobs

The Senior Community Service Employment program offers part-time training and employment opportunities for eligible low-income persons 55 years of age and older in a variety of public or private nonprofit community service settings, such as senior centers, nutrition programs, social service agencies, libraries, environmental projects, and many others.

The program provides seniors with income and the opportunity to learn new skills or improve the ones they already have. The program also helps you make the transition to the private job market through training, job search support and counseling.

Typical program participants work at such jobs as:
- activities coordinator
- bookkeeper
- cashier
- clerk typist
- custodian
- data entry clerk
- day care worker
- driver

- food service worker
- grounds keeper
- mechanic
- receptionist
- salesperson
- security guard
- teacher's aide

The Job Training Partnership Act program (JTPA) trains and places older workers in full- and part-time jobs with private businesses. Program participants not only receive on-the-job  experience, but also have an opportunity to develop job skills and good work habits.

Other services available to seniors in this program include job counseling, help writing your resume, job searches and classroom training. Participating businesses who hire JTPA graduates receive financial and tax incentives for doing so.

The offices listed below will help direct you to job training programs for older workers in your area. They are also great sources for information about general assistance programs for the elderly.

State Job Programs

Alabama
Commission on Aging
770 Washington Ave.
RSA Plaza, Suite 470
Montgomery, AL 36130
205-242-5743
This office can refer to Senior Community Service Employment Program (Title V) sites in your area and general programs and benefits available to older Americans. By calling the National Council on Senior Citizens (phone 202-347-8800) for regional help with Title V through the Senior Aides Program. The National Caucus on Black Aging (205-265-1451) can give you regional assistance with Title V in nine counties, including Montgomery.

Department of Economic and Community Affairs
401 Adams Ave.
P.O. Box 5690
Montgomery, AL 36103-5690
205-242-5300
This office will refer you to Job Training Partnership Act (JTPA) sites in your area.

Alaska
Older Alaskans Commissions
P.O. Box 110209
Juneau, AK 99811

333 Willoughby Ave.
Juneau, AK 99801
907-465-3250

907-465-4873
These offices can refer you to Senior Community Service Employment Program (Title V) sites in your area, and give you information on other programs and benefits available to older Americans. They can also send you the *1992 Directory for Older Alaskans.*

Department of Community and Regional Affairs
150 Third St.
P.O. Box 112100
Juneau, AK 99811-2100
907-465-4814
This office will refer you to Job Training Partnership Act (JTPA) sites in your area.

Arizona
Department of Economic Security
Aging and Adult Administration, 950A
1789 W. Jefferson
Phoenix, AZ 85007
602-542-4446
This office will refer you to Senior Community Service Employment Program (Title V) and Job Training Partnership Act (JTPA) sites in your area. They can also send you the free resource guide, *Senior Pages*, and information about other programs and benefits available to older Americans.

Arkansas
Arkansas Division of Aging and Adult Services
P.O. Box 1437
Slot 1412
Little Rock, AR 72203
501-682-2441
501-682-8525
This office can refer you to Senior Community Service Employment Program (Title V) sites in your area. By calling the Arkansas Able program (501-374-1318), you can also get more information on senior employment opportunities.

JTPA
Department of Labor
500 West Markham
220 West Wing
Little Rock, AR 72201
501-371-4484
This office will refer you to Job Training Partnership Act (JTPA) sites in
your area.

California
California Department of Aging
Administrative Services Branch
Senior Employment (Title V) Section
1600 K St.
Sacramento, CA 95814
916-323-0217
916-323-7515
This office will refer you to Senior Community Service Employment
Program (Title V) sites in your area and to regional Private Industry
Council offices (phone 800-FOR-A-JOB) for employment information.
They will also send you fact sheets on Title V, JTPA, and Older
Workers. The Job Training Coordinating Council (phone 916-322-2116)
can also provide information on job training for older Americans.

JTPA
·State of California
Employment Development Department
750 N St., Mic 69
Sacramento, CA 95814
916-654-7110
This office will refer you to Senior Community Service Employment
Program (Title V) sites in your area, and provide you with information
on programs and benefits available to older Americans.

Colorado
Governors Job Training Office
720 S. Colorado Building, Suite 550
Denver, CO 80222
303-758-5020

This office will refer you to Job Training Partnership Act (JTPA) sites in your area.

Connecticut

Department of Social Services
Elderly Services Division
175 Main St.
Hartford, CT 06106
800-443-9946
203-566-2768
This office will refer you to Senior Community Service Employment Program (Title V) and Job Training Partnership Act (JTPA) sites in your area. They can also give you information on the Older Worker Support Network for employment and training programs for low-income persons age 55 and older (state funded program).

Delaware

Division of Aging
Health and Social Services Department
1901 North DuPont Hwy.
Main Building, 2nd Floor Annex
New Castle, DE 19720
302-577-4660, ext. 24
This office will refer you to Job Training Partnership Act (JTPA) sites in your area. They also have information on the Career Exploration Program, Prime Time, a program for workers are 55 and older to provide workshops, training and job placement (phone 302-573-2474)

District of Columbia

DC Office on Aging
1424 K St. NW, 2nd Floor
Washington, DC 20005
202-724-5622
202-724-3662
This office will refer you to Senior Community Service Employment Program (Title V) and Job Training Partnership Act (JTPA) sites in your area. They also have information on the Over 60 Employment program information.

Department of Employment Service
500 C St. NW, Room 327
Washington, DC 20001
202-724-7073
This office will refer you to the Senior Aid Program which can in turn
refer you to Senior Community Service Employment Program (Title V)
and Job Training Partnership Act (JTPA) sites in your area.

Florida
Aging and Adult Services
1317 Winewood
Building 2, Room 323
Tallahassee, FL 32399
904-922-2078
This office will refer you to Senior Community Service Employment
Program (Title V) and Job Training Partnership Act (JTPA) sites in
your area.

Georgia
Department of Human Services
Division of Aging Services
2 Peachtree St.
18th Floor
Atlanta, GA 30303
404-657-5258
404-657-5330
This office will refer you to Senior Community Service Employment
Program (Title V) and Job Training Partnership Act (JTPA) sites in
your area.

Hawaii
Executive Office on Aging
Office of the Governor
335 Merchant St.
Suite 241
Honolulu, HI 96813
808-586-0100
This office will refer you to Job Training Partnership Act (JTPA) sites in
your area.

Office of Employment and Training
Department of Labor
830 Punchbowl, Room 316
Honolulu, HI 96813
808-586-9054/9055
This office will refer you to Senior Community Service Employment
Program (Title V) sites in your area.

Idaho
Office on Aging
Statehouse, Room 108
Boise, ID 83720
208-334-3833
This office will refer you to Senior Community Service Employment
Program (Title V) and Job Training Partnership Act (JTPA) sites in
your area (free brochures are available). Call the ElderCare Locator to
provide community services, including local employment contacts (800-
677-1116). Also, an Older Worker Employment Program staff listing is
available.

Illinois
Department on Aging
421 East Capitol Ave.
Springfield, IL 62701
217-785-0117
800-252-8966
This office will refer you to Area Agencies on Aging that can in turn
provide you with Senior Community Service Employment Program
(Title V) sites in your area.

Department of Commerce and Community Affairs
620 East Adams
Springfield, IL 62701
217-782-7500
217-785-6006
This office will refer you to Job Training Partnership Act (JTPA) sites in
your area.

Indiana
Disability, Rehabilitation and Aging Services
Family and Social Services Administration
402 West Washington St.
Indianapolis, Indiana 46207
317-232-7000
317-232-7459
This office will refer you to Job Training Partnership Act (JTPA) sites in your area.

Iowa
Department of Elder Affairs
914 Grand, 2nd Floor
Des Moines, IA 50309
512-242-4778
This office will refer you to Job Training Partnership Act (JTPA) sites in your area.

Kansas
Department of Aging
Docking State Office Building, 1st Floor
915 SW Harrison
Topeka, KS 66612
913-296-4986
This office will refer you to Senior Community Service Employment Program (Title V) and Job Training Partnership Act (JTPA) sites in your area. They can also refer you to Older Kansans Employment Program (same services as JTPA, but is state funded) sites in your area. Three other programs receive local or private funds for job referral and training: New Directions Program, Services for Seniors, Inc., and Project EARN. Ask for the free booklet, *Employment Services for Workers 55 and Over.*

Kentucky
Aging Services Division
Department for Social Services
275 East Main St., 6th Floor W.
Frankfort, KY 40621

502-564-6930
This office will refer you to Senior Community Service Employment Program (Title V) sites in your area. The free booklet, *Senior Community Service Employment Program,* will explain the benefits under this program.

JTPA Coordinator
Cabinet for Human Resources
Department for Employment Services
275 East Main St.
Frankfort, KY 40621
502-564-5360
This office will refer you to Job Training Partnership Act (JTPA) sites in your area.

Louisiana
Office of Elderly Affairs
Office of the Governor
P.O. Box 80374
Baton Rouge, LA 70898
504-925-1700
This office will refer you to Senior Community Service Employment Program (Title V) and Job Training Partnership Act (JTPA) sites in your area. Ask for the free fact sheet on employment programs.

Maine
Bureau of Maine's Elderly
Department of Human Services
State House Station #11
Augusta, ME 04333
207-624-5335
This office will refer you to Senior Community Service Employment Program (Title V) sites in your area.

Bureau of Employment and Training
Department of Labor
Hospital St.
Station #55
Augusta, ME 04333

207-287-3377
This office will refer you to Job Training Partnership Act (JTPA) sites in your area.

Maryland
Maryland Office on Aging
301 Preston St., Room 1004
Baltimore, MD 21201
410-225-1102
800-AGE-DIAL
This office will refer you to Senior Information and Assistance Office in each county that can in turn refer you to Senior Community Service Employment Program (Title V) and Job Training Partnership Act (JTPA) sites in your area. Be sure to ask for the free booklet, *Senior Information and Assistance on Benefits and Services for Older Persons.*

Massachusetts
Executive Office of Elder Affairs
One Ashburton Place
Boston, MA 02108
617-727-7750
800-882-2003
This office will refer you to special employment services in the area.

Michigan
Office of Services to the Aging
P.O. Box 30026
Lansing, MI 48909
517-373-4068
This office will refer you to Senior Community Service Employment Program (Title V) sites in your area.

Michigan Job Team
201 N. Washington Square
Victor Office Center, 4th Floor
Lansing, MI 48913
517-373-6227

This office will refer you to Job Training Partnership Act (JTPA) sites in your area.

Minnesota

Minnesota Board on Aging
Human Service Building, 4th Floor
444 Lafayette Rd.
St. Paul, MN 55155
612-296-2770
800-456-8519
This office will refer you to general programs and services for older Americans in your area.

Program Specialist
Community Based Services
Department of Jobs and Training
390 N. Robert St., Room 125
St. Paul, MN 55101
612-297-1054
This office will refer you to Senior Community Service Employment Program (Title and Job Training Partnership Act (JTPA) sites in your area.

Missouri

Division of Aging
Department of Social Services
P.O. Box 1337
Jefferson City, MO 65102
314-751-3082
This office will refer you to Senior Community Service Employment Program (Title V) sites in your area.

Division of Job Development and Training
221 Metro
Jefferson City, MO 65109
314-751-7896
800-877-8698
This office will refer you to Experienced Worker Program (JTPA) sites in your area.

Montana

Green Thumb
Box 2587
Great Falls, MT 59403
406-761-4821
This office will refer you to Senior Community Service Employment
Program (Title V) sites in your area.

Montana JTP, Inc.
101 N. Last Chance Gulch
Helena, MT 59601
406-444-1309
This office will refer you to Job Training Partnership Act (JTPA) sites in
your area.

Aging Coordinator
Governor's Office on Aging
Capitol Station
Helena, MT 59620
406-444-3111
This office will refer you to programs and benefits available to older
Americans, including job training.

Nebraska

Department on Aging
301 Centennial Mall S.
P.O. Box 95044
Lincoln, NE 68509
402-471-2306
This office will refer you to Senior Community Service Employment
Program (Title V) and Job Training Partnership Act (JTPA) sites in
your area. They'll also refer you to Older Worker Initiatives in
Nebraska.

Nevada

AARP
330 W. Washington, Suite 10
Las Vegas, NV 89106
702-648-3356

This office will refer you to Senior Community Service Employment Program (Title V) sites in your area.

Nevada Business Services
930 W. Owens
N. Las Vegas, NV 89106
702-647-7618
This office will refer you to Job Training Partnership Act (JTPA) sites in your area.

Division for Aging Services
340 N. 11th St., Suite 114
Las Vegas, NV 89101
702-486-3545
This office will refer you to general programs and benefits available to older Americans.

New Hampshire
AARP
P.O. Box 398
Main and Grove Sts.
North Conway, NH 03860
603-356-3117
800-652-8808
This office will refer you to Senior Community Service Employment Program (Title V) sites in your area. They will also send you free copies of the *New Hampshire Older Worker Employment Network Directory* and the *Senior Employment Program* brochure.

Job Training Council
64 Old Suncook Rd.
Concord, New Hampshire 03301-5134
800-772-7001 (NH only)
603-228-9500
This office will refer you to Job Training Partnership Act (JTPA) sites in your area.

Division of Elderly and Adult Services
Department of Health and Human Services
115 Pleasant St., Annex Bldg., #1
State Office Park South

Concord, NH 03301-3843
603-271-4680
This office will refer you to general programs and benefits available to older Americans.

New Jersey
New Jersey Division on Aging
Department of Community Affairs
101 South Broad St., CN 807
Trenton, NJ 08625
609-292-4833
This office will refer you to Senior Citizens Information and Referral Service (phone 800-792-8820) and your Area Agency on Aging that in turn can refer you to Senior Community Service Employment Program (Title V) sites in your area. This office also has information on ACTION programs that offer volunteer opportunities through the Foster Grandparent Program (FGP) and the Senior Companion Program (SCP). Ask for the free guide, *Federal Programs for Older Persons.*

Department of Environmental Protection and Energy
Division of Personnel
Recruitment Unit
440 East State St., CN 408
Trenton, NJ 08625-0408
609-295-6453
This office will refer you to Senior Environmental Employment Program (SEEP) site in your area.

New Jersey Department of Labor
Division of Employment and Training, CN 055
Trenton, NJ 08625-0055
609-292-5005
This office will refer you to Job Training Partnership Act (JTPA) sites in your area.

New Mexico
State Agency on Aging
224 East Palace Ave., 4th Floor
Santa Fe, NM 87503

505-827-7640
800-432-2080
This office will refer you to Senior Community Service Employment
Program (Title V) sites in your area (free brochure available).

State Department of Labor
Job Training Division
1596 Pacheco St.
Santa Fe, NM 87504
505-827-6827
This office will refer you to Job Training Partnership Act (JTPA) sites in
your area.

New York

State Office For the Aging
2 Empire State Plaza
Albany, NY 12223-0001
518-474-4425
518-474-1946
800-342-9871
This office will refer you to local offices for the aging that in turn can
refer you to Senior Community Service Employment Program (Title V)
and Job Training Partnership Act (JTPA) sites in your area (free
briefing books available).

North Carolina

Department of Human Resources
Division of Aging
693 Palmer Dr.
Raleigh, NC 27626-2531
919-733-3983
This office will refer you to Senior Community Service Employment
Program (Title V) sites in your area. A free program description and
history is available.

Department of Commerce
Division of Employment and Training
111 Seaboard Ave.
Raleigh, NC 27604

919-733-6383
This office will refer you to Job Training Partnership Act (JTPA) sites in your area.

North Dakota
Department of Human Services
Aging Services Division
1929 North Washington
Bismarck, ND 58501
701-224-2577
701-224-2825
This office will refer you to Job Training Partnership Act (JTPA) sites in your area.

Green Thumb
1424 West Century Ave.
P.O. Box 7068
Bismarck, ND 58501
701-258-8879
This office will refer you to Senior Community Service Employment Program (Title V) sites in your area.

Ohio
Department of Aging
50 West Broad St., 9th Floor
Columbus, OH 43266-0501
614-466-5500
614-466-1242
This office will refer you to Senior Community Service Employment Program (Title V) sites in your area.

JTPA Division
Ohio Employment Service Division
145 S. Front St.
P.O. Box 1618
Columbus, OH 43216-1618
614-466-3817
This office will refer you to local contact for Job Training Partnership Act (JTPA) sites in your area.

Oklahoma

Employment Security Commission
1401 N. Lincoln
Will Rogers Building, Room 408
Oklahoma City, OK 73105
405-557-5328
This office will refer you to Senior Community Service Employment Program (Title V) and Job Training Partnership Act (JTPA) sites in your area.

Department of Human Services
Aging Services
P.O. Box 25352
Oklahoma City, OK 73125
405-521-2327
This office will refer you to programs and benefits available to older Americans, and information on the Older Americans Act.

Oregon

Department of Human Services
Senior and Disabled Services Division
500 Summer St., NE
Salem, OR 97310
503-378-4728
503-945-6413
This office will refer you to Senior Community Service Employment Program (Title V) sites in your area.

JTPA
State Economic Development
775 Summer St., NE
Salem, OR 97310
503-373-1995
This office will refer you to Job Training Partnership Act (JTPA) sites in your area.

Pennsylvania

Department of Aging
400 Market St.

State Office Building, 6th Floor
Harrisburg, PA 17101
717-783-1550
717-783-6007
This office will refer you to Senior Community Service Employment
Program (Title V) sites in your area.

Department of Labor and Industry
Bureau of Employment Services and Training
7th and Forster Sts.
11th Floor
Harrisburg, PA 17120
717-783-0142
This office will refer you to local contact who in turn can refer you to
Job Training Partnership Act (JTPA) sites in your area.

Rhode Island
Department of Elderly Affairs
160 Pine St.
Providence, RI 02903
401-277-6157
This office will refer you to Senior Community Service Employment
Program (Title V) and Job Training Partnership Act (JTPA) sites in
your area.

South Carolina
Governors Office
Division on Aging
400 Arbor Lake Dr., Suite B-500
Columbia, SC 29223
803-735-0210
This office will refer you to Senior Community Service Employment
Program (Title V) sites in your area. They also have information on
Operation Able, a worker/job match service.

JTPA SAU
Employment Security Commission
P.O. Box 1406
Columbia, SC 29202

803-737-2611
This office will refer you to local contacts that in turn can refer you to Job Training Partnership Act (JTPA) sites in your area.

South Dakota

Adult Services and Aging Division
700 Governors Dr.
Pierre, SD 57501
605-332-7991
This office will refer you to Senior Community Service Employment Program (Title V) sites in your area.

JTPA
Department of Labor
700 Governors Dr.
Pierre, SD 57501-2291
605-773-5017
This office will refer you to Job Training Partnership Act (JTPA) sites in your area.

Tennessee

Commission on Aging
706 Church St., Suite 201
Doctors Building
Nashville, TN 37243-0860
615-741-2056
This office will refer you to Senior Community Service Employment Program (Title V) sites in your area.

JTPA
Department of Labor
4th Floor, Gateway Plaza
710 James Robertson Pkwy.
Nashville, TN 37243-0658
615-741-1031
This office will refer you to Job Training Partnership Act (JTPA) sites in your area.

Texas
Senior Texans Employment Program
P.O. Box 7186
Waco, TX 76714
817-776-4700
This office will refer you to Senior Community Service Employment Program (Title V) sites in your area. Texas also has a state funded program identical to Title V that provides the elderly with job training.

Workforce Development Division
First City Center
816 Congress Ave.
Austin, TX 78701
512-320-9800
This office will refer you to Job Training Partnership Act (JTPA) sites in your area.

Utah
Department of Human Services
Division of Aging and Adult Services
120 North 200 West
Room 401
4th Floor
Salt Lake City, UT 84103
801-538-3910
This office will refer you to Senior Community Service Employment Program (Title V) sites in your area. Call the Senior Employment (phone 801-468-2785) for additional Title V program assistance.
Ask for a free copy of the *Senior Resource Directory*, which includes referral numbers for numerous older worker programs.

JTPA
Economic Development and Training Division
2001 South State, S1600
Salt Lake City, UT 84190-3730
801-468-3247
This office will refer you to Job Training Partnership Act (JTPA) sites in your area.

Vermont
Department of Aging and Disabilities
Waterbury, VT 05671-2301
802-241-2400
This office will refer you to employment resources.

Vocational Rehabilitation
Senior Community Service Employment Program
103 S. Main St.
Waterbury, VT 05671-2303
802-241-2184
This office will refer you to Senior Community Service Employment
Program (Title V) in your area.

Virginia
Department For the Aging
700 East Franklin St., 10th Floor
Richmond, VA 23230
804-367-9818
This office will refer you to Senior Community Service Employment
Program (Title V) and Job Training Partnership Act (JTPA) sites in
your area. Ask for a Title V and JTPA directory with complete list of
local contacts.

Washington
Employment Security Department
Employment and Training Division
P.O. Box 9046
Olympia, WA 98506-9046
206-438-4643
This office will refer you to Job Training Partnership Act (JTPA) sites in
your area.

West Virginia
Commission on Aging
1900 Kanawha Building E.
Charleston, WV 25305-0160
304-558-3317

This office will refer you to Senior Community Service Employment Program (Title V) sites in your area.

JTPA
Employment Services
States College University System
1018 Kanawha Building E, Suite 700
Charleston, WV 25301
204-558-2664
This office will refer you to Senior Community Service Employment Program (Title V) sites in your area.

Wisconsin
Division of Jobs, Employment, and Training Services
Department of Industry
Labor and Human Relations
P.O. Box 7972
Madison, WI 53707
608-266-6886
This office will refer you to Job Training Partnership Act (JTPA) sites in your area.

Wyoming
Wyoming Senior Citizens, Inc.
413 West 18th St.
Cheyenne, WY 82001
307-635-1245
This office will refer you to Senior Community Service Employment Program (Title V) and Job Training Partnership Act (JTPA) sites in your area.

Department of Health
Division on Aging
139 Hathaway Building
Cheyenne, WY 82002
307-777-7986
This office will refer you to programs and benefits available to older Americans.

Get A Job With
The Forest Service

If you are over 55 years of age and meet some income eligibility guidelines, you may be a candidate for the Senior Community Service Employment Program (SCSEP).

This program provides part-time outdoor and indoor employment and training opportunities, while providing community services to the general public. Employees work an average of 20 hours per week at a nearby Forest Service Office in their local community. They are paid at least the federal or state minimum wage, receive training and skill upgrading, health programs, and more.

SCSEP supplements the permanent Forest Service workforce. You can be assigned a variety of jobs including visitor information, receptionist, computer aide, carpenter, researcher, or more.

To learn about the program, contact your local Forest Service office or U.S. Forest Service, U.S. Department of Agriculture, Human Resource Programs, P.O. Box 96090, Washington, DC 20090; 703-235-8855.

Make $15/hr With The EPA

The Environmental Protection Agency (EPA) has a special program for hiring senior citizens 55 years and over. When an EPA regional office has a shortage of workers, they  notify one of the organizations listed below, which in turn recruit workers.

Senior citizens get involved in all kinds of activities from conducting national surveys to fulfilling general administrative tasks. The jobs carry unemployment, workmen's compensation, Social Security, and health benefits.

There are 4 levels of pay:

Level 1 - Xerox operators, messengers, telephone assistants; $6-$8
Level 2 - secretaries, administrative assistants; $7.25-$10
Level 3 - writers and editors; $8.50-$11

Level 4 - professionals with relevant
degrees; $10.50-$15

For general information contact: Senior
Environmental Employment Program
(SEE), U.S. Environmental Protection
Agency, Office of Research and
Development of Exploratory Research,
Washington, DC 20460; 202-260-2574.

For recruitment information contact:
American Association of Retired Persons,
601 E St., NW, Washington, DC 20049;
202-434-6153.

National Association for Hispanic Elderly,
2727 West 6th St., Los Angeles, CA
90057; 213-487-1922.

National Caucus and Center on Black
Aged, Suite 500, 1424 K St., NW,
Washington, DC 20005; 202-637-8400.

National Council of Senior Citizens, 1331 F
St., NW, Washington, DC 20004;
202-627-9500.

National Council on the Aging, 409 Third
St., SW, Washington, DC 20024;
202-479-1200.

National Pacific/Asian Resource Center on Aging, Suite 410, 2033 6th Ave., Seattle, WA 98121; 216-448-0313.

☆ ☆ ☆

You Are Not The Only One

Feel like you are in the minority at work because you are over 60? You won't feel that way for long.

A report from the General Accounting Office (GAO) shows that the 55 and older age group will be the fastest growing group in the labor force. The report also outlines some options employers are considering in order to deal with the changing demographics, and looks at some different types of retirement. You can also learn from GAO reports that 28% of all the cases filed with the Equal Employment Opportunity Commission (EEOC) deal with age discrimination. You can find out how the EEOC handles complaints, their procedures, and more.

The GAO is the investigative arm of the Congress and conducts audits and evaluations of government programs and activities. The following are reports dealing with employment issues:

- *Multiple Employment Training Programs: Overlap Among Programs Raises Questions About Efficiency* (HEHS 94-193)
- *Federal Personnel: Employment Policy Challenges Created by an Aging Workforce* (GAO/GGD 93-138)
- *The Changing Workforce: Demographic Issues Facing Employers* (GAO/T-GGD 92-61)
- *Age Employment Discrimination: EEOC's Investigation of Charges Under 1967 Law*
- *EEOC: An Overview* (GAO/T-HRD 93-30)

All reports are free and can be requested by contacting U.S. General Accounting Office, P.O. Box 6015, Gaithersburg, MD 20884; 202-512-6000.

☆ ☆ ☆

Work Or Retire? It's Up To You

For many people over 60, their job is something they love and enjoy. For others work is what helps pay the bills.

Many seniors look forward to retirement. You can find out how the work force is changing, and that if you keep working your age group will soon control the watercooler.

If you retire, the retirement plans are becoming more complex and varied in order to meet the needs of both the companies and their employees. You can learn about various retirement options on how to make the transition from work to retirement.

The Congressional Research Service (CRS) writes reports which provide an understandable overview of the topic and provide relevant newspaper articles and bibliographies. These reports are free but must be requested through your Congressman. CRS reports dealing with employment include:

- *Age Discrimination in Employment Act: Recent Enforcement Actions by the EEOC* (87-783A)
- *Early Retirement Incentive Plans under the Age Discrimination in Employment Act of 1967* (88-608A)
- *A Demographic Portrait of Older Workers* (88-636E)

- *Older Workers: The Transition to Retirement* (89-28E)
- *Age Discrimination in Employee Benefit Plans* (89-478A)

You can get these and other CRS reports by contacting Your Senator or Representative, The Capitol, Washington, DC 20510; 202-224-3121.

☆ ☆ ☆

Working and Caring

As the population ages, many workers are finding that they need to take care of their parents or spouse. Caregiving for elderly dependents can involve things such as transporting to doctors appointments, paying bills, or even helping with bathing, dressing, and meal preparation.

Eldercare is a concern to both employers and employees because of the time and stress involved in caregiving can be enormous.

The Family and Medical Leave Act allows employees to take up to 12 weeks of unpaid leave in any 12 month period for the birth or adoption of a child; acquiring a foster child; the serious illness of a child, spouse, or parent; and the serious illness of the employee. Employees must have been working for one year, at least 1,250 hours to qualify, and employers must have at least 50 workers.

The Work and Family Clearinghouse has a free Work and Family Resource Kit which provides an overview and options for eldercare. The Clearinghouse can show you how companies similar to yours have established resources and programs to help out this population.

AT&T, Stride-Rite, and Travelers have begun to design innovative programs to decrease employee caregiver problems; your company can too. The Clearinghouse can also answer your Family and Medical Leave questions.

For more information, contact Work and Family Clearinghouse, U.S. Department of Labor, Women's Bureau, 200 Constitution Ave., NW, Washington, DC 20210; 800-827-5335.

Free and Low Cost Dental Care

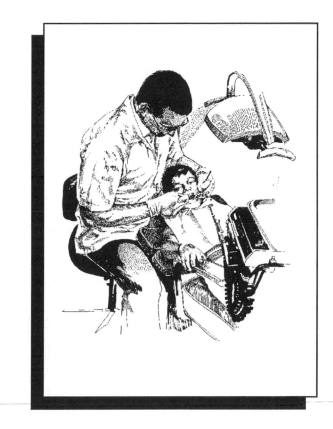

Don't let your teeth fall out just because you can't afford to go to a dentist. There are hundreds of programs across the country that offer free and low-cost dental care for seniors and practically anyone else who needs it, *often regardless of your income level*. If you know where and when to look, you may be able to get:

- free or low-cost dentures and repairs,
- automatic senior discounts of 15% to 80%,
- free at-home dental care if you can't get out,
- free dental implants by the best doctors in the world.

Most health insurance plans don't include dental coverage, and this means people often go without regular dental care simply because they think they can't afford it. But you may not be aware of the hundreds of programs that are designed for people like you — programs that actually require that you *don't* have dental insurance so that you can qualify to receive free or largely discounted dental care.

Here are some general examples of the kinds of programs funded all across the country:

Dental Care for the Elderly

You'll find that most states have special programs just for the elderly, especially those who have trouble finding money to pay for dental care on a limited income. Often dentists donate their time and services to make sure the elderly are taken care of. See the state-by-state listing on page 52.

☆ ☆ ☆

Dental Schools for Everyone

The best-kept secrets about low-cost dental care are the 53 dental schools across the country. They offer quality dental care at a fraction of the cost of private dentists. Many will even set up a repayment plan for you if you can't afford to pay the bill.

Also, researchers at many dental schools receive big money from the federal government to do cutting edge dental research, and these researchers often need patients to work on for free. Be sure to ask about any clinical research underway at the dental school nearest you. See state-by-state listing on page 52.

Free and Low Cost
Dental Clinics

Many state and local health departments
support dental clinics that offer their
services for free or on a sliding fee scale
basis. Services are usually limited to those
with limited income or those with special
needs. See state-by-state listing on page
52.

Free Dental Care
For Children

Almost every state runs some kind of
dental care
program to make
sure that kids
keep their teeth
in good shape.
Many of these
programs offer
their services for
free or at huge
discounts based
upon your ability
to pay. Your grandkids should know about
this. See state-by-state listing on page 52.

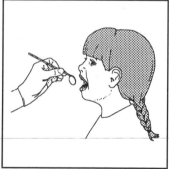

Dental Care for Disabled and Handicapped

There are special programs just for those with mental or physical disabilities, including those with mental retardation, cerebral palsy, multiple sclerosis, and much more.

Many states also have special programs that offer free care for children born with cleft palates. See the state-by-state listing on page 52.

☆ ☆ ☆

Free Dentures for Seniors

Don't sit around with false teeth that keep falling out when you eat or hurt so badly that you can't keep them in your mouth.

Many states have discount denture programs where you can receive big savings on false teeth, no matter what your age. See the state-by-state listing on page 52.

Information USA, Inc.

Free Tooth Implants and Impacted Molar Removal

These are just two of the many subjects that top dental researchers are studying at the National Institute of Dental Research which is part of the National Institutes of Health in Bethesda, Maryland. Also underway are studies on facial pain, taste disorders, herpes simplex, and dry mouth conditions.

Patients who participate in these clinical trials receive their dental care free of charge. For information about the clinical studies program at the National Institutes of Health, you or your doctor can contact: Clinical Center, National Institutes of Health, Bethesda, MD 20892, 301-496-2563.

☆ ☆ ☆

Dentists Who Get Government Grants to do Work for Free

Washington is not the only place where doctors receive government grants to conduct dental research and treat patients for free. Each year hundreds of dental schools and other dental research facilities around the country receive money to work on everything from gum disease to denture satisfaction.

You can contact the following office to receive information about on-going or up-coming dental research in your area.

National Institute of Dental Research
Research Data and Management
Information Section
5333 Westbard Ave., Room 539
Bethesda, MD 20814
301-594-7645

Another method of finding these doctors is by contacting the "Dental Schools" and "State Institutions Receiving Government Grants for Dental Research" in the state-by-state listing on page 52. Dental schools normally receive a good portion of available research, and the other listing represents those who received grant money last year.

Dentists on Wheels

If you have trouble getting around because of a handicap or other infirmity, some states, like Illinois, Arizona, and Missouri, have mobile dental vans that will actually come to your home or nursing home and provide you with dental care right there on the spot. See the state-by-state listing on page 52.

Dental Societies - Dentists Who Volunteer

Each state's Dental Society keeps track of free and low-cost dental programs in their state, so it's a good idea to call them if you have any questions or if you're interested in learning about any new dental programs that start up.

Some Dental Societies also act as a clearinghouse for identifying dentists who volunteer their services to those facing emergencies or those who have other special problems. See the state-by-state listing on page 52.

State-by-State Listing

Alabama
Dental Programs
Department of Public Health
Dental Health Division
434 Monroe St.
Montgomery, AL 36130
205-242-5760
Call your nearest Community Health Center or Clinic for information on reduced fees for dental care. Usually clinics offer a sliding fee scale-- qualifications vary. For example, some clinics will treat only children and senior citizens.

Dental School
School of Dentistry
University of Alabama
1919 Seventh Ave., South
Birmingham, AL 35394
205-934-2700
205-934-4546 (children)
Annual patient visits: 49,617.

Dental Society
Alabama Dental Association
836 Washington Ave.
Montgomery, AL 36104-3893
205-265-1684

Government Grants for Dental Research
Oakwood College
Grants: $4,644

University of Alabama at Birmingham
Birmingham, AL
Grants: $4,502,593

Alaska
Dental Programs
Social Services

Department of Public Health
P.O. Box 110610
Juneau, AL 99811-0610
907-561-4211
Limited dental care is available. Call your Community Health Center to get information about whether they offer dental.

Anchorage Neighborhood Health Center
1217 East 10th Ave.
Anchorage, AK 99501
907-257-4600
Call or write Anchorage Neighborhood Health Center to get information on reduced-fee dental services for adults and children. A sliding fee scale based on income is available.

Senior Citizen Discounts
Anchorage Dental Society
3400 Spenard Rd., Suite 10
Anchorage, AK 99503
907-279-9144
There are no special programs through the Dental Society; however, they do keep a list of referrals of dentists who will give discounts to senior citizens.

Dental Society
Alaska Dental Society
3400 Spenard Rd., Suite 10
Anchorage, AK 99503-3783
907-277-4675

Arizona
Dental Programs
Department of Health Services
Office of Dental Health
1740 West Adams St.
Phoenix, AZ 85007
602-542-1866
Low cost dental services are available through various Dental Clinics. Individuals must contact the Office of Dental Health to get eligibility requirements.

Fluoride and Sealant Programs are also available through the public schools. Some Indian Health Centers offer dental for tribal members.

McDowell Clinic
1314 E. McDowell St.
Phoenix, AZ 85006
602-252-1909
The McDowell Clinic provides basic dental work for individuals with HIV. The Area on Aging has contracted with the Office of Dental Health to provide dental services using portable equipment set up at local Senior Centers. Eligibility to access these services is determined by AAA.

Dental Society
Arizona State Dental Association
4131 N. 36th St.
Phoenix, AZ 85018-4761
602-957-4777

Arkansas
Dental Programs
Department of Health
Dental Division
4815 West Markham
Little Rock, AR 72201
501-661-2279
Limited dental care is available. Three clinics offer dental care at a reduced fee. Low-income is a major factor in determining eligibility. They will also see anyone who is in severe pain due to an emergency. All hospitals keep a listing of dentists who volunteer to treat emergencies. No special programs are available for handicapped or elderly.

Dental Society
Arkansas State Dental Association
920 W. 2nd St., #103
Little Rock, AR 72201-2125
501-372-3368

Government Grants for Dental Research
University of Arkansas at Fayetteville

Fayetteville, AR
Grants: $102,389

California
Dental Programs
Health Services Department
Oral Health
714 P St.
Sacramento, CA 95814
916-445-0174
Very limited dental care is available through some local Health Centers or Clinics on a sliding fee scale. You'll have to call each individually to see if dental is available.

Senior-Dent
California Dental Association
1201 K Street Mall
P.O. Box 13749
Sacramento, CA 95853
916-443-0505
800-736-7071
The *Senior-Dent Program* offers dental care at reduced fees to all qualified senior citizens. To qualify you must meet three eligibility requirements: 1) be 60 or older; 2) have an annual income of $16,000 or less; 3) not be receiving dental benefits from Denti-Cal or a dental insurance plan. Participating dentists offer at least a 15% discount. Call for additional information and a participating dentist.

Dental Schools
School of Dentistry
University of California, San Francisco
707 Parnassus Ave.
San Francisco, CA 94143
415-476-1891
Annual patient visits: 52,017.

School of Dentistry
University of California, Los Angeles
School of Dentistry
10833 LeConte Ave.
Los Angeles, CA 90024-1668

310-206-3904
Annual patient visits: 71,627.

School of Dentistry
University of Southern California
325 W. 34th St.
Los Angeles, CA 90089
213-740-2800
Annual patient visits: 31,000.

School of Dentistry
Loma Linda University
11092 Anderson St.
Loma Linda, CA 92350
909-824-4675
Annual patient visits: 105,500.

Dental Society
California Dental Association
P.O. Box 13749
Sacramento, CA 95853-4749
916-443-0505

Government Grants for Dental Research
University of California Davis
Davis, CA
Grants: $206,426

University of California Irvine
Irvine, CA
Grants: $156,173

University of California Los Angeles
Los Angeles, CA
Grants: $2,114,827

University of California San Diego
San Diego, CA
Grants: $296,906

University of California San Francisco
San Francisco, CA
Grants: $4,932,104

Children's Hospital of Los Angeles
Los Angeles, CA
Grants: $321,069

Molecular Research Institute
Grants: $39,936

Xoma Corporation
Grants: $248,538

Society for the Advancement of Chicanos/Native Americans
Grants: $20,000

Scripps Research Institute
Grants: $248,333

University of Southern California
Grants: $4,680,275

SRI International
Grants: $131,726

Colorado
Dental Programs
Department of Health
Family and Community Health Services
Dentistry
4300 Cherry Creek Dr., South, A4
Denver, CO 80222
303-692-2360

Call your local Health Department or Clinic to get information about reduced fee dental care. When dental care is offered, it is usually on a sliding fee scale based on income. Some will treat both children and adults.

Dental Care for the Handicapped
Donated Dental Services

1800 Glenarm Pl., Suite 500
Denver, CO 80202
303-298-9650
Certain handicapped individuals who meet the following guidelines may
be eligible to receive free or low-cost dental care. Patients must meet
the following guidelines: 1) mentally or physically disabled including
mental retardation, cerebral palsy, MS, or other disabilities; 2) Colorado
resident; 3) each patient is screened to find those in most need; limited
income due to handicap is a major factor. Call for additional
information.

Old Age Pension Dental Program
Family and Community Health Services
Dentistry, Ptarmigan Building
4300 Cherry Creek Dr. North
Denver, CO 80222
303-692-2360
The *Old Age Pension Dental Program* is a cooperative effort to provide
dental services to a segment of elderly that have an urgent need. Most
services offered are denture-related. Individuals must be low income
and at least 60 years old. Call to get additional information.

Dental School
School of Dentistry
University of Colorado Medical Center
4200 East Ninth Ave.
Denver, CO 80262
303-270-8751
Annual patient visits: 36,770.

Dental Society
Colorado Dental Association
3690 S. Yosemite Ave.
Suite 100
Denver, CO 80237-1808
303-740-6900

Government Grants for Dental Research
University of Colorado Health Sciences Center
Grants: $386,078

Connecticut
Dental Programs
Department of Health
Dental Health Division
150 Washington Street
Hartford, CT 06106
203-566-4800
Call your nearest Local Health Department or Clinic to find out information about reduced fees for dental care. Most clinics offer a sliding fee schedule and will accept Medicaid and insurance, though low-income is usually a requirement. Handicap access is also available. Preventive programs are run through the various public school systems and nursing homes. Area dentists volunteer their services to provide low-income elderly with reduced-fee dental care.

Dental School
School of Dental Medicine
University of Connecticut
263 Farmington Ave.
Farmington, CT 06032
203-679-3400 (adult)
203-679-3231 (children)
Annual patient visits: 19,496.

Dental Society
Connecticut Dental Association
62 Russ St.
Hartford, CT 06106-1589
203-278-5550

Government Grants for Dental Research
University of Connecticut Health Center
Grants: $2,199,626

Yale University
Grants: $347,094

Delaware
Dental Programs
Division of Public Health
William Center Dental Clinic

805 River Rd.
Dover, DE 19901
302-739-4755
Children in pain, as well as children on Medicaid, are treated. There is
very limited reduced fee dental care available in Delaware; however,
there are two clinics that treat children and adults on a sliding fee
scale. Call 302-428-2269 to get additional information and
qualifications.

Nemours Health Clinic
1801 Rockland Rd.
Wilmington, DE 19803
800-292-9538
302-651-4400
The Nemours Health Clinic offers a Dental Program for senior citizens
over 65. There are income requirements, so be sure to call for
additional information.

Dental Society
Delaware Dental Society
1925 Lovering Ave.
Wilmington, DE 19806-2147
302-654-4335

Government Grants for Dental Research
University of Delaware
Grants: $114,322

District of Columbia
Dental Programs
Department of Public Health
Dental Health Division
1660 L St., NW
Washington, DC 20036
202-673-6765
Low income is a major factor in determining eligibility for free and low-
cost dental care through the DC government. For information on this
very limited dental care, you'll need to call your local clinic. You must
be under 21 for most dental clinic programs, and a sliding fee scale is
used, based on your ability to pay.

Dental School
College of Dentistry
Howard University
600 W St., NW
Washington, DC 20059
202-806-0100
Annual patient visits: 128,886.

Dental Society
District of Columbia Dental Society
502 C St., NE
Washington, DC 20002-5810
202-547-7613
The Society will give referrals to clinics that offer low-cost dental care.
There are no programs for the elderly.

Government Grants for Dental Research
American Association for Dental Research
Grants: $40,000

Georgetown University
Grants: $333,083

Florida
Dental Programs
Department of Health and Rehabilitative Services
Public Health Dental Program
1317 Winewood Blvd.
Tallahassee, FL 32399-0700
904-487-1845
Call your local County Health Department or Clinic for information on
low cost dental care. Clinics usually offer a sliding fee scale.
Qualifications vary and emphasis is on children. Guidelines are 200%
of poverty standards but offer sliding fee scale based on ability to pay.

Dental School
College of Dentistry
University of Florida
Gainesville, FL 32610
904-392-4261

Geriatric Clinic: 904-392-9820
Annual patient visits: 47,441.

Dental Society
Florida Dental Association
1111 E. Tennessee St., Suite 102
Tallahassee, FL 32308-6914
800-877-9922
904-681-3629

Government Grants for Dental Research
Florida State University
Grants: $312,249

University of Florida
Grants: $5,023,030

University of South Florida
Grants: $156,335

Mount Sinai Medical Center
Miami Beach, FL
Grants: $182,058

Georgia
Dental Programs
Department of Human Resources
Oral Health Section
Two Peachtree St., 6th floor
Atlanta, GA 30303
404-657-2574
Call your local Health Department or Clinic to get information on low-cost dental care. Most will treat children and adults, but low-income is a major factor in determining your eligibility. Fluoride and Sealant Programs are available through various public school systems.

Dental School
School of Dentistry
Medical College of Georgia
1459 Laney Walker Blvd.
Augusta, GA 30912

706-721-2696
Annual patient visits: 16,676.

Dental Society
Georgia Dental Association
2801 Duford Hwy., Suite T00
Atlanta, GA 30329
404-636-7553

Government Grants for Dental Research
University of Georgia
Grants: $129,312

Georgia Institute of Technology
Grants: $237,653

Medical College of Georgia
Grants: $1,310,555

Morehouse School of Medicine
Grants: $95,875

Emory University
Grants: $1,191,993

Hawaii
Dental Programs
Department of Health
Dental Health Division
1700 Lanakila Ave., Room 203
Honolulu, HI 96817
808-832-5710
Dental care is available for very low income individuals who are in the GAP Group, which includes children and adults. A sliding fee scale is used to determine what you pay based on your income. Dental care is also available for the mentally or physically handicapped, as well as homeless individuals. To be treated, you must meet certain criteria, which you can get by calling your local clinic.

Dental Society
Hawaii Dental Association

1000 Bishop St., Suite 805
Honolulu, HI 96813-4281
808-536-2135

Idaho
Dental Programs
Department of Health and Welfare
Dental Program
P.O. Box 83720
Boise, ID 83720-0036
208-334-5966
Idaho has a limited dental care program for low-income individuals, but it is very limited for adults. Some restorative dental work is performed. Emergency service for women or children under the age of 21 is available. Call for eligibility requirements. Also, contact your nearest Community Health Center or Clinic to see if they offer dental assistance. Their fee scales are usually a sliding fee schedule, based on your ability to pay. *Preventive Programs* are offered through the public school system and some nursing homes, which are designed to help educate these groups on the importance of preventing dental problems before they occur.

Senior Care Program
Boise City/Ada County
3010 W. State St., Suite 120
Boise, ID 83703-5949
208-345-7783
The *Dental Access Program* helps low-income people receive assistance with the cost of dentures, denture repair, and extractions. Those eligible include: 1) Age 60 or older; 2) Residents of southwest Idaho; 3) Have limited or fixed income and no available resources to pay for dental work; 4) Must have a dental need that is denture related, 5) No Medicaid.

Dental Society
Idaho Dental Association
1220 W. Hays St.
Boise, ID 83702-5315
208-343-7543

Illinois
Dental Programs
Department of Public Health
Dental Health Division
535 West Jefferson St.
Springfield, IL 62761-0001
217-785-4899
Call your local clinics or health centers to get information about reduced fee dental services. Income is a major factor used to determine your eligibility, and sliding fee schedules are used based your ability to pay. Preventative programs are available for children through the various school systems.

Total Dent Program
Illinois Dental Society
P.O. Box 376
Springfield, IL 62705
800-252-2930
The *Total Dent Program* is designed to help low- or fixed-income individuals receive needed dental care at a discount rate. To qualify, you must meet ALL of the following requirements: 1) You cannot be eligible for the Public Aide Dental Program or other dental insurance coverage; 2) You must meet Title 20 income requirements; 3) You must be willing to sign a form certifying the above. Dentists who participate in this program offer a fee reduction of at least 20% to participating Illinois residents. Call for additional information.

Denture Referral Service
Illinois Dental Society
P.O. Box 376
Springfield, IL 62705
217-523-8495
The Illinois Retired Teachers Foundation sponsors the *Denture Referral Service* program, which provides dentures to eligible participants. Although you do NOT have to be a retired teacher to participate, you do need to fulfill the following requirements: 1) Resident of Illinois; 2) 65 years or older; 3) Have no public assistance or private dental insurance; 4) You must qualify for the Illinois *Circuit Breaker Program* which requires earnings of less than $14,000 per year.

Portable Dental Equipment
Illinois Dental Society
P.O. Box 376
Springfield, IL 62705
217-525-1406
In order to provide needed dental care for the homebound, elderly and physically and mentally handicapped, the Illinois State Dental Society maintains ten portable dental equipment units located throughout the state. Any licensed dentist in the state of Illinois may use the equipment to provide on-site dental care to these special individuals.

Dental Schools
Dental School
Northwestern University
240 E. Huron, 1st Floor
Chicago, IL 60611
312-908-5950
Annual patient visits: 96,044
This school has a geriatric clinic.

School of Dental Medicine
Southern Illinois University
2800 College Ave., Building 263
Alton, IL 62002
618-474-7000
Annual patient visits: 33,258

College of Dentistry
University of Illinois
801 S. Paulina
Chicago, IL 60612
312-996-7558
Annual patient visits: 70,510
This school also has a program for geriatrics. A doctor with an assistant will visit nursing homes and retirement homes.

Dental Society
Illinois Dental Society
P.O. Box 376
Springfield, IL 62705-0376
217-525-1406

Government Grants for Dental Research
American Dental Association Health Foundation
Grants: $1,582,463

University of Illinois at Chicago
Chicago, IL
Grants: $478,079

University of Illinois Urbana-Champaign
Grants: $289,735

College of Medicine at Rockford
Grants: $192,754

Southern Illinois University at Edwardsville
Edwardsville, IL
Grants: $96,135

University of Health Science/Chicago Medical School
Grants: $141,680

University of Chicago
Chicago, IL
Grants: $116,230

Northwestern University
Grants: $955,631

Rosary College
Grants: $66,838

Indiana
Dental Programs
Department of Public Health
Dental Health Division
P.O. Box 1964
Indianapolis, IN 46206
317-383-6417
The Dental Program offers reduced-fee dental care. Anyone with low income is eligible. Comprehensive care is available for children, and

some limited care for adults. Call your local heath center for more information.

Senior Smile Program
Dental Care for Senior Citizens
Indiana Dental Association
P.O. Box 2467
Indianapolis, IN 46204
317-634-2610
Dental care at reduced fees is available at participating dentists to those who meet the following guidelines: 1) 65 or older; 2) have no private dental insurance nor federal, state or other dental health insurance; 3) income no more than $10,000/single or $14,000 for married couples. Call the Indiana Counsel on Aging at 317-254-5465 for more information.

Donated Dental Services
Dental Care for Handicapped
P.O. Box 872
Indianapolis, IN 46206
317-631-6022
Participating dentists provide free and low-cost dental care to handicapped individuals who meet the following guidelines: 1) mentally or physically disabled including mental retardation, cerebral palsy, MS, or other disabilities; 2) live in Indiana; 3) each patient screened to find those in most need. Limited income due to handicap is a major factor in determining eligibility.

Dental School
School of Dentistry
Indiana University
1121 West Michigan St.
Indianapolis, IN 46202
317-274-7957
Annual patient visits: 58,495.
Clinic: 317-274-8111 (children)
          317-274-3547 (adults)

Dental Society
Indiana Dental Association
P.O. Box 2467

Indianapolis, IN 46206-2467
317-634-2610

Government Grants for Dental Research
Indiana University-Purdue University at Indianapolis, Indianapolis, IN
Grants: $1,310,525

Iowa
Dental Programs
Department of Public Health
Dental Division
Lucas State Office Building
Des Moines, IA 50319-0075
515-281-5787
Call local Clinics or Health Centers to get information about reduced-
fee dental services. A sliding fee schedule is most often used, and
most services are for children. Very limited adult care is available with
low-income levels used to determine eligibility.

Iowa Dental Elderly Access Program (IDEA)
Iowa Dental Association
505 Fifth Ave., Suite 333
Des Moines, IA 50309-2379
515-282-7250
This program makes dental services available to Iowa Senior Citizens
with limited financial means. Those eligible: 1) 65 or older; 2)
Residents of Iowa; 3) Income is 225% or less of the Federal income
poverty level; 4) Have no medical or dental insurance coverage for the
dental procedures being requested. Discounts off the dentists regular
fee will be made available and are determined on an individual basis in
consultation with a participating dentist. Call to get more information
and an application.

Dental School
College of Dentistry
University of Iowa
Dental Building
Iowa City, IA 52242-1001
319-335-7499
Annual patient visits: 56,817.
Special care clinic for Geriatrics and Handicapped: (319) 335-7373

Dental Society
Iowa Dental Association
505 Fifth Ave., Suite 333
Des Moines, IA 50309-2379
515-282-7250

Government Grants for Dental Research
University of Iowa
Grants: $3,178,529

Iowa State University of Science and Technology
Grants: $153,010

Kansas
Dental Programs
Department of Health and Environment
Dental Program
Landon State Office Building
900 SW Jackson, Room 665
Topeka, KS 66612-1290
913-296-1500
A Health Clinic in Wichita offers reduced-fee dental services for individuals with low income. A sliding fee scale is used. There is also a Fluoride Rinse Program available in the public school systems where needed. Dental care for children on Medicaid is available.

Senior Care Program
Kansas Dental Association
5200 SW Huntoon St.
Topeka, KS 66604-2398
800-432-3583
913-272-7360
Dental care at reduced fees is available by participating dentists to those who meet the following guidelines: 1) 60 years or older; 2) have no private, federal or state dental insurance; 3) income no more than $10,000/single or $15,000 for married couples. Fees vary but are reduced. Call for additional information.

Dental Society
Kansas Dental Association
5200 SW Huntoon St.

Topeka, KS 66604-2398
913-272-7360

Government Grants for Dental Research
University of Kansas Medical Center
Grants. $260,451

Kentucky
Dental Programs
Department of Health
Dental Health Division
275 East Main St.
Frankfort, KY 40621-0001
502-564-3246
Call your nearest Health Clinic for information on who offers free and
low-cost dental care. Income is a major factor used in determining
eligibility. There are three such programs now running in Kentucky. All
ages are treated using a sliding fee scale to determine ability to pay.

Jefferson County Dental
Park Duval Health Facility
1817 South 34th St.
Louisville, KY 40211
502-774-4401
Those eligible to participate in the dental care program at this facility
must meet the following guidelines: 1) Must be a resident of Jefferson
County; 2) Must meet low-income guidelines; 3) Must pay on a sliding
fee scale based on income level.

Kentucky Physicians Program
Kentucky Health Care Access Foundation
125 E. Maxwell St.
Lexington, KY 40508
800-633-8100
Under the Kentucky Physicians Program, all dental work is done by
volunteer dentists. Those eligible to receive treatment include: 1)
Individuals with no insurance, no Medicaid and be within the Federal
Poverty Guidelines; 2) Must be registered as a program participant.
The first visit is free. Pharmacies donate medication based on need.
Call to get additional information.

Denture Access Program
Kentucky Dental Association
1940 Princeton Dr.
Louisville, KY 40205-1873
502-459-5373
The Denture Access Program offers full dentures at a reduced rate.
There are no age requirements to participate. Call for additional
information and a referral to a participating dentist.

Dental Schools
College of Dentistry
University of Kentucky
801 Rose St.
Lexington, KY 40536
For appointments to the college clinic: 606-323-6525
Annual patient visits: 38,723.
The university has some programs for the elderly, and a few satellite
programs where they go to nursing homes.

Kentucky Clinic Dentistry
A219 Kentucky Clinic
740 South Limestone
Lexington, KY 40536-0284
606-233-5562 (adults)
606-233-6261 (children)
The residency program includes pediatric and general practice
residency. They will also see medical card patients. The program is not
income-based.

University of Louisville
School of Dentistry
Louisville, KY 40292
502-852-5096 (adult)
502-852-5642 (children)
Annual patient visits: 65,914.

Dental Society
Kentucky Dental Association
1940 Princeton Dr.
Louisville, KY 40205-1873
502-459-5373

Government Grants for Dental Research
University of Kentucky
Grants: $279,052

University of Louisville
Louisville, KY
Grants: $346,981

Louisiana
Dental Programs
Department of Public Health
Dental Health Division
1300 Perdido Street AE13
New Orleans, LA 70112
504-896-1337
The Dental Program offers reduced-rate dental care through your nearest clinic. Louisiana State University offers dentures for those in need, and also restorative work for those under 18 years of age. Anyone with low income under the age of 21 is eligible for these programs. This office also provides referrals for patients with AIDS. For the 24-hour Emergency Dental Service, call 504-897-8250 for more information.

Donated Dental Services
Dental Care for Handicapped
NFDH-Louisiana
LSDU Dept. Pediatric Dentistry
1100 Florida Ave. Box 139
New Orleans, LA 70119
504-948-6141
Certain handicapped individuals who meet the following guidelines can receive reduced-rate and free dental care through this programs: 1) mentally or physically disabled including mental retardation, cerebral palsy, MS, or other disabilities; 2) live in Louisiana; 3) each patient must be screened to find those in most need — limited income due to handicap is a major factor in determining eligibility.

Dental School
School of Dentistry
Louisiana State University
1100 Florida Ave.

Building 101
New Orleans, LA 70119
504-947-9961
Annual patient visits: 47,247.

Dental Society
Louisiana Dental Association
320 Third St., Suite 201
Baton Rouge, LA 70801
504-336-1692

Government Grants for Dental Research
Louisiana State University Medical Center
New Orleans, LA
Grants: $780,684

Louisiana State University A&M College
Baton Rouge, LA
Grants: $115,951

Optimizing Corrosion Testing of Dental Alloys
Tulane University of Louisiana
Grants: $127,461

Maine
Dental Programs
Department of Human Services
Division of Dental Health
Bureau of Health
State House Station #11
Augusta, Maine 04333
207-287-3121
Call your nearest Community Health Center or Clinic for information on
reduced fees for dental care. Usually fees are based on a sliding scale.
Insurance is accepted. Both children and adults are eligible. *American
Indian/Alaska Native Tribal Programs* offer direct and/or referral
medical/dental services for registered members of federally recognized
American Indian/Alaska Native Tribes. These are tribally-directed
programs and may differ significantly in eligibility requirements and
services.

Senior Dent Program
Maine Dental Association
P.O. Box 215
Manchester, ME 04351
207-622-7900
The Senior Dent program offers comprehensive dental care to low-income elderly at reduced fees. Those eligible must: 1) be residents of Maine; 2) be 62 or older; 3) Have no dental benefits under a private insurance plan or the Medicaid program; 4) Have an annual income that qualifies them for *Maine's Low Cost Drug Program*. Those eligible will receive at least a 15% discount from the usual and customary fees.

Dental Society
Maine Dental Association
P.O. Box 215
Manchester, ME 04351-0215
207-622-7900

Maryland
Dental Programs
Maryland State Health Department
Dental Health Division - Baltimore
201 West Preston St.
Baltimore, MD 21201-2399
800-492-5231
Under the Maryland Access to Care program, low-income individuals under 21 or over 65 years of age. The program offers reduced fee dental care. Fee schedule for care is based on ability to pay.

Senior Dent Program
Dental Care for Senior Citizens
Maryland State Dental Association
6450 Dobbin Rd.
Columbia, MD 21045-5824
410-964-2880
Senior citizens over 65 years of age living in MD and who meet certain income eligibility requirements may qualify for low-cost dental care. Call for qualifications and more information.

Dental Care for Handicapped
Donated Dental Services

6450 Dobbin Rd.
Columbia, MD 21045-5824
410-964-1944
Certain handicapped individuals who meet the following guidelines may
be eligible to receive free or low-cost dental care: 1) mentally or
physically disabled including mental retardation, cerebral palsy, MS, or
other disabilities; 2) Maryland resident; 3) each patient is screened to
find those in most need: limited income due to handicap is a major
factor. Call Lois Bidel for more information.

Dental School
Baltimore College of Dental Surgery
University of Maryland
666 W. Baltimore St.
Baltimore, MD 21201
410-706-5603
Annual patient visits: 57,865.

Dental Society
Maryland Dental Association
6450 Dobbin Rd.
Columbia, MD 21045-5824
410-964-2880

Government Grants for Dental Research
U.S. National Institute of Dental Research
Grants: $138,800

University of Maryland Baltimore Co. Campus
Baltimore, MD
Grants: $237,488

University of Maryland Baltimore Prof. School
Baltimore, MD
Grants: $1,319,996

Henry M. Jackson Foundation for the Advancement Mil/Med
Grants: $35,500

Quantex Corporation
Grants: $355,486

Federation of American Soc. for Experimental Biology
Grants: $3,000

American Society for Cell Biology
Grants: $3,000

Johns Hopkins University
Grants: $687,693

U.S. PHS Public Advisory Groups
Grants: $200,000

Massachusetts
Dental Programs
Department of Health and Hospitals
Community Dental Programs
1010 Massachusetts Ave.
Boston, MA 02118
617-534-4717
Eighteen Health Center Programs throughout Boston offer low-cost
dental care usually on a sliding fee scale based on your income.
Requirements vary, so be sure to call to get additional information.
Some hospitals offer limited dental. They also operate an HIV referral
and treatment program.

Developmentally Disabled Program
150 Tremont Street
Boston, MA 02111
617-727-0732
This program offers dental care for individuals who are mentally
retarded, have cerebral palsy, and those who are physically disabled.
Call for additional information.

Dentistry for All
Massachusetts Dental Society
83 Speen St.
Natick, MA 07160-4144
508-651-7511
The *Dentistry for All Program* is a reduced-fee dental program for low-
income individuals who have no dental coverage of any kind. Call to
get additional information.

Dental Schools
Harvard School of Dental Medicine
188 Longwood Ave.
Boston, MA 02115
617-432-1423
Annual patient visits: 26,270.

School of Graduate Dentistry
Boston University
100 E. Newton St.
Boston, MA 02118
617-638-4671
Annual patient visits: 34,324.

School of Dental Medicine
Tufts University
One Kneeland St.
Boston, MA 02111
617-956-6547
Annual patient visits: 87,522.

Dental Society
Massachusetts Dental Society
83 Speen St.
Natick, MA 01760-4144
508-651-7511

Government Grants for Dental Research
New England Medical Center Hospitals, Inc.
Grants: $421,987

Hampshire College
Grants: $98,921

Beth Israel Hospital
Boston, MA
Grants: $113,085

University of Massachusetts Medical School
Grants: $866,893

Boston University
Boston, MA
Grants: $1,192,463

Children's Hospital
Boston, MA
Grants: $234,721

Abiomed, Inc.
Grants: $260,373

Spire Corporation
Grants: $308,131

Cambridge Scientific, Inc.
Grants: $232,579

Forsyth Dental Center
Grants: $6,008,592

Endicott College
Grants: $102,457

Health Programs International, Inc.
Grants: $50,000

Harvard University
Harvard, MA
Grants: $2,522,817

Massachusetts General Hospital
Grants: $124,137

CBR Laboratories, Inc.
Grants: $396,191

Tufts University Boston
Boston, MA
Grants: $477,341

Michigan
Dental Programs
Department of Public Health
Dental Health Division
3423 Martin Luther King Jr., Blvd.
P.O. Box 30195
Lansing, MI 48909
517-335-8898
There are no direct dental services through the State Health
Department. You must call your local or county health department for
participating clinics and qualifications.

Senior Dent Program
Michigan Dental Association
230 North Washington Square, Suite 208
Lansing, MI 48933
800-589-2632
Dental care at reduced fees are available to senior citizens who meet
the following guidelines: 1) 65 or older; 2) have no private dental
insurance nor federal, state or other dental health insurance; 3) meet
certain low-income requirements. Fees vary, and procedures covered
include all types of dental care except full dentures. Over 800 dentists
in Michigan participate.

Discount Dentures
Michigan Dental Association
230 North Washington Square, Suite 208
Lansing, MI 48933
800-589-2632
Under the *Professionally Acceptable Economy Denture Service
(PAEDS)*, qualified patients can receive reduced-fees on full dentures
(upper, lower or both) provided by licensed dentists. It also includes
examination and x-rays. Those: 1) no age or income eligibility
requirements. 2) must call the above number for additional information.
Fees vary but are always at a reduced rate. Payment is handled
through patient and dentist.

Dental Schools
School of Dentistry
University of Detroit-Mercy
2985 E. Jefferson Ave.

Detroit, MI 48207
313-446-1800
Annual patient visits: 47,152.

School of Dentistry
University of Michigan
1011 North University
Ann Arbor, MI 48109-1078
313-763-6933
Annual patient visits: 88,035.

Dental Society
Michigan Dental Association
230 Washington Square North, Suite 208
Lansing, MI 48933-1392
517-372-9070

Government Grants for Dental Research
University of Michigan at Ann Arbor
Ann Arbor, MI
Grants: $5,108,084

Wayne State University
Grants: $367,880

Minnesota
Dental Programs
State Health Department
Dental Division
717 Delaware Street SE
Minneapolis, MN 55440
612-623-5441
Call your Local Health Clinic to find out who offers dental care on a reduced-fee scale. Also contact "First Call for Help," 612-224-1133, for additional information on clinics. Low-income is a major factor in determining eligibility.

Senior Partners Care Dental Program
Minnesota Senior Federation
Iris Park Place
1885 University Ave. W. Suite 190

St. Paul, MN 55104
800-365-8765
612-642-1398
The *Senior Partners Care Dental Program* is designed to bridge the
Medicare gap, with participating dentists agreeing to provide a 20%
discount for all professional dental services. Those eligible must: 1) join
the Minnesota Senior Foundation; 2) be 55 or older and retired; 3)
meet the annual income criteria of less than 200% of poverty
($1100/single or $1500/ couple per month in 1992); 4) have less than
$21,000 in liquid assets (cash savings, stocks, CDs, etc.); 5) NOT be a
part of any dental plan.

Wilder Senior Dental Program
516 Humboldt Ave.
St. Paul, MN 55107
612-220-1807
This program is for those 65 years old and older. It is not income-
based and they will set up payment plans.

Senior Hi-Rise Program
612-625-1417
This program goes into senior citizen apartment buildings and does
dental work. It is not income-based and they do not go to nursing
homes.

Dental School
School of Dentistry
University of Minnesota
515 SE Delaware St.
Minneapolis, MN 55455
612-625-2495
612-625-7171 (children)
612-625-8400 (adults)
Annual patient visits: 34,078

Dental Society
Minnesota Dental Association
2236 Marshall Ave.
St. Paul, MN 55104-5792
612-646-7454

Government Grants for Dental Research
University of Minnesota Twin Cities
Grants: $3,548,413

LAI Laboratories, Inc.
Grants: $241,190

Mississippi
Dental Programs
Low-Cost Denture Referral Program
Mississippi Dental Association
2630 Ridgewood Rd.
Jackson, MS 39216-4920
601-982-0442
Under this denture program, patients and dentists negotiate the reduced cost for services based on the patients' ability to pay. Call for additional information.

Dental School
School of Dentistry
University of Mississippi
2500 North State St.
Jackson, MS 39216
601-984-6155
Annual patient visits: 15,097.

Dental Society
Mississippi Dental Association
2630 Ridgewood Rd.
Jackson, MS 39216-4920
601-982-0442

Government Grants for Dental Research
University of Mississippi
Grants: $71,765

University of Mississippi Medical Center
Grants: $70,833

Missouri
Dental Programs
Department of Public Health
Dental Health Division
P.O. Box 570
Jefferson City, MO 65102
314-751-6247
Call your nearest health center or clinic for information on reduced fees
for dental care. Usually clinics offer a sliding fee scale, and
qualifications vary, though low income is a major factor considered.
Fluoride Rinse Programs are available through the public school
system.

Missouri Elks Program for the Handicapped
Truman Medical Center East
7900 Lee's Summit Rd.
Kansas City, MO 64139
816-373-1486
This program offers dental care for physically challenged adults and
children through three mobile units, which provide in-home care for
those unable to get out on their own. Call for information on eligibility
guidelines.

Dental Care for Senior Citizens
Senior Care Program
Missouri Dental Association
230 W. McCarty
P.O. Box 1707
Jefferson City, MO 65102-1707
800-688-1907
314-965-5960 (in St. Louis)
816-333-5454 (in KC)
This program provides low-cost dental care to seniors who meet the
following eligibility requirements: 1) 60 years or older; 2) income no
more than $15,000 (single) or $20,000 (for married couples); 3) you
cannot be currently receiving dental care through any public aid
program or insurance plan. Participating dentists have agreed to
provide a minimum of a 25% discount on services; however, the
dentist may charge the usual fee for the initial office visit and
examination.

Dental School
School of Dentistry
University of Missouri
650 E. 25th St.
Kansas City, MO 64108-2795
816 235 2100
Annual patient visits: 7,500.

Dental Society
Missouri Dental Association
P.O. Box 1707
Jefferson City, MO 65102-1707
314-634-3436

Government Grants for Dental Research
University of Missouri Columbia
Columbia, MO
Grants: $453,079

University of Missouri Kansas City
Kansas City, MO
Grants: $1,449,322

Jewish Hospital of St. Louis
St. Louis, MO
Grants: $231,507

St. Louis University
St. Louis, MO
Grants: $217,071

Washington University
Grants: $838,516

Montana
Dental Programs
Health Services Division
Dental Department
Health and Environment Sciences
P.O. Box 200901
Cogswell Building

Helena, Montana 59620-0901
406-444-0276
Through the Maternal and Child Health department, counties can
choose how they wish to use funds for dental care, so call your county
health department to find out about treatments. Also Fluoride and
Mouthrinse Programs are available for those who are in need.

Dental Society
Montana Dental Association
P.O. Box 1154
Helena, MT 59624-1154
406-443-2061

Nebraska
Dental Programs
Health Department
Dental Health Division
301 Centennial Mall South
P.O. Box 95007
Lincoln, NE 68509-5007
402-471-2822
Call your local Clinic to find out if they offer dental care. Low-income is
a major factor in determining eligibility, and fees are usually based on
a sliding scale. Children are a first priority.

Senior Dent Program
Nebraska Dental Association
3120 O Street
Lincoln, NE 68510-1599
402-476-1704
The *Senior Dent Program* offers dental care at a reduced fee for senior
citizens. There are eligibility requirements that include being at least 65
years of age. Cal to find out additional information.

Dental Schools
School of Dentistry
Creighton University
2802 Webster Ave.
Omaha, NE 68178
402-280-2865
Annual patient visits: 61,218.

College of Dentistry
University of Nebraska Medical Center
40th and Holdrege Sts.
Lincoln, NE 68583
402-472-1333 (adult)
402-472-1305 (children)
Annual patient visits: 17,599.

Dental Society
Nebraska Dental Association
3120 O St.
Lincoln, NE 68510-1599
402-476-1704

Government Grants for Dental Research
University of Nebraska Lincoln
Lincoln, NE
Grants: $115,576

Creighton University
Grants: $198,704

Nevada
Dental Programs
Nevada Health Department
Family Services
505 East King St.
Carson City, NV 89710
702-687-4740
Call your County Health Department to see if they offer dental. Only
very limited, low-cost dental care is available to adults other than
possibly extractions due to pain. Most often, programs are only for
children. *First Call for Help* will refer you for assistance based on what
is available. In Reno, call 702-329-4630. In Las Vegas, call 702-369-
4397. Clark County Dental Society keeps a list of dentists who offer
discounts to senior citizens. Call 702-255-7873 to get a referral.

Geriatric Health Clinic
1001 East 9th St.
Reno, NV 89512

702-328-2482
This clinic does referrals only.

Dental Society
Nevada Dental Association
6889 W. Charleston #B
Las Vegas, NV 89117
702-255-4211

New Hampshire
Dental Programs
Department of Health and Welfare
Dental Division
6 Hazen Dr.
Concord, NH 03301
603-271-4685
New Hampshire has a very limited dental care program for those of
low-income. Children are a first priority. Call the toll-free Helpline at
800-852-3345, ext. 4238 to find out about other possible dental
assistance. Some state technical colleges offer dental Hygiene
Programs.

Denture Program
New Hampshire Dental Society
P.O. Box 2229
Concord, NH 03302-2229
603-225-5961
The *Denture Program* offers dentures to anyone who needs them at a
reduced rate. There are financial guidelines that need to be met, but
the program is for all ages. Call the above number for additional
information.

Dental Society
New Hampshire Dental Society
P.O. Box 2229
Concord, NH 03302-2229
603-225-5961

New Jersey
Dental Programs
Department of Health

Dental Health Division
CN 364
Trenton, NJ 08625-0364
609-292-1723
Some area hospitals offer dental care on a sliding fee scale based on income, but most services offered are for children. Only limited care is available for adults. Also a limited number of clinics in some towns offer dental care, also using a sliding fee scale.

Senior Dent
New Jersey Dental Association
One Dental Plaza
P.O. Box 6020
North Brunswick, NJ 08902-6020
908-821-9400
The *Senior Dent* program offers increase access to Dental Care for senior citizens by offering at least a 15% discount on services. Those eligible: 1) you must have a PAA (Pharmacy) card; 2) be age 65 or older; 3) have annual income of less than $15,700 (single) or $19,250 (married couple; 4) have no dental insurance or Medicaid benefits. Call the State Division on Aging for additional information at 800-792-8820.

Donated Dental Services
One Dental Plaza
North Brunswick, NJ 08902-4313
908-821-2977
Donated Dental Services offers comprehensive dental care for handicapped individuals. Those eligible: 1) the mentally or physically disabled including mental retardation, cerebral palsy, MS or other disabilities; 2) New Jersey residents; 3) each patient is screened to find those in most need. Limited income due to disability is a major factor in determining eligibility.

Dental School

New Jersey Dental School
University of Medicine and Dentistry
110 Bergen St.
Newark, NJ 07103
201-982-4300
Annual patient visits: 58,615.

Information USA, Inc.

Dental Society
New Jersey Dental Association
One Dental Plaza
P.O. Box 6020
North Brunswick, NJ 08902-6020
908-821-9400

Government Grants for Dental Research
University of Medicine and Dentistry of NJ
Grants: $932,720

University of Med/Dent NJ
R.W. Johnson Medical School
Grants: $90,991

Rutgers The State University New Brunswick
New Brunswick, NJ
Grants: $46,424

New Mexico
Dental Programs
Department of Health
Dental Division
1190 Saint Francis Dr.
Santa Fe, NM 87502-6110
505-827-2389
Call your nearest Community Health Center or Clinic for information on reduced fees for dental care. Most clinics will charge according to ability to pay, and children are usually a priority. Carrie Tingley Hospital treats mentally disadvantaged and disabled; call 505-843-7493 for additional information. There are also some Indian Health Centers that offer dental care to tribal members.

Community Dental Services, Inc.
2116 Hinkle SE
Albuquerque, NM 87102
505-765-5683
Community Dental Services offers reduced-fee dental services based on income.

Dental Society
New Mexico Dental Association
3736 Eubank Blvd., NE, #1A
Albuquerque, NM 87111-3556
505-294-1368

Government Grants for Dental Research
Lovelace Medical Foundation
Grants: $395,309

University of New Mexico Albuquerque
Albuquerque, NM
Grants: $161,584

New York
Dental Programs
New York City Department of Health
Dental Health
93 Worth Street, Room 1001
New York, NY 10013
212-566-8166
Clinics throughout the city boroughs offer free dental care to children.
Call the above number to get additional information about services
offered. A recording will give you phone numbers of clinics so that you
can choose the one most convenient. Also, some private and city
hospitals offer reduced-fee dental services on a sliding fee scale for
adults based on income. Call your nearest hospital to get additional
information and see if they offer dental care.

Senior Citizens Dental Access Program
Dental Society of New York State
7 Elk St.
Albany, NY 12207-1023
518-465-0044
The *Dental Access Program* offers reduced-fee dental services for
senior citizens. Those eligible: 1) 65 or older; 2) have no public
assistance or private insurance; 3) live in New York.

Dental Schools
School of Dental and Oral Surgery
Columbia University

630 W. 168th St.
New York, NY 10032
212-305-5665
Annual patient visits: 53,255.

College of Dentistry
New York University
345 E. 24th St.
New York, NY 10010
212-998-9800
Geriatric Clinic: 212-998-9767
Annual patient visits: 269,095.

School of Dental Medicine
State University of New York at Stony Brook
Rockland Hall
Health Science Center
Stony Brook, NY 11794
516-632-8989
516-632-8967 (children)
516-632-8974 (adults)
516-632-9245 (geriatric clinic)
Annual patient visits: 15,321.

School of Dental Medicine
State University of New York at Buffalo
325 Squire, 3435 Main St.
Buffalo, NY 14214-3008
716-829-2821
716-829-2723 (children)
716-829-2720 (adults)
Annual patient visits: 78,000.

Dental Society
Dental Society of New York
7 Elk St.
Albany, NY 12207-1023
518-465-0044

Government Grants for Dental Research
Beth Israel Medical Center

New York, NY
Grants: $667,312

Cornell University Ithaca
Ithaca, NY
Grants: $213,700

Cornell University Medical Center
Grants: $173,364

Mount Sinai School of Medicine
Grants: $211,600

Columbia University New York
New York, NY
Grants: $1,640,918

Eastman Dental Center
Grants: $1,614,286

Hospital for Special Surgery
Grants: $291,266

Montefiore Medical Center
Bronx, NY
Grants: $300,452

New York Academy of Sciences
Grants: $10,000

State University of New York at Albany
Albany, NY
Grants: $142,942

State University New York Stony Brook
Stony Brook, NY
Grants: $946,316

State University of New York at Buffalo
Buffalo, NY
Grants: $5,741,273

Health Science Center at Syracuse
Syracuse, NY
Grants: $94,120

New York University
Grants: $1,189,424

Rensselaer Polytechnic Institute
Grants: $42,963

University of Rochester
Rochester, NY
Grants: $3,480,294

Naylor Dana Institute for Disease Prevention
Grants: $148,457

North Carolina
Dental Programs
Health and Natural Resources Environment
Dental Department
1815-8 Capital Blvd.
Raleigh, NC 27604
919-733-3853
Call your nearest County Health Clinic to see if they offer dental care
at a reduced cost. When offered, it is usually on a sliding fee scale and
most often for children. Prevention and education are the main focus
with *Fluoride and Sealant Programs* throughout the various public
school systems.

Senior Smile Program
North Carolina Dental Association
P.O. Box 12047
Raleigh, NC 27605-2047
919-832-1222
The *Senior Smile Program* offers reduced-fee dental care for senior
citizens. This program works under the American Dental Association
(ADA). The ADA toll-free number for this program is 800-621-8099.
Call for more information.

Dental School
School of Dentistry
University of North Carolina
104 Brauer Hall
Chapel Hill, NC 27599
919-966-1161
Annual patient visits: 30,395.

Dental Society
North Carolina Dental Society
P.O. Box 12047
Raleigh, NC 27605-2047
919-832-1222

Government Grants for Dental Research
University of North Carolina Charlotte
Charlotte, NC
Grants: $96,650

University of North Carolina Chapel Hill
Chapel Hill, NC
Grants: $5,219,258

Winston-Salem State University
Winston-Salem, NC
Grants: $6,179

Duke University
Grants: $424,146

North Dakota
Dental Programs
Health Department
Maternal and Child Health Department
600 E. Blvd. Ave.
Bismarck, ND 58505-0200
701-224-2372
Crippled Children Services offers dental and health care for those in need. Some Indian Health Centers offer dental for tribal members. The Fargo Homeless Project offers emergency dental work for the

homeless. No programs other than Medicaid offer dental care, and no clinics offer dental care.

Senior Dent
North Dakota Dental Association
Box 1332
Bismarck, ND 58502
701-223-8870
The *Senior Dent* program makes a full range of Dental Services available to financially eligible North Dakotans age 55 or older at a reduced fee. Those eligible must: 1) be 55 or older; 2) Not be covered by medical assistance or enrolled in a dental insurance plan; 3) have income that is 125% or less of federal poverty guidelines. Fees vary, but dentists have agreed to offer at least a 33% discount off their regular fees. Contact your local Senior Citizen Center for more information.

Dental Society
North Dakota Dental Association
P.O. Box 1332
Bismarck, ND 58502-1332
701-223-8870

Ohio
Dental Programs
State Health Department
Dental Health Division
246 North High
Columbus, OH 43215
614-466-4180
Ohio offers a *Sealant and Fluoride Mouthrinse Program* through the public school system.

Access to Dental Care Programs
Ohio Dental Association
1370 Dublin Rd.
Columbus, OH 43215-1098
800-MY-SMILE
The Ohio Dental Association coordinates numerous Access to Dental Care Programs. Free or low-cost dental care is available through the *Access to Dental Care for Children with Special Health Care Needs*

(CSHCN) program. This program assists local agencies to increase access to needed oral health services for this special needs group. Funds are also used to provide comprehensive services for high risk children and/or women of childbearing age, otherwise known as *Child and Family Health Projects (CFSHP)*. Primary Care is also available through some County Health Departments and Clinics. Call for additional information and qualifications.

Dental Services for the Handicapped
Donated Dental Services
421 E. 4th St.
Cincinnati, OH 45202
513-621-2517
Free and low-cost dental care is available to the handicapped and elderly is they meet the following guidelines: 1) Mentally or physically disabled including mental retardation, cerebral palsy, MS or other disabilities; 2) individuals may also be elderly living on a fixed income; 3) each patient is screened to find those in most need. Limited income due to handicap is a major factor in determining eligibility.

Greater Cincinnati Oral Health Council
635 W. Seventh St.
Cincinnati, OH 45203
513-621-0248
A charter agency of the United Way, the Public Dental Service Society's dental care programs help special groups such as children from low-income families, the homeless, the aging and those with disabling conditions. 1) *Dental Sealant Program*: sealants are applied to low-income and handicapped children of Cincinnati. 2) *Head Start*: provides dental education, consultation and preventive treatment for children of disadvantage families. 3) *Homeless Program*: provides dental care for homeless adults and children. 4) *Dental Registry for the Elderly and Handicapped*: a computerized referral service matches patients with special needs with a dentist who can accommodate these needs.

Dental Schools
College of Dentistry
Ohio State University
305 W. 12th Ave.
Columbus, OH 43210

614-292-2751
Annual patient visits: 51,476.

School of Dentistry
Case Western Reserve University
2123 Abington Rd.
Cleveland, OH 44106
216-368-3200
Annual patient visits: 86,630.

Dental Society
Ohio Dental Association
1370 Dublin Rd.
Columbus, OH 43215-1098
614-486-2700

Government Grants for Dental Research
Case Western Reserve University
Grants: $597,100

Medical College of Ohio at Toledo
Toledo, OH
Grants: $642,940

University of Cincinnati
Cincinnati, OH
Grants: $344,197

Ohio State University
Grants: $801,513

Oklahoma
Dental Programs
State Department of Health
Dental Health Services
1000 Northeast Tenth St.
Oklahoma City, OK 73117-1299
405-271-5502
Call your local Health Center or hospital to see if dental is offered.
When offered, it is usually on a sliding fee scale, and in some
instances only for children.

Care-Dent Program
Oklahoma Dental Society
629 West I-44 Service Rd.
Oklahoma City, OK 73118
800-876-8890
Care-Dent offers savings to those who need denture service. Dentists
also provide a thorough examination. Call for a participating dentist and
more information.

Senior Dent Program
Oklahoma Dental Society
629 West I-44 Service Rd.
Oklahoma City, OK 73118
800-876-8890
405-848-8873
The *Senior Dent Program* offers complete, professional dental care at
a reduced fee to those seniors who meet the following guidelines: 1)
65 or older; 2) have no dental insurance; 3) income no more than
$8,000/single or $12,000 for a married couple. Dentists offer a 20%
discount to qualifying senior citizens. Call for more information.

Disabled Program
4024 North Lincoln Blvd., Suite 101
Oklahoma City, OK 73105-5220
800-522-9510
405-424-8092
The *D-Dent Program* offers free dental care for the physically disabled.
You must apply, and applicants are carefully screened.

Dental School
College of Dentistry
University of Oklahoma
Health Sciences Center
P.O. Box 26901
Oklahoma City, OK 73190-3044
405-271-6056
Annual patient visits: 45,615.

Dental Society
Oklahoma Dental Association
629 W. Interstate 44 Service Rd.

Oklahoma City, OK 73118-6032
405-848-8873

Government Grants for Dental Research
University of Oklahoma Health Sciences Center
Grants: $338,458

Oregon
Dental Programs
Department of Health
Dental Health Division
800 NE Oregon St.
Portland, OR 97232
503-731-4098
Community Access Programs offer reduced-fee dental care to low-income individuals using a sliding fee schedule. Call your nearest Health Clinic for more information. The program requires enrollment at most clinics before treatment can begin. Under the *King Fluoride Program*, children are provided school-based fluoride mouthrinses and tablets.

Low-Cost Denture Program
107 Oakway Center, Suite C
Eugene, OR 97401
503-686-1175
Under this program, residents of Lake County, 55 years or older, and who meet the following guidelines may be eligible to receive low-cost denture care, including full upper and lower dentures, partials, reclines and repairs: 1) receive no public assistance; 2) income no more than $7,500 (single) or $10,500 (married couples). Call for additional qualifications and information.

Dental Care for Senior Citizens
Senior Smile Dental Service
Multnomah Dental Society
1618 W. First
Suite 317
Portland, OR 97201
503-223-4738
Under this program, low income seniors over 60 years old, who live in Multnomah County may be eligible to receive both general and

specialized dental care at a 50% reduced fee. Call for more information and to register.

Dental Care for Handicapped
Donated Dental Services
CDRC
P.O. Box 574, Room 2205
Portland, OR 97207
503-241-7075
Certain Oregon residents who are mentally or physically handicapped (cerebral palsy given first priority), or elderly may qualify for low-cost dental care under this program. Eligibility screening is required.

Dental School
School of Dentistry
Sam Jackson Park
Oregon Health Sciences University
611 SW Campus Dr.
Portland, OR 97201
503-494-8867
Annual patient visits: 44,900.

Dental Society
Oregon Dental Association
17898 SW McEwan Rd.
Portland, OR 97224-7798
503-620-3230

Government Grants for Dental Research
University of Oregon
Grants: $207,311

Oregon Health Sciences University
Grants: $636,122

Pennsylvania
Dental Programs
Department of Public Health
Dental Health Division
500 South Broad Street
Philadelphia, PA 19146

215-875-5666
The Dental Program offers reduced-rate dental care through your
nearest clinic. Insurance is accepted and fee set according to financial
situation. Anyone with low income is eligible, but children are first
priority.

Dental Care for Senior Citizens
Access to Care Program
3501 North Front St.
Harrisburg, PA 17110
717-234-5941
Under this program, individuals 65 or over can receive at least a
minimum of 15% discount on dental care through 1,700 participating
dentists across PA. To be eligible, you must: 1) have no private dental
insurance nor federal, state or other dental health assistance; 2) have
income no more than $13,000 (single) or $16,200 (married couples).
Call the PA Counsel on Aging at 800-692-7256 for more program
information.

Dental Care for Handicapped (Philadelphia only)
Donated Dental Services
Fidelity Bank Bldg.
123 S. Broad St., 22nd Floor
Philadelphia, PA 19109-1022
215-546-0300
Certain low-income mentally or physically handicapped residents of
Philadelphia may qualify to receive free or low-cost dental care. Each
patient is screened to find those most in need: limited income due to
handicap is a major factor.

Dental Schools
School of Dentistry
Temple University
3223 N. Broad St.
Philadelphia, PA 19140
215-707-2900
Annual patient visits: 77,665.

School of Dental Medicine
University of Pennsylvania
4001 W. Spruce St.

Philadelphia, PA 19104
215-898-8961
Annual patient visits: 85,000.

School of Dental Medicine
University of Pittsburgh
3501 Terrace St.
Salk Hall
Pittsburgh, PA 15261
412-648-8760
Annual patient visits: 59,570.

Dental Society
Pennsylvania Dental Association
P.O. Box 3341
Harrisburg, PA 17105-3341
717-234-5941

Government Grants for Dental Research
Pennsylvania State University-University Park
University Park, PA
Grants: $379,184

University of Pittsburgh at Pittsburgh
Pittsburgh, PA
Grants: $1,509,555

Drexel University
Grants: $122,068

Thomas Jefferson University
Grants: $616,651

University of Pennsylvania
Grants: $4,312,531

Philadelphia College of Osteopathic Medicine
Philadelphia, PA
Grants: $104,491

Temple University
Grants: $498,997

Medical College of Pennsylvania
Grants: $94,254

Rhode Island
Dental Programs
Department of Public Health
Oral Health Division
3 Capital Hill
Providence, RI 02908-5097
401-277-2588
The dental program offers reduced-fee basic dental care (not crowns
or bridges, for example). Call your nearest clinic for more information.
Most insurance are accepted and the pay schedule is according to
situation. Anyone with low-income can qualify.

Travelers Aide Society for the Homeless
177 Union St.
Providence, RI 02903
401-521-2255
The Travelers Aid Society offers dental care for the homeless. Call
Linda Dziobeck for more information.

Dental Care for Handicapped
Independence Square
500 Prospect St.
Pawtucket, RI 02860
401-728-9448
Through the *Donated Dental Services Program*, free and low-cost
dental care is available to the handicapped that meet the following
guidelines: 1) mentally or physically disabled including mental
retardation, cerebral palsy, MS, or other disabilities; 2) live in Rhode
Island; 3) each patient must be screened to find those in most need.
Limited income due to handicap is a major factor in determining
eligibility.

South County
Health Center of South County
One River St.

Wakefield, RI 02879
401-783-0853
Basic dental treatments for all ages are available. Call Herb Manfield for more information.

Dental Society
Rhode Island Dental Association
200 Centerville Rd.
Warwick, RI 02886-4339
401-732-6833

Government Grants for Dental Research
Gordon Research Conferences
Grants: $9,000

South Carolina
Dental Programs
Department of Health and
 Environmental Control
2600 Bull St.
Columbia, SC 29201
803-734-4972
A program through the public school system offers dental care for children. Applications are picked up at participating schools, but not during the summer. Call your local Health Center or Clinic to find out if they offer dental care. Dental usually is for children.

Primary Care Center
P.O. Box 6923
Columbia, SC 29260
803-738-9881
Some Primary Care Clinics or Centers offer dental on a sliding fee scale based on income. Call to get additional information.

Senior Care Dental Program
South Carolina Dental Association
120 Stonemark Ln.
Columbia, SC 29210-3841
803-750-2277
The *Senior Care Program* offers dental care to senior citizens at a reduced fee. The minimum discount is 20%, and there are specific

eligibility guidelines, which you can get from your local Council on Aging or Commission on Aging (Buford: 803-524-1787) or the Dental Society at 803-750-2277.

Dental School
College of Dental Medicine
Medical University of South Carolina
171 Ashley Ave.
Charleston, SC 29425
803-792-2611
Annual patient visits: 25,315.

Dental Society
South Carolina Dental Association
120 Stonemark Ln.
Columbia, SC 29210-3841
803-750-2277

Government Grants for Dental Research
University of South Carolina at Columbia
Columbia, SC
Grants: $113,498

Medical University of South Carolina
Grants: $180,824

South Dakota
Dental Programs
Department of Health
Dental Division
Anderson Building
445 E. Capitol Ave.
Pierre, SD 57501
605-773-3361
Although comprehensive dental care is not offered through local Health Centers, the *Emergency Care Referral Program* can put you in touch with dental care in emergency situations.

Indian Health Program
Indian Health Services
Federal Building

115 4th Ave. SE
Aberdeen, SD 57401
605-226-7501
Dental care is available at no charge for Indians enrolled in a tribe. Call the office above for additional information and find out locations for treatment.

Dental Society
South Dakota Dental Association
P.O. Box 1194
Pierre, SD 57501-1194
605-224-9133

Tennessee
Dental Programs
Department of Health
Oral Health Services
Tennessee Tower, 11th Floor
3128 Ave. North
Nashville, TN 37247-5410
615-741-7213
Contact your Local Health Center or Clinic to find out if they offer reduced-fee dental services. Low income is a major factor in determining eligibility, and a sliding fee scale is most often used. Qualifications vary, and care is primarily for children. Emergency care is offered to adults to alleviate pain. Although there are no special programs for the elderly or disabled, they will be treated based on the above income criteria.

Dental Schools
School of Dentistry
Meharry Medical College
1005 D.B. Todd Blvd.
Nashville, TN 37208
615-327-6669
Annual patient visits: 7,972.

College of Dentistry
University of Tennessee
875 Union Ave.
Memphis, TN 38163

901-448-6257
Annual patient visits: 52,551.

Dental Society
Tennessee Dental Association
P.O. Box 120188
Nashville, TN 37212-0188
615-383-8962

Government Grants for Dental Research
University of Tennessee at Memphis
Memphis, TN
Grants: $488,255

Meharry Medical College
Grants: $319,364

Texas
Dental Programs
Senior Dent
Texas Dental Association
1946 South Interregional
Austin, TX 78704
Senior Dent offers reduced-cost dental care to those who are: 1) 65 or
older; 2) not be receiving federal, state, or other dental health
insurance; 3) have a total household income of less than $12,000 or
acceptance by the participating dentist because of special
circumstances. Call for more information.

In Texas, several regional offices of the Texas Public Health Office
have additional information on reduced-fee dental care in their regions.
Call or write the appropriate region to get additional information.

Region 1
Texas Public Health
1109 Kemper St.
Lubbock, TX 79403
806-744-3577

Region 3
Texas Public Health

2561 Matlock Road
Arlington, TX 76015-1621
817-792-7224

Region 4 & 5 North
Texas Public Health
1517 West Front St.
Tyler, TX 75702
903-595-3585

Region 6
Texas Public Health
10500 Forum Place Drive, Suite 123
Houston, TX 77036-8599
713-995-1112

Region 7
Texas Public Health
2408 South 37th St.
Temple, TX 76504
817-778-6744

Region 8
Texas Public Health
1021 Garnerfield Rd.
Uvalde, TX 78801
210-278-7173

Region 11
Texas Public Health
601 West Sesame Drive
Harlingen, TX 78550
210-423-0130

Dental Schools
Baylor College of Dentistry
3302 Gaston Ave.
Dallas, TX 75246
214-828-8100
Annual patient visits: 75,411.

Health Science Center
Dental Branch
University of Texas
6516 John Freeman Ave.
Houston, TX 77030
713-792-4056
Annual patient visits: 113,153.

Health Science Center
Dental School
University of Texas
7703 Floyd Curl Dr.
San Antonio, TX 78284
210-567-3222
Annual patient visits: 124,783.

Dental Society
Texas Dental Association
P.O. Box 3358
Austin, TX 78764-3358
512-443-3675

Government Grants for Dental Research
Baylor College of Medicine
Grants: $93,118

Texas College of Osteopathic Medicine
Grants: $106,601

University of Texas Medical Center Br Galveston
Galveston, TX
Grants: $309,649

University of Texas MD Anderson Cancer Center
Grants: $149,455

University of Texas Health Science Center Houston
Houston, TX
Grants: $1,777,299

University of Texas Health Science Center
San Antonio, TX
Grants: $4,409,412

Baylor College of Dentistry
Grants: $563,581

Utah
Dental Programs
Department of Health
Dental Health Division
288 North 1460 West
Salt Lake City, UT 84116
801-538-6179
A few Community Health Centers offer dental care for people with low
income, usually using a sliding-fee scale. The Homeless Shelter in
Utah has a dental clinic that offers free dental care for the homeless.
The Indian Health Care Clinic offers dental for Native Americans.
Under the *Dental House Calls Program*, reduced-fee dental care is
available from volunteer dentists for the handicapped or elderly who
are unable to leave their homes. The Medicaid dental program is very
extensive for children and adults.

Dental Society
Utah Dental Association
1151 E. 3900 South, #B160
Salt Lake City, UT 84124-1216
801-261-5315

Government Grants for Dental Research
University of Utah
Grants: $424,976

Vermont
Dental Programs
Island Pond Health Center
P.O. Box 425
Island Pond, VT 05846
802-723-4300
This nonprofit Health Center in northeastern Vermont offers eligible
residents of specific towns dental care for a reduced fee based on a

sliding scale based on their income from the previous year. Fees range from 100% coverage for preventive dental services and 50% coverage for all other services that they provide. No specialty services, such as orthodontics, are available. Call to get additional information and to find out if Health Care Inc. has reduced fee dental care available in your town.

Dental Society
Vermont Dental Society
132 Church St.
Burlington, VT 05401-8401
802-864-0115

Government Grants for Dental Research
University of Vermont and State Agricultural College
Grants: $417,410

Virginia
Dental Programs
Health Department
Dental Division
1500 E. Main
Room 239
Richmond, VA 23219
804-786-3556
Community Health Centers offer dental care at a reduced-fee based on income. Although children are a first priority, adults are treated on an emergency basis. There are approximately 90 such Centers across VA that offer dental care.

Dental School
School of Dentistry
Virginia Commonwealth University
Box 980566
Richmond, VA 23298
804-828-9095
Annual patient visits: 61,722

Dental Society
Virginia Dental Association
P.O. Box 6906

Richmond, VA 23230-0906
804-358-4927

Government Grants for Dental Research
Virginia Commonwealth University
Grants: $2,609,933

University of Virginia Charlottesville
Charlottesville, VA
Grants: $378,373

Hampton University
Grants: $3,294

Virginia Polytechnic Institute and State University
Grants: $238,172

Washington
Dental Programs
State Health Department
Dental Division
P.O. Box 47867
Olympia, WA 98504-7867
206-664-3427
Call your nearest Health Department or Clinic to find out if they offer
free or discount dental care. When dental care is offered, it is usually
for children and senior citizens, with only limited care for adults. A
sliding fee scale is used, and low income is a factor in determining
what you're charged. Ask to speak with Connie Mix or Bob Blacksmith
to get additional information on these programs.

Seattle-King County Dental Society
2201 Sixth Ave., Suite 1306
Seattle, WA 98121-1832
206-443-7607
The Seattle-King County Dental Society has a listing of clinics and
programs that offer free or minimal cost dental care. Contact them for
a free copy.

Elderly and Disabled
Washington State Dental Association

2033 Sixth Avenue #333
Seattle, WA 98121
206-448-1914
Under the *Access Program for the Elderly and Disabled*, dental care at a reduced cost is available from participating dentists who meet the following guidelines: 1) 65 or older; 2) have no dental insurance; 3) income no more than $15,670/single or $19,765 for a family; 4) for the disabled, the same criteria for eligibility applies, but there is no age restriction. Eligibility must be re-certified every 12 months. Fees are reduced by at least 25% for patients meeting the criteria. Call or write for an application.

Dental School
School of Dentistry
University of Washington
Health Science Building
Northeast Pacific St.
Seattle, WA 98195
206-543-5830
Annual patient visits: 45,500.

Dental Society
Washington Dental Association
2033 6th Ave., Suite 333
Seattle, WA 98121-2514
206-448-1914

Government Grants for Dental Research
Gemtech, Inc.
Grants: $264,000

Washington State University
Grants: $76,250

University of Washington
Grants: $6,038,456

West Virginia
Dental Programs
Department of Health and Human Resources
Dental Information

State Capital Complex, Bldg. 6
Charleston, WV 25305
304-926-1700
Very limited dental care is available through the Health Department
other than Medicaid: however, below you'll find other contacts that do
offer reduced fee services.

Low-Income Adults, Linkline
One United Way Square
Charleston, WV 25301
800-540-8659
304-340-3510
Linkline offers reduced-fee dental services for adults 19 to 59, but you
must first apply to the program and be accepted. Low income is a
major factor in determining your eligibility.

Tiskewah Dental Clinic
600 Florida St.
Charleston, WV 25302
304-348-6613
This dental clinic treats children year-round, and senior citizens during
the summer free of charge. Call to find out if you might qualify.

Dental School
School of Dentistry
West Virginia University
The Medical Center
Morgantown, WV 26505
304-598-4810
Annual patient visits: 27,522.

Dental Society
West Virginia Dental Association
1002 Kanawha Valley Building
300 Capitol St.
Charleston, WV 25301-1794
304-344-5246

Government Grants for Dental Research
West Virginia University
Grants: $196,600

Wisconsin
Dental Programs
Division of Health
1 West Wilson
Madison, WI 53701
608-266-5152
Very limited reduced-fee dental care is available in Wisconsin. Call your local Health Center or Clinic to find out if dental is available.

Wisconsin Dental Society
111 East Wisconsin Ave., Suite 1300
Milwaukee, WI 53202
414-276-4520
The Wisconsin Dental Society has been working with County Dental Society's to come up with programs to assist the underserved with reduced fee dental services. Keep in contact with them to find out of any new programs that you might qualify for.

Dental School
School of Dentistry
Marquette University
604 N. 16th St.
Milwaukee, WI 53233
414-288-6500
Annual patient visits: 48,235.

Dental Society
Wisconsin Dental Association
111 E. Wisconsin Ave.
Suite 1300
Milwaukee, WI 53202-4811
414-276-4520

Government Grants for Dental Research
University of Wisconsin Madison
Madison, WI
Grants: $483,738

Marquette University
Grants: $109,378

Wyoming
Dental Programs
State Health Department
Dental Division
Hathaway Building, 4th Floor
Cheyenne, WY 82002
307-777-7945
The *Marginal Program* for low-income children provides dental care up to 10 years of age. You must apply and be accepted to be eligible. The *Cleft Palate Clinic* offers free diagnostic treatment and referrals. The *Sealant Program* provides sealant treatment for children of low-income families. The *Elderly Program* offers reduced fees for those low-income adults 65 or older. There is no reduced-fee dental care for those individuals 20 to 64 except through *Title 19 Emergency Care* program.

Dental Society
Wyoming Dental Association
330 S. Center St., Suite 322
Casper, WY 82601-2875
307-234-0777

Help With
Diet and Exercise

NOTES

Stop the insanity of throwing your money away on diet programs, books, and infomercial products. Why pay big money to some diet guru, who maybe spent a few years of his or her life and a few thousand bucks coming up with the latest health fad? Instead, you can contact a government office who spent millions of dollars and hundreds of man years developing the latest scientific information on weight, diet, nutrition, and exercise. And it'll only cost you the price of a stamp or phone call.

☆ ☆ ☆

From Food Pyramids To Nutritious Snacks

Did you know it takes five servings of fruit and vegetables a day to stay healthy? Or that low fat on a label of a can really means 3g or less of fat per serving?

The Food and Drug Administration (FDA) is the agency that spends all the money coming up with the latest scientific evidence to support findings like these. So if you want the latest answer to your food question, call the FDA and not your mother-in-law. They have a whole lot of information, publications, and brochures waiting to send to you, including:

- *Nutrition and the Elderly*
- *An FDA Guide to Dieting*
- *Fiber: Something Healthy To Chew On*
- *Food and Drug Interactions*
- *Keep Your Food Safe*

All these and more are free by contacting Office of Consumer Affairs, Food and Drug Administration, 5600 Fishers Lane, HFE88, Rockville, MD 20857; 301-443-3170.

☆ ☆ ☆

A Cookbook For Diabetics

If you are sick of those tasteless meals that you're forced to eat because you are a diabetic, the National Diabetes Information Clearinghouse can turn you on to wonderful recipes that don't have to taste like your laundry. Also, if you are wondering how some diabetics are able to keep their condition in check without taking insulin, they can provide you with information on that, as well.

This Clearinghouse is probably the world's best source for anything you need to know about the causes, cures, and treatment for diabetics.

For more information or a complete list of publications, contact National Diabetes Information Clearinghouse, 1 Information Way, Bethesda, MD 20892-3560; 301-654-3327.

☆ ☆ ☆

How To Pump Up Your Heart

You mean there really is good cholesterol? Yes. It's called high density lipo-proteins. To get more of the good stuff, you need to change your diet, exercise, and lose weight. A

serving of eggs has more cholesterol than a serving of rice. With just a bit of new information, you can easily plan a meal that has less cholesterol and probably tastes twice as good as what you've been eating.

This is the kind of information you can get by contacting the National Heart, Lung, and Blood Institute. They offer free publications on just about anything to do with heart disease, even information on the latest treatments and cures. Publications dealing with food and nutrition include:

- *Eating Right to Lower Your High Blood Cholesterol*
- *Eat Right To Help Lower Your High Blood Pressure*
- *Step by Step: Eating to Lower Your High Blood Cholesterol*
- *Recipes. A Low-Fat Diet*

For your free copies, contact National Heart, Lung, and Blood Information Center, P.O. Box 30105, Bethesda, MD 20824; 301-251-1222.

☆ ☆ ☆

Free Food At Uncle Sam's House

Now that's a great meal we can all relate to. But it's only for groups that are helping others, like meals for seniors, church groups, school programs, childcare centers, etc.

If you are a nonprofit and trying to improve the nutrition of others, you may be able to get free food from the government. Surplus commodities are distributed to the needy through food banks, charitable institutions, and local government agencies. Contact your local social services agency (look in the blue pages of your phone book) to find out more about these programs. Or contact U.S. Department of the Agriculture, Public Information Office, Food and Consumer Service, 3101 Park Ctr. Dr., Park Office Center Bldg., Alexandria, VA 22302; 703-305-2276.

☆ ☆ ☆

Slimming Down Without Health Riders, Thigh Masters, or Screaming Fitness Instructors

You can quit making the boat payment of your personal trainer and grab a free book instead. There are titles that will tell you how to exercise in water and save your joints from developing arthritis, how to develop walking as the only exercise you will need, or how seniors can pep up their life with an easy to do fitness program.

They are all from the office that Arnold Schwarzenegger used to run during the Bush Administration. Some of their free publications include:

- *Pep Up Your Life (a fitness book for older people)*
- *Fitness Fundamentals (guideline for personal exercise)*
- *Exercise and Weight Control*
- *Walking for Exercise and Pleasure*

For these publications and more information, contact President's Council on Physical Fitness and Sports, Suite 250, 701 Pennsylvania Ave., NW, Washington, DC 20004; 202-272-3421.

☆ ☆ ☆

Weight Watchers Get Competition From Uncle Sam

AND IT'S FREE. Weight Watchers may have prepared meals in the supermarket for dieters living a harried lifestyle, but the government and nonprofit organizations will provide meals to those on low-incomes who find shopping, meal preparation, and cleanup a problem.

There is the Meals-On-Wheels program that delivers to your door, or the congregate meal program run by many churches or senior centers.

To learn what meal options you may have, contact your local senior citizens organization, or the ElderCare Locator, National Association of Area Agencies on Aging, 1112 16th St., NW, Washington, DC 20024; 800-677-1116, which can refer you to a local resource.

☆ ☆ ☆

Hey! Liver Can Be BAD For You

Kids can call the Food and Nutrition Information Clearinghouse and get the facts so that Mom won't serve something like liver for dinner. And if you want to try and talk Mom into having pizza every night, they can also send you information on how a pizza has more nutritional value than an apple. There

is even a free listing of diet videos and free publications on almost any nutrition related topic you can think of. Some of the subjects include:

- *Diet and Cancer*
- *Nutrition and Cardiovascular Disease*
- *Nutrition and Diabetes*
- *Nutrition and the Elderly*
- *Nutrition and the Handicapped*
- *Sensible Nutrition*

For more information or for your copies, send an self-addressed, stamped envelope to Food and Nutrition Information Center, U.S. Department of Agriculture, National Agricultural Library, Room 304, Beltsville, MD 20705; 301-504-5719.

☆ ☆ ☆

Who Says Seniors Are Full Of It?

Constipation can be a serious problem for seniors or it can just be a matter of finding the right diet or exercise program. Curing constipation with the right diet and exercise is a lot easier and cheaper than doctor visits and medication. You can make a simple call to the Aging Information Center and find information on both.

This Center has dozens of free fact sheets and publications that will help seniors with their food and nutrition concerns. Some of the titles include:

- *Be Sensible About Salt*
- *Constipation*
- *Digestive Do's and Don'ts*
- *Hints For Shopping, Cooking, and Enjoying Meals*
- *Nutrition: A Lifelong Concern*

They are available by contacting National Institute on Aging Information Center, P.O. Box 8057, Gaithersburg, MD 20898-8057; 800-222-2225.

☆ ☆ ☆

Will Taking More Vitamins Make You Forget About Getting Alzheimer's?

Will drinking more milk prevent osteoporosis? Or what about eating more oysters as you get older — will that keep up your sex drive? There is a research center that spends a lot of money studying the latest scientific evidence on almost anything to do with food, nutrition, and the issues of aging, and they may be looking for volunteers. Call them and see what they are working on, which can help you live a longer, happier, and maybe even sexier life.

For more information about current research being undertaken, contact Human Nutrition Research Center on Aging at Tufts University, 711 Washington St., Boston, MA 02111; 617-556-3330.

☆ ☆ ☆

Up To $800 For Food

Call your local social service agency listed in the blue pages of your local telephone book and ask about the Food Stamp Program. Senior citizens are given special consideration.

For example, seniors unable to go to the food stamp office to be interviewed may request a phone or home interview instead. Seniors can even be living with others and still qualify as a separate household in order to receive this assistance. They can even go to school and still receive food stamps.

Contact your local social services agency to find out more about special food stamp rules for the elderly.

Contact U.S. Department of the Agriculture, Food and Consumer Service, Public Information Office, 3101 Park Ctr. Dr., Park Office Center Bldg., Alexandria, VA 22302; 703-305-2276.

☆ ☆ ☆

Two Carts For The Price Of One

Let Uncle Sam help you with your grocery shopping with some tips on how to get the most out of your nickels and dimes. Your grocery cart can cost you less and be better for your health with just a little planning.

If you are worried about the foods you are eating, and want to make sure your diet is a healthy one, then request some of the consumer information publications available from the Agriculture Research Service. They conduct research on the nutritive value of foods and the nutritional adequacy of diets and food supplies. Some of the publications they have available include:

- *Nutrition and Your Health: Dietary Guidelines for Americans (free)*
- *Food Facts For Older Adults: Information on How To Use the Dietary Guidelines ($4)*
- *Preparing Foods and Planning Menus Using the Dietary Guidelines ($2.50)*
- *Your Money's Worth in Foods ($2.25)*
- *The Sodium Content of Your Food ($2.25)*
- *Thrifty Meals for Two: Making Your Food Dollars Count ($2.50)*

A complete list of publications and ordering information is available by contacting Public Information Officer, Agriculture Research Service, U.S. Department of Agriculture, Federal Building, 6505 Belcrest Rd., Room 363, Hyattsville, MD 20782; 301-436-8617.

☆ ☆ ☆

Jog The Dog

Is your family always telling you to slow down? Is mall walking part of your life (or would you like it to be)? What about those $100 jogging shoes the kids got you for Christmas that are sitting in your closet?

The National Institute on Aging has an Exercise Packet containing articles and other helpful information on how exercise can help you live a longer, healthier life. So put on your walking shoes and get moving. Contact the National Institute on Aging Information Center, P.O. Box 8057, Gaithersburg, MD 20898-8057; 800-222-2225.

☆ ☆ ☆

Take A Free Cooking Class With Julia Child's Sister

You can spend $200 for a cooking class at a local school; a cooking video at the bookstore goes for $19.95; or you can take a free cooking class at your local County Cooperative Extension office. This is your local hotline on food where the person won't try to sell you a Butterball turkey.

Your local County Cooperative Extension office frequently has pamphlets, classes, and helpful advice on cooking, good nutrition, and weight loss. Some even offer videos on the subject.

To learn more about what your local office has to offer, look in the blue pages of your phone book for the office nearest you, or you can find the main state office in the state-by-state directory at the end of the book.

For more information, contact Extension Service, U.S. Department of Agriculture, Room 3328, Washington, DC 20250; 202-720-4111.

Free Legal Help and Consumer Advice

NOTES

Information USA, Inc.

Fire your lawyer! Instead, you can use government resources to answer most of your legal questions for free. You can learn how to write a "Living Will", take on big companies for age discrimination, and even resolve disputes with local stores, just by putting your tax dollars to work for you. If you do need an attorney, you can use the government to even help you find one that you really can afford.

The Pension Tax Guys

No need to pay an attorney money to interpret the tax issues surrounding retirement and pension plans. You can talk to the guys who wrote the law! The Internal Revenue Service operates a hotline service that allows you to speak to tax attorneys specializing in retirement and pension plan issues.

They are available Monday through Thursday, from 1:30 p.m. to 4 p.m. They can be reached at Employee Plans Technical and Actuarial Division, Internal Revenue Service, U.S. Department of the Treasury, Room 6550, CP:E:EP, 1111 Constitution Ave., NW, Washington, DC 20224; 202-622-6074 or 6075.

How To Handle the Power-of-Attorney

Sometimes you need to focus on the big picture of living and let someone else manage the details. There may come a time when you no longer feel able to handle all the responsibilities of managing your own finances.

In many cases, you can sign over a Power-of-Attorney form to a trusted relative or friend that will allow them to make financial decisions in your behalf. When it involves handling your Social Security check, you need to designate the person as a Representative Payee.

This will allow the person to receive your Social Security check, so that they can in turn pay your bills for you. A person can petition the courts to be designated a Representative Payee if their loved one cannot do so themselves due to a physical or mental condition.

To learn more about becoming a Representative Payee, contact your local Social Security office or you may call the Social Security Hotline at 800-772-1213.

Free Legal Services

You don't have to go to your neighbor's brother's cousin's kid who is an attorney, unless you want to pay for his legal advice. Uncle Sam has set up law offices all across the

country to help those who cannot afford standard legal fees.

It is the Legal Services Corporation's job to give legal help to low-income individuals in civil matters. They are staffed by over 6,400 attorneys and paralegals, and have handled over 1.5 million cases. Each program follows certain guidelines as to what cases it accepts and specific financial eligibility that possible clients must meet.

To learn about the program nearest you, look in the blue pages of your phone book, or contact Legal Services Corporation, 750 First St., NE, 11th Fl., Washington, DC 20002; 202-336-8800.

Free Help In Writing Your Will

Fill in the blanks, sign on the line. You've seen those *How To Write A Will* books in the bookstore. Why not save your money for your grandkids, instead? Many County Cooperative Extension Offices offer classes, pamphlets, and even general forms to help you along the way.

To learn what your local office has to offer, look in the blue pages of your phone book for the office nearest you, or you can find the main state office in the state-by-state directory at the end of the book.

☆ ☆ ☆

Lots More Free Legal Help

Don't waste time trying to learn the confusing ins and outs of Social Security or Medicare. Talk directly to an attorney who is on a first name basis with the people who run these programs, and can help you deal with your problem or concern without spending time getting up to speed on the complicated statutes surrounding these programs.

The following is a list of hotlines designed specifically to serve the needs of senior citizens. Services may vary from organization to organization. Some will refer you to lawyers who will offer legal assistance on a sliding fee scale; some will handle your case for you. If your state is not listed below, contact your state Department of Aging listed in the Directory of State Information at the end of this book.

Don't overlook law schools that may be nearby. Many offer legal clinics staffed by law students, although they are supervised closely by top level lawyer professors.

Arizona
Legal Hotline for the Elderly
Southern Arizona Legal Aid
160 Alameda St.
Tucson, AZ 85701
800-231-5441
602-623-5137

They give advice and referrals. Some senior centers in Arizona have attorneys that volunteer their time to give legal advice.

California
Senior Legal Hotline
Legal Services of Northern California
1004 18th St.
Sacramento, CA 95814
800-222-1753
916-442-1212

They will give legal advice and referrals. Some lawyers offer services on a reduced scale based on income. For seniors in northern California only.

District of Columbia
Legal Council for the Elderly
601 E St., NW
Building A, Fourth Floor
Washington, DC 20049
202-434-2120

They give advice and referrals.
Services are offered on a
reduced fee scale based on
age and income.

Florida
Legal Hotline for Older
Floridians
3000 Biscayne Blvd.
4th Floor
P.O. Box 370705
Miami, FL 33137
800-252-5997
305-576-5997

Lawyer Referral Service
Florida Bar Association
650 Apalachee Parkway
Tallahassee, FL 32399-2300
800-342-8011

This is strictly a referral service
for attorneys willing to work for
reduced fees.

Maine
Legal Service for the Elderly
Maine Legal Services
P.O. Box 2723
Augusta, ME 04338-2723
800-750-5353
207-623-1797

They will give advice and
referrals. Services offered to
anyone 65 or older, regardless
of income.

Michigan
Senior Alliance Inc.
3850 Second St.
Suite 160
Wayne, MI 48184
800-347-LAWS (MI only)
517-372-5959

They give advice and referrals
over the telephone. They have
a list of attorneys that will work
pro bono for people 60 or
older.

New Mexico
Lawyer Referral Services for
the Elderly
P.O. Box 25883
Albuquerque, NM 87125
800-876-6657
505-842-6252

They give advice and referrals.
Some attorneys offer sliding
fee scales based on income.

Ohio
ProSeniors Inc.
105 E. Fourth St.
Suite 1715
Cincinnati, OH 45202-4008
800-488-6070
513-621-8721

They give advice and referrals over the telephone. Actual legal services can be done on a sliding scaled based on income. ProSeniors also offers an ombudsman service if you are having any long-term health care problems. For example, if you are having trouble with the care given in a nursing home, this agency can investigate the problem.

Pennsylvania
Legal Hotline for Older Americans
Legal Council for the Elderly
P.O. Box 23180
Pittsburgh, PA 15222

800-262-5297
412-261-5297

They will give legal advice and referrals. Some lawyers offer services on a reduced scale based on income.

Texas
Legal Hotline for Older Texans
State Bar of Texas
P.O. Box 12487
Austin, TX 78711-2487
800-622-2520
512-463-1463

They will give legal advice and referrals. Some lawyers offer services on a reduced scale based on income.

☆ ☆ ☆

Free Legal Help With Age Discrimination

If the unemployment line is beginning to look like a gathering of the Gray Panthers, then maybe it's time to step back and re-evaluate. For some reason, those layoffs at work seem to affect mostly workers over 40. Do you feel as if your age was a factor in not getting a job for which you were qualified? Age-based discrimination is a serious and growing problem for older adults who depend on their income from working.

Persons 40 years of age or older are protected by the Age Discrimination in Employment Act of 1967. The law prohibits age discrimination in hiring, discharge, pay, promotions, and other terms and conditions of employment. Retaliation against a person who files a charge of age discrimination, participates in an investigation, or opposes an unlawful practice also is illegal.

Last year, the Equal Employment Opportunity Commission received 12,536 complaints of age discrimination, which accounted for over 25% of all the discrimination cases they received. Contact Equal Employment Opportunity Commission, 1801 L St., NW, Washington, DC 20507; 800-669-4000.

☆ ☆ ☆

You Have Rights

There's no need to take harassment or bullying on the job sitting down. Here is your chance to fight back. Remember, if your boss or another employee is discriminating against you, they are probably doing it to others and will continue to do it until someone forces them to stop.

If you believe you have been discriminated against by an employer, labor union, or employment agency when applying for a job or while on the job because of race, color, sex, religion, national origin, age, or disability, you may file a charge with the Equal Employment Opportunity Commission (EEOC).

The toll-free number will direct you to the appropriate EEOC number for more information and to file a complaint.

The EEOC also distributes a variety of publications including:

- *The American Disability Act: Questions and Answers*
- *Fact Sheet: National Origin Discrimination*
- *Fact Sheet: Religious Discrimination*
- *Sexual Harassment Resource Kit*
- *Information For The Private Sector*

For more information, contact Equal Employment Opportunity Commission, 1801 L St., NW, Washington, DC 20507; 800-669-4000.

Legal Help Locator

There's one phone number that can hook you up with more services for seniors than there are flavors of ice cream: the Eldercare Locator. This hotline provides access to an extensive  network of organizations serving older people at state and local community levels.

The service can connect you to a variety of services, including legal assistance and other advocates and ombudsmen. In some cases, the legal assistance services may actually come to your home or nursing home to help you complete paperwork.

To find out what's available near you, contact the Eldercare Locator, National Association of Area Agencies on Aging, 1112 16th St., NW, Washington, DC 20024; 800-677-1116. The phone lines are open between 9 a.m. and 8 p.m. EST.

Be Your Own Consumer Expert

You'd never guess by watching all those slick ads on TV that one of the most frequent things people complain about is the sale and repair of new cars.

Or what about the health club that gets you to sign up for a life-time membership only to close down the next day? Or even the store that advertises a great deal on a new T.V. only to claim to be "out of stock?"

If you feel you have been deceived or taken advantage of in some way, contact your state Consumer Protection Offices.

Depending on the circumstances, the office may contact the offending company and try to resolve the complaint on your behalf. If there are several complaints against a particular company, the Consumer Protection Office may even take legal action.

Look in the Directory of State Information at the back of this book to find the Consumer Protection Office nearest you.

When You Get Caught In The Legal Runaround

Because of a slip-up by your lawyer, you went to jail for a parking ticket. What about the lawyer to whom you paid an expensive retainer only to learn that she seems to have moved to Tahiti permanently? Don't think you're stuck just because they know more about the law than you do.

Often affiliated with the State Bar Associations, Attorney Grievances offices can help you resolve ethical, billing, and theft complaints against lawyers in your state. They can also tell you if an attorney has been sanctioned in any way before you even start to do business with them.

The Attorney Grievance programs deal with ethical complaints; the Fee Arbitration programs will help resolve billing complaints; and the Client Security Trust Funds provides money to clients who have had money stolen from them by their lawyers.

Look in the Directory of State Information at the back of this book to find the program nearest you.

When All Else Fails

You have done your best, written letters, documented phone calls, yet you still feel as if you haven't been helped.

Use the power of the voting booth, and call your Senator or Representative. Each one has support staff set up to solve the problems of the people who voted them into office and keep them happy so that they'll keep voting for them. Offices are located in both Washington, D.C. and in their home districts.

Remember, these are the people who vote to renew an agency's budget, so they can usually have their way with government agencies. Businesses also know laws and regulations can help them or hurt them, so they are not going to want to bite the hand that feeds them.

To locate your U.S. Senator or Representative, look in the blue pages of your phone book, or contact The Capitol, Washington, DC 20510; 202-224-3121.

Mug the Muggers

Victims of Crimes have united in an effort to get criminals to repay their victims.

Millions of people and their families are victimized by crime every year. Congress enacted a law to establish a Crime Victims Fund to compensate innocent victims of violent crime. Part of the money is given to help compensate victims or their families for costs relating to such crimes as muggings, and even murder.

One of the nice things about this money is that it does not come out of the pockets of taxpayers; rather it is collected from the criminals themselves through criminal fines, forfeited bail bonds, penalty fees, and forfeited literary profits.

To learn who you need to talk to in your state, contact Office of Congressional and Public Affairs, Office of Justice Programs, U.S. Department of Justice, 633 Indiana Ave., NW, Washington, DC 20531; 202-307-0781.

Money and Help
For Your Home
or Apartment

F or many people over 65, their homes are their only asset. What if you can't afford the taxes, will you be kicked out on the street? The house didn't seem so big when you had four kids, but now that you are all alone, you have to struggle just to keep it up.

What about if you are trying to find an affordable apartment? If you know where to look, there are all kinds of information about different housing opportunities for the older crowd, along with help to fix up your house or get a home equity loan, and much more.

Did you know:
- Almost 21 million households in the U.S. are headed by people 65 years or older.
- 8.9 million are headed by persons over 75.
- Two-thirds of renters are single.
- 4 million households spend more than 35 percent of their incomes on housing.
- 45% of public housing units are occupied by older adults.

Your Home Cash Machine

Just because the house you bought 30 years ago for $30,000 is now worth $500,000, doesn't mean that you are living on easy street. In fact, chances are that if you are over 65, you are struggling to make ends meet.

But it just doesn't have to be this way. To make your life easier, you can convert the value of your home into ready cash without having to sell your house and move. You can use this cash to get in-home care, someone to cut your lawn, pay for a new furnace or roof, get a new T.V., or even take your grandkids to McDonald's. But you have to be careful in the way that you do it.

To help you out, the Federal Trade Commission has several free publications that explain more about the different types of mortgage options:

- *Home Equity Credit Lines*
- *Home Financing Primer*
- *Mortgage Money Guide*
- *Reverse Mortgages*

For your copies or more information, contact Public Reference, Room 130, Federal Trade Commission, Washington, DC 20580; 202-326-2222.

☆ ☆ ☆

Choosing The Best Way To Live

Maybe your house is too large to manage. Maybe you need someone to come in and clean and cook. Or just maybe a roommate's the answer.

A free copy of *Your Home, Your Choice (Living Choices for Older Americans)* will help you make the right decision and show you where to get more help for any decision you make.

Contact Public Reference, Room 130, Federal Trade Commission, Washington, DC 20580; 202-326-2222.

Rent at Big Discounts

Want to find an apartment you can afford in a building is filled with people your own age? No need to look any further than your local public housing office. They have a special program called, Supportive Housing for the Elderly (Section 202).

If you meet certain income guidelines, your rent will be no higher than 10-30% of your adjusted income. An added plus is that many of these buildings also offer Service Coordinators, the concierge of special services for seniors. They can hook you up with special transportation, medical programs, food assistance, and more.

If your nonprofit or consumer cooperative sees a need for housing services for elderly persons, you can take advantage of the Section 202 program. Capital advances are made to eligible private, nonprofit sponsors to finance the development of rental housing with supportive services for the elderly.

The advance is interest free and does not have to be repaid as long as the housing remains available for very low-income elderly persons for at least 40 years. You can also take advantage of the fact that the Service Coordinators are an eligible expense under this program.

Contact the HUD field office nearest you to learn how you can apply. The HUD FIeld Offices for each state are listed in the Directory of State Information in the back of this book.

☆ ☆ ☆

A Thousand Bucks To Fix Up Your House

Need money to widen your doorway for wheelchairs, install ramps or grab bars, or even put on a new roof? There's a free money program that awards grants of AT LEAST $1,000 to help a senior citizen fix up and repair their home.

As part of the HOME Investment Partnership Program, the HOME Repair/Modification Programs For Elderly Homeowners program makes funds available to low-income individuals for home repair services. Money is distributed through over 500 sites, so to locate the closest program and application information, contact the American Communities, P.O. Box 7189, Gaithersburg, MD 20898; 800-998-9999.

Park It In A Trailer Park

Join the crowd of over 1,227,000 seniors who own or rent trailer homes. No lawn to mow, no big house to clean.

Many senior citizens live in trailer homes for the convenience and camaraderie of trailer park living. The U.S. Department of Housing and Urban Development (HUD) insures loans for people to finance the purchase of manufactured homes and/or lots. The loans, called Title 1, are made by private lending institutions, and are available to any person able to make the cash investment and the loan payments.

To learn more about this insurance program, contact the HUD Field office near you, or Assistant Secretary for Housing-Federal Housing Commissioner, U.S. Department of Housing and Urban Development, Washington, DC 20410; 202-708-3600.

☆ ☆ ☆

Get Cash From Your Home

Do you have a home, but no money to pay for repair bills or even your own medical bills?

The Home Equity Conversion Mortgage (HECM) allows a homeowner, 62 years of age or older, to borrow against the equity in his or her home and free up cash for home improvements, medical costs, or other living expenses. Loans do not have to be repaid until the homeowner moves from the home, sells the home, or dies.

The HECM program enables older Americans to continue living independently in their own homes. This program is now available in 47 states and is often referred to as a reverse mortgage.

If you would like more information on applying for the program, contact the HUD field office near you (listed in the Directory of State Information in the back of this book), or contact Assistance Secretary for Single Family Housing, U.S. Department of Housing and Urban Development, Washington, DC 20410.

☆ ☆ ☆

Money To Pay The Rent

Almost 25% of seniors rent the places they live in. But if you are struggling to pay rent, there is a U.S. Department of Housing and Urban Development (HUD) program that may be able to help you. Under the Section 8 Rental Assistance Program, low-income renters can receive special vouchers to cover part of their rent.

Low-income doesn't have to mean poor. For example, in some parts of Ohio the eligible income for a single person can go up to $24,700. With the vouchers, the most you will have to pay is 30% of your adjusted income for rent.

To apply for this type of assistance, contact your local public housing agency (look in the blue pages of your phone book), or the HUD field office for your state. The HUD Field Offices for each state are listed in the Directory of State Information in the back of this book.

☆ ☆ ☆

Apply for Valets and Room Service

No, you are not living in a luxury hotel, but actually in your own apartment. For many seniors, as they get older, they need help with housekeeping, bathing, and more.

The Congregate Housing Services Program (CHSP) is a demonstration program designed to help the elderly remain in rented dwellings as they age. Some public housing agencies and nonprofit Section 202 sponsor meals and other support services such as housekeeping, aid in grooming, dressing, and other activities to maintain personal appearance and hygiene for frail elderly and nonelderly handicapped residents.

Each participant must pay 10 to 20 percent of their income for the meals program, plus they may have to pay a flat fee for other supportive services. Total fees can be no more than 20% of his/her adjusted income.

There is a listing below of those who participate in the program, as well as the local U.S. Department of Housing and Urban Development or Rural Housing and Community Development Service offices. Keep in mind that many other elderly housing facilities offer similar services to residents.

For more information, contact the program nearest you from the list below, or contact Assistant Secretary for Housing-Federal Housing Commissioner, U.S. Department of Housing and Urban Development, Washington, DC 20410; 202-708-2730.

Congregate Housing Services Program
Grantee List

Arkansas
HUD/RHCDS Field Office Little
Rock
North Arkansas Human
Services
P.O. Box 2578
Batesville, AR 72503

California
HUD/RHCDS Field Office Los
Angeles
Los Angeles County Housing
Authority
4800 Cesar Chavez Ave.
Los Angeles, CA 90022-1307
213-260-2064

HUD/RHCDS Field Office San
Francisco
Marin County Housing
Authority
30 N. San Pedro Rd.
P.O. Box 4282
San Rafael, CA 94913
415-383-3131

Spanish Speaking Unity
Council
1900 Fruitvale Ave., Suite 2A
Oakland, CA 94601-2468
510-534-7764

Monterey County Housing
Authority
123 Rico St.
Salinas, CA 93907
408-424-2892 x610

Colorado
HUD/RHCDS Field Office
Denver
Sunset Towers, Inc.
1865 Larimer St.
Denver, CO 80202
303-297-0408

Francis Heights, Inc.
2626 Osceola St.
Denver, CO 80212-1258
303-433-7143

Archdiocesan Housing
Committee
1580 Logan, #700
Denver, CO 80203
303-830-0215

Connecticut
HUD/RHCDS Field Office
Hartford
Mansfield Retirement
Community
One Silo Circle
Storrs, CT 06268-2018
203-429-9933

HUD/RHCDS Field Office
Amherst, MA
State of CT
Dept. of Social Services
25 Sigourney St.
10th Floor
Hartford, CT 06106
203-424-5283

Delaware
Wilmington Housing Authority
400 Walnut St.
Wilmington, DE 19801
302-429-6700

Florida
HUD/RHCDS Field Office
Jacksonville
Ft. Pierce Housing Authority
601 Avenue B
Fort Pierce, FL 34950-4501
407-595-0239

Metro Dade County Housing
Authority
P.O. Box 350250
Miami, FL 33135-0250
305-644-5293

Dowling Park Apartments, Inc.
P.O. Box 4327
Dowling Park, FL 32060
904-658-3333

Dowling Park Home, Inc.
P.O. Box 4327
Dowling Park, FL 32060
904-658-3333

Kinneret Inc. & Kinneret II
515 S. Delaney Ave.
Orlando, FL 32801-3841
407-425-4537

Hawaii
HUD/RHCDS Field Office
Honolulu
Hale Mahaolu, 200 Hina Ave.
Kahului, Maui, HI 96732-1821
808-871-4782

Illinois
HUD/RHCDS Field Office
Chicago
The Lambs, Inc.
P.O. Box 520
Libertyville, IL 60048-0520
708-362-4636

Bloomington Housing Authority
104 E. Wood St.
Bloomington, IL 61701-6768
309-829-3360

Indiana
HUD/RHCDS Field Office
Indianapolis
Muncie Housing Authority
Agency
409 E. First St.
Muncie, IN 47302

Iowa
HUD/RHCDS Field Office Des
Moines
Ecumenical Housing, Inc.
2671 Owen Court
Dubuque, IA 52002

Alverno Apartments, Inc.
3525 Winsor Ave.
Dubuque, IA 52001-0419

Charles City Housing
Commission
1000 S. Grand Ave.
Charles City, IA 50616

HUD/RHCDS Field Office Des
Moines
Waterloo Housing Authority
620 Mulberry St. Carnegie

Waterloo, IA 50703
319-233-0201

Kansas
HUD/RHCDS Field Office
Kansas City
HA of the City of Atchison
103 S. 7th St.
Atchison, KS 66002

Louisiana
HUD/RHCDS Field Office New
Orleans
New Orleans Housing
Authority
918 Carondelet St.
New Orleans, LA 70130-3912
504-552-4127

Evangeline Council Housing f/t
1001 North Reed St.
Ville Platte, LA 70581

Maine
HUD/RHCDS Field Office
Manchester
Methodist Conference Home
39 Summer St.
Rockland, ME 04841-2939
207-596-6477

Old Town Housing Authority
100 S. Main St., P.O. Box 404
Old Town, ME 04468-1572
207-827-6151

Brunswick Housing Authority
30 Water St.
Brunswick, ME 04011-1541
207-725-8711

Summer Street Housing
Preservation, Inc.
39 Summer St.
Rockland, ME 04841-2939
207-596-6477

Maryland
HUD/RHCDS Field Office
Baltimore
Baltimore City DHCD
417 E. Fayette St., Room 265
Baltimore, MD 21202-3431
410-396-4271

St. Mary's ARC
P.O. Box 338
Leonardtown, MD 20650-0338
301-475-3122

Massachusetts
HUD/RHCDS Field Office
Boston
Bethany Homes
10-12 Phoenix Row
Haverhill, MA 01832
508-372-7597

MI Residential
189 Maple St.
Lawrence, MA 01841-3761
508-682-7575

Jewish Community Housing
30 Wallingford Rd.
Brighton, MA 02135-4753
617-254-8008 x41

Michigan
HUD/RHCDS Field Office
Detroit
Jewish Federation Apts., Inc.

15100 W. Ten Mile Rd.
Oak Park, MI 48237
810-967-4240

Detroit Int. Stake Adult
Housing
16651 Labser Rd.
Detroit, MI 48219

Plymouth Opportunity Non-
Profit Housing
593 Deer St.
Plymouth, MI 48170-1701
313-455-2669

HUD/RHCDS Field Office
Grand Rapids
Moore Non-Profit Housing
Corp.
401 W. Jolly Rd.
Lansing, MI 48910-6607
517-393-4442

Potential Development Homes,
I
P.O. Box 1978
Jackson, MI 49204

Minnesota
HUD/RHCDS Field Office
Minneapolis
St. Paul Housing Authority
480 Cedar St., Suite 600
St. Paul, MN 55101-2240
612-298-4487

Duluth Housing Redevel.
Authority
P.O. Box 16900
Duluth, MN 55816-0900
218-726-2857

HRA City of South St. Paul
125 Third Avenue North
South St. Paul, MN 55075
612-455-1560

Mississippi
HUD/RHCDS Field Office
Jackson
MS Regional Housing
Authority No. 5
P.O. Box 419
Newton, MS 39345-0419
601-683-3530

Mississippi Regional HA
P.O. Box 419
Newton, MS 39345-0419
601-683-3530

Missouri
HUD/RHCDS Field Office St.
Louis
The Delcrest
8350 Delcrest Dr.
St. Louis, MO 63124-2166
314-991-2055

St. Louis Housing Authority
5655 Kingsbury
St. Louis, MO 63112
314-361-1920

Murphy-Blair Senior Commons
2600 Hadley St.
St. Louis, MO 63106
314-539-9571

Community Housing
Association
10 Millstone Campus
St. Louis, MO 63146

B'nai B'rith Covenant House I
10 Millstone Campus
St. Louis, MO 63146

Montana
HUD/RHCDS Field Office
Denver
Northern Cheyenne Housing
Authority
P.O. Box 3207
Lame Deer, MT 59043

Nebraska
HUD/RHCDS Field Office
Omaha
Falls City Housing Authority
800 E. 21st St.
Falls City, NE 68355-2349
402-245-4204

Lincoln Area Agency on Aging
129 N. 10th St.
Room 222
Lincoln, NE 68508

New Hampshire
HUD/RHCDS Field Office
Manchester
198 Hanover St.
Manchester, NH 03104-6125
603-624-2100 x109

Manchester HRA
198 Hanover St.
Manchester, NH 03104-6125
603-624-2100 x109

Laconia HRA
25 Union St.
Laconia, NH 03246-3558
603-524-2112

Keene Housing Authority
105 Castle St.
Keene, NH 03431

Somersworth Housing
Authority
9 Bartlett Ave.
Somersworth, NH 03878

Nashua Housing Authority
101 Major Dr.
Nashua, NH 03060

Manchester Housing Authority
198 Hanover St.
Manchester, NH 03104-6125
603-624-2100 x109

New Jersey
HUD/RHCDS Field Office
Newark
Plainfield Housing Authority
510 E. Front St.
Plainfield, NJ 07060-1424
908-753-3439

Congregation Brothers of
Israel
511 Greenwood Ave.
Trenton, NJ 08609-2108
609-394-0093

New York
HUD/RHCDS Field Office New
York
New York City Housing
Authority
250 Broadway
Room 1503
New York, NY 10007
212-306-3330

HUD/RHCDS Field Office
Buffalo
Schenectady Municipal HA
375 Broadway
Schenectady, NY 12305-2519
518-372-3346

North Carolina

HUD/RHCDS Field Office
Greensboro
Bell House, Inc.
2400 Summit Ave.
Greensboro, NC 27405-5014
910-621-0938

High Point Housing Authority
500 E. Russell Ave.
P.O. Box 1779
High Point, NC 27261-1779
910-887-2661 x60/35

East Salem Homes, Inc.
8 W. Third St., Suite 400
Winston Salem, NC 27101
910-725-3564

Winston-Salem Housing
Foundation
8 W. Third St.
Suite 400
Winston-Salem, NC 27101-
3923
910-725-3564

Carolina Christian Village
Homes
8 W. Third St.
Suite 400
Winston-Salem, NC 27101-
3923
910-725-3564

North Dakota

HUD/RHCDS Field Office
Denver
Fargo Housing Authority
2525 N. Broadway
Fargo, ND 58102-1439
701-293-7870

HUD/RHCDS Field Office
Bismarck
Senior Meals & Services, Inc.
P.O. Box 713
Devil's Lake, ND 58330

Ohio

HUD/RHCDS Field Office
Cincinnati
Cincinnati Metrop. Housing
Authority
16 W. Central Pkwy. Zone 10
Cincinnati, OH 45210
513-961-5788

HUD/RHCDS Field Office
Cleveland
Alpha Phi Alpha Homes
695 Dunbar Dr.
Akron, OH 44311-1315
216-376-8787

HUD/RHCDS Field Office
Columbus
Columbus Recreation & Parks
Department
174 E. Long St.
Columbus, OH 43215
614-645-3865

Oklahoma

HUD/RHCDS Field Office
Oklahoma City

Cherokee Nation
P.O. Box 948
Tahlequah, OK 74465-0948
918-456-0671 x241

HUD/RHCDS Field Office
Tulsa
Muskogee Fairhaven Manor,
Phase I
500 Dayton
Muskogee, OK 74403
918-682-4300

Oregon
HUD/RHCDS Field Office
Portland
Housing Authority of Portland
335 NW 19th St.
Portland, OR 97209
503-241-7229

Pennsylvania
HUD/RHCDS Field Office
Pittsburgh
HA of the County of Elk
P.O. Box 100
Johnsonburg, PA 15845-0100
814-781-3428

Riverview Towers, Phase II,
Inc.
52 Garetta St.
Pittsburgh, PA 15217-3231
412-647-7407

Riverview Towers, Phase I,
Inc.
52 Garetta St.
Pittsburgh, PA 15217-3231
412-647-7407

Mid ACV Housing Corp.
P.O. Box 367
East Brady, PA 16028

HUD/RHCDS Field Office
Philadelphia
Philadelphia Housing Authority
801 Arch St., 5th Floor
Philadelphia, PA 19107
215-684-4421

OIC Housing
1717/27 W. Honey Park Ave.
Philadelphia, PA 19140
215-229-2329

Rhode Island
HUD/RHCDS Field Office
Providence
United Methodist Retirement
Center
40 Irving Ave.
East Providence, RI 02914
401-438-4456

South Dakota
South Dakota HDA
221 South Central
Pierre, SD 57501
605-773-3181

Tennessee
HUD/RHCDS Field Office
Nashville
St. Peter Manor
108 North Auburndale
Memphis, TN 38104-6405
901-278-8200

HUD/RHCDS Field Office
Knoxville

Orange Grove Center
615 Derby St.
Chattanooga, TN 37404-1632
615-493-2919

Texas
HUD/RHCDS Field Office
Houston
W. Leo Daniels Towers
8826 Harrell St.
Houston, TX 77093
713-692-8598

HUD/RHCDS Field Office San
Antonio
REAL, Inc.
301 Lucero
Alice, TX 78332
512-668-3158

Utah
HUD/RHCDS Field Office

Omaha
Episcopal Management Corp.
514 North 300 West
Kaysville, UT 84037-3103
801-544-4231

Wisconsin
HUD/RHCDS Field Office
Milwaukee
Residential Care
424 Washington Ave.
Oshkosh, WI 54901
414-236-6560

Wyoming
HUD/RHCDS Field Office
Denver
RENEW
2 North Main
Suite 406
Sheridan, WY 82801
307-674-4200

☆ ☆ ☆

Small Town Rent Money

Senior citizens have enough to worry about without wondering if they have the money to pay the rent.

If you live in a rural area and need some help with rent, contact the Rural Housing and Community Development Services (formerly Farmers Home Administration), which provides payments to make up the difference between the tenants' payments and the Rural Housing-approved rents for the housing.

To be eligible, low-income families must occupy Rural Rental Housing, Rural Cooperative Housing, and Farm Labor Housing projects financed by the Rural Housing and Community Development Services.

To learn more, contact your local office of Rural Housing and Community Development Services (look in the blue pages of your phone book), or Rural Housing and Community Development Services, U.S. Department of Agriculture, Washington, DC 20250; 202-720-1599.

☆ ☆ ☆

How Safe Is Your Home?

Every day there are stories in the paper about the dangers of lead paint, radon, or carbon dioxide. The Environmental Protection Agency is responsible for controlling environmental pollution and can answer all your questions. They have brochures and pamphlets describing how to check for radon and what should be done about it; the proper use of pesticides; how to garden chemically free; recycling;

how to find and use safe drinking water; and indoor and outdoor air pollution.

For all your environmental questions, contact Public Information Center 3404, U.S. Environmental Protection Agency, 401 M St., SW, Washington, DC 20450; 202-260-2080.

☆ ☆ ☆

No Down Payment Necessary

You don't even have to wear your uniform to qualify. If you are a veteran or an unmarried surviving spouse of a vet, you may be eligible for a loan guarantee for the purchase and refinancing of a home, condo, or manufactured home.

Veterans Affairs (VA) guarantees part of the total loan so a veteran may obtain a mortgage on a home or condominium with a competitive interest rate — and without a down payment, if the lender agrees. VA requires a down payment for the purchase of a manufactured home.

To learn who can qualify, details of financing, and more, contact Veterans Assistance Office, U.S. Department of Veterans Affairs, 810 Vermont Ave., NW, Washington, DC 20420; 800-827-1000.

$15,000 To Spruce Up Your Home

Need a new furnace, roof, water heater, or even plumbing in your house? Don't let your house deteriorate around you.

If you live in a small town and don't make much money, you can apply for a grant to fix up your home from the Rural Housing Preservation Grants (Section 504). The average grant is $7,500, but you can get up to $15,000. The money comes from the government, but is given to local groups who in turn give it out to local homeowners.

To learn more about the program, to identify local groups giving out the money, or to learn eligibility requirements, contact your local Rural Housing and Community Development Services (formerly Farmers Home Administration).

You may also contact Multiple Family Housing Loan Division, Rural Housing and Community Development Services, U.S. Department of Agriculture, Washington, DC 20250; 202-720-1606.

1% Loans To Move To The Country

You can move away from congestion, nosy neighbors, and smog by checking out a program designed to help you get a home in the country. The program is called Section 502, and it's set up just for  low-income families to buy new or existing houses in rural areas. Borrowers may reduce the interest rate to as low as 1 percent, and for some borrowers the loan term may be as long as 38 years. There are income requirements you must meet to qualify.

For information on the loans and eligibility requirements, contact your local Rural Housing office (formerly Farmers Home Administration) or Rural Housing and Community Development Services, U.S. Department of Agriculture, Washington, DC 20250; 202-720-1474.

Continuing Care Communities

Many elderly choose to move from their homes and into continuing care retirement communities (CCRCs), also called life-care communities. Typically these provide housing, personal care, nursing home care, and a range of social and recreation services as well as congregate meals. Residents enter into a contractual agreement with the community to pay an entrance fee and monthly fees in exchange for benefits and services. The contract usually remains in effect for the remainder of a resident's life.

The definition of these communities continues to be confusing and inconsistent due to the wide range of services offered, differing types of housing units, and different contracts. There have been some problems with refunds or of cancelling the contract if someone changes their mind.

The American Association of Homes for the Aging has a consumer guidebook which provides information about the various contracts and services, as well as outlines the benefits and risks.

Continuing Care Retirement Communities Guidebook is available for $10.95 by contacting American Association of Homes for the Aging, Suite 500, 901 E St., NW, Washington, DC 20004; 202-783-2242.

☆ ☆ ☆

Can't Pay Your Property Taxes?

There is no need to gripe about the local school board voting in another tax increase for the schools when your kids have long since graduated. Many seniors own houses mortgage free, yet cannot afford to pay their property taxes. Property tax deferral programs are popular in many states, and enable older home owners to postpone paying their taxes until they sell their homes or die. Many states even offer property tax relief of varying amounts to seniors.

The state pays taxes to the local government for the homeowner. These payments accrue with interest as a loan from the state to the homeowner, secured by equity in the home. Upon death or prior sale of the home, the loan is repaid to the state from the proceeds of the sale of the estate. To learn more about this program, contact your State Department of Taxation.

Roommate Hotline

Maybe you haven't had a roommate other than your spouse since college, but it may be time to reconsider. An option for many elderly so they can stay in their homes is to get a roommate. Shared housing is a way to help with bill payments, as well as the social benefits of having someone else around. According to statistics, 670,000 people over 65 share housing with nonrelatives; that's a 35 percent increase from over a decade ago.

There are a number of shared housing projects in existence today. One of the largest is called Operation Match, which is a division in the housing offices of many cities. It helps match people looking for an affordable place to live with those who have space in their homes and are looking for someone to aid with their housing expenses.

To learn more about this type of program, contact the housing office in your area (look in the blue pages of your phone book), or contact the ElderCare Hotline for a referral to an appropriate agency at 800-677-1116.

Save Your House Profit From The Tax Man

Say you want to sell your house in Ohio for $150,000 and buy a condo in Florida for $30,000. The law says that when you sell your home, you are required to buy a new home of equal

or greater value, or pay tax on the difference.

In order to provide extra assistance to those over age 55, the Internal Revenue Service provides a once-in-a-lifetime tax break. Those who are selling their personal residence may qualify for the exclusion of up to $125,000 of gain on the home sale.

Certain use and ownership restrictions apply to this one-time exclusion. For more information, request Publication 523, *Selling Your Home* from the Internal Revenue Forms Line, 800-829-3676.

$1,800 To Keep You Warm This Winter

Storm windows, insulation, and even weather stripping, can help reduce your fuel bill. The elderly can receive assistance to weatherize their homes and apartments at no charge if they meet certain income guidelines. States allocate dollars to nonprofit agencies for purchasing and installing energy-related repairs, with the average grant being $1800 per year.

Contact your State Energy Office or the Weatherization Assistance Programs Branch, EE532, U.S. Department of Energy, 1000 Independence Ave., SW, Washington, DC 20585; 202-426-1698.

☆ ☆ ☆

Can't Pay Your Energy Bill?

Get a break, and be part of over 1,500,000 seniors who get a deal on their heating and cooling bill. Even if you own or rent your home or apartment, you may be eligible for Low Income Home Energy Assistance Program (LIHEAP).

Although eligibility requirements vary from state to state, the household's income must not exceed 150% of the poverty level or 60% of the state median income. Payments may be made directly to eligible households or to home energy suppliers, and may take the form of cash, vouchers, or payments to third parties, such as utility companies or fuel dealers.

To learn more about the program, you may contact the State LIHEAP coordinator from the list below, or Administration for Children and Families, Office of Community Services, 370 L'Enfant Promenade, SW, Washington, DC 20447.

LIHEAP Coordinators

Alabama
Mr. Gareth D. Whitehead
LIHEAP Coordinator
Department of Economic and
Community Affairs
401 Adams Ave.
P.O. Box 5690
Montgomery, AL 36103-5690
205-242-5365

Alaska
Ms. Mary Riggen-Ver
Energy Assistance Coordinator
Department of Health and
Social Services
Division of Public Assistance
400 W. Willoughby Ave., #301
Juneau, AK 99801-1731

907-465-3058
Fax: 907-465-3319

Arizona
Ms. Juanita Garcia
Program Manager
Arizona Department of
Economic Security
Community Services
Administration, 086Z-A
P.O. Box 6123-010A
Phoenix, AZ 85005
602-542-6611
Fax: 602-229-2782

Arkansas
Ms. Cathy Rowe, LIHEAP Unit
OCS/Division of Economic and

Medical Services
Dept. of Human Services
P.O. Box 1437/Slot 1330
Little Rock, AR 72203-1437
501-682-8726

California
Ms. Toni Curtis
Deputy Director of Programs
California Department of
Economic Opportunity
700 N. 10th St., Room 272
Sacramento, CA 95814
916-323-8694
Fax: 916-327-3153

Colorado
Mr. Glenn Cooper
LIHEAP Administrator
Division of Self Sufficiency
Department of Social Services
1575 Sherman St., 3rd Floor
Denver, CO 80203
303-866-5972
Fax: 303-866-4214

Connecticut
Ms. Marion Wojick
Program Supervisor
Energy Services Unit
Department of Social Services
25 Sigourney St., 6th Floor
Hartford, CT 06106
203-424-5891
Fax: 203-566-3098

Delaware
Ms. Leslie Lee, Energy
Program Manager
Department of Health and
Social Services

Div. of State Service Centers
Carvel State Office Building
4th Floor, P.O. Box 8911
Wilmington, DE 19801
302-577-3491
Fax: 302-577-2383

District of Columbia
Mr. Richard Kirby, Chief
Citizen Energy Resources Div.
DC Energy Office
613 G St., NW, Suite 500
Washington, DC 20001
202-727-9700
Fax: 202-727-9582

Florida
Mr. Ray Smith
Program Coordinator
Bureau of Community
Assistance
Dept. of Community Affairs
2740 Centerview Dr.
Tallahassee, FL 32399-2100
904-488-7541

Georgia
Mr. Preston Weaver
Director
Office of Community Services
Division of Family and Children
Services
Two Peachtree St., NW
Atlanta, GA 30334-5600
404-656-6697

Hawaii
Ms. Patricia Williams
LIHEAP Coordinator
Hawaii Department of Human
Services

810 Richards St., Suite 500
Honolulu, HI 96809
808-586-5734
Fax: 808-586-5744

Idaho
Ms. Neva Kaufman
LIHEAP Program Specialist
FOO, Division of Welfare
Dept. of Health and Welfare
450 W. State St., Statehouse
Boise, ID 83720
208-334-5732

Illinois
Mr. Wayne Curtis, Chief
Office of Human Services
Department of Commerce and
Community Affairs
620 E. Adams St., B-4
Bressmer Building
Springfield, IL 62701
217-785-6135

Indiana
Mr. Thomas Scott
LIHEAP Coordinator
Family and Social Services
Administration
Division of Family and Children
P.O. Box 7083
Indianapolis, IN 46207-7083
317-232-7015

Iowa
Ms. Sue Downey
Chief, Bureau of Energy
Assistance
Division of Community Action
Agencies
Department of Human Rights

Lucas State Office Building
Des Moines, IA 50319
515-281-3838/3943
Fax: 515-242-6119

Kansas
Ms. Kathy Valentine
Energy Program Administrator
Division of Income
Maintenance, DSRS
Docking State Office Bldg.
6th Floor
915 SW Harrison Street
Topeka, KS 66612-1570
913-296-3349
Fax: 913-296-1158

Kentucky
Mr. Patrick Bishop, Manager
Energy Assistance Branch,
DMD
Dept. of Social Insurance
Cabinet for Human Resources
275 E. Main St., 2nd Floor
Frankfort, KY 40621
502-564-4847

Louisiana
Mr. Lonnie Didier
Program Manager
Department of Social Services
Office of Community Services
P.O. Box 3318
Baton Rouge, LA 70821
504-342-2274

Maine
Ms. Jo-Ann Choate
LIHEAP Coordinator
Maine State Housing Authority
353 Water St.

P.O. Box 2669
Augusta, ME 04338-2669
207-626-4600
Fax: 207-626-4678

Maryland
Ms. Sandra Brown, Director
Energy Assistance Program
Community Services
Administration
Dept. of Human Resources
311 W. Saratoga St.
Baltimore, MD 21201
410-767-7218
Fax: 410-333-0256

Massachusetts
Mr. James A. Hays
Director
EOCD/BEP
Saltonstall Bldg., Room 1803
100 Cambridge St.
Boston, MA 02202
617-727-7004, ext. 533
Fax: 617-727-4259

Michigan
Ms. Shirley Nowakowski
Director, Energy Services
Department of Social Services
325 S. Grand Ave.
P.O. Box 30037
Lansing, MI 48909
517-373-8023

Minnesota
Mr. Mark D. Kaszynski
Energy Assistance Program
Coordinator
Division of Community Based
Services, EPU

390 N. Robert St., Room 125
St. Paul, MN 55101
612-297-2590

Mississippi
Mr. Godwin Agulanna
LIHEAP Branch Director
Division of Community
Services
Mississippi Department of
Human Services
750 N. State St.
Jackson, MS 39202-3524
601-359-4769

Missouri
Mr. Charles F. Wright
Administrator
Division of Family Services
P.O. Box 88
Jefferson City, MO 65103
314-751-0472
Fax: 314-526-5592

Montana
Mr. Jim Nolan, Chief
Division of Family Assistance
Department of Social and
Rehabilitation Services
P.O. Box 4210
Helena, MT 59604-4210
406-444-4546
Fax: 406-444-4519

Nebraska
Mr. Bill Davenport
Public Asst. Unit
Program and Planning
Specialist
Department of Social Services
310 Centennial Mall South

5th Floor
P.O. Box 95026
Lincoln, NE 65809
402-471-9172
Fax: 402-471-9455

Nevada
Ms. Vickie DeKoekkoek
LIHEAP Program Manager
Nevada Department of Human
Services, Welfare Division
2527 N. Carson St.
Carson City, NV 89710
702-687-6919

New Hampshire
Mr. Richard M. Johnson
Fuel Asst. Program Manager
Governor's Office of Energy
and Community Services
57 Regional Dr.
Concord, NH 03301-8506
603-271-2611
Fax: 603-271-2615

New Jersey
Mr. John R. Simzak
Coordinator
Home Energy Assistance Unit
DHS, Division of Economic
Assistance, CN 716
Trenton, NJ 08625
609-588-2488
Fax: 609-588-3369

New Mexico
Ms. Dorian Dodson
Planner Director
Division of Income Support
Department of Human
Services

P.O. Box 234B, Pollen Plaza
Santa Fe, NM 87504-2348

New York
Mr. John Fredericks
Director, Bureau of Energy
Programs
NY State Department of Social
Services
40 N. Pearl St.
Albany, NY 12243-0001
518-474-9321
Fax: 518-474-9347

North Carolina
Ms. Kay Fields, Chief
Public Assistance Section
Division of Social Services
Dept. of Human Resources
325 N. Salisbury St.
Raleigh, NC 27603
919-733-7831

North Dakota
Ms. Gail Erickson
LIHEAP Coordinator
Energy Assistance and
Emergency Services
Department of Human
Services
State Capitol Bldg., 3rd Floor
Bismarck, ND 58505
701-224-4056
Fax: 701-224-2359

Ohio
Ms. Vicky Mroczek
Program Administrator
Home Energy Assistance
Program
Ohio Dept. of Development

77 South High, 25th Floor
Columbus, OH 43215
614-644-6858

Oklahoma
Mr. Ron Amos
Program Supervisor
Division of Family Support
Services
Department of Human
Services
P.O. Box 25352
Oklahoma City, OK 73125
405-521-4089

Oregon
Ms. Donna Crawford
LIHEAP Coordinator
Community Services
Oregon Housing and
Community Services
1600 State St.
Salem, OR 97310-0161
503-986-2094

Pennsylvania
Ms. Joan Brenner, LIHEAP
Director
Div. of Cash Assistance, DPW
Complex 2, Room 224
Willow Oak Building
P.O. Box 2675
Harrisburg, PA 17105
717-772-7907
Fax: 717-772-6451

Puerto Rico
Ms. Lucila B. Rivera
Specialist
Division of Policy and
Procedures

Department of Social Services
P.O. Box 11398
San Juan, Puerto Rico 00910
809-722-7361
Fax: 809-722-4605

Rhode Island
Mr. Matteo Guglielmetti
Energy Assistance Program
Manager
Governor's Office of Housing,
Energy and Intergovernmental
Relations
275 Westminster Mall
Providence, RI 02903
401-277-6920
Fax: 401-277-1260

South Carolina
Mr. Douglas Keisler
Deputy Director for Energy
Programs
Division of Economic
Opportunity
1205 Pendleton St.
Columbia, SC 29201
803-734-0672

South Dakota
Ms. Abbie Rathbun
Program Administrator
Office of Energy Assistance
Department of Social Services
206 W. Missouri Ave.
Pierre, SD 57501-4517
605-773-4131
Fax: 605-773-6657

Tennessee
Mr. Steve Neece
LIHEAP Coordinator

Dept. of Human Services
Citizens Plaza Bldg.
400 Deaderick St.
Nashville, TN 37219
615-741-6640

Texas
Mr. J. Al Almaguer
Director, Energy Assistance
Texas Department of Housing
and Community Affairs
P.O. Box 13941
Austin, TX 78711-3941
512-475-3935

Utah
Mr. Sherm Roquiero
Home Energy Assistance
Target Program
Office Family Support
Administration
120 N. 200 West, 3rd Floor
P.O. Box 45000
Salt Lake City, UT 84145-0500
801-538-4091
Fax: 801-538-4212

Vermont
Mr. Ed Pirie
LIHEAP Block Grant Manager
Department of Social Welfare
103 S. Main St.
Waterbury, VT 05676
802-241-2889
Fax: 802-241-2830

Virgin Islands
Ms. Juel C. Molloy
Commissioner
Dept. of Human Services
Knud Hansen Complex

Building A
1003 Hospital Ground
Charlotte Amalie, Virgin
Islands 00802
809-774-1166

Virginia
Ms. Charlene Chapman
Energy and Emergency
Assistance Unit
Virginia Department of Social
Services
Theater Row Building
730 E. Broad St., 7th Floor
Richmond, VA 23219-1849
804-692-1750
Fax: 804-692-1704

Washington
Mr. William Graham
EAP/ECIP Coordinator
Department of Community
Development
Division of Community
Services
9th and Columbia Building -
N/X GH51
Olympia, WA 98504
206-753-3403

West Virginia
Mr. Robert R. Kent, HHR
Specialist, Sr.
Income Maintenance Bureau
Department of Health and
Human Resources
Building 6, Room B-617
State Capitol Complex
Charleston, WV 25305
304-558-8290
Fax: 304-558-2059

Wisconsin
Mr. Steve Tryon
Energy Assistance Program
Supervisor
Division of Economic Support
Department of Health and
Social Services
P.O. Box 7935
Madison, WI 53707-7935
608-266-7601

Wyoming
Mr. Guy Noe
Consultant, LIHEAP Program
Department of Family Services
Room #343 Hathaway Building
Cheyenne, WY 82002-0490
307-777-6078
Fax: 307-777-7747

☆ ☆ ☆

There Is More Than Hope

You can stay in your home a little longer with a new program called HOPE for Elderly Independence. You can receive help with dressing, bathing, grooming, eating, and cleaning at little cost to you, as well as help with paying the rent through Section 8 rental certificates. This is a demonstration program designed to combine rent certificates along with support services to help the frail elderly remain in their homes.

To learn if the project is currently being undertaken in your town, contact your local public housing office, or you may contact the Rental Assistance Division, Office of the Assistant Secretary for Public and

Indian Housing, U.S. Department of
Housing and Urban Development,
Washington, DC 20410.

☆ ☆ ☆

Some Housing Reports

Want to know about the different housing
options available to seniors? What are the
pros and cons of congregate housing for
the elderly? Is the government actually
doing anything to help this group find
affordable housing? Want to know what
your congressman knows about housing
for the elderly?

Most likely they got most of their
information from reading reports done by
the Congressional Research Service
(CRS). These reports are written by
experts in various fields (usually PhDs) at
the request of Congress, but are great
resources for everyone. They provide an
understandable overview of the topic and
provide relevant newspaper articles and
bibliographies. These reports are free but
must be requested through your
Congressman.

CRS reports dealing with housing include:

- *Congregate Housing: The Federal Program and Examples of State Programs* (86-918E)
- *Description of Residential Facilities for the Elderly* (84-19 EPW)
- *Elderly and Handicapped Housing: Recent Developments in Section 202* (89-667E)
- *Federal Housing Programs Affecting Elderly People* (88-576E)
- *Housing for the Elderly and Handicapped: Section 202*, Issue Brief (IB84038)

You can get these and other reports by contacting Your Senator or Representative, The Capitol, Washington, DC 20510; 202-224-3121.

Free Health Information and Treatment

Access the Best Research on How to Live Longer

To live longer and healthier lives. From everything you hear on the T.V. and read in the paper you'd think otherwise. But findings show that the heart adapts well to the effects of age; that memory and problem solving remain strong; and that older adults are no more conservative or cranky or prone to complaining about their health than they were when young.

Where does this new information come from? You can learn how to live longer, get a good night's sleep, and even start an exercise program just by contacting the National Institute on Aging (NIA). NIA researches all kinds of subjects on aging, as well as the diseases and special problems of older people. They are also conducting the longest running scientific examination of human aging ever undertaken called the *Baltimore Longitudinal Study of Aging*.

On top of that, NIA can answer your questions and provide you with all kinds of free publications on a wide variety of topics including:

General Information
- *NIA Fact Sheet*
- *Extramural Training and Career Opportunities in Aging Research*
- *Research Training in Geriatrics and Gerontology*
- *With the Passage of Time: The Baltimore Longitudinal Study of Aging*
- *Publications List*

Health Information
- *Accidental Hypothermia*
- *Hyperthermia: A Hot Weather Hazard for Older People*
- *In Search of the Secrets of Aging*
- *What's On Your Mind? A Quiz on Aging and the Brain*
- *What's Your Aging IQ?*
- *Who? What? Where? Resources of Women's Health and Aging*
- *Working With Your Older Patient: A Clinician's Handbook*

Information Packets
- *Caregiving Packet*
- *Exercise Packet*
- *Nutrition Packet*
- *Urinary Incontinence Packet*
- *Women's Age Page Packet*

Research Summaries
- *Research Bulletin*

NIA's Age Pages provide a quick, practical look at some of the health topics that interest older people. Selected titles are available in Spanish (S).

Diseases/Disorders
- *Arthritis Advice*
- *Cancer Facts of People Over 50*
- *Forgetfulness in Old Age: It's Not What You Think*
- *Constipation*
- *Dealing With Diabetes* (S)
- *Depression: A Serious but Treatable Illness*
- *Digestive Do's and Don'ts* (S)
- *High Blood Pressure: A Common But Controllable Disorder*
- *HIV, AIDS and Older Adults*
- *Osteoporosis: The Bone Thinner*
- *Prostate Problems*
- *Stroke Prevention and Treatment* (S)
- *Urinary Incontinence*
- *What to Do About Flu*

Health Promotion
- *Aging and Alcohol Abuse*
- *A Good Night's Sleep*

- *Life Extension-Science or Science Fiction*
- *Don't Take It Easy - Exercise!*
- *Managing Menopause*
- *Smoking: It's Never Too Late To Stop*

Medical Care
- *Considering Surgery?*
- *Finding Good Medical Care for Older Americans*
- *Hospital Hints*
- *Who's Who in Health Care* (S)

Planning for Later Years
- *Getting Your Affairs in Order*
- *When You Need a Nursing Home*

Medications
- *Arthritis Medicines*
- *Safe Use of Medicines by Older People*
- *Safe Use of Tranquilizers*
- *"Shots" for Safety*
- *Should You Take Estrogen?*
- *The Pneumonia Vaccine: It's Worth A Shot*

Nutrition
- *Be Sensible About Salt*
- *Dietary Supplements: More is Not Always Better*

- *Hints for Shopping, Cooking, and Enjoying Medals*
- *Nutrition: A Lifelong Concern* (S)

Safety
- *Accident Prevention* (S)
- *Crime and Older People* (S)
- *Health Quackery*
- *Heat, Cold, and Getting Old* (S)
- *Preventing Falls and Fractures*
- *Safety Belt Sense*

The Body
- *Aging and Your Eyes*
- *Foot Care* (S)
- *Hearing and Older People*
- *Sexuality in Later Life*
- *Skin Care and Aging* (S)
- *Taking Care of Your Teeth and Mouth*

Contact National Institute on Aging, Public Information Office, 9000 Rockville Pike, Building 31, Room 5C27, Bethesda, MD 20892; 800-222-2225.

Get Your Own Facts On Your Own Heart

Although we're not sure whose mother it was, but someone once said that whoever controls your heart controls your head. Now it is time to take some action on your own.

Don't let high blood pressure or cholesterol rule your life. With some help from the National Heart, Lung, and Blood Institute you can learn about the target numbers you need to shoot for, as well as how to eat better to put you in control.

The National Heart, Lung, and Blood Institute (NHLBI) conducts research on these topics and more, and responds to questions on cholesterol, high blood pressure, blood resources, sleep disorders, obesity, and asthma. They can conduct database searches to locate materials, and they distribute a wide variety of educational publications for both the consumer and professional. Some of the publications available include:

- *Eat Right To Help Lower Your High Blood Pressure*

- *High Blood Pressure: Treat It For Life*
- *Facts About How To Prevent High Blood Pressure*
- *So You Have High Blood Pressure*
- *Step by Step: Eating To Lower Your High Blood Cholesterol*
- *Recipes — A Low Fat Diet*
- *Check Your Weight and Heart Disease IQ*
- *The Healthy Heart Handbook For Women*
- *Breathing Disorders During Sleep*

Many other publications are also available. Request a free catalog. Contact National Heart, Lung, and Blood Institute information Center, P.O. Box 30105, Bethesda, MD 20824; 301-251-1222; 800-575-WELL (recorded message line).

☆ ☆ ☆

Taking the Scare Out of Cancer

No one likes to think about the "C" word. But think about this: the earlier cancer is found, the better your chances of beating it.

There are simple tests you can take that can help find cancer early, long before any symptoms appear. Research is showing that this has helped increase the survival rate dramatically for certain types of cancer.

The toll-free Cancer Information Service (CIS) can provide accurate, up-to-date information about cancer and cancer-related resources near you. Information is also available about treatment studies currently accepting patients and is available to doctors through a database known as PDQ (Physician Data Query).

The National Cancer Institute also distributes free publications on specific types of cancer, treatment methods, coping with cancer, and other cancer-related subjects. Just a few of the publications available include:

- *Cancer Tests You Should Know About: A Guide For People 65 And Over*
- *A Mammogram: Once A Year For A Lifetime*
- *Anticancer Drug Information Sheets*
- *Advanced Cancer: Living Each Day*
- *Chemotherapy and You: A Guide To Self Help During Treatment*

- *Questions and Answers About Pain Control*
- *What Are Clinical Trials All About?*
- *Radiation Therapy And You*
- *Facing Forward: A Guide for Cancer Survivors*
- *Eating Hints: Recipes and Tips*

Contact National Cancer Institute, Office of Cancer Communications, Building 31, Room 10A16, 9000 Rockville Pike, Bethesda, MD 20892; Cancer Information Service 800-4-CANCER.

☆ ☆ ☆

When Aspirin Isn't Enough

If you suffer from chronic headaches, sometimes even several doses of aspirin may not do the trick. Believe it or not, in the Ninth Century the recommended treatment involved drinking a concoction of elderseed, cow's brain, and goat's dung dissolved in vinegar.

Although that may sound appealing to some of you out there, for the rest of us, new treatment options have greatly improved our lives. Drug therapy, biofeedback training, stress reduction, and elimination of certain foods from the diet are just a few of the most common methods of preventing and controlling migraines and other types of headaches. The National Institute of Neurological Disorders and Stroke has put together a Headache Information Packet that provides journal articles, research reports, and other resources for headache suffers. For your free copy, contact the National Institute of Neurological Disorders and Stroke, Information Office, Building 31, Room 8A06, 9000 Rockville Pike, Bethesda, MD 20892; 800-352-9424.

Keep Your Own Choppers

Just because you're over 65 doesn't necessarily mean you should be watching those commercials for denture cleaners more closely. In fact, who would ever have guessed that a majority of seniors still have their

own set of pearly whites, and with each passing year fewer and fewer are losing them.

This is due in large part to water fluoridation, brushing and regular visits to the dentist, not to mention the exciting new research on the causes, prevention, diagnosis, and treatment of dental disease.

The National Institute on Dental Research can answer your questions about problems with your teeth and send you all kinds of free publications to keep them healthy and happy. Contact National Institute of Dental Research, Information Office, Building 31, Room 2C35, 9000 Rockville Pike, Bethesda, MD 20892; 301-496-4261.

☆ ☆ ☆

Sugar Alert

Sugar doesn't need to be a four letter word to those 11 million Americans who have diabetes. In fact, it doesn't even have to be a five letter word to those who can spell.

With the proper diet and exercise program, in many cases you can actually reverse or reduce insulin resistance, which is one of the underlying causes of diabetes. And how about this: some formerly overweight diabetics no longer have the disease after shedding pounds.

The National Diabetes Information Clearinghouse can answer any of your questions regarding diabetes and will send you the Diabetes Dateline newsletter and a calendar of meetings and educational programs. They also have a wonderful collection of free publications on diabetes and how it can be controlled:

- *Diabetes in Adults*
- *Insulin Dependent Diabetes*
- *Monitoring Your Blood Sugar*
- *Non-insulin Dependent Diabetes*
- *Periodontal Disease and Diabetes: A Guide for Patients*

A complete list of publications is available by contact the Clearinghouse at National Diabetes Information Clearinghouse, 1 Information Way, Bethesda, MD 20892-3560; 301-654-3327.

Prostate Solutions

Research shows that if a man lives long enough, he's almost certain to have some kind of non-cancerous problem with his prostate. Fortunately, there are also many effective treatments.

To learn more about prostate problems and treatment options other than prostate cancer, contact the National Kidney and Urologic Diseases Information Clearinghouse. They can answer questions, provide publications, and can conduct a search on the Combined Health Information Database (CHID) for more information. Some of the free publications include:

- *Prostate Enlargement: Benign Prostatic Hyperplasia*
- *Age Page: Prostate Problems*

For more information, contact National Kidney and Urologic Diseases Information Clearinghouse, 3 Information Way, Bethesda, MD 20892-3580; 301-654-4415.

Should You Get Your Flu Shot?

Each winter, millions of people suffer from the unpleasant effects of the "flu." For most people, a few days in bed, a few more days of rest, aspirin, and plenty to drink will be the best treatment. For older people though, the flu can be life-threatening.

A flu shot can give your body time to build the proper immunity. To better understand infectious diseases and the immune system, the National Institute of Allergy and Infectious Diseases conducts research and clinical trials. They have a free publication titled, *Flu*, that can give you some great tips for the Flu season.

For more information, contact National Institute of Allergy and Infectious Diseases, Office of Communications Building 31, Room 7A50, 9000 Rockville Pike, Bethesda, MD 20892; 301-496-5717.

Aches and Pains

If your joints ache, join the crowd. Over 50% of people over 65 suffer from some form of arthritis, whether it is a mild stiffness in your joints when it rains to full-blown osteoarthritis. But for many, a simple change in diet and exercise could result in an improvement in their condition.

The National Institute of Arthritis and Musculoskeletal and Skin Diseases (NIAMS) conducts research on a number of chronic, disabling diseases, including osteoarthritis, rheumatoid arthritis, muscle diseases, osteoporosis, Paget's disease, back disorders, gout, and more.

The Clearinghouse can answer questions, provide you with publications, and search the Combined Health Information Database (CHID) for other references on specific topics. Some of the free publications include:

- *Medicine for the Layman: Arthritis*
- *Understanding Paget's Disease*
- *Arthritis, Rheumatic Diseases, and Related Disorders*

For more information contact National Arthritis and Musculoskeletal and Skin Diseases Information Clearinghouse, P.O. Box AMS, 9000 Rockville Pike, Bethesda, MD 20892; 301-495-4484.

☆ ☆ ☆

Stroke Clearinghouse

Here's some great news: strokes can be prevented today. In fact, the death rate from stroke has fallen as much as 50% since 1970.

This decline has come about, in part, because of new tests and treatments. There is even some evidence that common aspirin can reduce your chances of stroke. In addition, many people are adopting sensible health habits such as controlling their high blood pressure.

The free publication, *Stroke: Hope Through Research*, outlines some of the causes, tests and treatments for strokes. The National Institute of Neurological Disorders and Stroke (NINDS) supports and conducts research and research training on the cause, prevention, diagnosis and treatment of hundreds of neurological disorders. Some of their studies involve

Alzheimer's disease, Parkinson's disease, Huntington's disease, multiple sclerosis, and amyotrophic lateral sclerosis.

Some of the other free publications they have available include:

- *Dizziness: Hope Through Research*
- *Multiple Sclerosis: Hope Through Research*
- *Parkinson's Disease: Hope Through Research*
- *Shingles: Hope Through Research*

Contact the National Institute of Neurological Disorders and Stroke, Information Office, Building 31, Room 8A06, 9000 Rockville Pike, Bethesda, MD 20892; 800-352-9424.

☆ ☆ ☆

Incontinence Is Not Inevitable

You would think from the humiliating diaper commercials that incontinence is the Number 1 problem faced by seniors today. But in reality only 1 in 10 suffer from it, and in most cases it can be treated and controlled, if not cured.

Believe it or not, incontinence often results from the use of medications or certain common medical conditions. Once your doctor finds out the cause, there may be simple steps you can take to help correct this problem.

The National Kidney and Urologic Diseases Information Clearinghouse can answer questions and provide information about all kidney and urologic diseases. They have free publications and can conduct a search on the Combined Health Information Database (CHID) for more information on a specific subject. Some of the free publications include:

- *Urinary Tract Infections In Adults*
- *Kidney Stones in Adults*
- *End-Stage Renal Disease*
- *Age Page: Urinary Incontinence*

For more information, contact National Kidney and Urologic Diseases Information Clearinghouse, 3 Information Way, Bethesda, MD 20892-3580; 301-654-4415.

Help For Heartburn

No need to spend the rest of your life chugging antacids for that upset stomach. Besides tasting lousy, some recent research has shown a possible link between aluminum-based antacids and Alzheimer's.

But there are simple home remedies for heartburn. Just by avoiding some everyday foods such as peppermint, orange juice (naturally high in acid), and chocolate among other things, you can help control your heartburn. You can even try elevating the head of your bed six inches, although ask your spouse first.

Although they can't cure your heartburn or ulcer, the National Digestive Diseases Information Clearinghouse does offer helpful information about digestive diseases. They have free publications, and can conduct a search on the Combined Health Information Database (CHID) to provide you with references for further reading. Some of the fact sheets they have include:

- *Heartburn*
- *Constipation*

- *Hemorrhoids*
- *Pancreatitis*
- *Cirrhosis of the Liver*
- *Gallstones*

They also have information packets on many digestive diseases. For more information, contact National Digestive Diseases Information Clearinghouse, 2 Information Way, Bethesda, MD 20892-3570; 301-654-3810.

☆ ☆ ☆

Turn Down The Volume

Now you have the government backing you up when you tell the kids to turn down the rock-and-roll. Over one-third of people who have hearing impairments can trace the damage to exposure to loud sounds.

If you are currently shopping around for a hearing aid, you know that the choices you have are as varied as their price tags. You can learn more about the causes of hearing loss, hearing aid information, and the latest research on the topic from the National Institute on Deafness and Other Communication Disorder, which conducts research on the diseases and disorders of hearing, balance, smell, taste, voice, speech, and language.

They can answer your questions, and have publications which explain common problems and inform you of the latest research being undertaken. For a publications list or more information contact National Institute on Deafness and other Communication Disorders Clearinghouse, 1 Communication Way, Bethesda, MD 20892-3456; 800-241-1044.

☆ ☆ ☆

Sneezing?
Blame Your Parents

Most allergies can be blamed on inheriting them from your parents. You wanted their Louis IV chairs but instead ended up with their hay fever. Oh well.

Once you've finished yelling at them, there are some more effective steps you can take to improve your daily life. For example, the 1970's are over, and it's okay to get rid of the shag rug. Give the kid next door five bucks to mow your lawn for you. And if you're a real thrill seeker, give the cat a bath every week.

To learn about the different types of allergies and their treatment options, contact the National Institute of Allergy and Infectious Diseases, and they will send you free publications and information to help you survive the sniffle season.

- *Allergic Disease: Medicine for the Public*
- *Something in the Air: Airborne Allergens*
- *Drug Allergy*
- *Food Allergy and Intolerances*
- *The Immune System*

For more information, contact National Institute of Allergy and Infectious Diseases, Office of Communications Building 31, Room 7A50, 9000 Rockville Pike, Bethesda, MD 20892; 301-496-5717.

☆ ☆ ☆

Vision Blurry?

So you don't have 20/20 vision anymore. Look on the bright side, without your glasses your daughter-in-law is a far more attractive woman now.

Seriously, most people retain good eyesight well into their 80's and beyond. Some tips to help you see clearly include having regular health checkups to detect diseases that cause eye problems such as diabetes; having a complete eye exam every 2 or 3 years; and seeking eye health care more often if you have diabetes or a family history of eye problems.

The National Eye Institute (NEI) conducts research on the prevention, diagnosis, treatment, and pathology of diseases and disorders of the eye, and has free publications including:

- *Cataracts*
- *Don't Lose Sight of Glaucoma*
- *Don't Lose Sight of Diabetic Eye Disease*
- *Don't Lose Sight of Cataracts*
- *Don't Lose Sight of Age-Related Macular Degeneration*
- *Diabetic Retinopathy*

For more information, contact National Eye Institute, Information Office, Building 31, Room 6A32, Bethesda, MD 20892; 301-496-5248.

Drink Your Broccoli?

Well you don't have to drink it, but broccoli is a good source of calcium, in addition to cheese and milk. Getting enough calcium and maintaining a good exercise program are two steps you  can take to help prevent or delay the onset of osteoporosis.

To learn more about the causes, risk factors, and treatment of osteoporosis, contact National Resource Center on Osteoporosis and Related Disease, National Osteoporosis Foundation, 1150 17th St., NW, Suite 500, Washington, DC 20036; 202-223-0344.

Everyone Gets The Blues Now And Then

It's part of life. Being down in the dumps over a period of time is a common problem among the elderly, but it doesn't have to be a normal part of growing old. For most people, depression can be treated successfully, and while some depression may require drug treatments, many others require simple changes in diet and exercise.

The National Institute of Mental Health conducts research to learn more about the causes, prevention, and treatment of mental and emotional illnesses. They can answer your questions and have publications on a wide variety of topics, including:

- *Useful Information on Sleep Disorders*
- *Plain Talk About Aging*
- *Plain Talk About Depression*
- *Plain Talk About Wife Abuse*
- *Plain Talk About Handling Stress*
- *If You're Over 65 and Feeling Depressed...Treatment Brings New Hope*
- *Panic Disorder*

For more information, contact National Institute of Mental Health, Information Resources and Inquiries Branch, Room 7C02, 5600 Fishers Lane, Rockville, MD 20857; 301-443-4513.

☆ ☆ ☆

Don't Drink and Medicate

Many seniors are on drugs — serious prescription medications that when mixed with alcohol can cause serious problems, such as falls and broken bones, and even hard core addiction. And it's also not uncommon for some seniors to use alcohol to help them deal with the loneliness accompanied with being old.

The National Clearinghouse for Alcohol and Drug Information is a wonderful resource to learn more about alcohol and drug addiction. They can answer your questions and provide you with free publications on the safe use of prescription, drug and alcohol abuse, and treatment information.

To learn more, contact the National Clearinghouse for Alcohol and Drug Information, P.O. Box 2345, Rockville, MD 20847; 800-729-6686.

Quack Alert

Ignore those seductive ads in the supermarket tabloid newspapers. No amount of rubbing, wrapping, massaging, or scrubbing will cure your arthritis. And no over-the-counter  cream, lotion, or device can prevent baldness, induce new hair to grow, or cause hair to become thicker.

There are all kinds of miracle cure scams aimed at older people who are vulnerable to their unrealistic claims. The Federal Trade Commission has several pamphlets to help educate you about health fraud. Some of the free titles include *Health Claims: Separating Fact From Fiction*, and *Healthy Questions (To Ask Health Care Specialists)*.

To receive your copies, contact Public Reference, Room 130, Federal Trade

Commission, Washington, DC 20580;
202-326-2222.

☆ ☆ ☆

Information Clearinghouses on Problems With the Elderly

Would you like to learn more about nutrition and the elderly? What about how to help post-stroke patients rehab? Need videotapes to help your geriatric workers better understand the needs of the elderly?

As the elderly population grows each year, the need for doctors, nurses, and other health professionals trained in geriatrics also increases. The Bureau of Health Professions supports a nationwide network of Geriatric Education Centers whose purpose is to provide education and training opportunities in geriatrics.

Centers maintain resource clearinghouses and develop curriculum and teaching materials. A catalog of selected materials produced by the centers is available at no charge.

For additional information, contact Geriatric Education Centers Coordinator, Bureau of

Health Professions, U.S. Department of Health and Human Services, 5600 Fishers Lane, Room 8-103, Rockville, MD 20857; 301-443-6887.

The following is a list of the Geriatric Education Centers:

Alabama
University of Alabama at Birmingham Geriatric Education Center
CH-19, Suite 201
933 19th Street South
Birmingham, AL 35294-2041
205-934-5716
Fax: 205-934-7354

California
California Geriatric Education Center
Department of Medicine
University of California, Los Angeles
32-144 CHS
10833 Le Conte Ave.
Los Angeles, CA 90024-1687
310-312-0530
Fax: 310-312-0538

Stanford Geriatric Education Center
703 Welch Road
Suite H-1
Stanford, CA 94305-0151
415-723-7063
Fax: 415-723-9692

Pacific Geriatric Education Center
Los Angeles Caregiver Resource Center
3715 McClintock
Los Angeles, CA 90098-0191
213-740-8711
Fax: 213-740-1871

San Diego Geriatric Education Center
University of California
School of Medicine
Department of Medicine
200 West Arbor
San Diego, CA 92103-8415
619-543-6275
Fax: 619-543-3931

Colorado
Colorado Geriatric Education Center
Health Sciences Center
Office of Academic Affairs
Box A094
4200 E. 9th Ave.
Denver, CO 80262
303-270-8974
Fax: 303-270-7729

Connecticut

University of Connecticut
Geriatric Education Center
Travelers Center on Aging
University of Connecticut
School of Medicine
MC 5215
Farmington, CT 06030
203-679-3956
Fax: 203-679-1307

District of Columbia

Washington DC Geriatric
Education Center Consortium
George Washington University
Medical Center
Dept. of Health Care Sciences
2150 Pennsylvania Ave., NW
Room 5-425
Washington, DC 20037
202-994-4731
Fax: 202-994-7023

Florida

Miami Area Geriatric Education
Center
University of Miami
1425 NW 10th Ave.
Sieron Building, 2nd Floor
(D303)
Miami, FL 33136
305-547-6270
Fax: 305-548-4414

University of Florida Geriatric
Education Center
P.O. Box 100277
University of Florida
Gainesville, FL 32610-0277
904-395-0651
Fax: 904-338-9884

University of South Florida
Geriatric Education Center
Suncoast Gerontology Center
University of South Florida
Medical Center Box 50
12901 Bruce B. Downs Blvd.
Tampa, FL 33612
813-974-4355
Fax: 813-974-4251

Hawaii

Pacific Islands Geriatric
Education Center
347 N. Kuakini Street
Honolulu, HI 96817
808-523-8461
Fax: 808-528-1897

Illinois

Illinois GEC Network
University of Illinois at Chicago
College of Associated Health
Professions
808 S. Wood Street (M/C 778)
Room 166 CME
Chicago, IL 60612
312-996-1407
Fax: 312-413-4184

Great Lakes Geriatric
Education Center
Chicago College of
Osteopathic Medicine
5200 South Ellis Ave.
Chicago, IL 60615
312-947-2708
Fax: 312-947-3018

Indiana

Indiana Geriatric Education
Center

School of Medicine
Coleman Hall 120
1140 West Michigan Street
Indianapolis, IN 46202-5119
317-274-4702
Fax: 317-274-4723

Iowa
Iowa Geriatric Education
Center
Department of Internal
Medicine
University of Iowa Hospitals
and Clinics
Iowa City, IA 52242
319-356-1027
Fax: 319-356-7893

Kentucky
Ohio Valley Appalachia
Regional Geriatric Education
Center
University of Kentucky
20 Chandler Medical Center
Annex 1
Lexington, KY 40536-0079
606-233-5156
Fax: 606-258-2866

Louisiana
Louisiana Geriatric Education
Center
Louisiana State University
School of Medicine
1542 Tulane Ave.
New Orleans, LA 70112
504-568-5842
Fax: 504-568-2127

Massachusetts
Harvard Upper New England

Geriatric Education Center
Division on Aging
Harvard Medical School
643 Huntington Ave.
Boston, MA 02115
617-432-1463
Fax: 617-734-4432

Michigan
Geriatric Education Center of
Michigan
B-544 West Fee Hall
Michigan State University
East Lansing, MI 48824
517-336-2793
Fax: 517-355-7700

Minnesota
Minnesota Area Geriatric
Education Center
Box 197 Mayo
420 Delaware Street, SE
University of Minnesota
Minneapolis, MN 55455
612-624-3904
Fax: 612-624-8448

Mississippi
Mississippi GEC
University of Mississippi
Medical Center
2500 N. State Street
Jackson, MS 39216-4505
601-984-6190
Fax: 601-984-6659

Missouri
Missouri Gateway Geriatric
Education Center
St. Louis University
School of Medicine

1402 S. Grand Blvd.
Room M238
St. Louis, MO 63104
314-577-8462
Fax: 314-771-8575

Nebraska
Creighton Regional Geriatric
Education Center
3615 Burt Street
Omaha, NE 68131
402-390-9335
Fax: 402-390-9541

Nevada
Nevada Geriatric Education
Center
University of Nevada at Reno
Sanford Center of Aging
Mackay Science Bldg. /146
University of Nevada Reno
Reno, NV 89557-0133
702-784-1803
Fax: 702-784-1814

New Jersey
New Jersey Geriatric
Education Center
University of Medicine and
Dentistry of New Jersey
School of Osteopathic
Medicine
42 East Laurel Rd., Suite 3200
Stratford, NJ 08084-1504
609-566-7082
Fax: 609-556-6781

New Mexico
New Mexico Geriatric
Education Center
UNM Center for Aging

Research, Education and
Service
1836 Lomas Blvd., NE
University of New Mexico
Albuquerque, NM 87131-6086
505-277-5134
Fax: 505-277-6878

New York
Columbia University-New York
Geriatric Education Center
Columbia University
Center for Geriatrics and
Gerontology
100 Haven Ave., 3-30F
New York, NY 10032
212-305-4165
Fax: 212-305-6937

Hunter/Mt. Sinai Geriatric
Education Center
425 E. 25th St.
New York, NY 10010-2590
212-481-5142
Fax: 212-481-5069

Western New York Geriatric
Education Center
State University of NY at
Buffalo
Beck Hall, 3435 Main Street
Buffalo, NY 14214
716-829-3176
Fax: 716-829-2308

North Carolina
Appalachian Geriatric
Education Center
Bowman Gray School of
Medicine
Medical Center Boulevard

Winston-Salem, NC 27157-
1051
910-716-4284
Fax: 910-716-7359

Duke University Geriatric
Education Center
Center for the Study of Aging
and Human Development
Box 3003, Duke University
Medical Center
Durham, NC 27710
919-684-5149
Fax: 919-684-8569

North Dakota
Dakota Plains Geriatric
Education Center
University of North Dakota
501 N. Columbia Rd.
Grand Forks, ND 58203
701-777-3200
Fax: 701-777-3849

Oklahoma
Oklahoma Geriatric Education
Center
University of Oklahoma
O'Donoghue Rehabilitation
Institute
1122 NE 13th St.
Room C4201
Oklahoma City, OK 73117
405-271-8558
Fax: 405-271-3887

Oregon
Oregon Geriatric Education Ctr
Oregon Health Sciences
University
Portland VAMC Mail Code

(14G)
P.O. Box 1034
Portland, OR 97207-1034
503-721-7821
Fax: 503-721-7807

Pennsylvania
Geriatric Education Center of
Pennsylvania
University of Pittsburgh
121 University Place
Pittsburgh, PA 15260
412-624-9190
Fax: 412-624-4810

Delaware Valley Mid-Atlantic
Geriatric Education Center
Institute on Aging
3615 Chestnut Street
Philadelphia, PA 19104
215-898-3174
Fax: 215-898-0580

Puerto Rico
Geriatric Education Center of
University of Puerto Rico
School of Medicine
Medical Sciences Campus
G.P.O. Box 5067
San Juan, PR 00936
809-751-2478
Fax: 809-765-0514

Ohio
Western Reserve Geriatric
Education Center
12200 Fairhill Road
Cleveland, OH 44120
216-368-5433
Fax: 216-368-3118

Tennessee
Meharry Consortium Geriatric
Education Center
1005 D.B. Todd Boulevard
Nashville, TN 37208
615-327-6947
Fax: 615-327-6880

Texas
Texas Consortium of Geriatric
Education Centers
Baylor College of Medicine
One Baylor Plaza, Room M320
Houston, TX 77030-3498
713-798-6470
Fax: 713-798-6688

South Texas Geriatric
Education Center
Department of Dental
Diagnostic Science
7703 Floyd Curl Drive
San Antonio, TX 78284-7921
210-567-3370
Fax: 210-567-3337

Utah
Intermountain West Geriatric
Education Center
College of Nursing
University of Utah
25 South Medical Drive
Salt Lake City, UT 84112

801-582-1565, ext. 2475
Fax: 801-583-7338

Virginia
Virginia Geriatric Education
Center
Virginia Commonwealth
University
520 N. 12th Street
The Lyons Building
Richmond, VA 23298-0228
804-786-9060
Fax: 804-371-7905

Washington
Northwest Geriatric Education
Center
University of Washington
HL-23
Seattle, WA 98195
206-685-7478
Fax: 206-685-3436

Wisconsin
Wisconsin Geriatric Education
Center
Marquette University
Academic Support Facility
Room 160
735 N. 17th Street
Milwaukee, WI 53233
414-288-3712
Fax: 414-288-1973

Get The Inside Scoop on the Health Budget

Seems like all we hear about in the news these days is balancing the budget and lowering the deficit. Maybe at your expense.

Of course, one suggestion to accomplish this is to cap Medicare spending. How would this affect the everyday lives of older people? Will they be forced to join HMOs? Will new changes cover nursing home care or prescription drugs?

Before they vote on any issue, your Congressman usually looks over one of the reports written by the Congressional Research Service (CRS). These CRS reports provide an overview of an issue, and include bibliographies, newspaper articles, and more.

Copies of the CRS reports are free to the public, but you have to request them through your Representative or Senator. Some of the reports dealing with health include:

- *Health: Long-Term Health Care* (IP402H)

- *Medicare: An Overview* (IP467M)
- *Characteristics of Nursing Home Residents and Proposals for Reforming Coverage of Nursing Home Care* (90-471EPW)
- *Elderly Home Care: Tax Incentives and Proposals for Change* (89-662E)
- *Public Opinion on Long-Term Health Care Needs, Costs and Financing* (90-151GOV)

These and other titles dealing with older people are available by contacting Your Representative or Senator, The Capitol, Washington, DC 20510; 202-224-3121.

☆ ☆ ☆

Move To Florida and Look Even Older

Forget shoveling snow — you're moving to Arizona or Florida to enjoy the sunshine and feel younger. But you'd better think twice about enjoying the warm sun too much.

No matter what age you are, the sun can do all kinds of harmful things to your skin, not the least of which is accelerate aging.

Read up on tanning and suncare products through two free publications from the Federal Trade Commission, titled *Indoor Tanning* and *Sunscreens*. These will help you keep your skin beautiful and healthy.

To receive your copies, contact Public Reference, Room 130, Federal Trade Commission, Washington, DC 20580; 202-326-2222.

☆ ☆ ☆

What Treatment Is Best For You

Seems like everybody's got an opinion about how you should treat a condition or disease. Even doctors disagree with one another. That's when it gets really confusing. All you want to know is "What's best for me?"

To help both you and your doctor make the best treatment choices, the Agency for Health Care Policy and Research (AHCPR) has developed some practical guidelines that you can use to help you with your health care choices.

In addition, they also look at research on health services, health care, and home health care. Some of the publications they have available include:

- *Pain Control After Surgery: A Patient's Guide*
- *Cataract in Adults: A Patient's Guide*
- *Depression is a Treatable Illness: A Patient's Guide*
- *Preventing Pressure Ulcers: A Patient's Guide*
- *Urinary Incontinence in Adults: A Patient's Guide*
- *Annotated Bibliography, Long-Term Case Studies*
- *The Competing Demands of Employment and Information Caregiving to Disabled Elders*
- *The Elderly Population with Chronic Functional Disability: Implications for Home Care Eligibility*
- *Functional Disability Scales*
- *Relationship of Vision and Hearing Impairment to One-Year Mortality and Function Decline*
- *Tracing the Elderly Through the Health Care System*

For your free copies or more information, contact Agency for Health Care Policy and Research, P.O. Box 88547, Silver Spring, MD 20907; 800-358-9295.

Someone Else Is Also Checking Your Pulse

Many seniors worry that they don't have enough health coverage, so they spend billions on additional, and often unnecessary, insurance.

A recent government study looked into this issue, and what they found out might save you thousands of dollars on your insurance premiums. This free report from the General Accounting Office (GAO) looks at typical coverage that older Americans carry and potential problems.

The GAO publishes results of research into issues that face the elderly, including:

- *Health Insurance for the Elderly: Owning Duplicate Policies Is Costly and Unnecessary* (HEHS 94-185)
- *Medicare: Beneficiary Liability for Certain Paramedic Services May Be Substantial* (HEHS 94-122BR)
- *Medicare Part B: Inconsistent Denial Rates for Medical Necessity Across Six Carriers* (T-PEMD 94-17)
- *Cataract Surgery: Patient-Reported Data on Appropriateness and*

Outcomes (GAO/PEMD 93-14)
- *Home Health Care: HCFA Properly Evaluated JCAHO's Ability to Survey Home Health Agencies* (GAO/HRD 93-33)
- *Medicaid Estate Planning* (GAO/HRD 93-29R)
- *Retiree Health Plans: Health Benefits Not Secure Under Employer-Based System* (GAO/HRD 93-125)
- *Screening Mammography: Higher Payment Could Increase Costs Without Increasing Use* (GAO/HRD 93-50)

All reports are free and can be requested by contacting U.S. General Accounting Office, P.O. Box 6015, Gaithersburg, MD 20884; 202-512-6000.

☆ ☆ ☆

Medicare Medigap Medimess

One of the most burning questions facing older Americans today is: "Should I buy health insurance from Art Linkletter?" If only life were that simple.

For those who are covered by Medicare, the maze of questions about insurance coverage is confusing and frustrating, but the toll-free Medicare hotline can answer your questions and refer you to local offices if necessary. They also distribute free information booklets including:

- *Guide to Health Insurance for People with Medicare*
- *Medicare Hospice Benefits*
- *Medicare Highlights*
- *Hospital Stay Under Medicare's PPS*
- *Limits on Physician Charges*
- *Medicare Questions and Answers*
- *Medicare Second Surgical Opinion*
- *Medicare and Advanced Directives*
- *Medicare and Your Physician's Bills*
- *Medical and Other Health Benefits*
- *Financing Health Care for People with AIDS*
- *Medicare Savings for Qualified Beneficiaries*
- *Medicare Second Payer*
- *Medicare and Coordinated Care Plans*
- *Medicare Handbook*
- *Medicare Coverage of Kidney Dialysis and Transplants*
- *Medicare Pays For Flu Shots*
- *Medicaid and You*
- *Home Health Care*
- *Medigap*

For more information, contact the Medicare Hotline, Health Care Financing Administration, 6325 Security Blvd., Baltimore, MD 21207; 800-638-6833.

☆ ☆ ☆

More Health Insurance for the Poor

Being poor doesn't get you much in this country, but one of the things it may get you is free health insurance under the Medicaid program.

Medicaid is funded by the Federal and state governments to provides medical assistance for certain low-income persons. Each state designs and administers its own Medicaid program, setting eligibility and coverage standards.

Although originally intended to provide basic medical services to the poor and disabled, Medicaid has also become the primary source of public funds for nursing home care. Look in the blue pages of your phone book for your local Medicaid office.

Your Brain: Use It or Lose It

New studies show that people who don't have much education or high levels of job achievement have at least twice the risk for developing Alzheimer's disease as those who do.

Clearly this doesn't account for everyone who suffers from Alzheimer's — take Ronald Reagan for example — but there is a suggestion that when it comes to your brain, you need to use it or lose it. Other promising research is under way to find the causes and treatments of this disease.

And as for caring for a person with Alzheimer's, which can be emotionally, physically, and financially stressful, help is nearby. The Alzheimer's Disease Education and Referral (ADEAR) Center is a national resource that provides information on diagnosis, treatment issues, patient care, caregiver needs, long-term care, education and training and research activities. They also maintain a database which includes references to patient and professional materials. The ADEAR Center distributes a quarterly newsletter and other publications such as:

- *Alzheimer's Disease Fact Sheet*
- *Multi-infarct Dementia Fact Sheet*
- *Forgetfulness in Old Age: It's Not What You Think*
- *Progress Report on Alzheimer's Disease*
- *Alzheimer's Disease Centers Program Directory*
- *Differential Diagnosis of Dementing Diseases*
- *Working With Your Older Patient: A Clinician's Handbook*
- *Alzheimer's Disease: A Guide to Federal Programs*
- *Caring and Sharing: A Catalog of Training Materials from Alzheimer's Disease Centers*
- *Alzheimer's Disease Training Materials: An Annotated List of Resources*
- *Spanish-language Materials: An Annotated List of Resources*

For more information, contact Alzheimer's Disease Education and Referral Center, P.O. Box 8250, Silver Spring, MD 20907; 301-495-3311, 800-438-4380.

Free Treatment...Taking Part In Finding A Cure

Although there is currently no way to prevent or cure Alzheimer's disease, the research continues. In fact, a recent study has possibly located a genetic marker for Alzheimer's. Other areas of investigation range from the basic mechanisms of Alzheimer's disease to managing the symptoms and helping families cope with the effects of the disease.

The National Institute on Aging currently funds 28 Alzheimer's Disease Centers (ADC's) at major medical institutions across the nation. These centers offer free diagnosis and treatment for those who volunteer for the research. There are also support groups and other special programs for volunteers and their families.

Contact the Center nearest you from the list below and ask for information about services they may provide, as well as satellite clinics they may have at other locations.

Alzheimer's Disease Centers Program Directory

Alabama
University of Alabama at
Birmingham
Lindy E. Harrell, M.D., Ph.D.
Professor
Department of Neurology
University of Alabama at
Birmingham
1720 7th Ave., South
Suite 454
Birmingham, AL 35294-0017
Director: 205-934-3847
Fax: 205-975-7365
Information: 205-934-9775

California
University of California, Davis
William J. Jagust, M.D.
Associate Professor
Department of Neurology
University of California, Davis
Northern CA Alzheimer's
Disease Center
Alta Bates-Herrick Hospital
2001 Dwight Way
Berkeley, CA 94704
510-204-4530
Fax: 510-204-4524

University of California, Los
Angeles
Jeffrey L. Cummings, M.D.
Associate Professor
Department of Neurology and
Psychiatry
University of California, Los
Angeles
710 Westwood Plaza
Los Angeles, CA 90024-1769

Director: 310-824-3166
Fax: 310-206-5287
Information: 310-206-5238

University of California, San
Diego
Leon Ihal, M.D., Chairman
Department of Neuroscience
(0624)
University of California
San Diego School of Medicine
9500 Gilman Dr.
La Jolla, CA 92093-0624
Director: 619-534-4606
Fax: 619-534-1437
Information: 619-622-5800

University of Southern
California
Caleb E. Finch, Ph.D.
Division of Neurogerontology
Ethel Percy Andrus
Gerontology Center
University Park, MC-0191
3715 McClintock Avenue
University of Southern
California
Los Angeles, CA 90089-0191
Director: 213-740-1756
Fax: 213-740-8241
Information: 213-740-7777

Georgia
Emory University/VA Medical
Center
Suzanne S. Mirra, M.D.
Associate Professor
Department of Pathology and
Laboratory Medicine

Emory University School of
Medicine
VA Medical Center (113)
1670 Clairmont Rd.
Decatur, GA 30033
404-728-7714
Fax: 404-728-7771

Illinois
Rush-Presbyterian-St. Lukes
Medical Center
Denis A. Evans, M.D.
Professor of Medicine
Rush Alzheimer's Disease
Center
Rush-Presbyterian-St. Lukes
Medical Center
1653 West Congress Parkway
Chicago, IL 60612
Director: 312-942-3350
Fax: 312-942-2861
Information: 312-942-4463

Southern Illinois University
Robert E. Becker, M.D.
Center for Alzheimer's Disease
and Related Disorders
Southern Illinois University
School of Medicine
751 North Rutledge
P.O. Box 19230
Springfield, IL 62794-9230
Director: 217-785-6719
Fax: 217-524-2275
Information: 800-DIAL-SIU (in
IL) or 217-782-8249

Indiana
Indiana University
Bernardino Ghetti, M.D.
Professor of Pathology,

Psychiatry, Medical and
Molecular Genetics
Department of Pathology
MS A142
635 Barnhill Drive
Indianapolis, IN 40202-5120
Director: 317-274-7818
Fax: 317-274-4882
Information: 317-278-2030

Kansas
University of Kansas
William C. Koller, M.D., Ph.D.
Professor and Chairman
Department of Neurology
University of Kansas Medical
Center
39th and Rainbow Boulevard
Kansas City, KS 66103-8410
913-588-6925
Fax: 913-588-6948

Kentucky
University of Kentucky
William R. Markesbery, M.D.
Director
Sanders-Brown Research
Center on Aging
101 Sanders-Brown Building
University of Kentucky
800 S. Lime
Lexington, KY 40536-0230
606-233-6040
Fax: 606-258-2866

Maryland
The Johns Hopkins Medical
Institutions
Donald L. Price, M.D.
Professor of Pathology and
Neurology

Information USA, Inc.   *237*

The Johns Hopkins University
School of Medicine
558 Ross Research Building
720 Rutland Ave.
Baltimore, MD 21205
410-955-2750
Fax: 410-955-9777

Massachusetts
Harvard Medical School/
Massachusetts General
Hospital
John H. Growdon, M.D.
Department of Neurology
Massachusetts General
Hospital
ACC 830
Boston, MA 02114
617-726-1728
Fax; 617-726-7718

Michigan
University of Michigan
Sid Gilman, M.D.
Professor and Chair
Department of Neurology
Michigan Alzheimer's Disease
Research Center
University of Michigan
1914 Taubman St.
Ann Arbor, MI 48109-0316
Director: 313-936-9070
Fax: 313-936-8763
Information: 313-764-2190

Minnesota
Mayo Clinic
Ronald Petersen, M.D.
Associate Professor
Department of Neurology
Mayo Clinic

200 First St., SW
Rochester, MN 55905
Director: 507-284-4006
Fax: 507-284-2203
Information: 507-284-1324

Missouri
Washington University
Leonard Berg, M.D.
Alzheimer's Disease Research
Center
Campus Box 8111
Washington University School
of Medicine
660 S. Euclid Ave.
St. Louis, MO 63110
314-362-2881
Fax: 314-362-4763

New York
Columbia University
Michael L. Shelanski, M.D.,
Ph.D., Director
Alzheimer's Disease Research
Center
Columbia University
Department of Pathology
630 W. 168th St.
New York, NY 10032
Director: 212-305-3421
Fax: 212-305-5498
Information: 212-305-8056

Mr. Sinai School of Medicine/
Bronx VA Medical Center
Kenneth L. Davis, M.D.
Professor and Chairman
Department of Psychiatry
Mount Sinai School of
Medicine
Mount Sinai Medical Center

1 Gustave L. Levy Place
Box #1230
New York, NY 10029-6574
Director: 212-241-6623
Fax: 212-369-2344
Information. 212-241-8329

New York University
Steven H. Farris, Ph.D.
Aging and Dementia Research
Center
Department of Psychiatry
(THN314)
New York University Medical
Center
550 First Avenue
New York, NY 10016
212-263-5703
Fax: 212-263-6991
Information: 212-263-5700

University of Rochester
Paul D. Coleman, Ph.D.
Professor
Department of Neurobiology
and Anatomy, Box 603
University of Rochester
Medical Center
601 Elmwood Ave.
Rochester, NY 14642
716-275-2581
Fax: 716-422-8766

North Carolina
Duke University
Allen D. Roses, M.D.
Director and Principal
Investigator
Joseph and Kathleen Bryan
Alzheimer's Disease Research
Center

Memory Disorders Clinic
725 Broad St.
Durham, NC 27705
Director: 919-684-6274
Fax: 919-286-3406
Information: 919-286-7299

Ohio
Case Western Reserve
University
Peter J. Whitehouse, M.D.,
Ph.D., Director
Alzheimer's Disease Research
Center
University Hospitals of
Cleveland
11100 Euclid Ave.
Cleveland, OH 44106
216-844-7360
Fax: 216-844-7239

Oregon
Oregon Health Sciences
University
Earl A. Zimmerman, M.D.
Chairman
Department of Neurology
(L-226)
Oregon Health Sciences
University
3181 SW Sam Jackson Park
Rd.
Portland, OR 97201-3098
Director: 503-494-7321
Fax: 503-494-7242
Information: 503-494-6976

Pennsylvania
University of Pennsylvania
John Q. Trojanowski, M.D.,
Ph.D., Professor

Pathology and Laboratory
Medicine
University of Pennsylvania
School of Medicine
Room A009, Basement
Maloney/HUP
36th and Spruce Sts.
Philadelphia, PA 19104-4283
215-662-6921
Fax: 215-349-5909

University of Pittsburgh
Steven DeKosky, M.D.
Director
Alzheimer's Disease Research
Center
University of Pittsburgh
Suite 400
3600 Forbes Ave.
Pittsburgh, PA 15213
Director: 412-624-6889
Fax: 412-624-7824
Information: 412-647-2160

Texas
Baylor College of Medicine
Stanley H. Appel, M.D.
Director
Alzheimer's Disease Research
Center
Department of Neurology
Baylor College of Medicine

One Baylor Plaza
Houston, TX 77030
713-798-6660
Fax: 713-798-7434

University of Texas
Southwestern Medical Center
Roger N. Rosenberg, M.D.
Department of Neurology
Professor of Neurology and
Physiology
University of Texas
Southwestern Medical Center
at Dallas
5323 Harry Hines Blvd.
Dallas, TX 75235-9036
Director: 214-688-3239
Fax: 214-688-6824
Information: 214-648-3198

Washington
University of Washington
George A. Martin, M.D.
Professor
Department of Pathology
(SM-30)
University of Washington
1959 NE Pacific Ave.
Seattle, WA 98195
Director: 206-543-5088
Fax: 206-543-3644
Information: 206-543-6761

Healthy Hotline

People are living longer — a lot longer. In fact, the average life expectancy has almost doubled in the last hundred years in America.

But that doesn't necessarily mean that older people are spending their remaining years healthy and happy. In fact, because people are living longer, they are contracting some diseases in larger numbers than ever before. The report, *Healthy Older People*, finds that older people are very interested in maintaining and improving their health, but need information about specific habits and how they are connected to chronic disease.

You can learn about what programs public and private organizations have used to spread the word. The National Health Information Center serves as an information and referral service, directing people to organizations that can provide health information, and also distributing resource guides on popular health topics. A catalog of publications is available free, and the prices of the publications range from $1-$4. Some of the publications include:

- *Federal Health Information Centers and Clearinghouses* ($1)
- *Toll-Free Numbers for Health Information* ($1)
- *Healthy Older People: The Report of a National Health Promotion Program* ($2)
- *Locating Resources for Healthy People 2000 Health Promotion Projects* ($2)

For a catalog and referral information, contact National Health Information Center, Office of Disease Prevention and Health Promotion, Mary Switzer Building, Room 2132, 330 C St., SW, Washington, DC 20201; 800-336-4797.

☆ ☆ ☆

Taking Medication Safely

Swallow capsules whole. Don't chew tablets. Drink plenty of fluids. Do this, don't do that. Can't you read the label?

There are so many things to remember when taking medication, it's not surprising that many end up not taking them properly. Does it really matter if a tablet isn't taken at precisely the right time? What if you miss a dose?

The Food and Drug Administration's (FDA) Office of Consumer Affairs answers all these questions and more. They can refer you to other offices within the FDA for more information and has free publications that deal with drugs, medical devices, and health concerns. Some of the publications include:

- *Buying Medicine? Stop, Look, Look Again!*
- *How To Take Your Medicines: Acetaminophen-Codeine*
- *How To Take Your Medicines: Antihistamines*
- *How To Take Your Medicines: Beta Blocker Drugs*
- *How To Take Your Medicines: Cephalosporins*
- *How To Take Your Medicines: Diuretics*
- *How To Take Your Medicines: Erythromycin*
- *How To Take Your Medicines: Estrogens*
- *How To Take Your Medicines: Nonsteroidal Anti-inflammatory Drugs*
- *How To Take Your Medicines: Penicillins*
- *Testing Drugs In Older People*
- *When Medicines Don't Mix*

For these publications and more information, contact Office of Consumer Affairs, Food And Drug Administration, 5600 Fishers Lane, HFE 88, Rockville, MD 20857; 301-443-3170.

☆ ☆ ☆

Check Out The Drugs First

Since you started taking estrogen, you've been getting sudden headaches and gaining some weight. Coincidence or conspiracy? You don't have to wait for Oliver Stone to do a  movie about it — the Center for Drug Evaluation and Research does all kinds of research on side effects of prescription drugs, and can answer a whole variety of drug-related questions.

They are also the ones who make sure drug companies follow guidelines for warning labels. They can provide you with information on types of medications, such as estrogen, as well as send you the package insert for specific medications.

For more information, contact Center for Drug Evaluation and Research, Food and Drug Administration, 5600 Fishers Lane, Rockville, MD 20857; 301-294-1012.

☆ ☆ ☆

Free Hospital Care

Those annoying people from the collection agency won't leave you alone, even though you've told them a thousand times you don't have any money to pay for that gall bladder operation you had last year.

You might be able to get them off your back without having to pay a cent, simply by calling the Hill-Burton Hotline. Under this program, certain hospitals and other health care facilities provide free or low-cost medical care to patients who cannot afford to pay. You may qualify even if your income is up to double the Poverty Income Guidelines. You can apply before or after you receive care, and even after the bill has been sent to a collection agency.

Call the Hotline to find out if you meet the eligibility requirements and to request a list of local hospitals who are participating. For more information, contact Hill-Burton Hotline, Health Resources and Services Administration, 5600 Fishers Lane, Room 11-19, Rockville, MD 20857; 800-638-0742; 800-492-0359 (in MD).

☆ ☆ ☆

Health Stats

A majority of older adults rated their health as good, reported no problems in every day living, and are living longer than ever before. And only 1% of people admit cheating on their taxes. Just goes to show you make statistics say anything you want.

But if you are a statistics junkie who needs his fix, call up the National Center for Health Statistics and ask for the report, *Health Data on Older Americans: United States 1992*. You will be the hit of the next cocktail party. Or you'll be the first one shown to the door.

For a catalog of reports or more information, contact National Center for Health Statistics, 6525 Belcrest Rd., Hyattsville, MD 20782; 301-436-8500.

Get Free Medical Care

Each year over 150,000 patients receive free medical care by some of the best doctors in the world. Many are older patients suffering from common conditions, like Alzheimer's, cataracts, and heart disease.

Medical researchers get millions of dollars each year to study the latest causes, cures, and treatments to these diseases. If your condition is being studied somewhere, you might qualify for what is called a "clinical trial" and get treatment for free.

There are several ways to find out about ongoing clinical trials across the nation. Your first call should be to the National Institutes of Health (NIH) Clinical Center. NIH is the federal government's focal point for health research and is one of the world's foremost biomedical research centers. The Clinical Center is a 540-bed hospital with facilities and services to support research at NIH. Your doctor should contact the Patient Referral Line to find out if your disease is being studied, and to be put in contact with the primary investigator who can then tell if you meet the requirements for the study.

An information brochure is available describing the Clinical Center programs. For more information, contact Clinical Center, National Institutes of Health, Bethesda, MD 20892; 301-496-4891.

Quit Lighting Up

You can lower your risk of developing osteoporosis, having a heart attack, getting pneumonia, and setting your bed on fire. And earn $750 in savings to take a trip to the Bahamas. All you have to do is stop smoking for a year.

But you're probably wondering if it's really worth it after smoking for so long. It is, according to the Office on Smoking and Health. They collect and distribute information on the health risks associated with smoking and second hand smoke, as well as material on smoking cessation methods:

- *Clearing the Air*
- *Major Local Smoking Ordinances in the U.S.*
- *Good News For Smokers 50 and Older*
- *Health Benefits of Smoking Cessation*
- *Out of the Ashes*
- *Review and Evaluation of Smoking Cessation Methods*

The Office also has a fax service where they will fax you these and other articles. For a publications list or more information, contact Office on Smoking and Health, Centers for Disease Control, 4770 Buford Hwy., NW, Mail Stop K-12, Atlanta, GA 30341; 404-488-5705; 800-CDC-1311 (publications only); 404-332-4565 (fax service).

Your Medical Library

Want the latest medical research for your condition? What about doing a literature search?

The National Library of Medicine is the world's largest medical research library, containing more than 4.5 million journals, technical reports, books, photographs, audiovisual materials covering hundreds of biomedical areas and related subjects.

References to journal articles can be retrieved quickly through the MEDLARS databases. These computerized databases include hospital and health care literature, toxicology information, medical ethics information, cancer literature, and more.

You can learn about accessing MEDLARS, and receive a listing of regional medical libraries by contacting National Library of Medicine, 8600 Rockville Pike, Bethesda, MD 20894; 800-272-4787.

☆ ☆ ☆

Free Care From Those Getting The Money

If you don't trust your doctor about what he or she says about your arteries, you can conduct your own medical research. You can even learn who's being awarded research grants to study your health condition, simply by requesting a CRISP (Computer Retrieval for Information on Scientific Projects) search to be done by the Division of Research Grants.

The search can provide you with information on grants awarded by the National Institutes of Health, Food and Drug Administration, and other government research institution, universities, or hospitals that deal with the topic in which you are interested. In some cases, the researchers may be looking for people willing to take part in clinical trials.

To learn how to request a search, contact Research Documentation Section, DRG/NIH, Westwood Bldg., attn: Search Dept., 5333 Westbard Ave., Room 148, Bethesda, MD 20892; 301-594-7267.

Rehab Assistance

You hope it never gets to that point, but recovering from a stroke is a long struggle, including those who care for stroke victims. The National Rehabilitation Information Center provides information covering all types of physical and mental disabilities.

For example, do you need to find a special kind of wheelchair or communication board? What about handrails for the bathroom? The Center can conduct a search of their database to learn about research, journal articles, and more dealing with your topic of interest.

To learn more about the information and assistance this Center can provide, contact National Rehabilitation Information Center, Suite 935, 8455 Colesville Rd., Silver Spring, MD 20910; 301-588-9284; 800-227-0216.

☆ ☆ ☆

New Cancer Cure?

Ever seen a shark with cancer? You probably never wanted to get close enough to find out. Well, it's so rare that researchers have begun looking into what sharks have that we don't, and  they think they may have found it — in the sharks' cartilage. In a Cuban study, a number of cancer patients who received shark cartilage treatments showed significant improvement.

But before you go out and spend $115 on a bottle of shark cartilage pills, contact the National Cancer Institute. They'll send you a series of articles on this controversial treatment to help you better decide if it's for you. Contact: National Cancer Institute, Bldg. 31, Room 10A19, Bethesda, MD 20892; 1-800-4-CANCER.

☆ ☆ ☆

Prostate Cancer Treatment

The numbers aren't encouraging. Prostate cancer is on the rise, and more than 80% of cases occur in men over the age of 65.

But listen to the promising news: there's a new test to detect prostate cancer earlier, which could mean more lives will be saved. The test is called the Prostate-specific antigen test, or PSA. Right now, the government is sponsoring clinical trials at ten locations across the country to test how effective the PSA screening test is in men between the ages of 60 and 74.

If you're interested in participating in this free research project, call the National Cancer Institute's toll-free hotline at 1-800-4-CANCER.

Denied Again?

Did your insurance company claim a medical treatment was experimental or unnecessary, so they denied your claim? Have you been denied coverage, but you feel you qualify?

Contact your state's Insurance Commissioner. They handle complaints involving insurance policies, including premiums, deductibles, claims, or anything else related to your insurance coverage. They will review your complaint, and if they find that your insurance company has acted in an unlawful or unethical way, they have the power to force the insurance dealer to compensate you or correct whatever mistake they have made.

To locate your state Insurance Commissioner, look in the Directory of State Information at the end of this book.

☆ ☆ ☆

Can't Pay Your Premium?

For most elderly, Medicare takes care of a majority of their health care bills, but there is still the deductible and the Medicare Part B premium.

Information USA, Inc.

Many states have developed programs to provide coverage for low income elderly. Usually called Qualified Medicare Beneficiary Program, these programs provide benefits to individuals who do not qualify for Medicaid, but cannot afford some of the expenses of Medicare.

Most programs cover the premiums and annual deductible for Medicare Part B, plus the payment of co-insurance and deductible amounts for the services of Medicare.

To learn if your state has such a program, contact your state Department on Aging, located in the Directory of State Information at the end of this book.

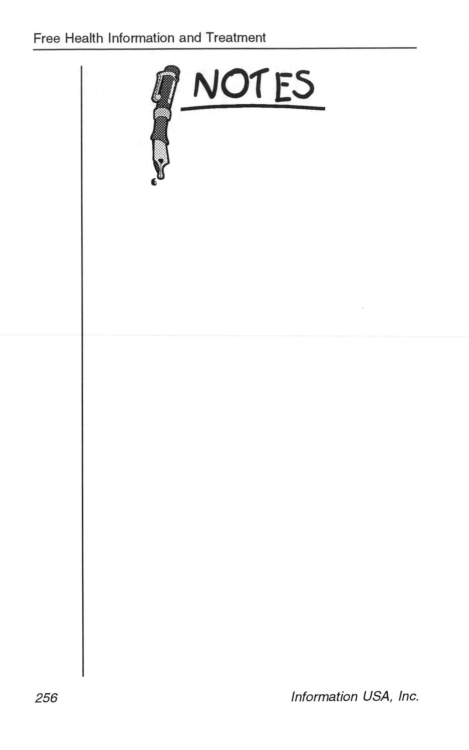

Travel Cheap

Information USA, Inc.

Now it's time to head out on the highway and look for some adventure. You probably have a few ideas of where you would like to go, but Uncle Sam can offer some valuable advice. Here you might find new ideas for your vacations that you might never hear from your travel agent.

☆ ☆ ☆

All Aboard For 15% Discounts

Traveling by train can make getting somewhere a lot more fun. We all know how adventurous AMTRAK can be at times — sit back and view the countryside, dream about the Orient Express, and if you are 62 or older you can save 15% on the lowest available fare to wherever you want to go.

By calling their toll-free hotline, AMTRAK will send you a free travel planner which offers travel tips and services, as well as a listing of their special vacation packages. Contact AMTRAK, 60 Massachusetts Ave., NW, Washington, DC 20002; 800-USA-RAIL.

Free Canoeing Courses

Whoever thought that spending time on property owned and operated by the U.S. Army could be fun? Boot camp for seniors? Far from it. For some strange reason, the Army owns thousands of  square miles of some of the best recreational areas in the country, with picnic areas, swimming beaches, hiking trails, boating, canoeing, fishing, ice fishing, hunting, and snowmobiling. They will even train you how to paddle a canoe and wear a life-preserver (yawn).

For a list of recreational areas, contact U.S. Army Corps of Engineers, Directorate of Civil Works, Natural Resources Management Branch, CECW-ON, 20 Massachusetts Ave., NW, Washington, DC 20314; 202-272-0247.

What Your Travel Agent Won't Tell You About Foreign Travel

Wouldn't it have been nice if someone had told you before you went to Rome that you should not have kept your money and your wallet together in your purse? Who knew that those little kids didn't really want to take your picture in front of St. Peter's but wanted your money instead?

This is just one piece of free advice you can read about in *Travel Tips for Seniors*, a free publication containing basic information on insurance, medication, travel warnings, and passports. And if you are unfortunate enough to run into problems overseas, the pamphlet also includes information on the kinds of assistance you can expect from U.S. embassies and consulates around the world.

For your copy, contact Overseas Citizens Services, U.S. Department of State, 2201 C St., NW, Room 4800, Washington, DC 20520; 202-647-5225.

George Washington Slept Here (Really)

Some people dream of seeing a baseball game in every major league city. For some reason (and we won't ask), you want to sleep in every bed George Washington slept in. To get some help in plotting out

your specific itinerary, contact the Advisory Council on Historic Places.

They will send you a free list of State Historic Preservation Officers who will no doubt know where George and all of his friends liked to hang out. They can also tell you about other historic and archeological sites in other states that you might want to check out.

Contact Advisory Council on Historic Preservation, 1100 Pennsylvania Ave., NW, Suite 809, Washington, DC 20004, 202-606-8503.

Hello Mrs. Jones...You've Just Won A Free Vacation

Many older people are especially vulnerable to the lure of cheap vacation offers. Before you sign up to take a cross-country flight for a free weekend in Las Vegas, you can get some free advice from a lawyer who specializes in dealing with travel schemes. Some of these opportunities really are too good to be true.

The Federal Trade Commission will send you this advice in a free pamphlet, *Telemarketing Travel Fraud.* It will provide you with information and tips to help prevent you from being taken by swindlers who are interested in only one thing — your money. Contact Public Reference, Room 130, Federal Trade Commission, Washington, DC 20580; 202-326-2222.

☆ ☆ ☆

Meaningful Memories For Vets

Commemorating the 50th anniversary of World War II can turn an overseas vacation into a meaningful experience.

World War II veterans and their families can honor their friends and family by visiting military burial grounds on foreign soil. The American Battle Monuments Commission maintains cemeteries around the world where 124,921 U.S. war dead are interred.

Each year the Commission publishes attractive, free pamphlets which highlight individual memorials, and include locations, site descriptions and photographs, brief histories of the battles in which the deceased fought, and directions from the nearest major airports. Free issues covering specific memorials are available.

For more information, contact American Battle Monuments Commission, Casimir Pulaski Building, 20 Massachusetts Ave., NW, Washington, DC 20314; 202-761-0533.

☆ ☆ ☆

Free Passports For Families Of Vets

It's hard to believe that a passport can cost up to $75, but did you know that you can get it free of charge if you are a member of a family visiting an overseas grave site of a veteran? So when you are planning your next trip to Paris, keep dear Uncle Harry in Normandy in mind.

Eligibility for these free passports includes widows, parents, children, sisters, brothers, and guardians of the deceased who are buried or commemorated in permanent American military cemeteries on foreign soil.

For additional information, write to the American Battle Monuments Commission, Room 5127, Pulaski Building, 20 Massachusetts Ave., NW, Washington, DC 20314.

☆ ☆ ☆

Enjoy The Outdoors

$10 will get you Yellowstone, Yosemite, and Mount Ranier. That's not bad considering that the U.S. Government paid $100 and three rabbit pelts for all of them!

Well, actually the $10 will get you the Golden Age Passport, which is a lifetime entrance pass to those national parks, monuments, historic sites, recreation areas, and national wildlife refuges. It entitles you to a 50% discount on fees for facilities and services, such as camping, swimming, parking, boat launching, and cave tours. The *Federal Recreation Passport Program* booklet describes the various passes to the parks which are available.

The National Parks Service (NPS) preserves historical, natural, and recreational areas of national significance. You can enjoy talks, tours, films, exhibits, publications, and other interpretive media about the parks.

The National Parks Service also operates campgrounds and other visitor facilities at the parks. Reservations can be made through MISTIX 800-365-2267. The NPS provides many publications about the various parks. They also have a map and guide which shows you the locations of the parks throughout the U.S. and the facilities each park offers.

For a complete catalog of free or for sale publications, contact the National Park Service, Office of Information, P.O. Box 37127, Washington, DC 20013; 202-208-4747.

Buffalo and Cattle Refuges

Maybe you hated watching Buffalo play in the Super Bowl, but you'll love them at the National Wildlife Reserve. And if buffalo don't do it for you, then there are plenty of Texas  longhorn cattle, as well as deer and elk who will gladly pose for pictures.

Wichita Mountains in Oklahoma and Fort Niobrara in Nebraska preserve these animals in their natural habitat. For more information, contact Fort Niobrara National Wildlife Refuge, Hidden Timber Route, HC 14, Box 67, Valentine, NE 69201; or 402-376-3789. Wichita Mountains Wildlife Refuge, Rt. 1, Box 448, Indiahoma, OK 73552; 405-429-3221. Another resource is National Bison Range, Moise, MT 59824; 406-644-2211.

Hotline to 10,000 "Rooms"

Maybe you don't need marble bathrooms or a king-size bed, or even room service for you to call it a vacation. All you need is a place to pull in for the night.

You can call the Forest Service toll-free hotline to make a reservation at one of the 156 National Forests, where you can hike, fish, camp, ski, or just relax on over 100,000 miles of trails and 10,000 recreation sites. Call the toll-free number to make reservations for any of the National Forests at 800-238-CAMP.

☆ ☆ ☆

Have Them Pay Your Ticket

Did you know that the government will pay you $50 a day to teach kids in Tanzania to throw a shot putt, or $100 a day to talk about women's rights in Bangladesh? And that includes round-trip airfare.

If you have had a unique American experience or hold a particular expertise, you can join the likes of Sandra Day O'Connor, Sally Ride, and John Updike who are just a few of those who have

Information USA, Inc.

taken part in the U.S. Speakers Program. You will get a chance to meet with government officials, journalists, labor leaders, students, entrepreneurs, and anyone who wants to know more about the United States.

Every year about 600 Americans are sent overseas for short-term speaking programs. If selected, you could be eligible to receive $100 a day, plus expenses. A U.S. Speaker's tour generally includes informal lectures or discussions, followed by questions and answers with a small group of experts.

For more information, contact U.S. Speakers Program, U.S. Information Agency, 301 4th St., SW, Washington, DC 20547; 202-619-4764.

☆ ☆ ☆

See Uncle Sam's Buffalo Herds Free

Land Between the Lakes offers recreation for tourists on over 300 miles of undeveloped shoreline. Three primary campgrounds offer over 1,000 sites and numerous informal shoreline campgrounds.

Land Between the Lakes also boasts their own resident buffalo herd — the largest publicly-owned herd east of the Mississippi River. For more information on recreation opportunities, contact Land Between the Lakes, Resource and Development, Tennessee Valley Authority, 100 Van Morgan Dr., Golden Pond, KY 42211; 502-924-5602.

☆ ☆ ☆

Camping On Uncle Sam's Land

The *Recreation Guide to Bureau of Land Management (BLM) Public Lands* features a map outlining all of the public lands used as recreational areas. Designations on the map include campgrounds, visitors centers, national wild and scenic rivers, national wilderness areas, and national historic and scenic trails.

Contact Office of Public Affairs, Bureau of Land Management, U.S. Department of the Interior, 18th and C Sts., NW, Washington, DC 20240; 202-208-5717.

Powwow With The Experts

You want to dance with some wolves? Maybe you would just settle for looking at ancient Indian artifacts in a glass case? The Bureau of Indian Affairs runs three museums full of all kinds of  Indian folk art. They'll send you free pamphlets and brochures about their respective programs and exhibition activities.

Contact the museums directly at Southern Plains Indian Museum, P.O. Box 749, Anadarko, OK 73005; 405-247-6221; Museum of the Plains Indian, P.O. Box 400, Browning, MT 59417; 406-338-2230; or Sioux Indian Museum, P.O. Box 1504, Rapid City, SD 57709; 605-348-0557.

See A Million Dollars

Do you want to know how to make a million dollars a day? Literally. Take a free self-guided tour at the Bureau of Engraving and Printing, which features actual money being made, cut, and counted.

Although the armed guards discourage sampling the goods, you can still enjoy yourself by buying uncut sheets of currency, engraved prints, small bags of shredded currency, and other neat stuff. For more information, contact the Bureau of Engraving and Printing, U.S. Department of Treasury, 14th and C Sts., SW, Washington, DC 20228; 202-874-3188.

☆ ☆ ☆

See Your Congressman Actually Work

You can now go to Washington, DC to see all your favorite T.V. stars — Sonny Bono, Gopher from Love Boat, and even Fred Thompson from the Tom Clancy movies.

The U.S. House of Representatives meets in the House Chamber in the south wing of the Capitol. You can be seated in the side and rear galleries while these well known personalities discuss cutting your benefits and increasing their salaries.

Seats are available to those who secure passes from their Representative on a first come, first serve basis: one helpful hint might be that rotten vegetables will not set off the metal detectors. Contact your member of Congress, U.S. House of Representatives, Washington, DC 20515; 202-224-3121.

☆ ☆ ☆

Get Your Own VIP White House Tour

Don't stand in that long line out back of the White House waiting to see Hillary's china pattern, or Bill's jogging shoes. Do what the insiders do: call your member of Congress and join the special VIP tours that are held every Tuesday through Saturday from 10 a.m. to 12 noon, unless the White House is closed for some official function. Who knows? You might even see Newt Gingrich's mother waiting in line with you.

You can get free passes that allow you to tour the White House earlier in the day to avoid the crowds, but you need to get these special passes from your member of Congress (call well in advance of your scheduled trip to Washington).

To learn about the White House tours contact, White House, 1600 Pennsylvania Ave., NW, Washington, DC 20500; 202-456-1414. Contact your Senator or Representative, The Capitol, Washington, DC 20515; 202-224-3121.

☆ ☆ ☆

Music At The Capitol

If listening to five hours of debate over Social Security cuts isn't music to your ears, then you might want to check out the American Festival/Concerts at the Capitol performed by the National Symphony during the spring and summer months.

The Armed Service bands and choral groups of the Air Force, Army, Marine Corps, and Navy provide summer nighttime entertainment in public concerts. Concerts are free, seating is on the lawn, and picnics are in order. Contact Architect's Office, Room SB-15, U.S.

Capitol Bldg., Washington, DC 20515;
202-225-1200.

☆ ☆ ☆

A Hotline For Your Cool Boat

Against your children's better advice, you sold the house, and bought a cabin cruiser.

Before you go tearing around the harbor terrorizing the locals, you'd better find out if you need a license to drive that thing, or maybe even learn the difference between starboard and starfish.

The Boating Safety Hotline can provide you with information on such topics of interest to boaters as safety recalls, publications, Coast Guard department contacts and addresses, public education courses, and free Coast Guard services.

A free consumer information packet is available. The hotline also takes consumer complaints about safety defects and violations.

Contact Boating Safety Hotline, Consumer and Regulatory Affairs Branch (G-NAB-5), Office of National Safety and Waterways

Services, U.S. Coast Guard, 2100 2nd St., SW, Room 1109, Washington, DC 20593; 800-368-5647.

☆ ☆ ☆

Is A Cheap Vacation In Haiti Worth Two Years In Jail?

The next time your travel agent calls with a cheap two weeks on some island in the Caribbean, first call the Overseas Citizens Service and make sure that the current political situation on that island won't turn your two weeks on the beach into two years behind bars. Believe it or not, some people in this world actually don't like Americans.

This office can provide financial and medical assistance when necessary, foreign visa and entry requirements, and they even issue travel warnings for countries where travel may be dangerous.

For more information, contact Overseas Citizens Services, Bureau of Consular Affairs, 2201 C St., NW, Room 4800, Washington, DC 20520; 202-647-5225.

☆ ☆ ☆

Know Before You Go

Before you get any big ideas about bringing back five boxes of cigars from Havana or 10 cases of vodka from Russia to sell to your friends, check it out first with the U.S. Customs Service. They can tell you how much duty you will have to pay, so you will know how much profit you can make from your scheme.

They can also tell you about the items that they will confiscate, quarantine, or even let you bring in free. For more information, contact Public Information Office, U.S. Customs Service, U.S. Department of the Treasury, P.O. Box 7407, Washington, DC 20044; 202-927-6724.

Picture Perfect Passports

If you are unclear about whether you need a passport to go to Mexico or if you need a vaccine to go to Nigeria, then contact Passport Services. You will hear a recorded message which explains the documents you need and application process for obtaining a passport, as well as reporting the loss or theft of your passport. It explains how to get any reports of a birth or death of any U.S. citizen who is in another country.

You will also be directed to the proper agencies for information regarding naturalization, travel warnings, customs regulations, and shots required by various countries. For more information, contact Passport Services, Bureau of Consular Affairs, U.S. Department of State, 2201 C St., NW, Room 5813, Washington, DC 20520; 202-647-0518.

Check Out The Plants

You never thought it would come to this, but you actually like watching the grass grow. The government knew this all along and that is why the Botanic Garden is open to the public from 9 a.m. to 9 p.m.

daily, June through August, and from 9 a.m. to 5 p.m. the rest of the year.

Of course, if you want to watch other things grow, that's okay too — they grow all kinds of plants that you and your green thumb have probably managed to kill over the years. They may even be able to give you some tips on how to spruce up your own yard.

Contact Public Programs Office, U.S. Botanic Garden, 245 1st., SW, Washington, DC 20024; 202-226-4082.

☆ ☆ ☆

Walk Pennsylvania Avenue

Besides dodging bullets and small engine aircraft in front of the White House, there are some other wonderful things happening on Pennsylvania Avenue. Really.

Throughout the year, various events are held, and you can hear a recorded message providing daily information about the events by calling 202-724-0009.

The Pennsylvania Ave. Development Corp. (PADC) also has a free guide called, *A*

Walker's Guide to Pennsylvania Avenue, which provides the locations and architects of the PADC projects.

For more information, contact Public Information Office, Pennsylvania Ave. Development Corp., 1331 Pennsylvania Ave., NW, Suite 1220 North, Washington, DC 200004; 202-724-9091.

☆ ☆ ☆

Foreign Travel Study

It is a little known fact, but there are actually some small countries in South America and the Middle East that require you to pass a trivia contest before they will allow you to enter their country. You know, questions like: what is the current population, what are the four leading industries, what is the gross national product?

The State Department has country desk officers who can tutor you before you go. To be directed to the right office, contact the Office of Public Affairs, U.S. Department of State, 2201 C St., NW, Washington, DC 20520; 202-647-6575.

Do You Have Your Shots?

Chances are that contracting an infectious disease like malaria, typhoid, or the plague isn't the point of that exotic vacation you're planning.

If it is you can skip this item, but for the rest of you who are going to be traveling outside the U.S., you might be interested in finding out about any disease outbreaks in the countries you will be visiting, along with any vaccine requirements you'll need to follow.

The Centers for Disease Control's Voice Information System allows anyone using a touchtone phone to get pre-recorded information on International Travelers' Health issues. The system can also transfer you to a public health professional if you need additional information.

The system is available 24 hours a day, although the health professionals are available Monday through Friday, 8 a.m. until 4:30 p.m. Contact Centers for Disease Control at 404-332-4555.

Hotlines For Some Hot Places

Before you plan your dream vacation to Arkansas to see Bill Clinton's birthplace, call the hotline listed below to learn about all kinds of special senior discounts for your hotel, restaurant, or theaters.

If you are scouting out destinations, or planning a visit to a particular city, each state's Travel and Tourism Office can be a great help. They can send you all kinds of maps, brochures, and other valuable information. If you want to know where to find hotels, motels, or restaurants, cafes, diners, movie theaters, supermarkets, drug stores or even churches, this is the place to start. They can even tell you if there are special discounts or programs for seniors.

Other information from state tourism offices might include highway conditions, weather advice, local hotel/motel rates, and the best places to eat. In general, each state will provide information packages containing a travel guide, a calendar of events, state maps, and brochures from private, state, and regional tourist attractions.

Information USA, Inc.

State Tourism Offices

Alabama
205-242-4169

Alaska
907-465-2012

American Samoa
684-633-1091-2-3

Arizona
602-542-4764

Arkansas
501-682-1088

California
916-322-2881

Colorado
303-592-5510

Connecticut
203-258-4286

Delaware
800-441-8846
302-739-5749

District of Columbia
202-789-7000

Florida
904-488-5607

Georgia
404-656-3553

Guam
671-66-5278-79

Hawaii
808-586-2550

Idaho
208-334-2470

Illinois
312-814-4732

Indiana
317-232-8860

Iowa
515-242-4705

Kansas
913-296-2009

Kentucky
502-564-4930

Louisiana
504-242-8110

Maine
207-289-5710

Marianas
670-234-8327

Maryland
410-333-6643

Massachusetts
617-727-3201

Michigan
517-373-0670

Information USA, Inc.

Minnesota
612-296-2755

Mississippi
800-647-2290
601-359-3297

Missouri
314-751-3051

Montana
406-444-2654

Nebraska
402-471-3794

Nevada
702-687-4322

New Hampshire
603-271-2665

New Jersey
609-292-6963

New Mexico
800-545-2040
505-827-7400

New York
518-474-4116

North Carolina
919-733-4171

North Dakota
800-437-2077
701-224-2525

Ohio
614-466-8844
800-BUCKEYE

Oklahoma
405-521-3981

Oregon
800-547-7842
503-378-3451

Pennsylvania
717-787-5453

Puerto Rico
89-721-1576-2402

Rhode Island
800-556-2484
401-277-2601

South Carolina
803-734-0136

South Dakota
800-843-1930
605-773-3301

Tennessee
615-741-7225

Texas
512-462-9191

Utah
801-538-1030

Vermont
802-828-3236

Virginia
804-786-2051

Virgin Islands
809-774-8784

Washington
206-753-5600

West Virginia
304-348-2286

Wisconsin
608-266-2345

Wyoming
307-777-7777

NOTES

Help With Your Retirement Fund and Pension Questions

Y ou gave your notice at the office, and now it is time to kick back and relax. Let Uncle Sam offer some assistance for those nagging financial questions that you might have. You can learn how to check on your retirement, pension, taxes, and more. All you need to do is pick up your phone and call.

☆ ☆ ☆

Little Known Tax Tidbits

Did you know that the IRS considers you 65 on the day before your 65th birthday? Why? I don't know, but you qualify for some added tax bonuses when you hit that magic number. It could be the only time you are actually happy to turn a year older!

Trying to fill out those simple tax forms each year can sometimes be a frustrating experience. The Internal Revenue Service has several different options to make things go a little smoother for you.

Do you need to file? Can you use the 1040EZ? Want to know how to figure out the donations you gave to your church?

The Information Line provides answers to all your tax questions, and can assist you in completing your income tax return. They can also refer your call to tax specialists for answers to your more detailed tax questions. You can also listen to pre-recorded answers on over 140 frequently asked tax questions on the Tele-Tax Line.

For more information on your taxes, contact Internal Revenue Service, U.S. Department of the Treasury, 1111 Constitution Ave., NW, Washington, DC 20224; 800-829-1040 Information Line; 800-829-3676 Forms Line; 800-829-4477 Tele-Tax Line.

☆ ☆ ☆

Special Tax Help For Seniors

The tax guys thought only of you when they wrote *Tax Information For Older Americans* (Pub. 554). It answers all those specific tax questions about your filing status, retirement benefits, life insurance proceeds, and more. It will even help you keep most of what you made (up to a point anyway) on the sale of your house if you meet certain requirements.

The IRS Forms Line distributes all of the IRS tax forms and instruction books. Some of the forms dealing with elderly concerns include:

- *Tax Information on Selling Your Home* (pub. 523)
- *Credit for the Elderly or Disabled* (pub. 524)
- *Comprehensive Tax Guide to U.S. Service Retirement Benefit* (pub. 721)
- *Pension and Annuity Income* (pub. 575)
- *Tax Information for Handicapped and Disabled Individuals* (pub. 907)
- *Social Security Benefits and Equivalent Railroad Retirement Benefits* (pub. 915)
- *Medical and Dental Expenses* (pub. 502).

For your copies, contact the IRS Forms Line at 800-829-3676.

☆ ☆ ☆

Learn How to Prepare Tax Forms

Are you the kind of person who has to see it before you believe it? The Internal Revenue Service distributes films and videos on a variety of tax topics.

For example, "A Vital Service" aims at enlisting groups and organizations into the Volunteer Income Tax Assistance Program in which IRS trains volunteers to help the low-income, elderly, non-English speaking, and the handicapped complete their tax returns.

This video is available from Audio/Visual Branch, Public Affairs Division, IRS, U.S. Department of the Treasury, 1111 Constitution Ave., NW, Washington, DC 20224; 202-622-7541.

Get Your Taxes Done For Free

But, don't worry, these guys from the IRS don't charge by the minute. And what's great about this group is that they go where they are needed — to nursing homes, community centers, and even to your home if you can't get out.

The program is called, Tax Counseling for the Elderly, and offers free tax help to people who are 60 years and older. Many of the volunteers are retired and are affiliated with nonprofit groups, so It's basically a nice group of people willing to lend a hand to others in completing those "simple" tax forms that are oftentimes not so simple to fill out.

The IRS Information Line can refer you to the closest program, so call 800-829-1040.

☆ ☆ ☆

A List of Little-Known Tax Deductions

We all feel like we pay, and we pay, and we pay. Now here is someone who is looking out for your needs for a change. If you are a senior citizen or know someone who is, it is important to get a copy of a free publication titled, *Protecting Older Americans Against Overpayment of Income Taxes*.

Designed to ensure that older Americans claim every legitimate income tax deduction, exemption, and tax credit, this publication is very easy to understand and provides many examples and checklists. It is updated annually in January and includes a section on income tax items which will change in the following year.

For your free copy, contact Special Committee on Aging, U.S. Senate, Washington DC 20410; 202-224-5364.

☆ ☆ ☆

Has Your Check Arrived?

Think you're not getting ahead? Think again. You're better off now than those folks who retired 30 years ago. The median income for married couples is now $23,817, and that's a 79% increase, even with an adjustment for inflation.

Today 92% of seniors receive Social Security which was designed to replace a portion of the income a person loses when they retire, die, or become disabled with monthly benefits based upon a worker's earnings. In August of 1992, the average check was for $630.

Social Security has established a hotline to answer all your questions. You can learn how to get a duplicate Social Security card, change your address, and even learn how much you would earn each month if you retired today.

It actually is very important to get a copy of your Personal Earnings and Benefits statement each year. The statement is free and records your income for each year from which your future benefits will be determined. Contact Social Security Hotline at 800-772-1213.

☆ ☆ ☆

Up to $5000 To Help You Pay Your Bills

If your check is to small to live on, don't be discouraged. If you don't qualify for Social Security, or if your benefits are very low, you may qualify for Supplement Security Income (SSI).

This program was established to help poor seniors over 65 and the blind and disabled meet basic living needs. To qualify you must meet a maximum monthly income test.

Some of the income and services you receive are excluded when they calculate your monthly income in relation to your personal expenses. Those who meet SSI's eligibility usually automatically qualify for Medicaid coverage and Food Stamps benefits.

Studies have found that only between 40 percent and 60 percent of seniors poor enough to qualify for SSI actually receive benefits under the program. To find out if you qualify, contact your local Social Security office or call the Social Security Hotline at 800-772-1213.

☆ ☆ ☆

Your Pension Watchdogs

There are a lot of pensions to watch as they grow or even lose value, as over 50 million workers and retirees are covered by employer-spo nsored pension plans. In fact, 19% of all income for seniors comes from private and government employee pensions.

Most private plan participants are covered under a defined-benefit plan, which generally bases the benefit paid in retirement either on the employee's length

296

of service or on a combination of his or her pay and length of service.

The Pension Benefit Guaranty Corporation (PBGC) keeps an eye on these different benefit plans and takes over those that are underfunded. They have several free publications concerning this issue to help you look out for your best interests.

Employer's Pension Guide provides a general overview of the responsibilities under federal law of employers who sponsor single-employer defined benefit pension plans.

Your Guaranteed Pension answers some of the most frequently asked questions.

Your Pension: Things You Should Know About Your Pension Plan serves as an explanation of pension plans: what they are, how they operate, and the rights and options of participants.

For more information, contact Public Affairs, Pension Benefit Guaranty Corporation, 1200 K St., NW, Washington, DC 20005; 202-326-4000.

For Those Who Served Our Country

Military veterans are entitled to retirement pay after 20 years of service. In 1990, 1.6 million retirees and survivors received military retirement benefits. There are actually three types of benefits provided by the military: standard retirement benefits, disability retirement benefits, and survivor benefits.

Service members who retire from active duty receive monthly payments based on a percentage of their final monthly base pay being received at the time of retirement. Base pay comprises 65-70 percent of total pay and allowances. The formula used to compute benefits varies depending upon when you entered the service, length of service, and age at retirement.

Full benefits begin immediately upon retirement; the average retiring enlisted member begins drawing benefits at 43; the average officer at 46. Benefits continue until the death of the participant. The Military Survivor Benefit Plan allows a military retiree to have a portion of his or her retired pay withheld to provide a benefit to his/her survivors.

Veterans may also be eligible for support if they have limited income when they have 90 days or more of active military service. They must be permanently and totally disabled for reasons not due to the military.

To learn more about the retirement plans, contact the U.S. Department of Veterans Affairs, 810 Vermont Ave., NW, Washington, DC 20420; 800-827-1000.

☆ ☆ ☆

For Those Employees Of The Big Guy

Uncle Sam takes care of those dutiful bureaucrats through the Federal Employees Retirement System (FERS). FERS is comprised of three parts: a defined-benefit plan, Social Security, and a Thrift Savings Plan.

In the defined-benefit plan, workers earn 1% of the average of their highest three consecutive years of wages for each year of service completed. You also contribute to Social Security. The Thrift Savings Plan (TSP) is similar to the 401(k) plans used by private employers. Sound complicated? It's not, once you do your required reading.

To learn more specific details about the plan and retirement information, contact Federal Employees Retirement System, Office of Personnel Management, 1900 E St., NW, Washington, DC 20415; 202-606-0490.

☆ ☆ ☆

I've Been Working On The Railroad

For all those engineers, conductors, linesmen, and caboose riders, the Railroad Retirement System is the one responsible for managing the retirement system. It covers all railroad firms and distributes retirement and disability benefits to employees, their spouses, and survivors.

Workers must amass 120 months of employment to qualify for a pension. In some cases, military service may be counted as railroad service. The average annuity paid in 1993 was $1,050.

The Board has several fact sheets including a booklet titled *Railroad Retirement and Survivor Benefits*, which explains who qualifies, how to apply, and more. For more information, contact Railroad Retirement Board, 844 North Rush St., Chicago, IL 60611; 312-751-4500.

☆ ☆ ☆

How To Check Up on Your Pension

It's a good idea to check its pulse, blood pressure, and heart rate. You want to make sure your pension is around longer than you are.

The Pension and Welfare Benefits Administration can help you do that. They require administrators of private pension and welfare plans to provide plan participants with easily understandable summaries of plans; to file those summaries with the agency; and to report annually on the financial operation of the plans.

Free publications include: *What You Should Know About The Pension Law*, which gives a summary of what is required of pension plans, and *How To File A Claim For Your Benefit*, which explains what you need to do to receive your benefit.

Contact Public Information, Pension and Welfare Benefits Administration, U.S. Department of Labor, 200 Constitution Ave., NW, Room N5656, Washington, DC 20210; 202-219-8921.

☆ ☆ ☆

Keeping An Eye On Your Pension Money

Sure, the Pension Benefit Guaranty Corporation (PBGC) says they will cover the pension plans that are underfunded, but what if several of the big ones collapse at the same time? Would they all be protected? A General Accounting Office (GAO) report showed that no one would get their check.

What if your company offers you a lump-sum retirement? A GAO report looks at several of these offers and examines the pros and cons.

Some of titles of the GAO reports focusing on income security issues include:

- *Financial Audit: Pension Benefit Guaranty Corporation's 1992 and 1991 Financial Statements* (GAO/AIMDD 93-21)
- *Lump-Sum Retirements* (GAO/GGD 93-2R)
- *Pension Plans: Hidden Liabilities Increase Claims Against Government Insurance Program* (GAO/HRD 93-7)
- *Pension Plans: Labor Should Not Ignore Some Small Plans That Report Violations* (GAO/HRD 93-45)
- *Pension Restoration Act* (GAO/HRD 93-7R)
- *Private Pensions: Protections for Retirees' Insurance Annuities Can Be Strengthened* (GAO/HRD 93-29)
- *Underfunded State and Local Pension Plans* (GAO/HRD 93-9R)

All reports are free and can be requested by contacting U.S. General Accounting Office, P.O. Box 6015, Gaithersburg, MD 20884; 202-512-6000.

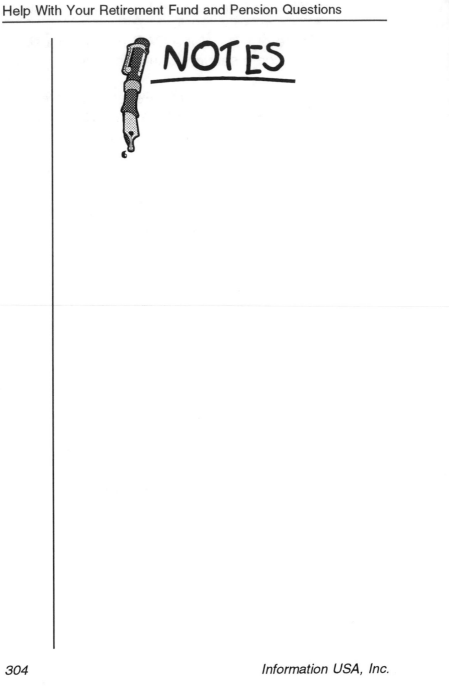

Free Prescription Drugs

Millions of older Americans are going without medications, even though they could be getting them for free. Why? Many do not have adequate insurance, and they understandably think that that is the end of the story.

An American Association of Retired Persons (AARP) report even found that about 8 million Americans over 45 now say that they have to cut back on necessary items such as food or fuel to pay for their medications. Of the top 20 most widely prescribed drugs taken by older Americans, most do not have lower-priced generic substitutes.

The average prescription price is about $20. In fact, if an older person with an average income of $8,700 took just 10 prescriptions a year, and had no insurance coverage, that individual would spend 27% of his/her income ($2,400/$8,781) on prescription drugs.

☆ ☆ ☆

Discount Drug Program

Help could be just a phone call away. Ten states have special drug programs that give huge discounts to seniors who are ineligible for Medicaid and who don't have private insurance. For example, seniors in New Jersey can get their prescriptions for only $5, and in Maine they can get them for as little as $2.

Often all it takes is a phone call and filling out a simple form. You will have to meet income eligibility, but you can make upwards of $23,000 a year and still be eligible in New York, for example. If your state is not listed below, contact your state Department of Aging listed in the Directory of State Information in the back of this book, but also check out the free drug programs sponsored by the drug manufacturers themselves. You will find a detailed description of this program following the listing of the state-by-state drug programs.

Connecticut
Conn PACE
P.O. Box 5011
Hartford, CT 06102
800-423-5026

Eligibility Requirements:
- You must be 65 years old or older.
- You must have lived in Connecticut for six months.
- Your income cannot exceed $13,800 if you are single, and $16,600 if you are married.
- You may not have an insurance plan that pays for all or a portion of each prescription, a deductible insurance plan that includes prescriptions, or Medicaid.

Cost:
- You pay a $15 one time registration fee.
- You pay $12 for each prescription.
- You must get generic drugs whenever possible, unless you are willing to pay the difference in price.

Delaware
Nemours Health Clinic
915 N. Dupont Blvd.
Milford, DE 1963
302-424-5420; 800-763-9326

Eligibility Requirements:
- You must be a Delaware resident.
- You must be U.S. citizen.
- You must be 65 or older.
- Income requirements for single $11,300; for married $15,500.

Cost:
- You must pay 20% of the prescription drug cost.

Illinois
Pharmaceutical Assistance Program
Illinois Department of Revenue
P.O. Box 19021
Springfield, IL 62794
800-624-2459

Eligibility Requirements:
- You must be 65 years of age or older, or over 16 and totally disabled, or a widow or widower who turned 63 before spouse's death.
- You must be a resident of Illinois.
- Your income must be less than $14,000.
- You must file a Circuit Breaker claim form.

Cost:
- Pharmaceutical Assistance card will cost either $40 or $80, depending upon your income.

- Your monthly deductible will be $15 if the cost of your card is $40, and $25 if the cost of your card is $80.
- You must choose the generic brand when available, unless you are willing to pay the difference in price.

Maine
Elderly Low-Cost Drug Program
Bureau of Taxation
State Office Building
Augusta, ME 04333
800-773-7895; 207-626-8475

Eligibility requirements:
- You must be a Maine resident.
- You may not be receiving SSI payments.
- You must be at least 62 years old or part of a household where one person is 62 years old.
- Your income may not exceed $9,700 if you live alone; $12,100 if you are married or have dependents.

Cost:
- Each drug will cost $2 or 20% of the price allowed by the Department of Human Services, whichever is greater.

Maryland
Maryland Pharmacy Assistance Program
P.O. Box 386
Baltimore, MD 21203-0386
410-225-5397; 800-492-1974

Eligibility:
- For anyone in the state who cannot afford their medications. Income requirements vary, so it is best to call.

New Jersey
Pharmaceutical Assistance to the Aged and Disabled (PAAD)
Special Benefit Programs
CN 715

Trenton, NJ 08625
800-792-9745; 609-588-7049

Eligibility:
- You must be a New Jersey resident.
- Your income must be less than $16,171 If you are single, or less than $19,828 if you are married.
- You must be at least 65 years of age.
- Drugs purchased outside the state of New Jersey are not covered, nor any pharmaceutical product whose manufacturer has not agreed to provide rebates to the state of New Jersey.

Cost:
- You pay $5 for each covered prescription. PAAD collects payments made on your behalf from any other assistance program, insurance, or retirement benefits which may cover prescription drugs.

New York
Elderly Pharmaceutical Insurance Coverage EPIC
P.O. Box 15018
Albany, NY 12212
800-332-3742; 518-452-6828

Eligibility Requirements:
- You must be 65 or older.
- You must reside in New York State.
- Your income must not exceed $17,500 if you are single; or $23,000 if you are married.
- You are not eligible if you receive Medicaid benefits.

Cost:
- You pay between $3-$23 per prescription depending upon the prescription cost.
- There are two plans for EPIC. You can pay an annual fee depending upon your income to qualify right away. The annual fee ranges from $20 to over $75, which can be paid in installments. The EPIC Deductible plan is that you pay no fee, but you pay full price for your prescriptions until you spend the deductible amount. The deductible amount also varies by income and starts at $468.

Pennsylvania
PACE Card
(Pennsylvania Pharmaceutical Assistance Contract For The Elderly)
Pennsylvania Department of Aging
P.O. Box 8806
Harrisburg, PA 17105
717-783-1550
800-225-7223

Eligibility Requirements:
- You must be 65 or older.
- Your income cannot exceed $13,000 if you are single; $16,200 for married couples.
- You must also live in the state for at least 90 days.

Cost:
- You pay a $6.00 co-payment for each prescription. You may not purchase drugs out of state.
- PACE limits drug amounts to no more than a 30-day supply or 100 pills. There are no vacation supplies allowed.

Rhode Island
Rhode Island Pharmaceutical Assistance to the Elderly (RIPAE)
Rhode Island Department of Elderly Affairs
160 Pine St.
Providence, RI 02903
401-277-3330

Eligibility Requirements:
- You must be a Rhode Island resident.
- You must be 65 years old.
- Your income must not exceed $13,860 if you are single; $17,326 if you are married.
- You cannot have any other prescription drug coverage.

Cost:
- Members pay 40% of the cost of prescription drugs used to treat certain illnesses.

Information USA, Inc.

Vermont
VScript program
Department of Social Welfare
Medicaid Division
103 South Main St.
Waterbury, VT 05070
802-241-2880
800-827-0589

Eligibility Requirements:
- You must be a resident of Vermont.
- You must be at least 65.
- You may not have income in excess of 175% of the federal poverty guidelines.
- You may not be in a health insurance plan that pays for all or a portion of the applicant's prescription drugs.

Cost:
- There will be a co-payment requirement. The amount will be a percentage of the charge for a drug, with the percentage amount determined at the beginning of each fiscal year.

☆ ☆ ☆

Free Medications Directly From Drug Companies

Zantac, Valium, Prozac, Dilantin, Insulin- these are just a few of the medications you can get FREE directly from the drug companies themselves.

That's right: drug companies don't want everybody to know this, but they will give certain people who can't afford their medications their drugs free of charge. I guess they don't want to tarnish their greedy bad guys image by publishing these benevolent programs.

So, what's the catch? It sounds too easy. All that many of these companies require for you to participate in these "indigent patient programs" is that your doctor write them a note stating that you cannot afford the drugs that you need. Your doctor is the one that needs to make the call.

Once the forms are filled out, you will be able to pick your drugs up directly from your doctor's office for free. Your doctor can call the toll-free Pharmaceutical Manufacturers Association (PMA) hotline to get more information about individual manufacturer indigent patient programs.

Call 800-PMA-INFO, or you can write Pharmaceutical Manufacturers Association, 1100 15th St., NW, Washington, DC 20005.

Directory of Pharmaceutical Manufacturers Programs

Adria Laboratories, Inc.
Contact: Adria Laboratories Patient Assistance Program, P.O. Box 9525, McLean, VA 22102; 1-800-366-5570. Adriamycin PFS, Adrucil, Folex, Idamycin, Neosar, Tarabine, and Vincasar. Two months supply. Physician must certify patient is unable to afford the cost of the drug, and is unable to obtain assistance elsewhere.

Allergan Prescription Pharmaceuticals

Contact: Judy McGee, 1-800-347-4500 Ext. 4280. Betagan, Bleph-10, Blephamide, FML, HMS, Oculinium, Pilogan, Propine, and some OTC tear products. Course of therapy, up to a maximum of 6 months supply. Eligibility criteria are at the physician's discretion.

Amgen, Inc.

Contact: Amgen Safety Net Programs, Medical Technology Hotlines, 1-800-272-9376 (202-637-6098 in Washington, D.C.). EPOGEN and NEUPOGEN. Amgen's program consists of a universal patient program and a variable cap program for uninsured patients. Enrollment in the program is based on a patient's insurance and financial status.

Astra

Contact: F.A.I.R. (FOSCAVIR Assistance and Information on Reimbursement) Program; 1-800-488-3247. Foscavir (Foscarnet Sodium). The physician must sign and complete the application and return it within seven days to the address indicated on the form. The qualification form must also be accompanied by a signed prescription.

Boehringer Ingleheim Pharmaceuticals, Inc.

Contact: PARTNERS IN HEALTH, 1-800-556-8317. Persantine, Atrovent, Alupent, and Catapres. Controlled substances are not covered. Maximum of three months. Patient cannot have prescription coverage, cannot be eligible for Medicaid/State assistance programs, and must meet annual income guidelines. Physician must initiate request.

Bristol-Myers Squibb #1

(General Indigent Patient Program)
Contact: Bristol-Myers Squibb, Indigent Patient Program, P.O. Box 9445, McLean, VA 22102-9998; 1-800-736-0003; 703-760-0049 (FAX). Duricef, Cefzil, BuSpar, Desyrel, Estrace, Ovcon-35, Ovcon-50, Natalins, Natalins RX, Vagistat-1, Mycostatin. Three months supply. Physician's request.

Bristol-Myers Squibb #2

(Cardiovascular Access Program)
Contact: Cardiovascular Access Program, P.O. Box 9445, McLean, VA 22102-998; 1-800-736-0003; 703-760-0049 (FAX). Program covers cardiovascular products, which include Capoten, Capozide, Corgard,

Corzide, Klotrix, K-Lyte, Monopril, Naturetin, Pravochol, Pronestyl-SR, Questran Light, Ranzide, Saluron, Salutensin, Vasodilan, and Betapen-VK. Three month's supply. The patient must work through an enrolled physician, cannot be eligible for other sources of drug coverage, such as Medicaid or private insurance, and must be deemed financially eligible, as determined by "means" and "liquid assets" tests.

Bristol-Myers Squibb #3
(Cancer Patient Access Program)
Contact: Bristol-Myers Squibb, Cancer Patient Access Program, 2400 West Lloyd Expressway, Evansville, IN 47721; Mail Code R-22; 1-800-437-0994. BICNU, CEENU, Lysodren, Mutamycin, Mycostatin Pastilles, Paraplatin, Platinol, Platinol-AQ, VePesid, Blenoxance, Cytoxan, Lyophilized Cytoxan, Ifex, Mesnex, and Megace. Two months supply. Internal financial screening on a case-by-case basis.

Burroughs-Wellcome
Contact: Patient Information Services, Burroughs-Wellcome Co., P.O. Box 52035, Phoenix, AZ 85072-9349; 1-800-722-9294 (Program Enrollment). Septra, Septra DS, Lanoxin, Mepron, AZT (Retrovir), Zovirax, Zyloprim, Imuran, and Wellcovorin. The products are available in a 30-day supply, with maximum of 90 days therapy. Eligibility criteria that have to be met: 1) Gross monthly income must be less than 200 percent of federal poverty guidelines. 2) All applications will be reviewed within established criteria and on a case-by-case basis. 3) Patients must be residents of the Untied States or territories. 4) All alternative funding sources must be investigated. 5) All required information must be provided for consideration of eligibility. 6) Patients may be approved (occasionally) by exception if extreme extenuating circumstances exist.

Ciba-Geigy Pharmaceuticals
Contact: Jackie LaGuardia, Senior Information Assistant, Ciba-Geigy Corporation, 556 Morris Ave., D2058, Summit, NJ 07091, 1-800-257-3273. All the company's products (including those distributed by Basal and Summit) are covered under the program, which include Lopressor, Lotensin, Slow K, Tegretol, Voltaren, Brethine, Estraderm, and Transderm Nitro. Ritalin, a controlled substance, is not covered under this program. Up to three months supply available.

DuPont Merck
Contact: Darlene Samis, DuPont Pharama, P.O. Box 80026, Wilmington, DE 19880-0026. 1-800-474-2762, 302-234-4327. Drugs covered: Coumadin, Lodosyn, Sinemet, Sinemet CR, Symmetrel, Trexan, and Vaseretic. Controlled substances are not covered, which include Percodan and Percocet. Thirty days supply. The patient must be indigent and ineligible for a federal or state government pharmaceutical assistance program.

Genentech, Inc.
Contact: Genentech Reimbursement Hotline, P.O. Box 2586, S. San Francisco, CA 94083-2586, 1-800-530-3083. Protropin (Human Growth Hormone), Activase (TPA, Tissue Plasminogen Activator), Actimmune (Interferon Gamma-lb), Nutropin, and Pulmozyme. Quantity provided and eligibility requirements are variable. Patients are asked to provide sufficiently detailed information to assure the company that they are uninsured and cannot afford the required payments. (For Activase: If an uninsured patient has gross family income of $25,000 or less, the company provides replacement product to the hospital).

Glaxo, Inc.
Contact: Laura N. Wright Supervisor, Glaxo Indigent Patient Program, Glaxo, Inc., P.O. Box 13438, Research Triangle Park, NC 27709; 1-800-452-9677; 919-248-7971 (FAX). Zantac, Ceftin, Ventolin, Beconase, Beconase AQ and Trandate. Maximum three months supply. Patient must be a private outpatient whom the physician considers medically indigent and who is not eligible for any other third-party reimbursement.

Hoechst-Roussel Pharmaceuticals, Inc.
Contact: Joyce Trotter, Field Forest Development, 1-800-422-4779. Prokine (sargramostim). Must show lack of insurance or ability to pay. The company indicated that it provides other products to indigents upon receipt of a prescription and a physician's letter certifying that the patient is indigent. Eligibility is on a case-by-case basis. This policy covers patients who are ineligible for a third-party payer or Medicaid coverage. Products include Lasix, Trental and Diabeta. One course of therapy (usually two to three weeks).

Hoffman-LaRoche, Inc.
Contact: Inge Shanahan, Medical Communications Associate, Roche

Laboratories, 340 Kingsland Street, Nutley, NJ 07110; 1-800-526-6367; Teleprompter #2; 201-235-2765 (FAX). They do not accept faxed applications. Valium, Librium, Limbritol, Dalmane, Hivid, Bactrim, Bactrim DS, Klonopin, Efudex (Fluorouracil Injectable), Gantrisin, Gantanol, Interferon 2A Recombinant, Rocephin Injectable, and Rocaltrol. Three months supply. Eligibility limited to private practice outpatients who are considered by the physician to be medically indigent and who are not eligible to receive Roche drugs through any other third-party reimbursement program. The physician's signature and DEA number are required for all applications, whether or not the request is for a controlled prescription drug. Drugs are shipped to registered DEA addresses only.

Immunex Corporation

Contact: Professional Services Immunex Corporation, 1-800-Immunex or 1-800-466-8639; 206-587-0430; 1-800-221-6820 (FAX). Leukine 250 meg., Leukine 500 meg, Hydraea, Rubex. Three cycles. Physician must attest that the patient requires the drug and that all the reimbursement options for the patient have been tried.

Janssen Pharmaceutica #1

Contact: Professional Services Department, Janssen Pharmaceutica Inc., 1125 Trenton-Harbourton Road, P.O. Box 200 Office A32000, Titusville, New Jersey 08560-0200; 1-800-526-7736: Hismanal, Alfenta, Sufenta, Sublimaze (1-800-652-6227 Risperdal). Varies by product, patient condition. Physician determines that patient is indigent and not eligible for health insurance. Physicians may request free medications by written or telephone requests, accompanied by a signed and dated prescription and letter stating financial status and need of patient.

Janssen Pharmaceutica #2

Contact: Janssen Patient Assistance Program. 1800 Robert Fulton Drive, Reston, VA 22091; 1-800-544-2987. Ergamisol (levamisole HCl), Nizoral, Sporanox, Duragesic. One or two months supply, varies by product. Patient must have less than $25,000 total annual household income and can have Medicare or private insurance, but cannot have prescription coverage.

Knoll Pharmaceuticals

Contact: Knoll Pharmaceuticals, Indigent Patient Program, 30 N. Jefferson Rd., Whippany, NJ 07981, 1-800-524-2474. Isoptin, Rythmol,

Santyl, Zostrix. Patients can enroll in the Heart-in Harmony program to receive educational information. Contact the local company sales representative, or call the patient help line.

Lederle Laboratories

Contact: Jerry Johnson, Pharm. D., Director, Industry Affairs, American Cyanamid, Inc., One Cyanamid Plaza, Wayne, New Jersey 07470, 1-800-533-2273, 1-201-831-4484 (FAX). Diamox, Artane, Minocin, Leucovorin, Calcium Loxapine, Verelan, Rheumatrex, Maxzide, and Myambutol. Physician has to make the request. Patients have to be financially indigent, and not eligible for coverage under third party insurance or Medicaid reimbursement.

Eli Lilly and Company

Contact: Indigent Patient Program Administrator, Eli Lilly and Company, Patient Assistance Program, P.O. Box 9105, McLean, VA 22102-0105; 1-800-545-6962. Ceclor, Keflex, Prozac, Dymelor, Axid and the insulin products Humulin and Iletin. The program does not cover controlled substances, which include Darvon and Darvocet products. Quantities are dependent upon the product and the physician's instructions. Patients eligibility is determined on a case-by-case basis in consultation with the prescribing physician. Patients are not required to complete enrollment forms. Physicians are asked to submit a written request containing specific information.

Marion Merrell Dow, Inc.

Contact: Indigent Patient Program, P.O. Box 8480, Kansas City, MO 64114, 1-800-362-7466. Cardizem, Cardizem CD, Cardizem SR, Carafate, Pavabid, Seldane, Seldane D, Nicorette, Rifadin, Quinamm, and Lorelco. Three months supply. The physician determines whether the patient is eligible for the program.

McNeil Pharmaceutical

Contact: Thomas Schwend, Manager, Medical Information, McNeil Pharmaceutical Corporation, P.O. Box 300, Route 202 South, Raritan, NJ 08869-0602; 908-218-6894. Pancrease, Parafon Forte DSC, Haldol, Vascor, Tolectin. Varies by product, patient condition. Physician determines that patient is indigent and not eligible for health insurance. Physicians may request free medications by written or telephone request, accompanied by a signed and dated prescription and letter stating financial status and need of patient.

Merck Sharp and Dohme

Contact: Complimentary Products Program, Merck & Co., Inc., P.O. Box 105534, Atlanta, GA 30348; 1-800-637-2579. Merck products covered include Mevacor, Plendil, Pepcid, Prilosec, Prinivil, Proscar, Timoptic, Timolol, Clinoril, Flexeril, Periactin, Noroxin, Cogentin, Indocin, Aldomet, Dolobid, Vasoretic and Vasotec; except injectables. Requests for three months; supply are generally honored. The patient's physician must provide a written statement of medical need; indicate the existence of financial hardship; indicate the lack of patient eligibility for prescription coverage from insurance or government assistance programs. Physician must also send a signed and dated written prescription with doctor's DEA number.

Miles Pharmaceuticals

Contact: Professional Services, Attention: Miles Indigent Patient Program, 400 Morgan Ave., West Haven, Connecticut 06516, 1-203-937-2373. Cipro, Nimotop, and Tridesilon Cream. Medication quantities and duration of support is determined on a case-by-case basis. Physician must certify that the patient is not eligible for or covered by government funded reimbursement or insurance programs for medication. Patient's income must be below federal poverty guidelines.

Ortho Biotechnology

Contact: Jacob Drapkin, Director, Health Care System, 908-704-5074; 908-526-4997 (FAX). Ortho Biotech Financial Assistance Program, 1800 Robert Fulton Drive, Reston, VA 22091. The assistance program covers PROCRIT (Epoetin alfa) and LEUSTATIN (cladribine) Injection. Programs criteria: 1) Financial Assistance Program (FAP) 1-800-447-3437 provides PROCRIT therapy free of charge to any qualifying nondialysis patient who cannot obtain insurance coverage, is uninsured, or cannot afford the cost of their treatment. 2) Cost Sharing Program 1-800-441-1366 limits the annual cost of PROCRIT expenditures for a patient exceeding approximately $8,500 for a calendar year, regardless of third party coverage. 3) LEUSTATIN Financial Assistance Program 1-800-447-3437 provides LEUSTATIN therapy free of charge to all persons who meet specific criteria and lack financial resources and third party insurance necessary to obtain treatment.

Ortho Pharmaceuticals

Contact: Thomas Schwend, Manager, Medical Information, Ortho

Pharmaceutical Corporation, P.O. Box 300, Route 202 South, Raritan, NJ 08869-0602; 1-800-682-6532. Flxin, Aci-jel, Ortho Dienestrol Cream, Monistat Vaginal Suppositories, Protostat Tablets, Sultrin Triple Sulfa Cream, Sultrin Triple Sulfa Vaginal Tablets, Terazol 3 Suppositories, Terazol 7 Cream, Spectazole Cream, Monistat-Derm Cream, Grifulvin Suppositories, Meclan Cream, Persa-gel, Persa-gel W, Erycette. Varies by product, patient condition. Physician determines that patient is indigent and not eligible for health insurance. Physician may request free medications by written or telephone request, accompanied by a signed and dated prescription and letter stating financial status and need of patient.

Parke Davis

Contact: Parke Davis Patient Assistance Program, P.O. Box 9945, McLean, VA 22102; 1-800-755-0120; 201-540-2000. All products are made available which include Cognex, Dilantin, Lopid, Mandelamine, Accupril, Pyridium, Nitrostat Sublingual, Tabron, Ponstel, Procan, Anusol HC, and Zarontin. All applications are taken over the phone. To apply, patient or doctor calls Parke Davis with the following information: Doctor's full name, address, phone number; Patient's name, address, phone number and financial status.

Pfizer Pharmaceuticals, Inc. Program #1

Contact: Mark Clark, Pfizer Indigent Patient Program, P.O. Box 25457, Alexandria, VA 22314, 1-800-646-4455. Antivert, Marax, Diabinese, Cardura, Minizide, Navane, Sinequan, Zithromax, Feldene, Procardia, Procardia XL, Vibramycin, Vistaril, Zoloft, Minipress, Minizide, and Glucotrol. Up to three months supply at one time, as prescribed by the physician. Any patient that a physician is treating as indigent is eligible. Patient must not be covered by third party insurance or Medicaid. Usually takes three to four weeks to receive medication. Refills are available upon request by doctor.

Pfizer Inc. Program #2: Roerig Division

Contact: Diflucan Patient Assistance Program; 1-800-869-9979. Diflucan (Fluconazole). Up to three months supply at one time and then can reapply. Patient must not have insurance or other third party coverage, including Medicaid. Patient must not be eligible for a state AIDS drug assistance program. Patient must have an income of less than $25,000 a year without dependents; or less than $40,000 a year with dependents.

Proctor & Gamble Pharmaceuticals Inc.

Contact: Customer Service, 17 Eaton Avenue, Norwich, NY 13815; 1-800-448-4878; 607-335-2998 (FAX). Asacol, Dantrium, and Macrodantin. The quantity varies depending upon the situation, but at least a one month supply can be obtained upon receipt of a physician's prescription. The company relies on the physician's appraisal of the patient need. The company also helps the patient identify other sources of financial help to pay for the patient's medications.

R & D Laboratories

Contact: R & D Laboratories, Inc., 4094 Glencoe Avenue, Marina del Rey, California 90292; 1-800-338-9066. Every R & D Laboratories pharmaceutical nutritional supplement has a special Indigent Patient Program sticker. Patients bring the stickers from their bottles of R & D products with them when they come to the dialysis unit. Stickers are attached to the back of a booklet supplied by the company and the completed booklet is returned to R & D Laboratories. For every 12 stickers they receive from a unit, R & D sends nutritional product of facility's choice for free distribution to indigent patients.

Sandoz Pharmaceuticals

Contact: Maria Hardin, Director, Sandoz Drug Cost Sharing Program, P.O. Box 8923, New Fairfield, CT 06812-1783. 1-800-447-6673 (for all drugs); 1-800-937-6673 (for Clozaril) The National Organization for Rare Disorders (NORD/Sandoz Drug Cost Share Program (DCSP) is solely administered by NORD. Sandimmune, Sandogobulin, Sandostatin, Parlodel, and Eldepryl are covered under one program. Clozaril is covered under a different program, as described below. Patient is awarded up to one year's supply of drug, which is shipped in three month supplies via the mail-order pharmacy utilized by the program. Clozaril-Patient is eligible to receive up to one year's supply of the drug, dispensed only one week at a time, per dispensing requirements of package label. NORD determines eligibility by medical and financial criteria, and applies a cost share formula. The patient/applicant must demonstrate financial need above and beyond the availability of federal and state funds, private insurance or family resources. NORD also determines patient eligibility for Clozaril program.

Sanofi Winthrop Pharmaceuticals

Contact: Sanofi Winthrop, Product Information Department, 90 Park

Avenue, New York, NY 10016; 212-907-2000; 1-800-446-6267 (Push #1 twice when automated answering machine picks up). Aralen, Danocrine, and Winstrol. One unit or one month supply, as required. Subject to acceptance by the company, patients can obtain medications by having their physician contact the company to request the product, provide a written order for the product, and confirm the patient's need.

Schering-Plough

Contact: For Intron/Eulexin Products: Roger D. Graham, Jr., Marketing Manager, Oncology/Biotech, Service Program, Schering Laboratories, 2000 Galloping Hill Road, Building K-5-2B2, Kenilworth, NJ 07033. For other Schering Products: Drug Information Services Indigent Program; 908-298-4000; 1-800-526-4099. Introl A-Initial supply is for three months; renewals available for three months at a time. Eulexin-Initial supply is for six months; renewals available for six months at a time. Other Schering products, which include Trinalin, Lotrimin, Lotrisone, Diprosone, Diprolene, Fulvicin, Proventil, Vancenase, Normodyne, and Optimine, are provided for an initial three months supply, with renewals available for up to three months at a time. Patient eligibility is determined on a case-by-case basis, on internal criteria. The consultation includes a review of the specific case, as well as the availability of other means of health care assistance.

G.D. Searle and Co.

Contact: "Patients in Need" Foundation, Searle Co., P.O. Box 5110, Chicago, IL 60680; 1-800-542-2526; 708-470-6719 (FAX). For general information about the program; Laura Leber, Associate Director, Public Affairs, 708-470-6280. Aldactazide, Aldactone, Calan, Calan SR, Cytotee, Kerlone, Nitrodisc, Norpace, and Norpace CR. Supply is based on the physician's assessment of the needs of the patient. The program is conducted through the physician, who determines the patient's eligibility based on medical and economic need. Searle provides suggested guidelines to the physician for determination of patient eligibility.

Sigma-Tau Pharmaceuticals

Contact: Michele McCourt, Carnitor Drug Assistance Program, Administrator, National Organization for Rare Disorders, P.O. Box 8923, New Fairfield, CT 06812-1783. 1-800-999-6673; 203-746-6518; 203-746-6481 (FAX). Carnitor (Levocarnitine). Three months supply, up to one year. The patient must have no other means for obtaining the drug through insurance or state or federal assistance, or liquid assets, and cannot afford to purchase the drug. Must be a U.S. citizen or permanent resident.

SmithKline Beecham: Program #1
Contact: SB Access to Care Program, SmithKline Beecham Pharmaceuticals, One Franklin Plaza-FP1320, Philadelphia, PA 19101. 1-800-546-0420 (patient requests) 215-751-5749 (physician requests). Tagamet, Augmentin, Relafen, Dyazide, Compazine, Bactroban, Amoxil, Ridaura, all other SmithKline Beecham prescription products. Individual physicians determine which patients are eligible and would benefit most from the Access to Care Program. Physicians are required to submit forms to enroll patients in the program. Three months supply is available at one time. Requests must originate from the physician.

SmithKline Beecham: Program #2
Contact: Eminase/Triostat Compassionate Care Programs, SmithKline Beecham Pharmaceuticals, One Franklin Plaza-FL1320, Philadelphia, PA 19101. 1-800-866-6273. Eminase and Triostat. Patient must demonstrate ineligibility for other forms of medical assistance and meet the program's income requirements (single patients with annual incomes of $18,000 or less will be eligible, and persons who are married or have at least one dependent will be eligible if their annual incomes of $18,000 or less will be eligible, and persons who are married or have at least one dependent will be eligible if their annual incomes are $25,000 or less). For each eligible patient, hospitals should submit a Hospital Consent Form and an Application Form with any one of the following documents: a copy of the patient's medical record, pharmacy record, or the patient's bill.

Syntex Laboratories, Inc.
Contact: Cytovene Medical Information Line, 1-800-444-4200 General telephone number to inquire about indigent patient programs: 1-800-822-8255. Cytovene (ganciclovir sodium) 500mg sterile powder. The company's other products include Naprosyn, Anaprox, Cardene, Synalar, Synemol, Ticlid, Toradol, Lidex and Nasalide. Up to 25 vials of Cytovene are available. Syntex provides Cytovene free of charge when it is prescribed for an immunocompromised patient who has been diagnosed as having cytomegalovirus (CMV) retinitis, if that patient

lacks the means to purchase the drug, and if that patient is ineligible for any form of third-party reimbursement to pay for the drug.

Upjohn Company

Contact: Patient Consumer Information, Upjohn Company, 7000 Portage Rd., Kalamazoo, MI 49001; 616-323-6004; 616-323-4551 (FAX). Health Care Professionals should contact their local Upjohn Representative. Ansaid, Motrin, Provera, E-Mycin, Halcion, Xanax, Medrol, Cleocin, Lincocin, Loniten, Micronase, Orinase, and Tolinase. Generally, a three months supply is provided. However, a physician can request a supply for a longer period of time. The physician determines the patient's needs, and if insurance or other social programs to help provide medications are available.

Wyeth-Ayerst Laboratories #1

Contact: Wyeth-Ayerst Laboratories Indigent Patient Program, Roger J. Eurbin, Professional Services IPP, P.O. Box 8299, Philadelphia, PA 19101; 1-800-568-9938. Sectral, Cyclospasmol, Premarin, Isordil, Phenergan, Orudis, Wytensin, and Cordarone. The company also makes three oral contraceptives: Triphasil, Lo/Ovral, and Nordette, which are primarily provided by family planning clinics. In general, one to two months supply or the closest trade package size available is provided. For Cordarone, one month supply or up to two bottles of 60 tablets is provided. The number of cycles of oral contraceptives given to the patient is determined by a health care provider or the family planning clinic. The patient must be medically indigent, with no form of coverage for pharmaceutical products. The family planning clinic determines eligibility for new and refill oral contraceptive cycles.

Wyeth-Ayerst Laboratories #2

Contact: Norplant Foundation, P.O. Box 25223, Alexandria, VA 22314; 703-706-5933. Norplant (levonorgestrel implants) five year contraceptive system. Eligibility determined on a case-by-case basis and limited to individuals who cannot afford the product and who are ineligible for coverage under private and public sector programs.

Zeneca Pharmaceuticals

Contact: Yvonne A. Graham, Manager, Professional Services, Zeneca Pharmaceuticals Group, P.O. Box 15197, Wilmington, DC 19850-5197; 302-886-2231. Nolvadex, Zestoretic, Bucladin-S, Kinesed, Sorbitrate, Tenormin, Tenoretic and Zestril. One to three months supply with application. 1-800-424-3727

Alphabetical Listing by Drug

This section identifies the name of medications frequently prescribed for older Americans and the manufacturers of the drugs which are covered under an indigent patient program listed in this directory. If a drug that you take is NOT listed here, it still may be provided under an indigent patient program; it is suggested that your physician call the company to determine if it is covered under a program.

If the manufacturer of a particular drug is not listed in this directory, it is suggested that the patient or physician call the company directly to determine if the company has an indigent patient program. Drug Manufacturer telephone numbers can be found in the *Physician's Desk Reference.*

Drug/Manufacturer

A
Aci-Jel/Ortho
Activase/Genentech
Actimmune/Genentech
Adriamycin PFS/Adria
Adrucil/Adria
Aldactone/Searle
Aldomet/Merck
Alupent/Boehringer
Anaprox/Syntex
Ansaid/Upjohn

Antivert/Pfizer#1
Anusol HC/Parke-Davis
Apresoline/Ciba-Geigy
Aralen/Sanofi-Winthrop
Artane/Lederle
Asacol/Procter & Gamble
Atrovent/Boehringer
Augmentin/SmithKline
Axid/Eli Lilly
AZT (Retrovir)/Burroughs-
Wellcome

B

Bactrim DS/Hoffman-LaRoche
Bactroban/SmithKline
Beconase/Glaxo
Beconase/AQ/Glaxo
Detagan/Allergan
BICNU/Bristol-Myers #3
Blenoxance/Bristol-Myers #3
Bleph-10/Allergan
Blephamide/Allergan
Bucladin-S/Zeneca
BuSpar/Bristol-Myers #1

C

Calan/Searle
Calan SR/Searle
Capoten/Bristol-Myers #2
Capozide/Bristol-Myers #2
Carafate/Marion Merrell Dow
Cardene/Syntex
Cardizem/Marion Merrell Dow
Cardura/Pfizer #1
Carnitor/Sigma-Tau
Catapres/Boehringer
Ceclor/Eli Lilly
CEENU/Bristol-Myers #3
Ceftin/Glaxo
Cefzil/Bristol-Myers #1
Cipro/Miles
Clinoril/Merck
Clozaril/Sandoz
Cogentin/Merck
Compazine/SmithKline
Cordarone/Wyeth-Ayerst
Corgard/Bristol-Myers #2
Corzide/Bristol-Myers #2
Coumadin/DuPont Merck
Cyclospasmol/Wyeth-Ayerst
Cytotec/Searle
Cytovene/Syntex
Cytoxan/Bristol-Myers #3

D

Dalmane/Hoffman-LaRoche
Danocrine/Sanofi-Winthrop
Dantrium/Procter & Gamble
Desyrel/Bristol-Myers #1
Diabinese/Pfizer #1
Diamox/Lederle
Dienestrol/Ortho
Diflucan/Pfizer #2
Dilantin/Park-Davis
Diprolene/Schering-Plough
Diprosone/Schering-Plough
Dolobid/Merck
Duricef/Bristol-Myers #1
Dyazide/SmithKline #1
Dymerlor/Eli Lilly

E

E-Mycin/Upjohn
Efudex (Fluorouracil
Inj)/Hoffman
Eldepryl/Sandoz
Eminase/SmithKline #2
Epogen/Amgen
Ergamisol/Janssen
Erycette/Ortho
Estrace/Bristol-Myers #1
Eulexin/Schering-Plough

F

Feldene/Pfizer #1
Flexeril/Merck
Floxin/Ortho
FML/Allergan
Fulvicin/Schering-Plough

G

Glucotrol/Pfizer #1

H

Halcion/Upjohn

Haldol/McNeil
Hismanal/Janssen
Hivid/Hoffman-LaRoche
HMS/Allergan

I
Idamycin/Adria
Ifex/Bristol-Myers #3
Imuran/Burroughs-Wellcome
Indocin/Merck
Insulin Humulin and Ilentin/Eli Lilly
Interferon-A Recomb/Hoffman
Intron-A/Schering-Plough
Isoptin/Knoll
Isordil/Wyeth-Ayerst

K
K-Lyte/Bristol-Myers #1
Keflex/Eli Lilly
Kerlone/Searle
Kinesed/Zeneca
Klonopin/Hoffman-LaRoche
Klotrix/Bristol-Myers #2

L
Lanoxin/Burroughs-Wellcome
Lasix/Hoechst-Roussel
Leucovorin Calcium/Lederle
Leukine/Immunex
Librium/Hoffman-LaRoche
Limbritol/Hoffman-LaRoche
Lioresal/Ciba-Geigy
Lithobid/Ciba-Geigy
Lo/Ovral/Wyeth-Ayerst
Lodosyn/DuPont-Merck
Lopid/Parke-Davis
Lopressor/Ciba-Geigy
Lotrimin/Schering-Plough
Lotrisone/Schering-Plough
Loxapine/Lederle

Lyophilized Cytoxan/Bristol-Myers #3

M
Macrodantin/Procter & Gamble
Maxzide/Lederle
Medrol/Upjohn
Megace/Bristol-Myers #3
Mepron/Burroughs-Wellcome
Mesnex/Bristol-Myers #3
Mevacor/Merck
Micronase/Upjohn
Minipress/Pfizer #1
Minocin/Lederle
Monistat/Ortho
Monistat-Derm/Ortho
Monopril/Bristol-Myers #2
Motrin/Upjohn
Myambutol/Lederle
Mycostatin/Bristol-Myers #1

N
Naprosyn/Syntex
Nasalide/Syntex
Natalins RX/Bristol-Myers #1
Neosar/Adria
Neupogen/Amgen
Nicorette/Marion Merrell Dow
Nimotop/Miles
Nitrodisc/Searle
Nizoral/Janssen
Nolvadex/Zeneca
Nordette/Wyeth-Ayerst
Normodyne/Schering-Plough
Norpace/Searle
Noroxin/Merck
Norplant System/Wyeth-Ayerst
Nutropin/Genentech

O
Oculinium/Allergan

Optimine/Schering-Plough
Orinase/Upjohn
Orudis/Wyeth-Ayerst
Ovcon/Bristol-Myers #1

P
Pancrease/McNeil
Parafon Forte DSC/McNeil
Paraplatin/Bristol Myers #3
Parlodel/Sandoz
Pavabid/Marion Merrell Dow
Pepcid/Merck
Periactin/Merck
Persantine/Boehringer
Persa-Gel/Ortho
Pilogan/Allergan
Platinol/Bristol-Myers #3
Plendil/Merck
Ponstel/Parke-Davis
Pravochol/Bristol-Myers #2
Premarin/Wyeth-Ayerst
Prilosec/Merck
Prinivil/Merck
Procan/Parke-Davis
Procardia/Pfizer #1
Procrit/Ortho Biotechnology
Prokine/Hoechst-Roussel
Pronestyl SR/Bristol-Myers #2
Propine/Allergan
Proscar/Merck
Prostat/Ortho
Protropin/Genentech
Proventil/Schering-Plough
Provera/Upjohn
Prozac/Eli Lilly
Pulmozyme/Genentech
Pyridium/Parke-Davis

Q
Questran/Bristol-Myers #2
Quinamm/Marion Merrell Dow

R
Relafen/SmithKline
Rheumatrex/Lederle
Risperdal/Janssen #1
Rocaltrol/Hoffman-LaRoche
Rocephin/Hoffman-LaRoche
Rythmol/Knoll

S
Sandimmune/Sandoz
Sandoglobulin/Sandoz
Sandostatin/Sandoz
Santyl/Knoll
Sectral/Wyeth-Ayerst
Septra DS/Burroughs-
Wellcome
Seldane/Marion Merrell Dow
Sinemet/DuPont-Merck
Sorbitrate/Zeneca
Spectazole/Ortho
Sporanox/Janssen
Sultrin/Ortho
Symmetrel/DuPont Merck
Synalar/Syntex
Synemol/Syntex

T
Tagamet/SmithKline
Tarabine/Adria
Tenormin/Zeneca
Terazol/Ortho
Timolol/Merck
Timoptic/Merck
Tofranil/Ciba-Geigy
Tolectin/McNeil
Trandate/Glaxo
Trexan/DuPont-Merck
Tridesilon Cream/Miles
Triostat/SmithKline #2
Triphasil/Wyeth-Ayerst

Free Prescription Drugs

V

Vagistat/Bristol-Myers #1
Valium/Hoffman-LaRoche
Vascor/McNeil
Vasodilan/Bristol-Myers #3
Vasoretic/Merck
Vasotec/Merck
VePesid/Bristol-Myers
Verelan/Lederle
Vincasar/Adria
Voltaren/Ciba-Geigy

W

Wellcovorin/Burroughs-
Wellcome
Wytensin/Wyeth-Ayerst

X

Xanax/Upjohn

Z

Zantac/Glaxo
Zestril/Zeneca
Zestoretic/Zeneca
Zithromax/Pfizer #1
Zoloft/Pfizer #1
Zostrix/Knoll
Zovirax/Burroughs-Wellcome
Zyloprim/Burroughs-Wellcome

Help With Your Sex Life

Use it or lose it. Research shows that a pattern of regular sexual activity helps to preserve sexual ability in later life. So try to avoid those "Not tonight, I have a headache" days. Most older people want — and are able to lead — an active, satisfying sex life. There are some normal changes that may affect sex, but as long as you're aware of what is happening and why, your sex life can continue to be great! Read on to learn about physical changes and what to expect.

☆ ☆ ☆

Is Estrogen Really The Fountain Of Youth?

It will make you young, beautiful, and sexy. No, we are not talking about the latest hair care product. Estrogen is getting a lot of hype these days as a cure-all for aging women who wish to remain youthful and sexually active through menopause and beyond.

Estrogen is taken by millions of women and does help relieve symptoms of menopause such as hot flashes, and other vaginal changes that can cause problems during sex. Some vaginal changes can be treated with local applications of creams that contain estrogen, which may lower the risk to the rest of the body from estrogens that are taken orally.

The Food and Drug Administration (FDA) has information on estrogen to help women understand the benefits and risks of this drug when deciding the best course of therapy. Contact the Center for Drug Evaluation and Research, Food and Drug Administration, 5600 Fishers Lane, HFD-8, Rockville, MD 20857; 301-594-1012.

☆ ☆ ☆

Impotence...When Love Is A Let Down

It is not exactly an easy subject to talk to your doctor about, but many elderly men suffer from impotence.

You don't have to forgo sex in your remaining years because of this problem. Many types of sexual dysfunction can now be treated successfully. Close to 10 million men suffer from impotence and Uncle Sam can give you the latest on medical therapies, from penile implants to encounter sessions. There are 15 different models of penile implants and they all have a 90% success rate.

The National Kidney and Urologic Diseases Information Clearinghouse can answer questions and provide information about impotence and penile implants. They have free publications and can conduct a search on the Combined Health Information Database (CHID) for more information on a specific subject.

For more information, contact National Kidney and Urologic Diseases Information Clearinghouse, 3 Information Way, Bethesda, MD 20892-3580; 301-654-4415.

☆ ☆ ☆

Are your Hot Flashes Getting Hotter?

Menopause doesn't have to be the hormonal hurricane women have faced in the past. Mood swings, hot flashes, depression...the list goes on. But many women still rely on outdated information when trying to adjust to "the change." Taking estrogen and progesterone, known as HRT, can help relieve the problems of menopause, although they are not without problems of their own. Research is currently being undertaken regarding the use of these drugs.

The National Institute on Aging has a free booklet titled *Menopause* which explains the changes women go through as their bodies change. Lower estrogen levels can affect sexual intercourse, but there are steps you can take to make sex a pleasurable experience once again. For your copy, contact National Institute on Aging, Information Center, P.O. Box 8057, Gaithersburg, MD 20898; 800-222-2225.

☆ ☆ ☆

Bald Is Sexy

Don't look for some over-the-counter miracle to solve your balding pate. Bad hair days are bad hair days. Our government hair and drug experts say over-the-counter drugs don't work, but some prescription drugs and implant techniques can keep you from indulging in those "Hair Club" offers on late night TV. Get the facts. Contact Center for Drug Evaluation and Research, Food and Drug Administration, 5600 Fishers Lane, HFD-8, Rockville, MD 20857; 301-594-1012.

Find Your Lover On The Freeway

Looking for your future Mercedes Benz driving boyfriend? You can get a mailing list from your state Department of Motor Vehicles (DMV) which

includes information on men in your zip code who own BMWs and Mercedes Benzs. This information is available for a fee in 47 states. Contact your Department of Motor Vehicles in your state capital.

Also for a fee, your full service DMV can provide you with a person's current address if you have their full name, date of birth, and city. Most states have an office through which you can trace auto tags, but the request usually has to be made in writing. Each state operates the service a little differently, and may charge a small fee. You can receive information such as to whom the car is registered, their address, the year and make of car, and the serial number of the car. Contact your state Department of Motor Vehicles located in your state capital for more information.

☆ ☆ ☆

Sexy Seniors Do It, Too

A recent poll found that many Americans are enjoying each other's charms well into their seventies. Many of them even swear that sex, like wine, gets better with age.

With age, women do not ordinarily lose their physical capacity for orgasm nor men their capacity for erection and ejaculation. There is, however, a gradual slowing of response, especially in men. This slowing down is currently considered part of normal aging, but may be eventually treatable or even reversible.

A pattern of regular sexual activity (which may include masturbation) helps to preserve sexual ability. When problems occur, they should not be viewed as inevitable, but rather as the result of disease, disability, drug reactions, or emotional upset, and may require medical

Information USA, Inc.

care. Illness, disabilities, and even some medicines can affect sex or sexual desire.

The National Institute on Aging has a free publication titled *Age Page: Sexuality in Later Life* which provides information on normal physical changes, effects of illness or disability, and other factors that may affect sex for older adults. For your free copy, contact National Institute on Aging, Information Center, P.O. Box 8057, Gaithersburg, MD 20898; 800-222-2225.

☆ ☆ ☆

AIDS: Changing Sex In The Nineties

AIDS is not something that affects only the young, but is found in every age group. In fact, over 40,000 people received their AIDS diagnosis when they were 50 years or older.

And it's not just contracted from unprotected sex. Even having your gall bladder removed puts you at risk because of the possibility of being exposed to AIDS tainted blood. There is so much information out there regarding AIDS — how do you know what is true and what's not?

The National AIDS Hotline can answer questions about HIV transmission and prevention, HIV testing, and HIV/AIDS treatments. Callers can receive referrals to national, state, and local HIV/AIDS service organizations. There is a catalogue of brochures, pamphlets, reports, posters, and audiovisuals that are available free or at a very low cost.

For more information, contact National AIDS Hotline, P.O. Box 13827, Research Triangle Park, NC 27709; 800-342-AIDS; 800-458-5231 (publications).

Gifts, Bargains, and Hobbies

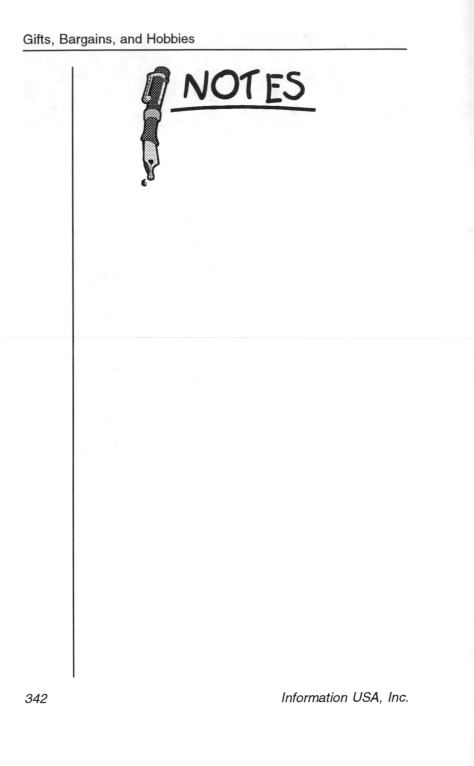

W ith your retirement, you may finally have some extra time now to enjoy your favorite pastimes. Whether it's gardening, sewing, shopping for bargains, watching videos, or even tracking down your family history, Uncle Sam can help you.

The government has videos on every topic imaginable for your viewing pleasure. Did you know that through government auctions you can get great gifts for the kids and grandkids? You can even improve your fishing technique with some lessons, courtesy of the government. All it takes is a few phone calls and you are on your way to getting much more out of your free time.

☆ ☆ ☆

Free Sewing Classes

You never know when it will come in handy to know 100 things to do with a yard of fabric.

If you are using your retirement time to get back into sewing, or even want to teach sewing classes to kids, a great resource is your County Cooperative Extension Office. They frequently offer courses, workbooks, and even videos about how to sew. Some even focus on certain projects like Christmas gifts or draperies.

To learn more about what is available in your area, look in the blue pages of your phone book for the office nearest you, or you can find the main state office in the Directory of State Information at the end of the book. For more information, contact Extension Service, U.S. Department of Agriculture, Room 3328, Washington, DC 20250; 202-720-4111.

☆ ☆ ☆

Free Photos of Bill, Hill, and Socks

Whether you are a Republican or Democrat, President Clinton is the one in charge these days.

You can get free photos of the President and/or the First Lady, and even get an 8x10 of First Feline Socks. Remember that they won't know if you are throwing darts at the picture or not.

All you need to do is send a letter with your request to Presidential Correspondence, White House, Photo

Department, Attention Jeff Riley, Old
Executive Office Building, Room 94,
Washington, DC 20500.

☆ ☆ ☆

Help for Model Ship Builders

If miniature ship building is a pastime for
you, then turn
to the
National
Archives for
help in
making your
replicas
accurate. The
brochure,
*Pictures of
United States
Navy Ships:*

1775-1941, lists pictures available covering
sailing ships to submarines, in addition to
steamships, aircraft carriers, battleships,
cruisers, destroyers, and torpedo boats.

For the brochure and ordering information,
contact Still Pictures Branch, National
Archives and Records Administration, 8601
Adelphi Rd., College Park, MD 20740;
301-713-6625, ext. 221.

WWII Memorabilia

General Douglas MacArthur storming the shores. Ships burning in Pearl Harbor. Inspirational posters. World War II can come alive again through slides, pictures, and posters from the National Archives.

Thousands of pictures are maintained by the Archives, so to help you with your selection they have developed a brochure, *Pictures of World War II*, which describes what is available.

For the brochure and ordering information, contact Still Pictures Branch, National Archives and Records Administration, 8601 Adelphi Rd., College Park, MD 20740; 301-713-6625, ext. 221.

☆ ☆ ☆

Borrow Old Faithful

For those armchair travelers who want to learn more before they go, or even for those that never got to see some of this country's natural wonders, the Park Service can bring them directly to you.

The photography library of the U.S. Park Service will lend you pictures and slides of national parks, monuments, battlefields, and other points of interest. This is a great resource for Civil War buffs.

Contact Photo Library, Office of Public Affairs, National Park Service, U.S. Department of Interior, 18th and C Sts., NW, Washington, DC 20240, 202-208-4997.

☆ ☆ ☆

Photos of the Natural Wonders

Volcanoes, earthquakes, the Grand Canyon, and Niagara Falls are just a few of the thousands of pictures available from the U.S. Geological Survey. Pictures date back to 1869, but unfortunately there is no real catalog to consult, so why not develop a wish list of your very own?

To obtain information on ordering or purchasing prints, negatives or transparencies, contact the library directly. Contact Photographic Library, MS914, U.S. Geological Survey, Box 25046, Federal Center, Denver, CO 80225, 303-236-1010; for the hearing impaired, 303-236-0998 TTY.

Free Videos of The One That Got Away

Back up your fishing adventures with evidence. The Fish and Wildlife Service lends slides and still photos to lend credibility to even the tallest tale that you can dream up to tell your buddies.

The Audio Visual Department of the Fish and Wildlife Service has a collection of both black and white pictures and color slides of fish and wildlife and there is no charge for their lending service. You can even contact your regional Fish and Wildlife office for free loaner films and videos to get you excited about the upcoming fishing season.

Contact Audio Visuals, Fish and Wildlife Service, 18th and C Sts., NW, Washington, DC 20240, 202-208-5611.

☆ ☆ ☆

Our African Heritage On Film

An exhaustive collection of photographs of African art and life is available from the Eliot Elisofon Photographic Archives.

The collection is divided into two major categories: art, which includes photographs of art objects in the permanent collection, as well as in public and private collections; and field, which contains images of African life. An overall guide to the collection and a price list are available upon request.

Contact National Museum of African Art, 950 Independence Ave., SW, Washington, DC 20560, 202-357-4654.

☆ ☆ ☆

A Picture For Those Who Served

If Mom or Dad ever served in the Armed Forces, surprise them on their next birthday with a photo of their base, aircraft, or ship. You can get them an 8x10, so that the next time they say, "When I was in the service we did things this way," you can understand what they're talking about.

The Still Media Records Center of the Defense Department has an archive of over 135,000 photographs. For a general information sheet and current price list, contact Still Media Records Center, Bldg. 168 Code SMRC, U.S. Department of

Defense, 2701 S. Capitol St., SW,
Washington, DC 20374-5080,
202-433-2166.

☆ ☆ ☆

A Fisherman's Dream

Did the movie *A River Runs Through It*
excite you about fly fishing? "Pathway to
Fishing" is a 12-part, hour-long
instructional program covering fish biology,
aquatic ecology, angler ethics, methods for
handling fish, and information about where
to go fishing.

Although a bit pricey at $61, it's packed
with a User's Guide, 12 support posters
and an instructional video. Contact U.S.
Fish and Wildlife Service, Pathway To
Fishing, 1849 C St., NW, ARLSQ-820,
Washington, DC 20240.

☆ ☆ ☆

When The Fish Aren't Biting

Everyone needs a little down time, so
when you are taking a break from the
fishing boat, you can at least read up on
the topic.

A free shopping list of government fishing publications (doc. number SB209) is available which provides information on fisheries and fish research, and another list (doc. number SB57) provides information on charts and marine posters.

For your copies, contact Superintendent of Documents, Government Printing Office, Washington, DC 20402, 202-512-1800.

☆ ☆ ☆

Bones And Fossils Headquarters

For all those fossil hunters out there, the government has an office just for you. The National Park Service provides technical assistance to federal and state agencies on the identification, evaluation, and preservation of archeological properties, and has a series

of technical publications and a database of archeology bibliographies.

For more information, contact Archeological Assistance Division, National Park Service, Department of the Interior, P.O. Box 37127, Suite 360, Washington, DC 20013-7127, 202-343-4101.

☆ ☆ ☆

For Archaeologists Who Won't Get Their Hands Dirty

Here is your own home study course to help you make your own rare find.

Participate in Archeology is a free brochure which provides some basic information on archeology, and lists magazines, books, videos, and agencies and organizations through which you can receive additional information.

Contact National Park Service, Archeological Assistance Division, U.S. Department of the Interior, P.O. Box 37127, Washington, DC 20013-7127, 202-208-4747.

Join In on a Free Archaeological Dig

Never liked staying on the sidelines? Well then, dig in. "Passport In Time" helps you open a window on the past by allowing you to join activities such as archaeological excavation, site mapping, drafting, laboratory and art work, collecting oral histories, restoration, and much more.

Projects vary in length and there is no registration cost or fee. You may even receive a small stipend to off-set your living expenses. For information on upcoming opportunities, contact Passport In Time Clearinghouse, CEHP, Inc., P.O. Box 18364, Washington, DC 20036, 202-293-0922.

Check Out The Past

No need to reinvent the wheel, if it has already been done before. You can find what has been going on in the field of archeological discoveries, and even get a directory of those professionals in the know.

LEAP (Listing of Education on Archeological Programs) is an annotated listing of programs, special tours, and publications done by archaeologists for the public and includes a contact person from whom additional and updated information can be obtained.

For your free copy, write LEAP Coordinator, DCA/ADD, National Park Service, P.O. Box 37127, Suite 210, Washington, DC 20013-7127.

☆ ☆ ☆

Free Help With Sick Pets

For most pet owners, their pets are like their children. You worry about what they are eating, and you worry when they are sick.

The Center for Veterinary Medicine can answer all your pet food and nutrition questions. They have fact sheets and articles about choosing food for your pets, as well as information sheets on common pet illnesses and veterinary terms.

Do what is right for your pet. To receive free copies of these fact sheets, contact Center for Veterinary Medicine, Food and

Drug Administration, 7500 Standish Place, Rockville, MD 20855; 301-295-8755.

☆ ☆ ☆

Learn About Endangered Species

You actually may not need to go any farther than your own backyard to find rare and wonderful things. If you are a card-carrying birder, the Fish and Wildlife Service has

information booklets on attracting birds to your yard, and even information on different homes for birds.

If you are worried about endangered species, they can provide you with information on the Endangered Species Act, a list of endangered and threatened species, as well as information sheets on many species. Contact U.S. Fish and

Wildlife Service, 4401 N. Fairfax Dr.,
Arlington, VA 22203; 703-358-1711.

☆ ☆ ☆

How to Care for Your Cat Or Cow

They are not just for livestock anymore. Many County Cooperative Extension Service Offices have information pamphlets, classes, or even videos on the care and feeding of animals.

Want to learn how to take better care of your pet? What about dog training classes?

To learn what your local office has to offer look in the blue pages of your phone book for the office nearest you, or you can find the main state office in the Directory of State Information at the end of the book.

For more information, contact Extension Service, U.S. Department of Agriculture, Room 3328, Washington, DC 20250; 202-720-4111.

Another Elvis Sighting

You may think you've seen Elvis around town, but don't think you're all that special — so have millions of others. What you probably saw was Elvis' face on millions of envelopes. What Elvis did for the Post Office is to make stamp collecting even more the rage.

Join the crowd with some help from the U.S. Postal Service, and request their free brochure, *Introduction to Stamp Collecting*, which will help you learn how to start and maintain a collection. Contact your local post office or write U.S. Postal Service, 475 L'Enfant Plaza West, SW, Washington, DC 20260.

☆ ☆ ☆

Get the Ship Passenger Logs of Ellis Island Arrivals

Gathering up all those branches, limbs, and splinters can be an incredible treasure hunt. If you are putting together your family tree, let the National Archives help you along.

They maintain ship passenger arrival records dating back into the 1800's, and they will even do the research for you! If they find your ancestor, they will send you a notice. The logs consist of 2x3 foot sheets listing age, amount of money, language spoken, even their height and weight. There is a cost of $10 if you want to purchase the log.

For more information, contact Reference Services Branch, National Archives and Records Administration, 8th St and Pennsylvania Ave., NW, Washington, DC 20408; 202-501-5400.

☆ ☆ ☆

Help Your Garden Grow

Rather not have your tomatoes glow in the dark? You can get your vegetables and flowers to be the talk of the neighborhood without using pesticides that may turn your insides into mush.

You can learn how to fertilize and protect your plants without adding harmful chemicals with some help from the Environmental Protection Agency. They have fact sheets and information booklets on pesticides, organic gardening, and even composting.

To learn more, contact Public Information Center, U.S. Environmental Protection Agency, 401 M St., SW, 3404, Washington, DC 20460; 202-260-7751.

☆ ☆ ☆

Bountiful Botany

Ferns, ivies, poinsettias, orchids, chrysanthemums.
Fact sheets to keep you reading and digging are available to answer some of your plant questions.
The Horticulture Services

Division of the Smithsonian Institution has a series of fact sheets, which includes information on how to help the plant grow, potential problems, fertilization, and cultivation.

For more information, contact Horticulture Services Division, Arts and Industries Building, Room 2282, MRC 420, Smithsonian Institution, Washington, DC 20560; 202-357-1926.

Call The Plant Doctor

Bring me your tired, sick, and decaying plants... Almost all Cooperative Extension Service offices (which are located in every county) have a horticulture hotline, where you can talk to gardening experts, and even bring in samples of your plants for diagnoses. There is usually no fee for this service.

They can even help you deal with squirrels digging up your bulbs, and deer eating your trees. Look in the blue pages of your phone book for the office nearest you, or find the main state office in the Directory of State Information at the end of this book.

For more information, contact Extension Service, U.S. Department of Agriculture, Room 3328, Washington, DC 20250; 202-720-4111.

☆ ☆ ☆

Free Books on Tape

You used to love reading, but since your eyes have started to get bad, you've all but given up enjoying a good book anymore.

Before you give up altogether, listen to this: the National Library Service (NLS) maintains a large collection of books, magazines, journals, and music materials In Braille, large type, and recorded formats for individuals who cannot read or use standard printed materials because of temporary or permanent visual loss or physical limitations. Reading materials and necessary playback equipment for books on record and cassette are distributed through a national network of cooperating libraries.

Books in the collection are selected on the basis of their appeal to a wide range of interests. Bestsellers, biographies, fiction, and how-to books are in great demand.

Contact your local library to find out what they have available to you, or you may contact Handicapped Readers Reference Section, National Library Service for the Blind and Physically Handicapped, Library of Congress, Washington, DC 20542; 202-707-9275.

Great Bargains at Uncle Sam's Shopping Mall

At one time or another everything is shipped by mail, including the latest CDs, videos, books, toys, ostrich eggs, and even suits of armor. When the government can't deliver something, it is collected in the back of the post offices and auctioned off around the country. I personally got 100 stuffed animals for $1.00 each.

The postal auctions are held at four Mail Recovery Centers across the U.S. To locate the center nearest you, contact your local postmaster.

Information USA, Inc.

Jewelry Cheaper Than Out of Someone's Trunk

No need to locate the nearest shady dealer to find a great deal. The U.S. Customs agents are on the lookout for you. These are the guys that confiscate items brought into this country illegally.

You can get diamond rings for half price, fancy cars for a fraction of their cost, and anything else you can imagine including airplanes, boats, and fine linens. These items are auctioned off all over the U.S. For information on auctions, contact EG&G Dynatrend, U.S. Customs Support Division, 2300 Clarendon Blvd., Suite 705, Arlington, VA 22201; 703-351-7887.

☆ ☆ ☆

Bargains on Bombs, Bases, and Butterfly Catchers

Everyone would love to have their own B-52, but there are just not enough to go around. But if you can't have that, what else does the Department of Defense have that you could use?

With the Defense cutbacks taking place, you can now buy tents, sporting equipment, computers, horses, furniture, telephone systems, photographic equipment, and even entire military bases. The merchandise is sold at over 200 locations worldwide.

Information on local and national sales is available in the free booklet *How To Buy Surplus Personal Property From DOD*. To obtain your booklet, contact Defense Reutilization and Marketing Service, National Sales Office, P.O. Box 5275 DDRC, 2163 Airways Blvd., Memphis, TN 38114; 800-222-3767, 901-775-6427.

☆ ☆ ☆

A Drug Confiscated Limo For $1.00

No. You can't get one for $1.00, but you can get one at bargain prices. (Just hope they don't want it back when they get out of jail). You can also get boats, planes, antiques, exquisite jewelry, and luxury homes that have been confiscated from drug traffickers or other criminals. Major sales are advertised the third Wednesday of every month in *USA Today*. For more information, write U.S. Marshals

Service, 600 Army-Navy Dr., Arlington, VA 22202; 202-307-9065.

☆ ☆ ☆

Get a Horse and Ride'em Cowboy

You don't have to go to the Wild West to re-enact the movie *City Slickers*. Horses roaming on government land can be adopted for only $125. Or you can get a burro for $75. And if you're lucky, you can get two for the price of one if a mare is with foal. For details, write the Bureau of Land Management, U.S. Department of the Interior, P.O. Box 12000, Reno, NV 89520; 702-785-6400.

☆ ☆ ☆

Cash In on Another's Banking Problems

Tired of putting money into a bank and not seeing much in return? The Federal Deposit Insurance Corporation (FDIC) sells a wide variety of assets from failed banks including loans, real estate such as undeveloped land, hotels, shopping malls, single-family homes, condominiums, and apartment complexes. They even sell personal property including computers, phone systems, furniture, fixtures, plants, and more.

For information about the sales, contact the FDIC, 550 17th St., NW, Washington, DC 20429-9990; 202-736-0000.

☆ ☆ ☆

Fly a Flag in Your Honor

No need to struggle with a gift idea for your "Made In America" relative. As a special gift for a loved one or for yourself, you can purchase an American flag that has been flown over the Capitol. It comes with a certificate verifying the date on which the flag was flown.

You can request a specific date, such as a birthdate, anniversary, or even the day someone was discharged from the Service. These flags cost between $6.50-$17 depending upon the size and material, and can be purchased through your Senator or Representative. To learn more, contact your Senator or Representative, The Capitol, Washington, DC 20510; 202-224-3121.

Money, Help, and Cheap Tickets for Art Lovers

Grandma Moses didn't start painting until her late seventies, and was still at it when she turned 100. Pablo Picasso was still drawing at 90. Even Tolstoy and George Bernard Shaw were productive writers well into their eighties. To find out where you can turn your talent into money for yourself or your group, as well as help in bringing in artists to inspire you, read on.

☆ ☆ ☆

Money From The Big Guys

The National Endowment for the Arts (NEA) may be fighting for their very existence these days, but don't fear — they've been on the government hit list for many years, and somehow have always managed to survive in one form or another.

The Endowment funds fellowships to individuals and grants to organizations in the fields of Arts in Education, Dance, Design Arts, Expansion Arts, Folk Arts, Literature, Media Arts, Museums, Music, Opera-Musical Theater, Presenting and Commissioning, Theater, and Visual Arts.

Individuals or organizations interested in applying for grants from the NEA should first check out whether they meet the basic eligibility requirements outlined in the free *Guide to the National Endowment for the Arts*. Potential applicants can then request application guidelines from the various offices.

For more information, contact Public Information Office, National Endowment for the Arts, Nancy Hanks Center, 1100 Pennsylvania Ave., NW, Washington, DC 20506; 202-682-5400.

☆ ☆ ☆

$25,000 For Interior Designers

Actually this grant money is available to individuals working in the fields of architecture, landscape architecture, urban design and planning, historic preservation, interior design, and more.

Grants are awarded to professional designers, nonprofit organizations, arts groups, and others to help encourage further development in their fields.

To learn more about the grant and eligibility requirements, contact Design Art Program, National Endowment For The Arts, Room 627, 1100 Pennsylvania Ave., NW, Washington, DC 20506; 202-682-5437.

☆ ☆ ☆

$45,000 To Go Dancing

If your dance group is now good enough that people will actually pay to see you perform, look at what the NEA has for you. The Dance Program provides support for professional  choreographers, dance companies, and to organizations and individuals that service dance. Money may be used to create new dance works, rehearsal support, presenting dance workshops, dance touring, and more.

To learn more about the program and eligibility requirements, contact Dance Program, National Endowment for the Arts, Room 620, 1100 Pennsylvania Ave., NW, Washington, DC 20506; 202-682-5435.

☆ ☆ ☆

$35,000 To Practice Singing

For those lucky enough to have perfect pitch, the Music Program offers fellowships and grants to help support excellence in music performance and creativity, and to develop informed audiences for music throughout the country.

Money can be used to assist talented individuals and a wide range of organizations including professional symphony orchestras, festivals that act as producers, national service organizations, choruses, chamber ensembles, jazz ensembles, and others.

For more information, contact Music Program, National Endowment for the Arts, Room 702, 1100 Pennsylvania Ave., NW, Washington, DC 20506; 202-682-5445.

$37,500 For Clowning Around

Well, not just clowns, but also puppeteers, mimes, storytellers, monologists, new vaudevillians, and others. There are even fellowships for playwrights, directors, actors, and designers.

The money can be used to support organizations and professional theater artists while they perform in their particular medium. For more information, contact Theater Program, National Endowment for the Arts, Room 608, 1100 Pennsylvania Ave., NW, Washington, DC 20506; 202-682-5425.

☆ ☆ ☆

$20,000 To Write The Great American Novel

For all those writers and poets out there, the Literature Program wants to support you. They offer fellowships to creative writers of fiction, poetry, and nonfiction, as well as translators of works into English.

The money can be used to cover expenses while you write, conduct research, or travel. It can also be used to sponsor residencies and reading series.

To learn more, contact Literature Program, National Endowment for the Arts, Room 772, 1100 Pennsylvania Ave., NW, Washington, DC 20506; 202-682-5451.

☆ ☆ ☆

Priceless Art For Your Home

Who needs expensive auction houses selling culture to the highest bidder? The National Gallery of Art can help people like you and me start our own collections. All you need is $5, and you can get a jump start on your collection.

Black and white photographs and 35 mm slides of works from the National Gallery of Art's permanent collections are available for sale (color transparencies for rental). For ordering information, contact National Gallery of Art, Office of Visual Services, Constitution and 6th St., NW, Washington, DC 20565, 202-842-6231.

$20,000 For
The Painter Within You

For all those painters, sculptors, photographers, crafts artists, printmakers, illustrators, and other visual artists, it's time to take note. The Visual Arts Program has money to help support you while you create your masterpieces.

For guidelines and application information, contact Visual Arts Program, National Endowment for the Arts, Room 729, 1100 Pennsylvania Ave., NW, Washington, DC 20506; 202-682-5448.

☆ ☆ ☆

Start a Local Theater
or Dance Company

If your arts group develops work reflective of your own community, you may be eligible for Expansion Arts grants.

These grants are to professionally directed arts organizations that are rooted in culturally diverse, inner-city, rural, or tribal communities. Matching grants are available to help create, exhibit, or present works representative of the culture of a community, and to provide a community with access to all types of quality art.

To learn more about eligibility requirements, contact Expansion Arts Program, National Endowment for the Arts, Room 711, 1100 Pennsylvania Ave., NW, Washington, DC 20506; 202-682-5443.

☆ ☆ ☆

$10,000 For Craftspeople and Storytellers

If you create works in a traditional art form, then look to the Folk Arts Program for assistance. This program supports traditional arts that have grown through time within the many groups that make up our nation — groups that share the same ethnic heritage, language, occupation, religion, or geographic area.

These folk arts include music, dance, poetry, tales, oratory, crafts, and various types of visual art forms. Money can be used for festivals, tours, workshops, residencies, exhibits, and more.

To learn about eligibility, contact the Folk Arts Program, National Endowment For The Arts, Room 710, 1100 Pennsylvania Ave., NW, Washington, DC 20506; 202-682-5449.

☆ ☆ ☆

Get a Smithsonian Exhibit For a Fundraiser

The Smithsonian can bring art to you, whether you live in a major metropolitan area or a rural one. The Smithsonian Institute Traveling Exhibition Services (SITES) sponsors 80 to 100 different exhibits at any given time in museums and other locations around the country.

The participation fee varies from $500 to $20,000. The exhibitions range from popular culture, to fine arts, photography, historical exhibits, or topics of interest to children. The collections are most frequently sent to other museums, libraries, historic homes, or even schools and community centers.

Request a free *SITES Updates* catalog to see what is currently available. Contact Smithsonian Institute Traveling Exhibition

Service, Smithsonian Institution, 1100 Jefferson Dr., SW, Room 3146, Washington, DC 20560; 202-357-3168.

☆ ☆ ☆

Get Your Local Gallery to Cater More to Seniors

Want to reach people of all ages and disabilities? In conjunction with the National Endowment for the Arts, the National Assembly of State Arts Agencies has compiled a comprehensive arts access book titled, *Design for Accessibility: An Art Administrator's Guide*. The book helps people design spaces and programs that accommodate individuals throughout their lives.

You can also learn about how to open up existing programs and outreach to people who would otherwise not experience your arts programs. For more information, contact the Office for Special Constituencies, National Endowment for the Arts, 1100 Pennsylvania Ave., NE, Washington, DC 20506; 202-682-5532.

Music That Will Bring Tears To Your Eyes

And not ringing to your ears. Tired of all that loud music, where you can't understand the words, and aren't sure you want to? The Folkways Records Archive has an incredible collection of music from around the world, and from America's past.

You can hear Jelly Roll Morton, Leadbelly, Pete Seeger, Woody Guthrie, great fiddlers, balladeers, gospel singers, and more. They even have recordings of the spoken word. Cassette tapes are available for under $10.

To receive a free catalog, contact Smithsonian/Folkways Recordings, Office of Folklife Programs, 955 L'Enfant Plaza, Suite 2600, Smithsonian Institution, Washington, DC 20560; 202-287-3262.

Free Loan of Famous Masters

You can tell your house guests to sit back and enjoy the show, as you move from masterpiece to masterpiece on your slide projector. They really didn't want to see those pictures of your vacation to Florida anyway.

The National Gallery's lending library of 50,000 images of art will impress your friends and influence your enemies. There is no catalog, so start a wish list and find out what the National Gallery can fulfill on it.

The slide images can be borrowed through inter-library loan. For the Public Lending Guide or more information, contact National Gallery of Art, Slide Library, Constitution and 6th St., NW, Washington, DC 20565, 202-842-6100.

☆ ☆ ☆

Get Paid To Take Art Classes

How do most struggling artists perfect their art? By working alongside masters in their specific craft, and believe it or not, there are money programs on the state level to help you do just that. There are apprenticeship programs which provide support for a master artist to train a practicing artist.

There are also money programs that support individual artists, allowing them to paint, draw, write, and much more. For instance, in Arizona you can get $7,500 for creative writing. In Idaho, you can get $5,000 to dance. Kansas gives awards up to $5,000 to outstanding painters.

To find out what your particular state has to offer and the eligibility requirements that you must meet, contact your State Arts group from the list below (see page 391).

☆ ☆ ☆

Free Videos and CDs of Famous Artists

While the Mortons are watching Top Gun for the hundredth time next door, you can be watching something with a little class and learning about Leonardo, Matisse, or Impressionism.

The National Gallery of Art has over 150 videos, films, and video-discs covering specific artists or time periods. These programs are loaned free of charge to you in an effort to bring the Gallery to the world.

To receive a complete catalog of programs, contact Department of Education Resources, Education Division, National Gallery of Art, 4th St. and Constitution Ave., NW, Washington, DC 20565; 202-842-6875.

☆ ☆ ☆

Artists and Performers Will Give You a Free Show

You won't be able to get Picasso or Warhol, but you will be able to get some incredible artists, musicians, actors, and craftsmen to come to your senior citizens' center, nursing home, or other nonprofit organization gathering.

Most states have Project Grants or Artist in Residence Programs to help cover some of the expenses involved in bringing various art forms to the community. To find out what programs are available and the requirements for each program, contact your State Arts group from the list below (see page 391).

Take Your Own Art Show On The Road

Grandparents Theater In The Round? High-Stepping Seniors? If you are part of an arts group that would like to go on tour, take advantage of the Touring Programs offered in many states.

These programs help share the cost of bringing artists, dancers, musicians, storytellers and others to local community organizations. Contact your State Arts group from the list below (see page 391) to learn more about the steps necessary to qualify.

☆ ☆ ☆

Money to Have Your Own Art Exhibit

If your work didn't get into the Metropolitan Museum of Art, don't give up. Your group can still have a show of its own. States offer grants to produce exhibits, workshops, and performances. Your senior citizen photography group, painting class, or even the art work created by nursing home residents may qualify.

Contact your State Arts group from the list below (see page 391) to learn more about the steps necessary to qualify.

☆ ☆ ☆

Free Art Speakers for Your Group

Want someone to come to your group and talk "Art?" You can get a certified (not certifiable) artist to come share words of wisdom about his or her craft, or you can even learn what special programs your local arts group offers to seniors.

Many State Arts Councils, as well as regional or local agencies will provide speakers to your group whenever possible. Contact the offices nearest you to see what they have to offer.

☆ ☆ ☆

Cheap Seats...Discounts on Theater Tickets

Take advantage of some special deals for those that hit the magic age of seniority. Many ballets, orchestras, museums, and art galleries offer discounted admission to senior citizens.

Here's a sample of nonprofit cultural organizations across the country that have received funding from either state arts councils and/or the National Endowment for the Arts and provide programs geared specifically toward older adults.

Arkansas
The Arkansas Symphony
Orchestra (ASO)
P.O. Box 7328
Little Rock, AK 72717
501-666-1761
The ASO provides discounted tickets to senior citizens. The String Quartet performs in retirement communities and community centers.

California
The Cornerstone Theater
Company
1653 18th St., #6
Santa Monica, CA 90404
Attn: Bill Rauch

National Institute of Art and
Disabilities
551 23rd St.
Richmond, CA 94804
510-620-0290
National Institute of Art and Disabilities provides an on-going, 40-hour week art program for adults with

developmental disabilities, many of whom are older and are developing careers as visual artists. Participants' work is facilitated by Master artist teachers.

Georgia
The Woodruff Arts Center
1280 Peachtree St., NE
Atlanta, GA 30309
404-733-4200
The Woodruff Arts Center provides discounted theater and museum tickets for senior citizens over age 65.

Kentucky
Appalshop
306 Madison St.
Whitesburg, KY 41858
606-633-0108
Appalshop provides programs that seek to break down cultural stereotypes of the Appalachian people. They have several programs that target older citizens. Roadside

Theater program draws together diverse groups to examine local heritage. The community radio program features programs such as "Deep in Tradition," an old-time mountain music show.

ElderSprites
1816 Frankfort Ave.
Louisville, KY 40205
502-451-7302
Attn: Mary Ann Maier

Elder Dance Express
1442 Rufer Ave.
Louisville, KY 40204
502-581-1976
Attn: Chris Doerflinger
ElderSprites, a theater troop of older adults; and Elder Dance Express, an ensemble of older dancers perform in schools, senior centers, and community centers, as well as in theaters throughout Kentucky.

Massachusetts
Boston-Fenway, Inc.
Elder Arts Project
590 Huntington Ave.
Boston, MA 02115
617-445-0047
Attn: Juanda Drumgold
This initiative involves older adults in the activities of the Boston Symphony Orchestra, New England Conservatory of Music, Huntington Theater, Stewart Garden and Museum, and Boston Museum of Fine

Arts. The program provides complimentary tickets and transportation to selected events and performances. The more than 500 older adults participating in the program live in elder care centers or low-income housing complexes in Boston's Roxbury and Back Bay neighborhoods.

Minnesota
St. Paul's Chamber Orchestra
Hamm Building
408 St. Peters St.
Suite 300
St. Paul, MN 55102
612-292-3248
The Saint Paul Chamber Orchestra provides "The Morning Coffee Series," which is geared towards older people, and is comprised of eight morning Baroque concerts opening with informative concert previews.

New Mexico
Very Special Arts New Mexico
P.O. Box 7784
Albuquerque, NM
505-768-5188
Very Special Arts New Mexico features the Buen Viaje Dancers, a modern dance troupe of all ages with multiple disabilities. They received a grant to produce, market, and distribute a video on working with individuals with disabilities in dance.

New York
Performance Space 122
150 1st Ave.
New York, NY
212-477-5288
Performance Space 122
provides dance tickets for
events at a cost of $8 for
eligible seniors.

Theater Development Fund
1501 Broadway Ave.
New York, NY 10036
212-221-0013 (recorded
message)
212-221-0885 (staff)
The Theater Development
Fund provides discounted
theater and dance tickets to
individuals and nonprofit
community and senior citizen
centers.

Elders Share the Arts (ESTA)
57 Willoughby St.
Brooklyn, NY 11201
718-488-8565
Attn: Susan Pearlstein
Elders Share the Arts
produces living history theater
workshops and performances
throughout New York's five
boroughs. They tour and
perform at city wide festivals,
schools, museums, and
community and senior centers.

Bronx Arts Ensemble
c/o Gulf House
Van Courtland Park
Bronx, NY 10471

718-601-7399
The Bronx Arts Ensemble
provides occasional free
concerts and a series of
concerts at reduced rates that
are available to senior adults.

North Carolina
Greensboro Symphony Society
P.O. Box 20303
Greensboro, NC 27420
910-333-7490
The Greensboro Symphony
Orchestra provides discounted
tickets to senior citizens.

Vermont
Grass Roots Art and
Community Effort (GRACE)
P.O. Box 324
Saint Johnsbury, VT 05819
802-525-3620
GRACE discovers, develops,
and promotes visual art
produced primarily by older
self-taught artists in rural
Vermont. GRACE has involved
older adults in arts programs,
many of whom are in nursing
homes and other residential
centers.

Washington, DC
Dance Exchange
1664 Columbia Rd., NW
Suite 21
Washington, DC 20009
202-232-0833
The Dance Exchange explores
the relation of movement to
language with an ensemble of

older dancers called Dancers of the Third Age.

Washington DC International Film Festival
P.O. Box 21396
Washington, DC 20009
202-274-6810

The Washington DC. International Film Festival provides two free matinee screenings for senior citizens at the Kennedy Center for Performing Arts during their May film festival each year.

☆ ☆ ☆

Attend the Symphony for Free

Many music groups offer special programs to older adults in the form of discounted tickets, free concerts, transportation, afternoon teas, and/or daytime events. Contact your state arts group (see page 391) or your state Department of Aging (listed in the Directory of State Information at the end of this book) to investigate the possibilities in your area. Some of the groups include:

Augusta Symphony in Augusta, GA
Boston Symphony Orchestra in
    Boston, MA
Bronx Arts Ensemble in Bronx, NY
Concert Royal in New York City, NY
Creative Opportunity Orchestra in
    Austin, TX

Eastern Connecticut Symphony in
New London, CT
Evansville Philharmonic Orchestra
in Evansville, PA
Flint Institute of Music in Flint, MI
Fort Wayne Philharmonic Orchestra in
Fort Wayne, IN
Goliard Concerts in Astoria, NY
Grand Rapids Symphony Society in
Grand Rapids, MI
Greensboro Symphony Society in
Greensboro, NC
Island Philharmonic in Melville,, NY
Jacksonville Symphony Association in
Jacksonville, FL
Kansas City Symphony in Kansas City, MO
La Jolla Chamber Music Society in
La Jolla, Ca
Lexington Philharmonic Society in
Lexington, KY
Long Island Baroque Ensemble in Locust
Valley, NY
Louisville Orchestra in Louisville, KY
Meet the Composer in New York City, NY
Memphis Orchestral Society in
Memphis, TN
Minnesota Composers Forum in
St. Paul, MN
Minnesota Orchestral Association in
Minneapolis, MN
Missouri Symphony Society in
Columbia, MO

Mississippi Symphony Orchestra
Association in Jackson, MS
Modesto Symphony Orchestra in
Modesto, CA
Musical Arts Association in Cleveland, OH
New Orchestra of Westchester
in Hartsdale, NY
Orpheon in New York City, NY
Performance Zone in New York City, NY
Philharmonic Symphony Society in
New York City, NY
Philomel Concerts in Philadelphia, PA
Pro Musicis Foundation in
New York City, NY
Robert W. Woodruff Arts Center in
Atlanta, GA
Rochester Philharmonic Orchestra
in Rochester, NY
Rockford Symphony Orchestra
in Rockford, IL
Rosewood Chamber Ensemble
in Sunnyside, NY
Saint Paul Chamber Orchestra Society
in St. Paul, MN
Santa Barbara Symphony Orchestra
Association in Santa Barbara, CA
Seattle Children's Home in Seattle, WA
Shreveport Symphony Society in
Shreveport, LA
South Carolina Orchestra Association
in Columbia, SC

Stamford Symphony Orchestra in
    Stamford, CT
Theatre Development Fund in
    New York City, NY
Trustees of Columbia University in
    New York City, NY
Tucson Symphony Society in Tucson, AZ
Westwind Brass in San Diego, CA

☆ ☆ ☆

State Arts Groups

The following is a state-by-state listing of
state arts groups. Each listing contains a
list of programs, a description of general
requirements, and an estimate of the total
money available.

Alabama
Alabama Arts Council
1 Dexter Ave.
Montgomery, AL 36130-5810
205-242-4076

Money Available: $378,000

Eligibility Requirements:
For individual artist programs state residency is required, unless
otherwise specified. Grants to organizations must be matched by at
least an equal amount from other sources located by the applicant.

Programs Available:
$5,000 To Art Administrators
    (Fellowship in Arts Administration)

$10,000 For Artists, Craftsmen, Photographers
    (Artists Fellowships)
$1,000 To Develop Administrative Skills
    (Technical Assistance)
Money To Be An Artist-In-Residence
    (Artist Residences)
$5,000 For Master Folk Artists
    (Folk Art Apprenticeships)
Grants To Large Arts Organizations
    (Advanced Institutional Assistance)
Money For Schools To Hire Artists
    (Arts in Education Projects)
$500 For Designers
    (Design Arts Projects)
$500 For Folk Artists
    (Folklife Program)
$7,500 For Local Arts Councils
    (Local Arts Councils)
Money To Put On A Show Or Exhibition
    (Presenter Program)
$1,000 For Community Arts Projects
    (Project Assistance Programs)

Alaska

Alaska State Council on the Arts
411 W. 4th Ave., Suite E
Anchorage, AK 99501-2343
907-269-6610

Money Available: $1,119,322

Eligibility Requirements:
State residency is required for individual grants to artists. The Council awards funds only to Alaskan non-profit organizations, schools or government agencies.

Programs Available:
$5,000 For Artists To Develop New Works
    (Individual Artist Fellowships)

$600 For Artists To Travel To Art Conferences
  (Travel Grant Program)
$2,000 To Study With A Master Craftsperson,
  Musician, Dancer, Or Storyteller (Master Arts and Apprentice
  Grants in Traditional Native Arts)
Money For Local Art Agencies
  (Grants to Local Arts Agencies)
Grants To Help Pay For Art Administration Costs
  (Season Support)
Money To Support a Local Art Project
  (Project Grants)
Money To Pay Artists To Speak At Workshops
  (Workshop Grants)
Money For Schools To Have An Artist-In-Residence
  Program (Artist Residency Grants)

Arizona
Arizona Arts Commission
417 W. Roosevelt St.
Phoenix, AZ 85003
612-255-5882

Money Available: $3,224,116

Eligibility Requirements:
Individual Artist Fellowships require state residency. Priority for
organizational funding is given to projects in rural areas of the state
and projects coordinated by ethnic-run organizations or those that
primarily serve ethnic communities.

Programs Available:
$7,500 For Artists and Writers
  (Fellowships)
$5,000 For Artists To Use For Research And Travel
  (Artist Projects)
Money To Support Special Art Projects
  (Project Support)
Grants To Help Run Art Organizations
  (Administrative/General Operating Support)

Money For Schools To Have Artists-In-Residence
    Programs (Artists-in-Residence)
Money For Schools With New Ideas In Art
    (Education Initiatives)
Help For Sponsors Who Wish To Contract With
    Artists (Project Support)

Arkansas
Arkansas Arts Council
1500 Tower Bldg.
323 Center St.
Little Rock, AR 72201
501-324-9150

Money Available: $1,046,233

Eligibility Requirements:
State residency is required for individual artist programs. Funds
awarded to non-profit organizations and educational institutions must
be at least equally matched by the applicant organization with cash
from sources other than the Council or National Endowment for the
Arts (NEA).

Programs Available:
$5,000 To Craftspersons and Artists
    (Individual Artist Fellowship Program)
Grants To Arts Organizations
    (General Operating Support Grants)
Grants To Put On Art Shows For The Public
    (Program Support Grants)
Money For Arts Organizations To Hire Consultants
    (Professional and Organizational Development Grant)
Money For Schools Or Communities To Have An Artist
    In Residence (Arts-in-Education)
$1,000 For Emergency Arts Funding (Mini-Grants)
More Money For Schools Or Communities To Have An
    Artist-In-Residence (Artists-In-Residence)
Money To Support Community Arts Activities
    (Community Arts Development Grants)

California
California Arts Council
Public Information Council
2411 Alhambra Blvd
Sacramento, CA 95817
916-227-2550

Money Available: $13,800,000

Eligibility Requirements:
State residency is required for individual artists programs.

Programs Available:
$2,500 Award To Artists, Choreographers, and Writers
    (Artists Fellowship Program)
Be An Artist-In-Residence And Get $1,300 For 80 Hours
    (Artists-in-Residence Program)
Money For Organizations Interested In Art-Related
    Activities (Organizational Support Program)
$6,000 For Multi-Cultural Arts Activities
    (Multi-Cultural Entry Grant Program)
$40,000 For Multi-Cultural Grant Activities
    (Multi-Cultural Advancement Program)
Money For Organizations To Hire Performing Artists
    (Performing Arts Touring and Presenting Program)
Matching Grants For Arts Organizations (California Challenge Program)

Colorado
Colorado Council on the Arts (CCAH)
750 Pennsylvania
Denver, CO 80203
303-894-2617

Money Available: $220,000

Eligibility Requirements:
For individual artist programs, state residency is required, unless
otherwise specified.

Programs Available:
Grants To Individual Artists
    (Colorado Visions Project Grants)
Grants To Learn From A Master Artist
    (Folk Arts Master/Apprentice Program)
$5,000 To Arts Groups Serving Minorities Or Rural
    Areas (Entry Grants)
Grants To Groups Who Have Been In Operation For
    Three Years Or More (Institutional Partnership Program)
Money For Special Projects (Project Grants)
Grants For Arts Programs In Small Towns
    (Rural Arts Initiatives)
Funding For Arts Programs In The Summer
    (Summer Activities Programs)
Free Help With Managing An Arts Organization
    (Organizational Assistance Program)
Grants To Local Arts Councils
    (Community Arts Development Grants)
Money For Schools To Have An Artist-In-Residence
    (Artists-in-Residence Program)

Connecticut

Connecticut Commission on the Arts
227 Lawrence St.
Hartford, CT 06106
203-566-4770

Money Available: $904,788

Eligibility Requirements:
Individual Artist Programs: State residency is required, unless
otherwise specified.

Programs Available:
$5,000 For Visual Artists (Artist Grants)
Money For Organizations To Hire An Artist-In-Residence
    (Artists Residencies)
Money To Help Art Organizations With Long Range
    Planning (Multi-Year Funding)

Grants To Arts Groups To Afford Administrative Help
    (Professional Development Funding)
$10,000 To Produce A Show, A Festival, Or A Book
    (Arts Project Grants)

Delaware
Delaware Division of the Arts
Carvell State Office Building
820 North French St.
Wilmington, DE 19801
302-577-3540

Money Available: $1,858,191

Eligibility Requirements:
Individual artist programs require state residency, unless otherwise
specified.

Programs Available:
Money For New Or Established Artists
    (Individual Artist Fellowships)
Matching Grants For Arts Groups
    (Project Support Grants)
Money For Operating Expenses
    (General Operating Support Grants)
$500 Emergency Money For Arts Groups (Emergency Grants)
Money For New Arts Groups To Help With Management
    (Grants to Emerging Organizations)
Money For Schools To Have An Artist-In-Residence
    (Arts in Education Residencies)

District of Columbia
District of Columbia Council of Arts
410 Eighth St., NW, 5th Floor
Stables Art Center
Washington, DC 20004
202-724-5613

Money Available: $710,000

Eligibility Requirements:
Individual artist programs require residency in the District of Columbia for at least one year prior to application deadline and the applicant must maintain residency during the grant period. Individuals and arts organizations may apply in one of the following disciplines: crafts, dance, interdisciplinary/performance art (individuals only), literature, media, multi-disciplinary, music, theater, and the visual arts.

Programs Available:
$5,000 For Theater, Visual, And Literary Artists
$40,000 For Art Groups (Organizational Funding)

Florida
Florida Arts Council
Division of Cultural Affairs
Department of State
Tallahassee, FL 32399
904-487-2980

Money Available: $2,373,800

Eligibility Requirements:
Individual Artist Programs: State residency is required, unless otherwise specified.

Programs Available:
$5,000 To Professional Artists
    (Individual Artist Fellowship Program)
$40,000 For Arts Groups (General Program Support)
$20,000 For Arts Related Activities
    (Specific Project Support)
Up To $100,000 For Arts Organizations
    (Challenge Grant Program)
$1,000 To Hire An Arts Consultant
    (Technical Assistance Grants)
$20,000 For Schools To Improve Their Arts Program
    (Arts Education Project Support)
$20,000 For School Teachers To Work With Artists
    (Special Projects)

Georgia
Georgia Council for Arts
530 Means St., NW, Suite 115
Atlanta, GA 30318
404-651-7920

Money Available: $2,727,660

Eligibility Requirements:
Individual artist programs require state residency, unless otherwise specified. In general, grant categories include: architecture/ environmental arts, dance, arts-related education, film-making, folk arts/heritage arts and crafts, arts-related historic preservation, literary arts, multi-media, museums, music, photography, public radio and television, theater and visual arts.

Programs Available:
$5,000 For Artists, Choreographers, And Playwrights
(Individual Artist Grants)
$150,000 To Arts Organizations
(Major Arts Organization Grants)
$55,000 For Arts Organizations
(Arts Organization Grants)
Grants To Schools, Local Governments, And Non-Profits
(Civic/Education Government/Other Grants)
Money To Set Up A Local Arts Council
(Arts Council/Agency Development Grants)
Grants For Art Groups To Tour (Georgia Touring Grants)
$500 To Hire An Arts Consultant
(Technical Assistance Grants)
Georgia Folklife Program (Georgia Folklife Program)
Money For Schools To Have An Artist-In-Residence
(Artist in Education Program)

Hawaii
Hawaii State Foundation on Culture and Arts (SFCA)
335 Merchant St., Room 202
Honolulu, HI 96813
808-586-0300

Money Available: $5,950,586

Eligibility Requirements:
No fellowships were awarded this year, although a new individual artist program is being developed.

Programs Available:
Grants For Concerts, Performances, Workshops, and
    Lectures (Organizational Funding)
$2,700 For Artists To Study As An Apprentice
    (The Folk Arts Program)

Idaho
Idaho Commission on Arts
304 West State St.
Boise, ID 83720
208-334-2119

Money Available: $614,547

Eligibility Requirements:
Individual artist programs require state residency, unless otherwise specified.

Programs Available:
$5,000 For Artists, Dancers, Designers, and Craftspersons
    (Fellowship Awards)
$5,000 For Artists To Work With A Master (Worksites Awards)
$1,000 To Support An Artist's Work
    (Sudden Opportunity Awards)
$1,000 Plus Travel To Study With A Master Craftsperson
    (Traditional Native Arts Apprenticeship Program)
$10,000 To Be A Writer-In-Residence
    (Writer-in-Residence)
$25,000 For An Arts Group
    (General Operating Support)
$10,000 For Special Art Projects (Project Support)
$5,000 For Touring Arts Groups
    (Performing Arts Touring)

Grants To Bring Art To Small Towns
  (Arts in Rural Towns)
Money For Running A Local Arts Council
  (Local Arts Council Salary Assistance)
$3,700 For An Arts Council In A Small Town
  (Arts in Rural Towns (ARTs))
FastFunds
Money To Build A Cultural Facility
  (Cultural Facilities Grants)
$500 To Artists and Schools To Improve Arts Education
  (Technical Assistance)
Money For Schools Or Nursing Homes To Have An
  Artist-In-Residence (Artists-in-Residence)
$600 For Creative Art Teachers
  (Master Teacher Awards)
$3,500 For New Ideas In Arts Education (Special Projects Awards)

Illinois
Illinois Arts Council
State Of Illinois Center
100 West Randolph, Suite 10-500
Chicago, IL 60601
312-814-6750

Money Available: $6,273,031

Eligibility Requirements:
Individual artist programs require state residency, unless otherwise
specified.

In addition to the programs detailed, grants are funded for choral music
and opera, dance, ethnic and folk arts, symphonies and ensemble,
theater, and visual arts programs.

Programs Available:
$10,000 for Artists, Photographers, Writers, and Poets
  (Fellowships)
Grants To Artists To Study As Apprentices
  (Apprenticeship Program)

$1,000 For Writers And Non-Profit Magazines
(Literary Awards)
Money To Provide Art To Communities Normally
Deprived Of Art (Access Program)
Grants To Groups That Support Creative Writers
(Literature Programs)
Money For Film and Video Production (Media Program)
Funding For Interdiscipline Art Programs
(Multi-Disciplinary Programs)
Grants For Performing Arts
(Presenters Development Programs)
Money For Touring Art Groups (ArtsTour)
Special Money For Arts Programs and Projects
(Special Assistance Grants)
Money For Schools Or Other Organizations To Have An
Artist-In-Residence (Artists-in-Residence)
Grants For Schools To Develop Special Art Classes
(Arts Resource)

Indiana
Indiana Arts Commission
402 W. Washington St., Room 072
Indianapolis, IN 46204
317-232-1268

Money Available: $2,597,319

Eligibility Requirements:
Individual Artist Programs: State residency is required, unless
otherwise specified. Grants are awarded in 16 categories: dance,
design arts, education, expansion arts, folk arts, literature, local arts
agencies, media arts, multi-arts, museums, music, presenters,
statewide arts service organizations, theater, and visual arts.

Programs Available:
Grants To Individual Artists
(Individual Artist Fellowships)
Grants To Arts Organizations
(General Operating Support)

Grants To Local Arts Organizations
(State and Local Partnership)
Grants To Run Special Art Projects
(Arts Projects and Series)
Money For Artists-In-Residence Programs
(Arts in Education Grants)
$2,000 To Bring Artists Into Schools
(Visiting Arts Program)
Money For Multi-Cultural Or Rural Art Activities
(Arts: Rural and Multi-Cultural (ARM) Program)
Money For Art Administrators To Attend Workshops
(Technical Assistance)
$4,000 To Put On An Art Show (Presenter Touring Program)

Iowa
Iowa Council On Arts
Capitol Complex
Des Moines, IA 50319
515-281-4451

Money Available: $437,205

Eligibility Requirements:
Individual artist programs require state residency, unless otherwise
specified.

Programs Available:
Money For Individual Artists
(Individual Artist Programs)
Money For Artists To Work On Special Projects
(Artist Project Grants)
Money To Help Artists With Financial, Legal, Or
Marketing Problems (Artist Professional Development Grants)
Money For Artists To Attend Out-Of-State Seminars
(Artist Training Grants)
Grants For Artists To Learn More About Their Craft
(Artist Arts Education Grants)
$1,000 For Local Artists To Show Their Work
(Community Folk Arts Residency Program)

$1,000 For Artists To Work Towards A College Degree
    In Art (Iowa Scholarship for the Arts)
$1,000 For Poets And Writers
    (Iowa Literary Awards Prospectus)
Money To Provide Art To Those Who Normally Don't Participate
    (Special Constituencies Program)
$3,000 To Produce Visual Or Performance Art
    (Arts to Go Presenter Program)
$500 To Help Art Groups
    (Technical Assistance)
Grants To Arts Organizations
    (Operational Support Grants)
$1,600 To Non-Profits To Develop Art Projects
    (Project Support)
$500 In Emergency Art Money For Organizations
    (Emergency Project Support)
$200 To Help Train Art Administrators
    (Training Grants)
$1,000 For Arts Education Programs
    (Area Education Agencies Grants)
Money For Schools To Have An Artist-In-Residence
    (Artists in Schools/Communities Residencies)
Money For Art Management Training (Arts Education Mini-Grants)

Kansas
Kansas Arts Commission
Jayhawk Tower
700 Jackson, Suite 1004
Topeka, KS 66603-3714
913-296-3335

Money Available: $983,748

Eligibility Requirements:
Individual Art programs require state residency. The Commission
provides direct or indirect funding to artists, schools, government units,
and cultural, social and educational organizations as well as non-profit
organizations. Major grants are awarded each May for the following
fiscal year.

Programs Available:
$5,000 For Artists And Writers
    (Fellowships in the Performing Arts)
$500 For Artists Creating Original Work
    (Professional Development Grant Program)
Money For Folk Artists To Work As Apprentices
    (Folk Arts Apprenticeship Program)
Money To Start A Community Arts Organization
    (Local Arts Agency Support)
Money To Support Local Art Agencies (Basic Program Support)
Grants To Produce Art Publications, Workshops, Exhibits,
    and Performances (Project Support)
Money To Groups That Help Artists
    (Statewide Arts Service Organizations)
$2,000 To Schools To Improve Their Art Education
    (Planning Education in the Arts in Kansas (PEAK))
Money For Schools and Organizations To Have An Artist-
    In-Residence (Artist-in-Residency and Visiting Artist Grants)

Kentucky
Kentucky Arts Council
31 Fountain Place
Frankfort, KY 40601
502-564-3757

Money Available: $1,067,466

Eligibility Requirements:
Matching grants from the Council are available to Kentucky non-profit
organizations committed to providing arts programs and services to the
public. Grant amounts vary from year to year and depend upon the
availability of funds. Non-matching fellowships are available to
Kentucky artists. Interim Grants are available in all program areas to
provide one-time funding for emergencies or for unexpected and
outstanding opportunities in the arts.

Programs Available:
Money To Produce Art Projects
    (Project and Touring Grants)

Money To Hire An Arts Management Consultant
(Consultant Grants)
Grants To Arts Organizations
(Challenge Grants)
Money To Help Pay Artists And Art Administrators
(Arts Development Grants)
Grants For Local Art Projects
(Project and Touring Grants)
Grants To Support Rural Art Projects
(Special Initiatives)
Money For Communities Which Have Little Access To
Art (Consultant Grants)
Money For Communities To Have An Artist-In-Residence
(Community Artist Residencies)
Money For Schools To Have An Artist-In-Residence
(Artists-in-Residence Grants)
Grants For Teachers To Put Art In Their Classrooms
(Teacher Incentive Project Grants)
Funding For Art Projects In Education
(Project and Touring Grants)

Louisiana
Louisiana State Division of the Arts
P.O. Box 44247
Baton Rouge, LA 70804
504-342-8180

Money Available: $493,303

Eligibility Requirements:
Individual artist programs require state residency.

Programs Available:
$5,000 For Artists, Craftspersons, Designers, and Musicians
(Artist Fellowships)
$5,000 For Artists To Work With A Master (Folklife Apprenticeships)
$15,000 For Art Organizations (Project Assistance Program)
$1,000 For Arts Management Training
(Technical Assistance)

Up To $350,000 For Local Arts Agencies
    (Local Arts Agency Program)
Up To $350,000 For Art Groups (General Operating Support)
Money For Schools To Develop Art Programs (Educational Funding)

Maine

Maine Arts Commission
State House Station 25
Augusta, ME 04333
207-287-2724

Money Available: $844,822

Eligibility Requirements:
Individual artist programs require state residency. Maine offers an
Institutional Support Program which provides two-year funding for
established professional, non-profit cultural organizations, schools, and
other organizations for specific local arts projects and programs.

Programs Available:
$3,000 To Artists (Fellowships)
$1,200 For Master Artists To Teach Others
    (Traditional Arts Apprenticeships)
Grants To Arts Organizations (Operating Support)
Up To $20,000 For Special Art Programs
    (Project Support)
$850 For Community Arts Programs (Regional Arts Program)
$2,500 For Multi-Cultural Arts Programs In Schools
    (Special Projects in Arts Education)
$2,000 For School Teachers To Go To Art Seminars
    (Professional Development for Teachers)

Maryland

Maryland State Arts Council
601 N. Howard St.
Baltimore, MD 21201
410-333-8232

Money Available: $5,525,792

Eligibility Requirements:
The Council provides direct grants to individual artists, offers professional advice, and initiates projects that provide services and opportunities for Maryland artists. State residency is required for participation. The Council's Community Arts Development program supports county arts council organizations in each of the 23 counties of Maryland and Baltimore City. Funds are used in each county to regrant to local arts organizations, support various arts programs, assist local arts groups with fund raising, publicity, promotion and planning, and to support the operating expenses of the county arts council.

Programs Available:
$6,000 For Creative Artists
    (Individual Artist Awards)
Money For Large Arts Organizations
    (Grants to Major Institutions)
Grants To Groups Who Provide Art To Children And
    Communities (General Operating Grants)
Money To Support Innovative Art Projects
    (Special Project Grants)
Grants To Non-Arts Groups
    (Grants to Non-Arts Organizations)
Help For Those Interested In Maryland Folklife
    (Maryland Folklife Program)
Money For Poets, Artists, and Performers To Be At
    Schools (Artists in Education Program)
Help With Managing Arts Organizations (Arts Advancement Program)

Massachusetts
Massachusetts Cultural Council
80 Boylston St., 10th Floor
Boston, MA 02116
617-727-3668

Money Available: $5,408,839

Eligibility Requirements:
Individual artist programs require state residency, unless otherwise specified.

Programs Available:
$5,000 To Creative Artists, Craftspersons, and Scientists
    (Individual Project Support)
$15,000 For Arts Organizations (General Project Support)
$15,000 To Provide Art To Children (Education Project Support)
Money To Provide Artist-In-Residence To Schools
    (Residency Program)

Michigan
Michigan Council for the Arts
1200 Sixth St.
Detroit, MI 48226
313-256-3731

Money Available: $4,094,908

The Council for the Arts was recently restructured. Grant programs are arranged in three general funding programs: Arts Organizations, Arts Projects, and Individual Artists. Any non-profit organization or institution, artist, local government, school, or community group in Michigan is eligible to apply for MCA grant funds. All funded activities must take place within the state and comply with Equal Opportunity Standards. Contact the Council for specific program guidelines.

Minnesota
Minnesota State Arts Board
432 Summit Ave.
St. Paul, MN 55102
612-297-2603

Money Available: $4,394,626

Eligibility Requirements:
Individual artist programs require state residency, unless otherwise specified.

Programs Available:
$6,000 For Visual, Literary, Or Performing Artists
    (Fellowships)

$1,000 For Artists To Improve Their Careers
(Career Opportunity Grants)
Money For Art Studio In Sausalito, California
(Headlands Residency Project)
$4,000 To Be An Apprentice Craftsperson
(Folk Arts Apprenticeship Grants)
$4,000 For Folk Art Research And Festivals
(Folk Arts Sponsorship Grants)
$3,000 For Artists To Travel More Than 60 Miles From
Home (Minnesota Touring Arts)
$10,000 To Organizations Who Help Artists
(Operating Support Program)
$5,000 To Organizations That Help More Than 5 Artists
(Series Presenters Programs)
Money For Schools To Improve Their Arts Program
(Organizational Support Grants)
Money For Schools To Have An Artist-In-Residence
(School Support Grants)

Mississippi

Mississippi Arts Commission
239 North Lamar St., Suite 207
Jackson, MS 39201
601-359-6030

Money Available: $645,839

Eligibility Requirements:
Individual artist programs require state residency.

Programs Available:
$5,000 For Writers, Composers, Video Producers
(Artist Fellowships)
$30,000 For Arts And Cultural Organizations
(General Operating Support)
$25,000 For Local Arts Agencies
(Local Arts Agencies)
$9,000 For New Arts Organizations
(Organizational Development)

$5,000 For Special Art Projects (Project Support)
$2,000 To Help Touring Artists
(Mississippi Touring Arts)
$7,000 For Local Schools To Improve Their Art
Programs (Arts in Education)

Missouri
Missouri State Council on the Arts
Wainwright Office Complex
111 N. 7th St., Suite 105
St. Louis, MO 63101
314-340-6845

Money Available: $4,414,799

Eligibility Requirements:
The Council offers financial assistance through seven art areas: dance, literature, media, multi-discipline, music, theater, and visual arts. A program administrator supervises applications in each area.

Programs Available:
Money For Smaller Arts Organizations
(Community Arts Program (CAP))
$2,000 For New Art Projects
(Community Arts Special Projects)
Money For Arts Groups Serving The Entire State
(Statewide Arts Service Organizations)
$2,000 To Help Art Organizations With Management
Development (Technical Assistance)
Money For Schools To Have An Artist-In-Residence
(Artist Residency Program)
Money To Learn From Folk Art Masters
(Traditional Arts Apprenticeship Program)

Montana
Montana Arts Council
48 N. Last Chance Gulch
Helena, MT 59620
406-444-6430

Money Available: $1,300,000

Eligibility Requirements:
Individual artist programs require state residency.

Programs Available:
$2,000 To Individual Artists
(Individual Artist Fellowships)
$6,000 For Arts Organizations
(Organizational Funding)
Grants For Arts Preservation, Media Arts, Archaeology,
and Folklore (Cultural and Aesthetic Project Grants)
Money For Schools To Have An Artist-In-Residence
(Artists in Schools/Communities)

Nebraska
Nebraska Arts Council
Jocelyn Castle Carriage House
3838 Davenport St.
Omaha, NE 68131
402-595-2122

Money Available: $1,384,453

Eligibility Requirements:
Individual artist programs require state residency.

Programs Available:
Money For Writers, Artists, and Performers
(Individual Artist Fellowships)
Grants To Arts Organizations (Basic Support Grant)
$2,000 For New Arts Organizations
(Community Challenge Grant)
$1,000 For High Risk Art Projects
(Director's Fund)
$10,000 For Art Festivals, Exhibitions, and Poetry
Readings (Special Projects)
Money For Touring Exhibits and Programs
(Nebraska Touring Program/Exhibits Nebraska)

Money For Educational Organizations To Use Art
    (Arts as Basic in the Curriculum/Community)
$500 For Artists and Groups To Tour
    (Nebraska Touring Program/Exhibits Nebraska (NTP) Technical
    Assistance Program)
Money For Art Projects At Schools
    Artists in Schools/Communities)

Nevada
Nevada State Council on the Arts
Capitol Complex
100 S. Stewart St.
Carson City, NV 89701
702-687-6680

Money Available: $545,594

Eligibility Requirements:
Individual artist programs require state residency.

Programs Available:
$10,000 For Artists To Create New Works
    (Artists Fellowships)
$2,500 For Master Folk Artists To Teach Apprentices
    (Folk Arts Apprenticeships)
$22,500 For Arts Organizations
    (Grants to Organizations)
$7,500 For Art Groups To Make Presentations
    (Grants to Presenters)
$15,000 To Bring Art To Small Towns
    (Rural Arts Development)
$30,000 To Help Art Organizations
    (Challenge Grant Program)
$1,000 For Artists Or Art Groups
    (Mini-Grants)
Money For Schools To Have An Artist-In-Residence
    (Artist-in-Residence Program)

New Hampshire
New Hampshire Division of Arts
Council of the Arts
40 North Main St.
Concord, NH 03301
603-271-2789

Money Available: $615,000

Eligibility Requirements:
Individual artist programs require state residency, unless otherwise specified.

Programs Available:
$3,000 For Individual Artists
    (Individual Artist Fellowships)
$500 For Individual Artists
    (Artist Opportunity Grants)
$500 For Artists Who Don't Normally Get Money
    (Discovery Award)
$8,000 To Help The Management Of Arts Groups
    (Operating Grants)
$4,000 To Community Arts Organizations
    (Program Grant)
$5,000 To Pay For Staff At Arts Groups
    (Salary Assistance Grants)
$4,000 For Special Art Projects (Special Project Grants)
$3,000 For Artist-In-Residence In Small Towns
    (Rural Residency Grants)
$500 For Groups To Hire Consultants (Technical Assistance Grants)
$16,000 To Help Art Groups With Fund Raising
    (Arts Institution (A1) Grants)
$4,500 Grants For Special Projects (Project Grants)
$4,000 For Schools To Bring In Artists
    (Artist-in-Residence Grants)
$5,000 For Arts Education In Schools
    (AIE Initiatives)
$1,490 For School Teachers To Develop Art Classes
    (Teacher/Artist Curriculum Collaborations)

New Jersey
New Jersey State Council on the Arts
20 West State St., CN 306
Trenton, NJ 08625
609-292-6130

Money Available: $9,541,209

Eligibility Requirements:
Individual artist programs require state residency, unless otherwise
specified.

Programs Available:
Grants For Artists, Mimes, Sculptors, Poets, and Opera
        Singers (Fellowships)
Grants To Arts Organizations (Organizational Funding)
Money For Regional and State-Wide Organizations
        (General Operating Support)
Grants To Support Special Art Projects (Special Project Support)
Money For Art Programs In Local Schools
        (Arts Basic to Education Awards)
Funding For Arts Organizations
        (Major Impact Arts Organizations)
Matching Grants To Arts Organizations (Challenge Grants)
Grants To Improve The Management Of Art
        Organizations (Technical Assistance)
Money For Public Or Parochial School Art Programs
        (Educational Funding: Arts in Education Programs (AIE))
Money For Jazz, Folk, And Theater Artists-In-Residence
        (Artists in Education Programs)
Summer Programs For Artists and Teachers (Artist/Teacher/Institute)

New Mexico
New Mexico Cultural Affairs Arts Division
228 East Palace Ave.
Santa Fe, NM 87501
505-827-6490

Money Available: $918,400

Eligibility Requirements:
The New Mexico Art Division is unable to fund fellowships to individuals. It strongly encourages applicant organizations to involve resident New Mexico artists. However, the Division does support local sponsorship of out-of-state artists or organizations to enrich a resident group or when the services fill a need that is not being met locally. Organizational Funding: New Mexico administers awards to non-profit organizations. Generally, award applicants must provide at least a one-to-one cash match.

Programs Available:
$120,000 For Arts Organizations
    (Established Arts Organizations)
$15,000 For Local Art Groups
    (Civic and Community Arts Organizations)
$15,000 For Ethnic Arts Projects
    (Culturally Diverse Organizations)
$5,000 For Folk Art Programs (Arts Projects)
Money For Artists To Tour The State
    (Incentives to Present New Mexico Touring Artists)
Money For An Artist-In-Residence For Schools And
    Community Homes (Artists Residencies)

New York
New York State Council on the Arts
915 Broadway
New York, NY 10010
212-387-7000

Money Available: $26,172,900

Eligibility Requirements:
Individual artist programs require state residency. Non-profit organizations can obtain support in 17 areas including: architecture, planning and design, arts in education, capital funding initiative, dance, electronic media and film, folk arts, individual artists, literature, museum, music, musical instrument revolving loan fund, presenting operations, special arts services, state local partnership, theater, and the visual arts.

Programs Available:
$25,000 For Artists (Individual Artist Programs)
Grants For Arts Organizations
    (General Operating Support)
Money For More Than One Year For Art Groups
    (Multi-Year Support)
$5,000 For Local Art Groups
Money For School Art Programs In Music, Theater, and
    Media (Arts in Education)

North Carolina
North Carolina Arts Council
Department of Cultural Resources
Raleigh, NC 27601
919-733-2821

Money Available: $3,519,696

Eligibility Requirements:
Individual artist programs require state residency. Money for arts
organizations is in eight categories: community development, dance,
folklife, literature, music, theater, touring/presenting, and the visual
arts. Support includes funding for program support,
interdisciplinary/special projects, and organizational development
grants.

Programs Available:
$8,000 For Artists, Dancers, Musicians, and Writers
    (Fellowships)
$8,000 For Specific Dance, Folk Art, or Literature
    Projects (Artist Project Grants)
Money For Artists To Work With Schools And
    Community Colleges (Residencies)
$3,000 For Local Folk Artists
    (Folk Heritage Awards)
$10,000 To Make A Documentary Of State Folk Artists
    (Folklife Documentary Project Grants)
Help For Local Artists To Tour The State
    (Touring Artists Roster)

$500 For Writers To Attend Conferences
    (Writers Scholarships)
Money To Train As An Art Administrator
    (Internships)
Money For Dance, Music, And Visual Arts Groups
    (Major Organization Support)
Money For Theater And Literary Organizations
    (General Support)
Money For Local Governments To Support Art Groups
    (Local Government Challenge)
Money For Statewide Arts Groups
    (Management Service Organization)
Grants To Schools For Art Projects
    (Arts in Education)

North Dakota
North Dakota Council On Arts
Black Building, #606
118 Broadway
Fargo, ND 58102
701-239-7150

Money Available: $642,000

Eligibility Requirements:
Individual artist programs require state residency, unless otherwise
specified.

Programs Available:
Money For Artists, Dancers, Opera Singers,
    Photographers, and Writers (Artists Fellowships Program)
Money To Hire Consultants Or Arts Advisors
    (Professional Development Program)
Grants To Small Arts Organizations (ACCESS Grant Program)
$500 For Special Art Projects
    (Institutional Support)
Grants For Arts Projects In Small Towns
    (Rural Arts Initiative)
Money For Artistic Touring Events (Touring Arts Program)

Money For Schools To Have An Artist-In-Residence
  (Artists-in-Residence)
Money For Schools To Develop Art Programs
  (Local Education in the Arts Planning: (LEAP))

Ohio
Ohio Council on Arts
727 East Main St.
Columbus, OH 43205
614-466-2613

Money Available: $6,119,360

Eligibility Requirements:
State residency is required, unless otherwise specified.

Programs Available:
$10,000 For Artists And Art Critics
  (Individual Artist Fellowships)
Study Your Art In Long Island, NY Or Sausalito, CA
  (Individual Artist Program)
$1,000 For Artists To Attend Workshops
  (Professional Development Assistance)
$2,000 For An Artist To Work With A Master
  (Traditional and Ethnic Arts Apprenticeship Program)
Grants To Arts Organizations
  (Major Institution Support)
Money To Support Special Projects
  (Project Support)
Money For Administrative Expenses (Operating Support)
$2,000 For Special Art Opportunities (Sudden Opportunity Grants)

Oklahoma
State Arts Council of Oklahoma
2101 N. Lincoln Blvd.
Oklahoma City, OK 73105
405-521-2931

Money Available: $2,844,042

Eligibility Requirements:
The Council is unable to fund individuals. Applications are accepted from non-religious, non-profit, tax exempt organizations. Colleges, schools, and universities which receive funding through the State Regents for Higher Education or substantial private sources, are a lower funding priority, except in areas where the university or college is the sole source of arts events in a community.

All funding for the Advanced Request, Over $2,000 and Under $2,000 Project Assistance categories must be matched dollar for dollar by the applicant. Fifty percent of the matching funds must be cash. The Council will fund personnel or administrative costs associated with a project. The Council does not fund general administrative expenses or general organizational support.

Programs Available:
Grants For Arts Organizations
    (Advanced Request Funding)
Money For Projects Over $2,000
    (Project Assistance Over $2,000)
Money For Projects Under $2,000
    (Project Assistance Under $2,000)
$5,000 For Minority Arts Organization
    (Minority Arts)
Grants For Community Arts Celebrations
    (Fairs and Festival Funding)
Money For An Artist-In-Residence In Schools Or
    Community Groups (Artists-in-Residences Program)
Money For Artists To Tour
    (Oklahoma Touring Program)

Oregon
Oregon Arts Commission
550 Airport Road, SE
Salem, OR 97310
503-986-0082

Money Available: $1,730,163

Eligibility Requirements:
Individual artist programs require state residency, unless otherwise specified.

Programs Available:
$3,000 To Artists, Photographers, And Performers
    (Artist Fellowships)
$7,000 For Artists Living In 13 Western States
    (Western States Regional Media Arts Fellowships)
Money For Authors and Publishers In 13 Western States
    (Western States Book Awards)
Grants For Arts Organizations
    (Economic Development Grants)
Grants For Artists and Small Art Groups
    (Regional Regranting)
Money To Be An Artist-In-Residence (Artist Residencies)
$3,000 For Arts Programs In Schools (Arts Education Project Grants)

Pennsylvania
Pennsylvania Council on the Arts
Room 216, Finance Bldg.
Harrisburg, PA 17120
717-787-6883

Money Available: $9,652,660

Eligibility Requirements:
For individual artist programs, applicants must have lived in Pennsylvania for two years prior to applying for funding and should have had a minimum of three years professional experience in their field. Organizational funding programs require that organizations must be non-profit, tax exempt corporations that provide arts programming and/or services to Pennsylvania. Categories include: broadcast of the arts, crafts, inter-disciplinary arts, dance, literature, local arts services, local government, media arts, museums, music, presenting organizations, theater, and visual arts. Non-profit organizations may apply on behalf of an unincorporated arts group. In this capacity, the organization becomes a "conduit" for grant funds and is financially, administratively, and programmatically responsible for a grant.

Programs Available:
Grants To Dancers, Jazz Composers, Writers, And Artists
(Fellowships)
Grants To Arts Organizations
(General Support)
$1,000 To Hire A Consultant For Your Art Group
(Technical Assistance)
$250 To Bus Artists To A Performance
(Busing Program)

Rhode Island
Rhode Island State Council on The Arts
95 Cedar St., Suite 103
Providence, RI 02903
401-277-3880

Money Available: $636,397

Eligibility Requirements
Applicants for the individual artist programs must be eighteen years of age or older and have lived in the state for at least one year prior to application. Minimum grants awarded to organizations is $100 and funds must be expended during the fiscal year of the award. Program grants, with the exception of general operating support, are divided into two categories. Level I grants range from $100 to $2,000. Level II grants range from $2,001 to $5,000. A dollar for dollar cash match is required.

Programs Available:
$5,000 For Artists To Create New Works
(Artist Projects)
$3,000 For Artists, Choreographers, Designers, and
Printmakers (Fellowships)
$2,000 For Folk Art Apprenticeships
(Folk Arts Apprenticeships)
Grants To Groups Providing Art To Underserved Groups
(Access Initiatives)
Grants For Special Art Projects
(Arts Programming)

Grants To Help Manage Art Organizations
(Organizational Development)
Money For Operating Expenses
(General Operating Support)
$12,000 To Have An Artist-In-Residence At A School
(Artist Residency Grants)
$2,500 To Develop Art For Schools
(Arts as Basic in Curriculum (ABC) Grants)
$2,000 For A Public School To Plan An Art Program
(Rhode Island Comprehensive Arts Planning Grants)

South Carolina

South Carolina Arts Commission
1800 Gervais St.
Columbia, SC 29201
803-734-8696

Money Available: $1,249,578

Eligibility Requirements:
Individual artist programs require state residency.

Programs Available:
$7,500 For Artists, Performers, Writers, And Craftsmen
(Fellowships)
$7,500 For Artists To Do Special Projects
(Project Support)
$1,000 To Be Used For Professional Development
(Quarterly Grants)
Up To $500,000 To Arts Groups
(General Support Grants)
$20,000 For Special Art Projects
(Project Support)
$1,000 To Help Develop Art Management Skills
(Quarterly Grants)
Money To Bring Art Programs To Schools
(Arts in the Basic Curriculum)
Money For Schools To Have An Artist-In-Residence
(Arts in Education)

$350 For Teachers To Work On Art Projects In School
  (Teacher Incentive Grants)
Grants To Bring Performances Or Screenings To Schools
  (Visiting Artists)

South Dakota
South Dakota Arts Council
230 S. Phillips Ave., Suite 204
Sioux Falls, SD 57102
605-339-6646

Money Available: $781,422

Eligibility Requirements:
Individual artist programs require state residency. All grants (except
Emerging Artist Grants and Fellowships) are intended as seed money.
Applicant organizations and individuals are funded up to 50% of
projected costs. Funding is available in the following arts disciplines:
dance, music, opera/music theater, theater, visual arts, design arts,
crafts, photography, media arts, literature, and folk arts.

Programs Available:
$5,000 For Artists In Any Arts Discipline
  (Artist Fellowship Grants)
$1,000 For Artists Who Want To Grow
  (Emerging Artists Grants)
Grants For Artists To Work On Specific Projects
  (Project Grants)
Grants To Arts Groups and Art Councils
  (General Operating Support)
Grants To Groups For Special Projects
  (Project Grants)
$500 For New Art Organizations
  (Interim Project Grants)
$500 For Art Groups Who Need Emergency Support
  (Emergency Grants)
$1,000 For A Community Art Project (Arts Bank)
$500 For Arts Groups To Hire Consultants
  (Technical Assistance)

$500 For Art Group Managers To Improve Their Skills
    (Professional Development)
Money For Touring Art Groups
    (Touring Arts)
Money For Schools To Have An Artist-In-Residence
    (Artists in Schools)
Grants For Teachers To Develop Art In Schools
    (Art Educator Grants)

Tennessee

Tennessee Art Commission
320 6th Ave., North, Suite 100
Nashville, TN 37243
615-741-1701

Money Available: $3,877,940

Eligibility Requirements:
Individual artist programs require state residency.

Programs Available:
$2,500 For Artists, Musicians, Writers, And Dancers
    (Individual Artists Fellowships)
Grants For Arts Organizations
    (Arts Build Communities)
$6,000 For Special Art Projects (Arts Projects)
$15,000 For Community Orchestras
    (Community Orchestra Challenge Grants)
Grants To Operate An Arts Organizations
    (General Operating Support)
$25,000 For Underserved Art Forms
    (Partnerships for Access and Appreciation)
$500 For Unexpected Art Activities
    (Special Opportunity Grants)
$2,500 To Hire Out-Of-Town Consultants
    (Technical Assistance Program)
$5,000 For Artists To Go On Tour (Touring Arts Program)
$10,000 For A Non-Profit Agency To Have An Artist-In-
    Residence (Artists Residencies)

Texas
Texas Commission on the Arts
920 Colorado
P.O. Box 13406
Capitol Station
Austin, TX 78711
512-463-5535

Money Available: $2,988,023

Eligibility Requirements:
Texas does not offer direct funding to individuals. Individual artists are funded indirectly through the Arts in Education and the Touring Programs. In addition, individual artists may apply to the Commission under the umbrella of a non-profit organization or government entity.

Programs Available:
Grants To Arts Organizations
     (Organizational Assistance)
Money To Support Art Projects (Project Assistance)
Grants For Artists To Go On Tour (Touring Assistance)
Money For Schools To Have An Artist-In-Residence
     (Arts in Education)

Utah
Utah Arts Council
617 E. South Temple
Salt Lake City, UT 84102
801-533-5895

Money Available: $1,000,349

Eligibility Requirements:
Individual artist programs require state residency, unless otherwise specified.

Programs Available:
$5,000 For Artists, Printmakers, Photographers, and
     Video Artists (Visual Artist Fellowships)

$2,500 For An Artist To Learn From A Master
  (Folk Arts Apprenticeship Program)
$5,000 For Creative Writers (Creative Writing Award)
$130,000 To Art Groups (Grants Program)
Money For Community Art Councils
  (Community/State Partnership Program)
Money For Performing Artists To Tour The State
  (Utah Performing Arts Tour)
$25 An Hour For Artists To Work At Local Schools
  (Arts in Education)

Vermont
Vermont Council on Arts
133 State St.
Montpelier, VT 05633
802-828-3291

Money Available: $576,930

Eligibility Requirements:
Individual artist programs require state residency.

Programs Available:
$1,000 For Artists To Attend Classes and Workshops
  (Artist Development Grants)
$3,500 For Artists (Fellowships)
Money To Support Special Art Projects (Project Grants)
$15,000 For Arts Groups (Operating Grants)
$3,000 For Special Art Projects (Project Grants)
$5,000 For Arts Organizations To Develop
  (Service Organization Grants)
$750 For Schools And Groups To Hire Artists (Options Programs)
Money To Have An Artist Perform For Your
  Organization (Touring Artists Program)
$160 A Day Plus Expenses To Be An Artist-In-Residence
  (Residency Program)
Grants To Develop Art-Related Courses (Development Grants)
Money To Have An Artist-In-Residence
  (Residency Grants for Sponsors)

Virginia
Virginia Commission for the Arts
Lewis House
223 Governor St.
Richmond, VA 23219
804-225-3132

Money Available: $1,400,000

Eligibility Requirements:
Individual artist programs require state residency.

Programs Available:
$5,000 For Professional Artists To Advance Their Careers
    (Project Grants)
$250 For Readings and Workshops Conducted By Writers
    (Writers in Virginia)
$15,000 To Run An Arts Organization
    (General Operating Support)
$1,500 To Hire Management Consultants
    (Technical Assistance Grants)
Money To Produce Music, Opera, Theater, and Dance
    (Performing Arts Endowment Matching Program)
$5,000 To Help Local Governments Support The Arts
    (Local Government Challenge Grants)
Money For Artists To Tour The State
    (Touring Assistance Programs)
Money For Schools To Have An Artist-In-Residence
    (Artist in Education Residencies)
Grants For Community Colleges To Have An Artist-In-
    Residence (Community College Artist Residencies)
Funding For Workshops and Consultants In Arts
    Education (Arts in Education Development Grants)
$300 For Teachers To Develop Innovative Art Programs
    (Teacher Incentive Grant Program)
Money To Hire Consultants Or Attend Conferences In
    Arts Education (Arts In Education Technical Assistance)

Washington

Washington State Arts Commission
110-9th and Columbia Bldg.
MS-GH11
Olympia, WA 98504
206-753-3860

Money Available: $1,212,000

Eligibility Requirements:
Individual artist programs require state residency.

Programs Available:
$5,000 To Professional Literary, Performing, and Two-
    Dimensional Artists (Artist Fellowship Awards)
Money For Outstanding Artists
    (Governor's Arts Awards)
Grants To Ethnic Heritage Artists
    (Governor's Ethnic Heritage Awards)
$2,000 For Short-Term Art Projects
    (Project Support)
$10,000 For Arts Organizations
    (Organizational Support)
Money To Support Arts Organizations
    (Institutional Support Program)
Money To Bring Performances To Schools
    (Cultural Enhancement Program (CEP))
Money For Schools To Have An Artist-In-Residence
    (Artists-in-Residence Program (AIR))

West Virginia

Arts and Humanities Division
Division of Culture and History
Cultural Center
1900 Kanawha Blvd. East
Charleston, WV 25305
304-558-0220

Money Available: $932,872

Programs Available:
Money For Individual Artists (Individual Artist Programs)
Money For The Professional Development Of Artists
(Support for Artists Program)
Artists Lists and Register
(West Virginia Artists List and Register)
Money For Craftsman and Artists
(West Virginia Juried Exhibition)
$15,000 For An Art Exhibition
(Presenting West Virginia Artists Program)
Money For Special Art Exhibits
(Showcase of Visual Arts Program)
$125,000 For Art Organizations
(Major Institutions Support Grant)
$25,000 For Theaters, Galleries, and Museums
(Support for Arts Institutions/Arts Organizations)
$10,000 To Pay For Performing Artists ((Residencies for
Performing Arts Organizations and Institutions)
Grants To Bring Art To Local Schools And Communities
(Arts in the Community)
Money To Fund Art Programs (Touring Program)
$10,000 For Film, Video, And Audio Projects
(Media Arts Projects)
Money To Support New Works Of Composers,
Playwrights, Writers, and Choreographers (Performing Arts)
Money To Artists and Art Administrators To Attend
Conferences (Travel Fund)
Grants For Groups And Communities To Develop Long
Range Arts Programs (Project 20/21)
Money to Develop Special Art Programs For Schools
(Arts in Education)

Wisconsin

Wisconsin Arts Board
101 E. Wilson St., Suite 301
Madison, WI 53702
608-266-0190

Money Available: $2,982,570

Eligibility Requirements:
Individual artist programs require state residency. For most programs, recipients must match state awards with cash or donated services.

Programs Available:
$5,000 For Artists, Writers, and Folk Artists
    (Fellowships)
$3,500 For New Artistic Works (New Work Awards)
$1,000 To Support An Artist's Professional Development
    (Development Grants)
Money For Artists To Work With A Master
    (Folk Art Apprenticeships)
Grants To Larger Arts Organizations
    (Artistic Program Support I)
Grants To Smaller Arts Organizations
    (Artistic Program Support II)
$3,000 For Small Groups And Individual Artists
    (Small Organization Support)
Grants To Community Art Programs
    (Community Arts Program)
Support For The Performing Arts Network
    (Performing Arts Network (PAN)-Wisconsin)
Money For Organizations To Bring In Professional
    Touring Artists (Wisconsin Touring Program)
$5,000 For Folk Artists (Folk Arts Opportunity Grants)
Grants For Culturally Diverse Art Projects
    (Cultural Diversity Initiative)
Money To Pay For Art Administrators
    (Salary Assistance Grants)
Money For Schools To Have An Artist-In-Residence
    (Artists in Education Residency)
Money For Schools To Bring Artists Into The Classroom
    (Educational Opportunity Grants)

Wyoming
Wyoming Arts Council
2320 Capitol Ave.
Cheyenne, WY 82002
307-777-7742

Money Available: $378,017

Eligibility Requirements:
Individual artist programs require state residency. For educational funding, grants require a one-to-one cash match.

Programs Available:
$2,500 For Artists, Mimes, And Costume Designers
    (Performing Arts)
$2,500 To Exhibit Wyoming Artists
    (Visual Arts)
$2,500 To Writers (Literature)
Grants For Arts Organizations
    (Organizational Funding)
Grants For Operating An Arts Organization
    (General Operating Support Grant)
Grants For One-Time Arts Events
    (Project Grants)
Grants For Art Productions
    (Presenting and Producing Grants)
Grants To Strengthen An Arts Organization
    (Technical Assistance)
Grants To Schools And Organizations To Plan Arts
    Programs (Art is Essential Grant)
Grants For Schools To Have An Artist-In-Residence
    (Artist-In-Residence Grants)
Money To Develop Art Courses In Schools
    (Project Grants)
Money To Bring Scholars and Experts To School Art
    Programs (Technical Assistance/In-Service Grants)
Money For Trailblazer Art Programs
    (Trailblazer Projects)

Choosing a Nursing Home...If You Want To

W e all know that a nursing home is not really a home, but for some folks the services that nursing homes provide are a necessary part of life.

Maybe you need some rehab after breaking your hip or having a stroke. Maybe your loved one is a little confused, and needs someone to keep a close eye on her. On any given day, approximately 5% of the elderly population is in a nursing home, but for most, the stay is only for a short time.

People want to stay at home, so new programs are springing up each day to fill the need for home care. But for those who do need a nursing home, who picks up the check for the $30,000 a year to stay in a nursing home is always an interesting discussion.

There are government resources to help you choose a good nursing home, look at your finances, and make this difficult step a little easier.

Your Very Own Strong Arm

You don't need to put up with cold food or rough care. Just make a call to your state's Nursing Home Ombudsman, and there will be another person on your side.

Ombudsmen are there to help people who are denied admission to nursing homes, improve the quality of the food, and even help report stolen property.

The Ombudsman Program is designed to investigate and resolve complaints made by or on behalf of residents of long-term care facilities. They also make sure these places are running properly and up to code.

Ombudsman act as mediators, but they are not enforcement agencies. They cannot force a nursing home to change or correct their practices. But it is in the best interest of the nursing home to work with you, before you refer your complaint elsewhere (which the Ombudsman can assist you with).

To locate the Nursing Home Ombudsman in your state, look in the Directory of State Information at the end of this book.

Where To Begin

All nursing homes are not created equal. Before you sign on the dotted line, you'd better make sure you understand what you're getting yourself into. The National Health Information Center publication, *Long Term Care*, lists a number of free publications dealing with choosing a nursing home, financing, identifying organizations that could be of assistance and more.

Who covers what cost? How do you check one of these places out? The publication costs $1 and is available from National Health Information Center, Office of Disease Prevention and Health Promotion, Mary Switzer Building, Room 2132, 330 C St., SW, Washington, DC 20201; 800-336-4797.

☆ ☆ ☆

Nursing Home Shopping List

It's not like shopping for groceries. You can't really walk into a nursing home's cafeteria and squeeze the fruit or check the expiration date on cereal boxes. But even if you could, it probably wouldn't tell you what you really need to know.

So what are the ways you can make sure you are getting your money's worth?

You might first ask these simple questions. Do residents seem well cared for and generally content? Is there an activity room? Is the home certified for Medicare and Medicaid programs?

Does the home have a security system to prevent confused residents from wandering away?

These are just some of the questions you will find from the nursing home checklist provided in the free publication, *When You Need A Nursing Home*. To receive your copy, contact National Institute on Aging, Information Center, P.O. Box 8057, Gaithersburg, MD 20898; 800-222-2225.

The Medicare Hotline also distributes a free publication titled, *A Guide to Choosing a Nursing Home*, which provides you with information and questions you should ask when looking at facilities. Contact the Medicare Hotline at 800-638-6833.

☆ ☆ ☆

Free Workshops to Help You Decide

The decision to enter a nursing home is never an easy one, but with some preparation, the move can go smoothly.

Many County Cooperative Extension offices offer pamphlets or workshops on choosing a nursing home, or planning for it financially. Some local offices have information on estate planning and the pros and cons of nursing home insurance.

To learn more about what your local County Cooperative Extension office has for seniors, look in the blue pages of your phone book for the office nearest you, or you can find the main state office in the state-by-state directory at the end of the book.

For more information, contact Extension Service, U.S. Department of Agriculture, Room 3328, Washington, DC 20250; 202-720-4111.

Who is Really Picking Up The Check?

A recent government study has discovered that a disturbingly large number of seniors who buy long-term care insurance will actually stop paying their premiums long before they get to the point where they need the insurance coverage the most. This trend is especially alarming given the fact that the price of nursing home care is expected to double in the next 25 years.

To find out more about this study and others on long-term care issues, contact the General Accounting Office (GAO). The GAO has a series of reports that deal with long-term care issues including:

- *Long-Term Care Insurance: High Percentage of Policyholders Drop Policies* (GAO/HRD 93-129)
- *Long-Term Care: The Need for Geriatric Assessment in Publicly Funded Home and Community-Based Programs* (T-PEMD 94-20)
- *Long-Term Care: Demography, Dollars, and Dissatisfaction Drive Reform* (T-HEHS 94-140)
- *Long-Term Care Insurance: Tax*

Preferences Reduce Costs More for Those in Higher Tax Brackets (GAO/GGD 93-110)

All reports are free and can be requested by contacting the U.S. General Accounting Office, P.O. Box 6015, Gaithersburg, MD 20884; 202-512-6000.

☆ ☆ ☆

Get Married And Move To Arizona

Who would have ever thought that this is what you could do to lower your chances of ever having to spend some time in a nursing home? Believe it or not, nursing home use is  different for each state, with Arizona being the lowest and Minnesota the highest. Must be all that dry desert air.

Research also shows that if you've been married you're less likely to use a nursing a home than if you haven't. So, you might want to reconsider the marriage proposal from that guy with the plaid jacket from Tucson.

Actually, the Agency for Health Care Policy and Research (AHCPR) looks into who pays for this care, and even if it is the right facility for certain people. Some of the free publications include:

- *Characteristics of Nursing Homes that Affect Resident Outcomes*
- *Case Management Agency Systems of Administering Long-Term Care: Evidence from the Channeling Demonstration*
- *Cognitive Impairment and Disruptive Behaviors Among Community-Based Elderly Persons: Implications for Targeting Long-Term Care*
- *A Lifetime Perspective on Proposals For Financing Nursing Home Care*
- *Long-Term Care Arrangements for Elderly Persons with Disabilities: Private and Public Roles*
- *Long-Term Case Studies*
- *Measuring Cognitive Impairment with Large Data Sets*

- *Nursing Home Reform and the Mentally Ill*
- *Nursing Home Use After 65 in the United States*
- *Nursing Home Use and Costs*
- *Public and Private Responsibility for Financing Nursing Home Care*
- *Quality of Board Care Homes Serving Low-Income Elderly*
- *Lifetime Use of Nursing Home Care*
- *The Risk of Nursing Home Use in Later Life*
- *Standardizing Nursing Home Admission Dates for Short-Term Hospital Stays*
- *Use of Formal and Informal Home Care by the Disabled Elderly*
- *Use of Psychoactive Drugs in Nursing Homes*

For your free copies or more information, contact Agency for Health Care Policy and Research, P.O. Box 88547, Silver Spring, MD 20907; 800-358-9295.

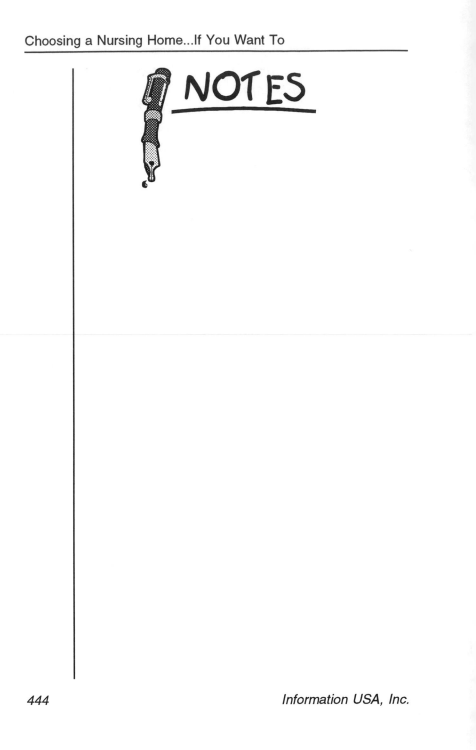

Neat Things to Do With Your Free Time

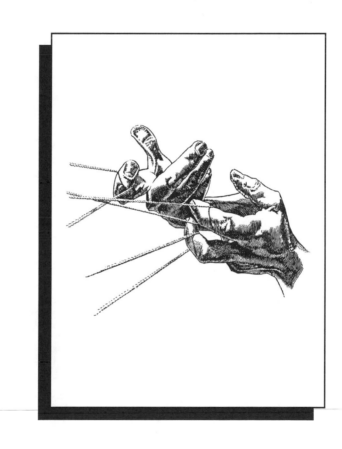

Shuffleboard, dominoes, bridge, and golf...Excited yet? Wouldn't you rather improve your neighborhood, lead nature walks, or teach Lech Walesa's kids to become little capitalists? Being retired doesn't have to mean spending your afternoons chasing a little white ball around a glorified cow patch. And just because now you might find yourself on a fixed income, it doesn't mean that you can't take that trip to Africa you've always dreamed about. The government has hundreds of ways to help you get excited about your new-found free time.

☆ ☆ ☆

Keep a Fellow Senior Out of a Nursing Home

Nursing homes have got to be one of the last places people want to spend the remaining years of their lives. Through a special program, you can be matched up with someone who needs just a little help to stay in the comfortable surroundings of their own home, and you can gain a friend in the bargain.

Through the Senior Companion program, Oscar Jones was matched up with a 93-

year old man named Joe, who was afflicted by everything from blindness, heart disease, lung and kidney problems, to a stroke. Before long, Oscar had Joe up, walking, and talking. Joe's family was amazed at the beautiful friendship that developed between Joe and Oscar.

As a participant in the Senior Companion Program, you will give individual care to other seniors who need help with transportation and shopping, or just sharing their reminiscences. Volunteers receive a small paycheck and other benefits.

There are fact sheets and brochures available outlining the program. For more information, contact National Senior Service Corps, 1201 New York Ave., NW, Washington, DC 20525; 800-424-8867.

☆ ☆ ☆

$3,000 to Help the Kids

After being retired for only a month, Lucy DePeppo just couldn't stand it anymore, and decided to become one of over 14,300 seniors who take part in the Foster Grandparent Program. Instead of watching soap operas, Ms. DePeppo spends her day caring for AIDS babies and babies born addicted to drugs — and she is even being paid for her work. Lucy's supervisor says she is a terrific role model for young parents.

The Foster Grandparent Program matches low-income seniors with young people who need various kinds of special help. Volunteers serve as mentors, tutors, and caregivers for  children and young kids with special needs, and can also work in schools, hospitals, and recreation centers in their communities. Volunteers work twenty hours per week, and receive a small paycheck and other benefits such as transportation costs or uniforms.

If you think you are up to a challenge like this, call the toll-free hotline listed below and have some free fact sheets and brochures sent to you.

For more information, contact National Senior Service Corps, 1201 New York Ave., NW, Washington, DC 20525; 800-424-8867.

☆ ☆ ☆

Share Your Know-How For Some Expense Money

You've got forty years of business experience out there with you on the golf course during your retirement. There are hundreds of businesses and even nonprofit groups starting up each day run by people who have the energy, but not the experience that you possess. You can lend your expertise to those who need your help the most.

Take John Moore, for example. He is a retired pastor who now uses his years of experience to serve as a mediator for a community program which gets criminals and victims to sit down to air their feelings, and reach an agreement on restitution.

This is only one example of how the Retired Senior Volunteer Program (RSVP) gives retired people a chance to continue using their professional experience by working with local service organizations doing such things as conducting employment workshops and acting as consultants to nonprofit organizations. You can even work in schools, libraries, hospitals, and other community service centers.

There are fact sheets and brochures available describing the program. For more information, contact National Senior Service Corps, 1201 New York Ave., NW, Washington, DC 20525; 800-424-8867.

☆ ☆ ☆

Give Of Your Time And Your Heart

Over 9 million seniors a year could use your help. Over half a million seniors volunteer each year to: deliver meals to shut-ins, help others get to doctor's appointments — whatever is needed to keep them functioning in their homes and communities.

If you have the time and want to get involved, contact your State Department on Aging which is listed in the Directory of State Information at the end of this book, and they will direct you to local organizations who would love to get you started.

If you have trouble locating an appropriate organization, the Eldercare Locator can refer you to various services that aid and assist the elderly. Contact Eldercare Locator, Administration on Aging, 330 Independence Ave., SW, Washington, DC 20201; 202-629-0641, 800-677-1116.

☆ ☆ ☆

Have Some Fun in the Woods

If you prefer saving spotted owls and counting woodchucks to playing bridge with the girls, then how about volunteering at one of our national forests? Since the government seems to be more interested in investing in obsolete bombers, volunteers are essential in managing the nation's natural resources.

That is where you can come in if you would like to help. Volunteer positions vary depending on the needs of your local forest, but can include everything from typing and filing, leading nature hikes, to conducting fascinating research.

For a list of national forests nearest you, contact U.S. Forest Service, U.S. Department of Agriculture, Human Resource Programs, P.O. Box 96090, Washington, DC 20090; 703-235-8855.

☆ ☆ ☆

15,000 Seniors Are Doing It in the Parks

Do you ever wonder why the National Parks seem so crowded in the summer? It might be because they are 80,000 people volunteering each year, 15,000 of whom are in the over 50 crowd! Whether it is timing Old Faithful with a stop watch, directing moose traffic, or luring grizzly bears away from stray children, the National Park Service will find something for you to do.

While some money is available for out of pocket expenses, and there is even limited housing opportunities at a few parks reserved for volunteers with special skills, this is strictly a volunteer program designed for those who love the great outdoors.

Contact your nearest park to discover an interesting way to spend your free time or to receive a free brochure, contact Office of Public Inquiries, National Park Service, U.S. Department of the Interior, P.O. Box 37127, Washington, DC 20013; 202-208-4747.

☆ ☆ ☆

Travel The World at Government Expense

The average roundtrip ticket to Nepal will cost you $2,800, Poland is $1,800, and Sudan is $2,100. Who can afford those prices on a fixed income? Bob and June Lindstrom managed to get to Poland for free by volunteering to teach those former communists how to become capitalists. Harriet Locke is teaching school in Nepal.

These are just a few of the 508 seniors who recently volunteered for the Peace Corps (out of a total of 6500). Even Jimmy Carter's mother once volunteered. Who else but Uncle Sam is going to pay all your expenses and give you a salary to boot?

As a volunteer you will serve for two years, living among the native people, and becoming part of the community. The Peace Corps sends volunteers throughout

Latin America, Africa, the Near East, Asia, the Pacific, and Eastern Europe to share their expertise in education, agriculture, health, economic development, urban development, and the environment.

To learn more about serving the world, contact Peace Corps, 1990 K St., NW, Washington, DC 20526; 800-424-8580.

☆ ☆ ☆

Fishing and Hunting Was Never Like This

When you hear a statistic like there are 10,318 salmon running upstream in Washington State, we hope you don't think that number was made up by some guy at a desk. In

fact, statistics such as this often come from volunteers who are needed to stand out in the middle of rivers and count those fish, one-by-one.

If you like fishing or hiking, you can serve as a volunteer where you can do this kind of work all the time. The U.S. Fish and Wildlife Service counts all kinds of things — fish, owls, cranes, herons. But if you're just not very good at math, they will find something else for you to do. Whatever it is that you do, it will look great on your resume.

To find out about volunteer opportunities at your local Fish and Wildlife Office, look in the blue pages of your phone book, or contact U.S. Fish and Wildlife Service, U.S. Department of the Interior, 4401 N. Fairfax Dr., Arlington, VA 22203; 703-358-1724.

☆ ☆ ☆

Be a Big Shot Executive

Your wife wants you to slow down now that you're retired, but every time you walk into a store, you embarrass your wife by demanding to see the manager. Then you proceed to tell the guy what's wrong with the way he's running his business. Your wife hides in the frozen food section.

Instead of getting kicked out of every place you shop, try volunteering with SCORE, Service Corps of Retired Executives.

SCORE volunteers are usually retired business professionals who want to share their expertise with the next generation of business owners.

You won't get paid as a volunteer, although you may get reimbursed for certain out-of-pocket expenses. SCORE even conducts seminars and workshops covering major considerations for running a business.

If you are interested in becoming one of over 13,000 SCORE members nationwide, contact them at SCORE, 409 Third St., SW, Fourth Floor, Washington, DC 20024; 202-205-6762; 800-634-0245.

Information USA, Inc.

Free Help With Your Investments

Y ou can't eliminate all the risks, but you sure can rest easier at night if you learn how to make use of government sources before you make your next big deal. Check out your broker and the information he provides by using resources available courtesy of your tax dollars.

☆ ☆ ☆

Hello — Gimme Your Money

Shady telemarketers and investment brokers have duped more than one unsuspecting consumer out of their life savings. At last count, the number of victims climbed into the millions.

You don't want to be among the big losers; all it takes is a little self-control and a call to the Federal Trade Commission. Several of their free publications can help you become a more informed investor, including *Telephone Investment Fraud*, *Investing in Rare Coins*, *Investing in Wireless Cable TV*, and more.

For more information, contact Federal Trade Commission, Public Reference Branch, 6th and Pennsylvania Aves., NW, Washington, DC 20580; 202-326-2222.

Foreign Investment Advice Straight From the Experts

Your broker tells you that the hottest investment in town is selling computers in Bangladesh. Your first thought is that poor people can't afford computers.

What about your friend who wants you to go in on a company that's importing nylons from Poland? Since when are Polish women known for their beautiful legs? You can find out a great deal of information about these countries simply by making a phone call.

State Department Country Officers can provide current political, economic, and background information on marketing and business practices for every country in the world. Although they can't tell you whether your computer deal is going to fly, they can give you enough information to help you better weigh your options.

Write to the U.S. Department of State, Coordinator for Business Affairs, 2201 C St., NW, Washington, DC 20520; 202-647-1625.

Buyer Beware
of Mutual Funds

Before you sink your money into that hot
new biotechnology company, wouldn't you
like to know if it's being sued for patent or
copyright infringement? And what about
the CEO of that new software enterprise —
didn't you see him avoiding news cameras
a couple of years ago outside the
courthouse?

You can do a full background check on
any company that's offering public stock
simply by making a call to the Securities
and Exchange Commission. They can tell
you if a broker or brokerage firm is being
investigated, and can provide general
information about the federal securities
laws, as well as information on investor
inquiries and complaints. They have many
free publications available including, *Invest
Wisely: An Introduction To Mutual Funds*,
The Work of the SEC, and *What Every
Investor Should Know*.

Contact Securities and Exchange
Commission, Office of Consumer Affairs,
450 5th St., NW, Washington, DC 20549;
202-942-7040.

Silver and Gold

Pennies are twelve cents a dozen, but you passed first grade math so you already know that. Since then, your investment concerns have become a little more sophisticated than that, and

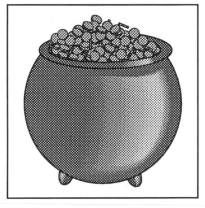

you now might find yourself looking into American Eagle Gold and Silver Bullion Coins produced by the U.S. Mint.

These gold coins are available in a variety of weights, while silver coins are minted only in a one ounce size. Check listings in your daily newspaper to find out current market value.

Coins may be purchased from brokerage companies, participating banks, coin dealers, and precious metal dealers. For a listing of sales locations in your area, write Customer Service, U.S. Mint, U.S. Department of the Treasury, 633 3rd St., NW, Washington, DC 20220, 202-283-COIN.

Know the Difference Between Junk Bonds and Junk Food?

Do people really invest in pork bellies? And if so, why don't you ever see people lined up in the supermarket waiting to buy them?

While the Commodities Futures Trading Commission (CFTC) may not be able to answer these sophisticated investment questions, they do offer several free booklets explaining how the commodities market operates.

Some of the titles they have include *Swindlers Are Calling*, *The CFTC*, *Before Trading Get the Facts*, and *Economic Purposes of Futures Trading*.

You can find out that commodity prices are tied to the weather, strikes, foreign exchange rates, and even storage factors. A small amount of money (the initial margin) controls a commodity futures contract worth a large amount of money.

The risk is high because a small change in the price of the commodity can either bring a large return on your money, or it can wipe out your initial margin and require that you immediately make additional margin payments. Follow that? Better get the publication yourself.

The CFTC will also send you a free copy of their annual report which includes a handy glossary of trading terms. For your copy, contact Commodities Futures Trading Commission, Office of Public Affairs, 3 Lafayette Center, 1155 21st St., NW, 9th Floor, Washington, DC 20581; 202-418-5080.

☆ ☆ ☆

Free Lesson on How To Buy a T-Bill

On the golf course, your investment adviser tells you that with interest rates what they are, maybe it's time to consider T-Bills, and he's not talking golf tees. Treasury bills, notes, and bonds are a way to invest in this country's future, he claims.

The T-Bill hotline provides general information on buying treasury bills, notes, and bonds, and can tell you how they can be purchased and when they will be auctioned. Contact Bureau of the Public Debt, U.S. Department of the Treasury, 13th and C Sts., SW, Washington, DC 20239-0001; 202-874-4000, ext. 231 and 232.

Is Your Bank Messing With Your Money?

Is Charles Keating or one of his friends sitting on your bank's Board of Directors? Before you and your friends make a run on the bank, you should check out how secure your savings are.

For example, many people have set up separate accounts to safeguard their money against bank failure, but unless they are under different types of ownership categories, such as single or joint ownership, the maximum limit per institution is $100,000. And you might not know that Treasury bonds or notes purchased through a particular institution are not covered by insurance.

The Federal Deposit Insurance Corporation's Office of Consumer Affairs answers questions and addresses complaints regarding FDIC regulated institutions and your FDIC insured deposit. A computerized system helps to track complaints from their initial filing to their resolution.

You can request information on financial reports and compliance of different institutions, as well as free brochures such as *Deposit Insurance* and *Consumer Protection*. The FDIC even publishes a quarterly newsletter which answers common questions, and informs you about what to do in the event of a problem.

Banking questions may be directed to your nearest regional FDIC office, or call the FDIC's toll-free hotline at 800-934-FDIC.

☆ ☆ ☆

Free Legal Help With a Franchise

Tipsy McSwiggers Restaurants claim to be the hottest franchise to come down the pike since McDonalds, and they are letting you in on the ground floor.

Before you get too flattered and lose your shirt, you should find out everything you can about this new business from the Franchise Hotline. They can tell you all the ins and outs of the franchise world and what you need to know to ask when you actually visit a couple of the franchises and talk to the owners.

Want to know what a franchise is required to disclose? Through this hotline you can find out which states have franchise laws and who you need to contact, as well as have an opportunity to discuss particulars with staff attorneys who helped write the franchise laws. Call Franchise Rule Information Hotline, Pennsylvania Ave. at 6th St., NW, Washington, DC 20580, 202-326-3128.

☆ ☆ ☆

When Your Banker Takes You To The Cleaners

Even though you have good credit and a good job, your bank won't give you a car loan because you're divorced. What if your bank makes unusual deductions from your bank account each month for maintenance charges you don't understand? What if you are having trouble with your bank issued credit card or mortgage?

Your State Banking Commissioner handles complaints about state-chartered banks doing business in their state. If you cannot resolve your problem with your bank, contact the Banking Commissioner and they will investigate for you. To locate your State Banking Commissioner, look in the Directory of State Information at the end of this book.

Money Lessons

If your bank tells you that they need to hold the amount of your Social Security check until the check clears, they are wrong. Certain checks, such as cashier's certified, or teller's checks, money orders, and electronic payments must be available on the next banking day from when they were deposited.

Teaching the grandkids about the value of money? Want to learn more about how bonds work? What about international economics? Or even consumer protection issues? The Federal Reserve has a free list of public information materials available from their various district offices. You can even learn about inflation, public debt, and macroeconomic data.

For your copy, contact Board of Governors of the Federal Reserve System,

Publications Service, MS-138, Washington, DC 20551; 202-452-3244.

☆ ☆ ☆

Free Financial Planning

Trying to live on a limited budget is never easy. Congress can't do it, but they somehow expect you to. With so many financial options available, it's not surprising that so many seniors are confused while trying to sort out the best financial plan. Your County Cooperative Extension Offices frequently have pamphlets or classes which can help you look at your bank book and savings, and make a plan you can live with.

For example, free publications in Ohio include *Estate Planning Considerations for Ohio Families*; *Evaluating Nursing Home Insurance*; *Financial Planning For Retirement*; and *Personal Property Inventory*.

To learn what your local office has to offer, look in the blue pages of your phone book for the office nearest you, or you can find the main state office in the Directory of State Information at the end of this book.

For more information, contact Cooperative State Research Education and Extension Service, U.S. Department of Agriculture, Room 3328, Washington, DC 20250; 202-720-3029.

☆ ☆ ☆

Funeral Home Funny Business

When you're planning a loved one's funeral, the last thing you want to worry about is whether or not you're being taken advantage of during this emotional time. But that's exactly what happens to hundreds of people each year.

You don't have to let that overly polite funeral director play upon your grief, and get you to spend more than you want. The Federal Trade Commission has a publication entitled *Caskets and Burial Vaults*, which helps you ask the right questions of the funeral home and points out issues which need to be addressed.

To receive your free copy, contact Public Reference, Room 130, Federal Trade Commission, Washington, DC 20580; 202-326-2222.

Make Sure You Have Credit Credibility

Securing credit is as important for older adults as it is for anyone else. Yet, older consumers, and particularly older women, may find they have special problems establishing credit.

For example, if you've paid for everything with cash all of your life, you may find it difficult to open a credit account, because you have "no credit history." If you now are living on a lower salary or pension, you may find it harder to obtain a loan because you have "insufficient income." Or, if your spouse dies, you may find that creditors try to close credit accounts that you and your spouse once shared.

To learn what legal rights and recourses you have, request the publication *Credit And Older Americans*, which explains the credit process, gives tips on establishing credit, and tells you what to do if you are denied credit.

To receive your free copy, contact Public Reference, Room 130, Federal Trade Commission, Washington, DC 20580; 202-326-2222.

Check Out Phony Charities

Starving children in Bolivia who won't live another day unless you give them the help they need today. It seems like every day someone calls or sends letters asking for donations for charity.

Don't fall for appeals, especially the ones over the phone that insist you send money right away. But it may be hard to decide who is most deserving.

There are several different organizations like the National Charities Information Bureau or the Philanthropic Advisory Service at the Council of the Better Business Bureau, where you can learn more about a particular charity's activities, finances, and fundraising practices.

The free publication *Charitable Giving* outlines steps you can take to check out any organization and make sure your money is put into good hands. For your copy, contact Public Reference, Room 130, Federal Trade Commission, Washington, DC 20580; 202-326-2222.

Take The Deduction

When you finally do find a good organization you'd like to donate money or gifts to, don't forget that you can take a tax deduction for that contribution. If you spend $50 to attend a special dinner for a cause, is the entire amount deductible? No, but part may be allowed.

What about if you pay $100 for a Golf for Gallstones benefit? Anything over and above the usual charge for golfing may be deductible.

Request the publication, *Charitable Contributions* (Publication 526), that explains which contributions you may deduct and what qualifies as a contribution. For your copy, contact the Internal Revenue Forms Line at 800-829-3676.

To get your copy, contact Public Reference, Room 130, Federal Trade Commission, Washington, DC 20580; 202-326-2222.

Information USA, Inc.

Free College Tuition For Seniors

NOTES

You're never too old to be the Big Man — or Big Woman — on Campus again, or get a degree in Renaissance art, or even carouse at a frat party. Don't waste any more time feeling nostalgic about how great it was to be a carefree student all those years ago. Or, if you never went to college in the first place, you can stop regretting it.

Believe it or not, more than 350 colleges and universities all across the country have special programs for seniors who are interested in going back to school. This often means free or low-cost tuition, discounts on fees and books, and even special deals on housing, if you feel like living in a dorm and blasting your Benny Goodman records to all hours of the night.

So why not go to college with your grandchildren? Sure, it will probably embarrass them to death, but you'll have loads of fun doing it, and at the same time...earn a diploma...graduate magna cum laude...or start a new business.

Maybe you never went to college because you couldn't stand doing homework. Even if that's still the case, you could still take an art appreciation class that requires only that you show up to a couple of times a week...or learn to swim...or draw nude women...or cook like a gourmet chef.

Tuition and basic fees for seniors are based on the lowest charged to all students (in-state, in-district, in-county, non-degree seeking, undergraduate etc.). Special fees may apply to some classes. Generally, lab, books and materials are additional, and vary depending upon the class. Some other additional fees include parking, health insurance, and a fee for degree seeking and graduate students.

Anyone interested should contact the school they wish to attend to find out how to apply for a discount or waiver. Some limitations and restrictions apply such as an income limit, residency, and space availability.

Alabama
Gadsden State Community
College
Admissions
P.O. Box 227
Gadsden, AL 35902-0227
205-549-8260
Minimum Age: 60
Tuition: free
Basic Fees: none
Credit: yes

Jefferson State Community
College
Admissions
2601 Carson Rd.
Birmingham, AL 35215-3098
205-853-1200
Minimum Age: 60
Tuition: free
Basic Fees: $4 per credit hour
Credit: yes

Livingston University
Station 2
Livingston, AL 35470
205-652-3400
Minimum Age: 55
Tuition: free
Basic Fees: $15 one time
application fee
Credit: no

University of Montevallo
Station 6065
Montevallo, AL 35115
205-665-6065
800-292-4349
Minimum Age: 65
Tuition: free
Basic Fees: $15 per class
Credit: no

Alaska
Prince William Sound
Community College
P.O. Box 97
Valdez, AK 99686
907-835-2678
Minimum Age: 60
Tuition: free
Basic Fees: $2.50 for 1-3
credit hours; $5 for 4-5 credit
hours; $25 for 7+ credit hours
Credit: yes

University of Alaska
Anchorage
Enrollment Services
3211 Providence Dr.
Anchorage, AK 99508
907-786-1525
Minimum Age: 60

Tuition: free
Basic Fees: $45 for 3 credit
hours; $57 for 6 credit hours
Credit: yes

University of Alaska Fairbanks
Admissions and Records
P.O. Box 757640
Fairbanks, AK 99775-0060
907-474-7821
Minimum Age: 60
Tuition: free
Basic Fees: $25 for 3 credit
hours; $155 for 12 credit
hours; parking and health
insurance can be waived if not
needed
Credit: yes

University of Alaska Southeast
11120 Glacier Hwy.
Juneau, AK 99801
907-465-6457
Minimum Age: 60
Tuition: free
Basic Fees: $5 for 1 credit
hour; $8 for 2 credit hours; $17
for 3+ credit hours
Credit: yes

Arizona
Arizona Western College
P.O. Box 929
Yuma, AZ 85366-0929
602-726-1050
Minimum Age: 60
Tuition: $16 per credit hour
Basic Fees: none
Credit: yes

Central Arizona College
Student Records
8470 North Overfield Rd.
Coolidge, AZ 85228
602-426-4444
Minimum Age: 60
Tuition: $18 per credit hour
with the 6th, 16th, 17th and
18th free
Basic Fees: none
Credit: yes

Arkansas
Arkansas State University
Admissions
P.O. Box 1630
State University
Jonesboro, AR 72467-1630
800-382-3030
Minimum Age: 60
Tuition: free
Basic Fees: $4 per credit hour
Credit: yes

Arkansas State University:
Beebe Branch
P.O. Drawer H
Beebe, AR 72012
501-882-6452
Minimum Age: 60
Tuition: free
Basic Fees: none (auto sticker
$5)
Credit: yes

Arkansas Tech University
Admissions
Russelville, AR 72801-2222
501-968-0343
Minimum Age: 60

Tuition: free
Basic Fees: none
Credit: yes

East Arkansas Community
College
1700 Newcastle Rd.
Forest City, AR 72335-9598
501-633-4480
Minimum Age: 62
Tuition: free
Basic Fees: $3 per credit hour
Credit: yes

Garland County Community
College
100 College Dr.
P.O. 3470
Hot Springs, AR 71914-3470
501-767-9371
Minimum Age: 60
Tuition: free
Basic Fees: $10 per session
Credit: yes

Henderson State University
Registrar
P.O. Box 7534
Arkadelphia, AR 71999-7534
501-246-5511
Minimum Age: 60
Tuition: free
Basic Fees: $36 for 3 credit
hours
Credit: yes

Northern Arkansas Community
College
Pioneer Ridge
Harrison, AR 72601
501-743-3000

Minimum Age: 60
Tuition: free
Basic Fees: none
Credit: yes

Phillips County Community
College
Campus Dr.
P.O. Box 785
Helena, AR 72342
501-338-6474
Minimum Age: 60
Tuition: free
Basic Fees: none
Credit: yes

California

California State University -
Sacramento
Re-Entry Services
6000 J St.
Sacramento, CA 95819-6048
916-278-6750
Minimum Age: 60
Tuition: $3 per session
Basic Fees: none (students
receive free public
transportation in the
Sacramento area)
Credit: yes

Colorado

Adams State College
Alamosa, CO 81102
719-589-7712
Minimum Age: 65
Tuition: free
Basic Fees: none
Credit: no

Colorado Mountain College:
Alpine Campus
1330 Bob Adams Dr.
Steamboat Springs, CO 80487
303-879-3288
Minimum Age: 62
Tuition: 50% off (regular tuition
$32 per credit hour)
Basic Fees: $50 for 0-9 credit
hours; $65 for 12+ credit hours
Credit: yes

Colorado State University
Admissions and Records
Administrative Annex Bldg.
Ft. Collins, CO 80523
303-491-6909
Minimum Age: 62
Tuition: free
Basic Fees: none
Credit: no

Metropolitan State College of
Denver
Adult Learning Services
P.O. Box 173362
Denver, CO 80217
303-556-8342
Minimum Age: 62
Tuition: free
Basic Fees: none
Credit: no

University of Colorado, Boulder
Regent Administrative Center
125
Office of Admissions
Campus Box 6
Boulder, CO 80309
303-492-6301
Minimum Age: 55

Tuition: member of alumni $5
per session; non-alumni
member $15 per session
Basic Fees: none
Credit: no

University of Colorado at
Denver
P.O. Box 173364
Campus Box 146
Denver, CO 80217-3364
303-556-2400
Minimum Age: 60
Tuition: free
Basic Fees: none
Credit: no

University of Northern
Colorado
Registration Center
Greeley, CO 80639
303-351-2881
Minimum Age: 60
Tuition: free
Basic Fees: none
Credit: no

Connecticut

Asnuntuck Community College
Admissions
170 Elm St.
Enfield, CT 06082
203-253-3043
Minimum Age: 62
Tuition: free
Basic Fees: none (lab fee also
waived)
Credit: yes

Central Connecticut State
University
Admissions Office
1615 Stanley St.
New Britain, CT 06050
203-827-7422
Minimum Age: 62
Tuition: free
Basic Fees: $37 per semester
Credit: yes

Eastern Connecticut State
University
Registrar
83 Windham St.
Willimantic, CT 06226
203-465-5389
Minimum Age: 62
Tuition: free
Basic Fees: $12 per credit
hour for part-time
Credit: yes

University of Connecticut,
Storrs
Box U-88
28 N. Eagleville Rd.
Storrs, CT 06269-3088
203-486-3137
Minimum Age: 62
Tuition: free
Basic Fees: $222 full-time per
semester
Credit: yes

University of Hartford
Adult Services
200 Bloomfield Ave.
West Hartford, CT 06117-0395
203-768-4457
Minimum Age: 70

Tuition: free
Basic Fees: $30 per semester
(1 class limit)
Credit: no

Western Connecticut State
University
Office of Continuing Education
181 White St.
Danbury, CT 006810
203-837-8230
Minimum Age: 62
Tuition: $10 per semester
(non-credit $10 per class)
Basic Fees: Part-time none
(full-time varies)
Credit: yes

Delaware

Delaware State College
Admissions
1200 N. Dupont Hwy.
Dover, DE 19901
302-739-4917
Minimum Age: 62
Tuition: free
Basic Fees: $25 per semester
Credit: yes

Delaware Technical and
Community College:
Southern Campus
P.O. Box 610
Georgetown, DE 19947
302-856-5400
Minimum Age: 60
Tuition: free
Basic Fees: none
Credit: yes

Delaware Technical and
Community College:
Stanton/Wilmington Campus
333 Shipley St.
Wilmington, DE 19801
302 571 5343
Minimum Age: 60
Tuition: free
Basic Fees: none
Credit: yes

Delaware Technical and
Community College:
Terry Campus
1832 N. Dupont Pkwy.
Dover, DE 19901
302-739-5412
Minimum Age: 60
Tuition: free
Basic Fees: none
Credit: yes

District of Columbia

University of the District of
Columbia
1100 Harvard St., Room 114
Washington, DC 20008
202-274-5010
Minimum Age: 65
Tuition: free (50% off if going
for a degree)
Basic Fees: $20 per semester
Credit: yes

Florida

Broward Community College,
Ft. Lauderdale
Registration
225 E. Lasolas Blvd.

Ft. Lauderdale, FL 33301
305-761-7465
Minimum Age: 65
Tuition: free
Basic Fees: the school will
cover up to $181.50 of basic
fees
Credit: yes

Florida Atlantic University
500 Northwest 20th St.
Boca Raton, FL 33431-0991
407-367-3294
Minimum Age: 60
Tuition: free
Basic Fees: none
Credit: no

Florida International University
University Park
Miami, FL 33199
305-348-2363
Minimum Age: 60
Tuition: free
Basic Fees: none
Credit: no

Florida State University
216 WJB
Tallahassee, FL 32306-1009
904-644-6200
Minimum Age: 62
Tuition: free
Basic Fees: none
Credit: no

Santa Fe Community College
P.O. Box 1530
3000 NW 83rd St.
Gainesville, FL 32602
904-395-5443

Minimum Age: 60
Tuition: free
Basic Fees: none
Credit: yes

University of Central Florida
P.O. Box 160111
Orlando, FL 32816-0111
407-823-3000
Minimum Age: 60
Tuition: free
Basic Fees: none
Credit: no

Georgia
Albany State College
504 College Dr.
Albany, GA 31705
912-430-4650
Minimum Age: 62
Tuition: free
Basic Fees: $10 per session
Credit: yes

Armstrong State College
11935 Abercorn St.
Savannah, GA 31419
800-633-2349
Minimum Age: 62
Tuition: free
Basic Fees: $10 per session
Credit: yes

Athens Area Technical Institute
US Highway 29 North
Athens, GA 30610-3099
706-542-8050
Minimum Age: 62
Tuition: free
Basic Fees: $12.50 per quarter
Credit: yes

Bainbridge College
Highway 84 East
Bainbridge, GA 31717
912-248-2500
Minimum Age: 62
Tuition: froo
Basic Fees: none
Credit: yes

Brunswick College
Admissions
3700 Altama Ave.
Brunswick, GA 31520-3644
912-264-7253
Minimum Age: 62
Tuition: free
Basic Fees: none
Credit: yes

Clayton State College
Admissions/Registrar
P.O. Box 285
Morrow, GA 30260
404-961-3400
Minimum Age: 62
Tuition: free
Basic Fees: none
Credit: yes

Columbus College
4225 University Ave.
Columbus, GA 31907-5645
706-568-2035
Minimum Age: 62
Tuition: free
Basic Fees: none
Credit: yes

Georgia College
Admissions and Records
Campus Box 023

Milledgeville, GA 31061
912-453-5004
Minimum Age: 62
Tuition: free
Basic Fees: none
Credit: yes

Georgia Southern University
Admissions
Landrum Box 8024
Statesboro, GA 30460-8024
912-681-5531
Minimum Age: 62
Tuition: free
Basic Fees: none
Credit: yes

Georgia Southwestern College
800 Wheatly St.
Americus, GA 31709-4693
912-928-1273
Minimum Age: 62
Tuition: free
Basic Fees: none
Credit: yes

Georgia State University
P.O. Box 4009
Atlanta, GA 30302-4009
404-651-2365
Minimum Age: 62
Tuition: free
Basic Fees: $82 per quarter
Credit: yes

Hawaii
University of Hawaii: Hawaii
Community College
200 West Kawili St.
Hilo, HI 96720

808-933-3611
Minimum Age: 60
Tuition: free (no summer
classes)
Basic Fees: none
Credit: yes

University of Hawaii: Honolulu
Community College
874 Dillingham Blvd.
Honolulu, HI 96817
808-845-9129
Minimum Age: 60
Tuition: free
Basic Fees: $10 per semester
Credit: yes

University of Hawaii: Kapiolani
Community College
4303 Diamond Head Rd.
Honolulu, HI 96816
808-734-9559
Minimum Age: 60
Tuition: free
Basic Fees: $10 per semester
Credit: yes

University of Hawaii: Kauai
Community College
3-1901 Kaomualii Hwy.
Lihue, HI 96766
808-245-8212
Minimum Age: 60
Tuition: free
Basic Fees: none
Credit: yes

University of Hawaii: Leeward
Community College
96-045 Ala Ike
Pearl City, HI 96782

808-455-0217
Minimum Age: 60
Tuition: free
Basic Fees: none
Credit: yes

University of Hawaii at Manoa
2530 Dole St.
Room C-200
Honolulu, HI 96822
808-956-8975
Minimum Age: 60
Tuition: free
Basic Fees: none
Credit: yes

University of Hawaii: Maui
Community College
310 Kaahumanu Ave.
Kahului, HI 96732
808-244-9181
Minimum Age: 60
Tuition: free
Basic Fees: $4 per session
plus .50 cents per credit hour
Credit: yes

University of Hawaii: West
Oahu
96-043 Ala Ike
Pearl City, HI 96782
808-456-5921
Minimum Age: 65
Tuition: free
Basic Fees: none
Credit: yes

University of Hawaii: Windward
Community College
45-720 Keaahala Rd.

Kaneohe, HI 96744
808-235-7432
Minimum Age: 60
Tuition: free
Basic Fees: none
Credit: yes

Idaho
Boise State University
1910 University Dr.
Boise, ID 83725
800-824-7017
Minimum Age: 60
Tuition: $5 per credit hour
Basic Fees: $20 per semester
Credit: yes

College of Southern Idaho
Admissions
P.O. Box 1238
Twin Falls, ID 83303-1238
208-733-9554
Minimum Age: 60
Tuition: free
Basic Fees: none
Credit: yes

Idaho State University
Enrollment Planning
Campus Box 8054
Pocatello, ID 83209
208-236-2123
Minimum Age: 60
Tuition: $5 per credit hour
Basic Fees: $20 per semester
Credit: yes

Lewis Clark State College
500 Eighth Ave.
Lewiston, ID 83501

208-799-5272
Minimum Age: 60
Tuition: $5 per credit hour
Basic Fees: $20 per semester
Credit: yes

North Idaho College
Business Office
1000 West Garden Ave.
Coeur d'Alene, ID 83814
208-769-3311
Minimum Age: 60
Tuition: 50% off (regular tuition
$50 per credit hour)
Basic Fees: $130 full-time
Credit: yes

Illinois
Belleville Area College
2500 Carlyle Rd.
Belleville, IL 62221
618-235-2700
Minimum Age: 60
Tuition: $2 per credit hour
Basic Fees: $10 one time
application fee
Credit: yes

Chicago State University
95th St. and King Dr.
Chicago, IL 60628
312-995-2513
Minimum Age: 65
Tuition: free (income limitation
of $12,000 annually)
Basic Fees: none (lab also
waived)
Credit: yes

College of Du Page
22nd St. and Lambert Rd.
Glen Ellyn, IL 60137
708-858-2800 ext. 2482
Minimum Age: 65
Tuition: $3.25 per credit hour
Basic Fees: none
Credit: yes

Illinois State University
Adult Services
Campus Box 4060
Normal, IL 61790-4060
309-438-2181
Minimum Age: 65
Tuition: free
Basic Fees: none
Credit: no

Northern Illinois University
Office of Admissions
101 Williston Hall
Dekalb, IL 60115-2857
815-753-0446
Minimum Age: 65
Tuition: free (income limitation
of $14,000 annually)
Basic Fees: $20-$40 per
session
Credit: yes

Indiana

Ball State University
Office of Admission
Lucina Hall
Muncie, IN 47306
317-285-8300
Minimum Age: 60
Tuition: 50% off (regular tuition
$430 for 0-3 credit hours; $574

for 4-5 credit hours; $906 for
6-8 credit hours)
Basic Fees: none
Credit: yes

Indiana University at Kokomo
P.O. Box 9003
Kokomo, IN 46904-9003
317-453-2000
Minimum Age: 60
Tuition: 50% off up to 9 hours
(regular tuition $78.95 per
credit hour)
Basic Fees: $15 maximum
activity fee plus $2 per credit
hour
Credit: yes

Indiana University-Purdue
University at Fort Wayne
Financial Aid
2101 Coliseum Blvd., East
Fort Wayne, IN 46805
219-481-6820
Minimum Age: 60
Tuition: 50% off (regular tuition
$80.25 per credit hour)
Basic Fees: none
Credit: yes

Indiana University Southeast
4201 Grant Line Rd.
New Albany, IN 47150
812-941-2212 ext. 2335
Minimum Age: 60
Tuition: 50% off up to 9 hours
(regular tuition $363 for 9
credit hours)
Basic Fees: none
Credit: yes

University of Southern Indiana
8600 University Blvd.
Evansville, IN 47712
812-464-1765
Minimum Age: 60
Tuition: $5 per class
Basic Fees: $10 ID fee per session
Credit: yes

Iowa

Clinton Community College
Enrollment Services
1000 Lincoln Blvd.
Clinton, IA 52732-6299
319-242-6841
Minimum Age: 62
Tuition: $3.65 per semester hour
Basic Fees: $5.50 per hour
Credit: yes

Des Moines Area Community College
Records and Services
2006 South Ankeny Blvd.
Ankeny, IA 50021
515-964-6241
Minimum Age: 65
Tuition: free
Basic Fees: none
Credit: yes

Indian Hills Community College
Admissions
525 Grandview St.
Ottumwa, IA 52501
515-683-5153
Minimum Age: 62

Tuition: 50% off (regular tuition $40 per credit hour)
Basic Fees: $4.50 per credit hour
Credit: yes

Iowa Western Community College
Business
923 East Washington St.
Clarinda, IA 51632
712-542-5117
Minimum Age: 55
Tuition: $15 per credit hour (3 credit hour limit per semester)
Basic Fees: $15 one time application fee plus $6 per credit hour
Credit: yes

Kansas

Allen County Community College
1801 North Cottonwood St.
Iola, KS 66749
316-365-5116
Minimum Age: 60
Tuition: $26 per credit hour (book rental and fees are free)
Basic Fees: none
Credit: yes

Barton County Community College
Registrar
Rt. 3
Great Bend, KS 67530-9283
316-792-2701 ext. 215
Minimum Age: 65
Tuition: free

Basic Fees: $10 per credit
hour
Credit: yes

Butler County Community
College
901 South Haverhill Rd.
Eldorado, KS 67042
316-321-2222
Minimum Age: 60
Tuition: free
Basic Fees: $10 per credit
hour
Credit: yes

Cloud County Community
College
221 Campus Dr.
P.O. Box 1002
Concordia, KS 66901-1002
913-234-1435
Minimum Age: 55
Tuition: $24 per credit hour
Basic Fees: none
Credit: yes

Coffeyville Community College
400 West 11th
Coffeyville, KS 67337
316-251-7700
Minimum Age: 60
Tuition: free
Basic Fees: $10 per credit
hour
Credit: yes

Emporia State University
Admissions
1200 Commercial
Emporia, KS 66801-5087
316-341-5465

Minimum Age: 60
Tuition: free
Basic Fees: none
Credit: no

Fort Hays State University
600 Park St.
Hays, KS 67601-4099
913-628-4222
Minimum Age: 60
Tuition: free
Basic Fees: none
Credit: no

Garden City Community
College
Dean of Admissions
801 Campus Dr.
Garden City, KS 67846
316-276-7611
Minimum Age: 65
Tuition: free
Basic Fees: $7 per credit hour
Credit: yes

Hutchinson Community
College
1300 North Plum St.
Hutchinson, KS 67501
316-665-3535
Minimum Age: 60
Tuition: $21 per credit hour
Basic Fees: none
Credit: yes

Kentucky
Ashland Community College
1400 College Dr.
Ashland, KY 41101
606-329-2999

Minimum Age: 65
Tuition: free
Basic Fees: none
Credit: yes

Eastern Kentucky University
Coates Box 2A
203 Jones Building
Richmond, KY 40475-3101
606-622-2106
Minimum Age: 65
Tuition: free
Basic Fees: none
Credit: yes

Elizabethtown Community
College
600 College Street Rd.
Elizabethtown, KY 42701
502-769-1632
Minimum Age: 65
Tuition: free
Basic Fees: none
Credit: yes

Lexington Community College
203 Oswald Bldg., Cooper Dr.
Lexington, KY 40506-0235
606-257-4872
Minimum Age: 65
Tuition: free
Basic Fees: none
Credit: yes

Madisonville Community
College
2000 College Dr.
Madisonville, KY 42431
502-821-2250
Minimum Age: 65
Tuition: free

Basic Fees: none
Credit: yes

Maysville Community College
1755 US 68
Maysville, KY 41056
606-759-7141
Minimum Age: 65
Tuition: free
Basic Fees: none
Credit: yes

Morehead State University
202 Howell McDowell
Morehead, KY 40351
606-783-2000
Minimum Age: 65
Tuition: free
Basic Fees: none
Credit: yes

Murray State University
Bursars Office
P.O. Box 9
Murray, KY 42071-0009
502-762-3741
800-272-4678
Minimum Age: 65
Tuition: free
Basic Fees: none
Credit: yes

Northern Kentucky University
Office of Admissions
Highland Heights, KY 41099
606-572-5220
800-637-9948
Minimum Age: 65
Tuition: free
Basic Fees: none
Credit: yes

University of Kentucky
100 Funkhouser Bldg.
Lexington, KY 40506-0054
606-257-2000
Minimum Age: 65
Tuition: free
Basic Fees: none
Credit: yes

University of Louisville
Admission AO
University of Louisville
Louisville, KY 40292
502-852-6531
Minimum Age: 65
Tuition: free (10% off non-academic)
Basic Fees: none
Credit: yes

Louisiana
Delgado Community College
615 City Park Ave.
New Orleans, LA 70119
504-483-4114
Minimum Age: 60
Tuition: 3 credit hours free per semester
Basic Fees: $15 per semester
Credit: yes

Grambling State University
P.O. Box 864
Grambling, LA 71245
318-274-2435
Minimum Age: 65
Tuition: free
Basic Fees: $15 per semester
Credit: yes

Louisiana State University and
Agricultural and Mechanical
College
Records and Registration
112 Thomas Boyd Hall
Baton Rouge, LA 70803
504-388-1175
Minimum Age: 65
Tuition: free
Basic Fees: none
Credit: yes

Louisiana State University at
Alexandria
Financial Aid
8100 Highway 71 South
Alexandria, LA 71302-9633
318-473-6423
Minimum Age: 65
Tuition: free
Basic Fees: none
Credit: yes

Louisiana State University -
Baton Rouge
Office of Admissions
Room 110 Thomas Boyd Hall
Baton Rouge, LA 70803
504-388-1175
Minimum Age: 65
Tuition: free
Basic Fees: none
Credit: yes

Louisiana State University at
Eunice
P.O. Box 1129
Eunice, LA 70535
318-457-7311
Minimum Age: 65
Tuition: free

Basic Fees: $10 per semester
Credit: yes

Louisiana State University in
Shreveport
Admissions and Records
One University Place
Shreveport, LA 71115
318-797-5207
Minimum Age: 65
Tuition: free
Basic Fees: $50 for part-time;
$65 for full-time
Credit: yes

Louisiana Tech University
P.O. Box 7924
Tech Station
Ruston, LA 71272
318-257-3036
Minimum Age: 65
Tuition: 1 class per quarter
free
Basic Fees: $20 per quarter
Credit: yes

McNeese State University
P.O. Box 92935
Lake Charles, LA 70609
318-475-5000
Minimum Age: 60
Tuition: 3 credit hours free per
semester
Basic Fees: $10 per semester
Credit: yes

Nicholls State University
P.O. Box 2004
College Station
Thibodaux, LA 70310
504-448-4139

Minimum Age: 62
Tuition: 3 credit hours free per
semester
Basic Fees: $10 per semester
Credit: yes

Northeast Louisiana University
Student Affairs
Office of the Registrar
Monroe, LA 71209-1710
318-342-5252
Minimum Age: 60
Tuition: 3 credit hours free per
semester
Basic Fees: $15 per semester
Credit: yes

Northwestern State University
Fiscal Affairs
Cashier Section
Natchitoches, LA 71497
318-357-4503
Minimum Age: 60
Tuition: 3 credit hours free per
semester
Basic Fees: $5 one time
application fee
Credit: yes

Southeastern Louisiana
University
Enrollment Services
P.O. Drawer 752
Hammond, LA 70402-0752
504-549-2123
Minimum Age: 60
Tuition: 3 credit hours free per
semester
Basic Fees: $10 per semester
Credit: yes

Maine

University of Maine
Admissions
Chadbourne Hall
Orono, ME 04469
207-581-1561
Minimum Age: 65
Tuition: free
Basic Fees: $9 for 3 credit
hours; $246.50 for 12 credit
hours
Credit: yes

University of Maine at Augusta
Admissions
46 University Dr.
Augusta, ME 04330
207-621-3020
Minimum Age: 65
Tuition: free
Basic Fees: $4.50 per credit
hour
Credit: yes

University of Maine at
Farmington
102 Main St.
Farmington, ME 04938
207-778-7052
Minimum Age: 65
Tuition: case-by-case basis
Basic Fees: case-by-case
basis
Credit: yes

University of Maine at Fort
Kent
Admissions
25 Pleasant St.
Fort Kent, ME 04743
207-834-7500

Minimum Age: 65
Tuition: free (2 course limit)
Basic Fees: $20 for 6 credit
hours
Credit: yes

Maryland

Alleghany Community College
Continuing Education
Willow Brook Rd.
Cumberland, MD 21502
301-724-7700
Minimum Age: 60
Tuition: free (non-academic
only)
Basic Fees: up to $3 per
course
Credit: no

Baltimore City Community
College
Registration
2901 Liberty Heights Ave.
Baltimore, MD 21215
410-333-5393
Minimum Age: 60
Tuition: free
Basic Fees: $20 per credit
hour (non-credit $10 per
course)
Credit: yes

Bowie State University
Human Resources
14000 Jericho Park
Bowie, MD 20715
301-464-6515
Minimum Age: 62
Tuition: free
Basic Fees: $83.50 for 0-11

credit hours; $369 for 12+
credit hours
Credit: yes

Coppin State College
Human Resources
2500 W. North Ave.
Baltimore, MD 21216
410-383-5990
Minimum Age: 60
Tuition: free
Basic Fees: part-time $47 plus
$8 per credit hour; $333 for 12
credit hours
Credit: yes

Frostburg State University
Admissions
Frostburg, MD 21532-1099
301-689-4201
Minimum Age: 60
Tuition: free (3 course limit)
Basic Fees: 9 credit hours
approximately $115
Credit: yes

Salisbury State University
Human Resources
Camden and College Avenues
Salisbury, MD 21801-6862
410-543-6035
Minimum Age: 60
Tuition: free (2 course limit)
Basic Fees: 6 credit hours
approximately $18
Credit: yes

St. Mary's College of Maryland
Admission
St. Mary's City, MD 20686
301-862-0292

Minimum Age: 65
Tuition: free
Basic Fees: $230 for 9-11
credit hours
Credit: yes

University of Maryland -
College Park
Golden ID Program
College Park, MD 20742
301-314-8237
Minimum Age: 65 (60 if
employed less than 20 hours
per week)
Tuition: $103.50 per semester
(3 class limit per semester)
Basic Fees: $30 one time
application fee
Credit: yes

Massachusetts
Berkshire Community College
1350 West St.
Pittsfield, MA 01201
413-499-4660
Minimum Age: 60
Tuition: free
Basic Fees: $25 per credit
hour
Credit: yes

Boston University
881 Commonwealth Ave.
6th Floor
Boston, MA 02215
617-353-2300
Minimum Age: 60
Tuition: $20 per course
Basic Fees: none
Credit: no

Bridgewater State College
Gates House
Bridgewater, MA 02325
508-697-1237
Minimum Age: 60
Tuition: free
Basic Fees: $201.42 for 3
credit hours; $491.25 for 12
credit hours
Credit: yes

Briston Community College
777 Elsbree St.
Fall River, MA 02720
508-678-2811
Minimum Age: 60
Tuition: $42 for 3 credit hours,
$55 for 4 credit hours
Basic Fees: none
Credit: yes

Bunker Hill Community College
250 New Rutherford Ave.
Boston, MA 02129-2991
617-241-228-2000
Minimum Age: 60
Tuition: free
Basic Fees: $35/credit hour
Credit: yes

Cape Cod Community College
Rt. 132
West Barnstable, MA 02668-
1599
508-362-2131
Minimum Age: 60
Tuition: free (one credit class
per semester)
Basic Fees: $138 for 3 credit
hours
Credit: yes

Salem State College
352 Lafayette St.
Salem, MA 01970
508-741-6200
Minimum Age: 60
Tuition: free
Basic Fees: $61 per credit
hour; full-time $743.50
Credit: yes

North Adams State College
Admissions
Church St.
North Adams, MA 01247
413-664-4511
Minimum Age: 65
Tuition: free
Basic Fees: none
Credit: yes

Michigan

Alpena Community College
666 Johnson St.
Alpena, MI 49707
517-356-9021
Minimum Age: 60
Basic Fees: $10 per session
plus $6 per credit hour
Tuition: free
Credit: yes

Central Michigan University
Admissions
105 Warriner Hall
Mount Pleasant, MI 48859
517-774-3076
Minimum Age: 60
Tuition: free
Basic Fees: none
Credit: no

Charles Stewart Mott
Community College
1401 East Court St.
Flint, MI 48503
810-762-0200
Minimum Age: 60
Tuition: free (50% off non-academic)
Basic Fees: none
Credit: yes

Delta College
Admissions
University Center, MI 48710
517-686-9092
Minimum Age: 60
Tuition: 50% off (regular tuition $65 per credit hour)
Basic Fees: $25 per session
Credit: yes

Glen Oaks Community College
62249 Shimmel Rd.
Centreville, MI 49032
616-467-9945
Minimum Age: 60
Tuition: free
Basic Fees: none
Credit: yes

Macomb Community College
2800 College Dr., SW
Sidney, MI 48885-0300
517-328-2111 ext. 215
Minimum Age: 60
Tuition: in-district free; out-of-district $22 per credit hour
Basic Fees: $1.50 per credit hour
Credit: yes

Oakland Community College
District Office
George AB
Administration Center
2480 Opdyke Rd.
Bloomfield Hills, MI 48304-2266
810-540-1567
Minimum Age: 60
Tuition: 20% off (regular tuition $47 per credit hour)
Basic Fees: $35 per session
Credit: yes

Wayne State University
Office of Undergraduate Admission
Detroit, MI 48202
313-577-3577
Minimum Age: 60
Tuition: 50% off (regular tuition $98 per credit hour)
Basic Fees: $70 per semester
Credit: yes

Western Michigan University
Office of Admission and Orientation
Kalamazoo, MI 49008-5120
616-387-2000
Minimum Age: 62
Tuition: free
Basic Fees: none
Credit: no

University of Michigan - Ann Arbor
515 East Jefferson
1220 Student Activities
Ann Arbor, MI 48109-1316
313-764-7433

Minimum Age: 65
Tuition: 50% off (regular tuition full-time $2,500)
Basic Fees: $87 per term
Credit: yes

Minnesota

Anoka-Ramsey Community College
11200 Mississippi Blvd., NW
Coon Rapids, MN 55433
612-427-2600
Minimum Age: 62
Tuition: $6 per credit hour
Basic Fees: $15 per session plus $1 per credit hour
Credit: yes

Austin Community College
1600 Eighth Ave., NW
Austin, MN 55912
507-433-0535
Minimum Age: 62
Tuition: $6 per credit hour
Basic Fees: 0-7 credit hours free; 8+ credit hours $15 plus $2 per credit hour
Credit: yes

Bemidji State University
1500 Birchmont Dr., NE
Bemidji, MN 56601
218-755-2040
Minimum Age: 62
Tuition: $6 per credit hour
Basic Fees: $15 per session
Credit: yes

Brainerd Community College
501 West College Dr.

Brainerd, MN 56401
218-828-2508
Minimum Age: 62
Tuition: $6 per credit hour
Basic Fees: $15 per session plus $2 per credit hour
Credit: yes

Fergus Falls Community College
1414 College Way
Fergus Falls, MN 56537
218-739-7501
Minimum Age: 62
Tuition: $6 per credit hour
Basic Fees: 0-7 credit hours free; 8+ credit hours $15 plus $3 per credit hour
Credit: yes

Hibbing Community College
1515 East 25th St.
Hibbing, MN 55746
218-262-6700
Minimum Age: 62
Tuition: $6 per credit hour
Basic Fees: 0-7 credit hours free; 8+ credit hours $15 plus $2 per credit hour
Credit: yes

Minnesota Universities - Twin Cities
Room 240, Pillsbury Dr., SE
Minneapolis, MN 55455
800-752-1000
Minimum Age: 62
Tuition: $6 per credit hour
Basic Fees: none
Credit: yes

Mississippi

Copiah-Lincoln Community
College
Financial Aid Office
P.O. Box 649
Wesson, MS 39191
601-643-8307
Minimum Age: 65
Tuition: free
Basic Fees: none
Credit: yes

Delta State University
Registrar
Cleveland, MS 38733
601-846-4656
Minimum Age: 60
Tuition: $10 for 1 course up to
3 credit hours
Basic Fees: none
Credit: yes

East Central Community
College
Admissions
Decatur, MS 39327
601-635-2111
Minimum Age: 65
Tuition: free
Basic Fees: none
Credit: yes

Holmes Community College
P.O. Box 369
Goodman, MS 39079
601-472-2312
Minimum Age: 65
Tuition: free
Basic Fees: none
Credit: yes

Itawamba Community College
Admissions
602 W. Hill St.
Fulton, MS 38843
601-862-3101
Minimum Age: 65
Tuition: free
Basic Fees: none
Credit: yoo

Jones County Junior College
Guidance Office
900 South Court St.
Ellisville, MS 39437
601-477-4025
Minimum Age: 65
Tuition: free
Basic Fees: none
Credit: yes

Meridian Community College
910 Highway 19 North
Meridian, MS 39307
601-483-8241
Minimum Age: 65
Tuition: $2.50 per class
Basic Fees: none
Credit: yes

Mississippi Gulf Coast
Community College: Jackson
County Campus
Business Services
P.O. Box 100
Gautier, MS 39553
601-497-9602
Minimum Age: 65 (62-64 also
qualify if retired)
Tuition: free
Basic Fees: none
Credit: yes

Missouri

Crowder College
601 LaClede Ave.
Neosho, MO 64850
417-451-3223
Minimum Age: 60
Tuition: free
Basic Fees: $12 per credit hour
Credit: yes

East Central College
Registration
P.O. Box 529
Union, MO 63048
314-583-5193
Minimum Age: 60
Tuition: free
Basic Fees: none
Credit: yes

Jefferson College
Continuing Education
1000 Viking Dr.
Hillsboro, MO 63050
314-789-3951
Minimum Age: 60
Tuition: 50% off (regular tuition $38 per credit hour)
Basic Fees: $1 for a Lifetime Card
Credit: no

Lincoln University
820 Chestnut St.
Jefferson City, MO 65102
314-681-5000
Minimum Age: 60
Tuition: $12 per course
Basic Fees: $17 per session
Credit: no

Longview Community College
500 Longview Rd.
Lee's Summit, MO 64081
816-672-2000
Minimum Age: 65
Tuition: free
Basic Fees: none
Credit: yes

Maple Woods Community College
Development Center
2601 Northeast Barry Rd.
Kansas City, MO 64156
816-437-3050
Minimum Age: 65
Tuition: free
Basic Fees: none
Credit: yes

Missouri Southern State College
Business Office
3950 East Newman Rd.
Joplin, MO 64801-1595
417-625-9300
Minimum Age: 60
Tuition: free
Basic Fees: none
Credit: yes

Missouri Western State College
4525 Downs Dr.
St. Joseph, MO 64507
816-271-4200
Minimum Age: 60
Tuition: free
Basic Fees: none
Credit: yes

Moberly Area Community
College
Financial Aid Office
College Ave. and Rollins St.
Moberly, MO 65270
816-263-4110
Minimum Age: 60
Tuition: free
Basic Fees: none
Credit: yes

St. Louis Community College
Office of Admission
11333 Big Bend Blvd.
Kirkwood, MO 63122
314-984-7601
Minimum Age: 62
Tuition: 50% off (regular tuition
$40 per credit hour)
Basic Fees: none
Credit: yes

Montana

Dawson Community College
Business Office
300 College Dr.
Glendive, MT 59330
406-365-3396
Minimum Age: 60
Tuition: free
Basic Fees: none (most books
can be borrowed)
Credit: yes

Flathead Valley Community
College
777 Grandview Dr.
Kalispell, MT 59901
406-756-3846
Minimum Age: 62

Tuition: $30.25 per credit hour
Basic Fees: none
Credit: yes

Fort Belknap College
P.O. Box 159
Harlem, MT 59526
406-353-2607
Minimum Age: 55 (must be a
member of a federally
recognized tribe)
Tuition: free
Basic Fees: none
Credit: yes

Fort Peck Community College
P.O. Box 398
Poplar, MT 59255
406-768-5551
Minimum Age: 60
Tuition: free
Basic Fees: $12 per credit
hour
Credit: yes

Miles Community College
2715 Dickinson St.
Miles City, MT 59301
406-232-3031
Minimum Age: 62
Tuition: free
Basic Fees: none
Credit: yes

Montana College of Mineral
Science and Technology
1300 West Park St.
Butte, MT 59701
406-496-4178
800-445-8324
Minimum Age: 62

Tuition: free
Basic Fees: $26.25 for 3 credit
hours; $171 for 12 credit hours
Credit: yes

Northern Montana College
P.O. Box 7751
Havre, MT 59501
406-265-3700
Minimum Age: 62
Tuition: free
Basic Fees: $80.25 for 3 credit
hours
Credit: yes

Western Montana College at
the University of Montana
Continuing Education
710 South Atlantic
Dillon, MT 59725
406-683-7537
Minimum Age: 62
Tuition: 1 credit hour $20; $3
for each additional credit hour
Basic Fees: $30
Credit: yes

University of Montana
Missoula, MT 59812
406-243-8636
Minimum Age: 62
Tuition: all state supported
costs waived (80% fee waiver)
Basic Fees: $30 one time fee
Credit: yes

Nebraska
Chadron State College
Admissions
1000 Main St.

Chadron, NE 69337
308-432-6263
Minimum Age: 62
Tuition: free
Basic Fees: $35 for 3 credit
hours
Credit: yes

McNook Community College
Registrar
1205 East Third St.
McNook, NE 69001
308-345-6303
800-348-5343
Minimum Age: 62
Tuition: free
Basic Fees: none
Credit: no

Metropolita Community
College
Student Accounts
P.O. Box 3777
Omaha, NE 68103
402-449-8418
Minimum Age: 62
Tuition: 50% off (regular tuition
$23 per credit hour)
Basic Fees: none
Credit: yes

Mid-Plains Community College
Accounting
1101 Halligan Dr.
North Platte, NE 69101
308-532-8740
Minimum Age: 60
Tuition: free
Basic Fees: $1.50 per credit
hour
Credit: yes

Nebraska Indian Community
College
Financial Aid Office
P.O. Box 752
Winnebago, NE 68071
402-878-2414
Minimum Age: 55
Tuition: free
Basic Fees: $10 one time
application fee
Credit: yes

Southeast Community College:
Beatrice Campus
Adult Education
Rt. 2, Box 35A
Beatrice, NE 68310
402-228-3468
Minimum Age: 62
Tuition: 50% off (regular tuition
$35.25 per credit hour)
Basic Fees: none
Credit: no

Southeast Community College:
Lincoln Campus
Cashier
8800 O St.
Lincoln, NE 68520
402-437-2600
Minimum Age: 62
Tuition: 50% off (non-credit
only)
Basic Fees: varies by class
Credit: no

Southeast Community College:
Milford Campus
Student Accounts
Rt. 2, Box D
Milford, NE 68405

402-761-2131
800-999-7223
Minimum Age: 65
Tuition: 50% off (non-credit
only)
Basic Fees: varies by class
Credit: no

Nevada

Community College of
Southern Nevada
3200 East Cheyenne Ave.
North Las Vegas, NV 89030
702-651-4060
Minimum Age: 62
Tuition: free
Basic Fees: none
Credit: yes

Northern Nevada Community
College
901 Elm St.
Elko, NV 89801
702-738-8493
Minimum Age: 62
Tuition: free
Basic Fees: none
Credit: yes

Truckee Meadows Community
College
7000 Dandini Blvd.
Reno, NV 89512
702-673-7000
Minimum Age: 62
Tuition: free
Basic Fees: none
Credit: yes

University of Nevada: Las
Vegas
4505 Maryland Pkwy.
Las Vegas, NV 89154-1021
702-895-3011
Minimum Age: 62
Tuition: free
Basic Fees: none
Credit: yes

University of Nevada: Reno
Records and Enrollment
Services
Reno, NV 89559
702-784-6865
Minimum Age: 62
Tuition: tuition waiver fall-
spring, 50% off during summer
Basic Fees: none
Credit: yes

Western Nevada Community
College
2201 West College Pkwy.
Carson City, NV 89703
702-887-3138
Minimum Age: 62
Tuition: free
Basic Fees: none
Credit: yes

New Hampshire
New Hampshire Technical
College: Berlin
2020 Riverside Dr.
Berlin, NH 03570
603-752-1113
800-445-4525
Minimum Age: 65
Tuition: free

Basic Fees: $16 for 3 credit
hours
Credit: yes

New Hampshire Technical
College: Claremont
One College Dr.
Claremont, NH 03743
603-542-7744
Minimum Age: 65
Tuition: free
Basic Fees: $10 per course
Credit: yes

New Hampshire Technical
College: Manchester
1066 Front St.
Manchester, NH 03102
603-668-6706
Minimum Age: 65
Tuition: free
Basic Fees: none
Credit: yes

New Hampshire Technical
College: Nashua
505 Amherst St.
Nashua, NH 03063
603-882-6923
Minimum Age: 65
Tuition: free
Basic Fees: none
Credit: no

New Hampshire Technical
College: Stratham
Tech Dr. and Rt. 101
277 Portsmouth Ave.
Stratham, NH 03885
603-772-1194
Minimum Age: 65

Tuition: free
Basic Fees: none
Credit: yes

New Hampshire Technical
Institute
Institute Dr.
Concord, NH 03301
603-225-1800
Minimum Age: 65
Tuition: free
Basic Fees: none
Credit: yes

Notre Dame College
2321 Elm St.
Manchester, NH 03104
603-669-4298
Minimum Age: 65
Tuition: free (2 course per
semester limit - 6 courses per
year)
Basic Fees: $60 per semester
Credit: yes

Plymouth State College of the
University System of New
Hampshire
Bursars
15 Halderness Rd.
Plymouth, NH 03264-1600
603-535-2237
Minimum Age: 65
Tuition: free
Basic Fees: $35/credit hour
Credit: yes

School for Lifelong Learning
Learner Services
NSNH
Dunlap Center

Durham, NH 03824
603-862-1692
Minimum Age: 65
Tuition: free
Basic Fees: $15 per session
Credit: yes

University of New Hampshire
at Manchester
220 Hackett Hill Rd.
Manchester, NH 03102
603-668-0700
Minimum Age: 65
Tuition: free up to 8 credit
hours, 8 credit hours or 2 non-
credit courses; no discount if
courses are being taken for
economic gain
Basic Fees: none
Credit: yes

New Jersey

Atlantic Community College
5100 Black Horse Pike
Mays Landing, NJ 08330
609-343-4922
Minimum Age: 62
Tuition: free
Basic Fees: $20 per session
Credit: yes

Bergen Community College
Admissions and Registration
400 Paramus Rd.
Paramus, NJ 07652
201-447-7857
Minimum Age: 65
Tuition: free
Basic Fees: $8.60/credit hour
Credit: yes

Brookdale Community College
765 Newman Springs Rd.
Lincroft, NJ 07738
908-842-1900
Minimum Age: 65
Tuition: free
Basic Fees: $28 for 3 credit hours
Credit: yes

Burlington County College
Admission
County Rt. 530
Pemberton, NJ 08068
609-894-9311
Minimum Age: 62
Tuition: $65 for 3 credit hours
Basic Fees: none
Credit: yes

Camden County College
P.O. Box 200
Blackwood, NJ 08012
609-227-7200
Minimum Age: 62 (55 if unemployed)
Tuition: free
Basic Fees: none
Credit: yes

County College of Morris
214 Center Grove Rd.
Randolf, NJ 07869
201-328-5100
Minimum Age: 65
Tuition: $5 per credit hour
Basic Fees: none
Credit: yes

Essex County College
303 University Ave.

Newark, NJ 07102
201-877-3100
Minimum Age: 60
Tuition: free
Basic Fees: none
Credit: yes

Glassboro State College
Oak Hall
Glassboro, NJ 08028
609-863-5346
Minimum Age: 55
Tuition: $13 per credit hour
Basic Fees: none
Credit: no

Gloucester County College
Business Office
Tanyard Rd.
Deptford Township
RR #4, Box 203
Sewell Post Office, NJ 08080
609-468-5000
Minimum Age: 60
Tuition: $5/credit hour
Basic Fees: $10/credit hour
Credit: yes

Jersey City State College
2039 Kennedy Blvd.
Bursars Office
Jersey City, NJ 07305
201-200-3234
Minimum Age: 62
Tuition: free
Basic Fees: $73.50 for 3 credit hours
Credit: yes

Kean College of New Jersey
1000 Morris Ave.

Union, NJ 07083
908-527-2195
Minimum Age: 62
Tuition: free
Basic Fees: $60 for 3 credit
hours
Credit: yes

Mercer County Community
College
1200 Old Trenton Rd.
Trenton, NJ 08690-1099
609-586-0505
Minimum Age: 65
Tuition: free
Basic Fees: none
Credit: yes

Middlesex County College
155 Mill Rd.
P.O. Box 3050
Edison, NJ 08818
808-906-2510
Minimum Age: 65
Tuition: $2.50 per credit hour
Basic Fees: $20 per semester
plus $6 per credit hour
Credit: yes

Montclair State College
Normal Ave. and Valley Rd.
Upper Montclair, NJ 07043
201-655-4136
Minimum Age: 65
Tuition: free
Basic Fees: $25 per session
Credit: yes

Ocean County College
College Dr.
CN 2001

Toms River, NJ 08754
908-255-0304
Minimum Age: 65
Tuition: $17.35 per credit hour
Basic Fees: $15 per semester
Credit: yes

Ramapo College of New
Jersey
505 Ramapo Valley Rd.
Mahwah, NJ 07430
201-529-7700
Minimum Age: 65
Tuition: free
Basic Fees: none
Credit: no

State University of New Jersey
- Rutgers
Office of University
Undergraduate Admissions
Administrative Services Bldg.
P.O. Box 2101
New Brunswick, NJ 08903-
2101
908-932-3770
Minimum Age: 62
Tuition: free
Basic Fees: none
Credit: no

New Mexico
Clovis Community College
417 Schepps Blvd.
Clovis, NM 88101
505-769-4025
Minimum Age: 65
Tuition: $13 first credit hour,
$5 for each additional credit
hour

Basic Fees: none
Credit: yes

New Mexico State College at
Carlsbad
1500 University Dr.
Carlsbad, NM 88220
505-885-8831
Minimum Age: 65
Tuition: $6 per credit hour
Basic Fees: $10 one time
admission fee
Credit: yes

New Mexico State University
Registrars Office
Las Cruces, NM 88003
505-646-3121
Minimum Age: 65
Tuition: $25 per hour (6 credit
hour limit in the fall)
Basic Fees: $15 per semester
for part-time (full-time free)
Credit: yes

New Mexico State University
at Alamogordo
Admissions
P.O. Box 477
Alamogordo, NM 88310
505-439-3600
Minimum Age: 65
Tuition: $8 per credit hour for
in-district, $13 per credit hour
out-of-district
Basic Fees: $10 one time
admission fee (6 credit hour
limit)
Credit: yes

New Mexico State University
at Grants
1500 North Third St.
Grants, NM 87020
505-287-7981
Minimum Age: 65
Tuition: $6 per credit hour
Basic Fees: $10 one time
application fee
Credit: yes

University of New Mexico
Cashier
Student Services Center
Room 140
Albuquerque, NM 87131
505-277-5363
800-225-5866
Minimum Age: 65
Tuition: $5 per credit hour (6
credit hour limit)
Basic Fees: none
Credit: yes

New York
Adirondack Community
College
Registrar
Bay Rd.
Queensbury, NY 12804
518-793-4491
Minimum Age: 60
Tuition: free
Basic Fees: none
Credit: no

Broome Community College
Student Accounts
P.O. Box 1017
Binghamton, NY 13902

607-778-5000
Minimum Age: 60
Tuition: free
Basic Fees: none
Credit: no

Cayuga County Community
College
Records Office
197 Franklin St.
Auburn, NY 13021
315-255-1743
Minimum Age: 60
Tuition: free
Basic Fees: none
Credit: no

City University of New York:
Baruch College
P.O. Box 279
17 Lexington Ave.
New York, NY 10010
212-447-3000
Minimum Age: 62
Tuition: free
Basic Fees: $52 per session
Credit: yes

City University of New York:
Bronx Community College
Bursars Office
W. 181st and University Ave.
New York, NY 10453
718-220-6450
Minimum Age: 65
Tuition: free
Basic Fees: $52 per session
Credit: yes

City University of New York:
Brooklyn College

1602 William James Hall
Brooklyn, NY 11210
718-220-6450
Minimum Age: 65
Tuition: free
Basic Fees: $52 per session
Credit: yes

City University of New York:
City College
Convent Ave. at 138th St.
New York, NY 10031
212-650-6977
Minimum Age: 65
Tuition: free
Basic Fees: $52 per session
Credit: yes

City University of New York:
College of Staten Island
Registrar
2800 Victory Blvd.
Bldg. 2A-110
Staten Island, NY 10314
718-982-2000
Minimum Age: 65
Tuition: free
Basic Fees: $52 per session
Credit: yes

City University of New York:
Hostos Community College
Admissions
500 Grand Concourse
Bronx, NY 10451
718-518-4444
Minimum Age: 65
Tuition: free
Basic Fees: $52 per session
Credit: yes

City University of New York:
Hunter College
Admissions
695 Park Ave.
Room 203, North Bldg.
New York, NY 10021
212-772-4490
Minimum Age: 65
Tuition: free
Basic Fees: $52 per session
Credit: yes

City University of New York:
Kingsborough Community
College
2001 Oriental Blvd.
Brooklyn, NY 11235
718-368-5079
Minimum Age: 65
Tuition: free
Basic Fees: $52 per session
Credit: yes

North Carolina

Alamance Community College
Student Services
P.O. Box 8000
Graham, NC 27253
910-578-2002
Minimum Age: 65
Tuition: free
Basic Fees: none
Credit: yes

Anson Community College
P.O. Box 126
Polkton, NC 28135
704-272-7635
Minimum Age: 65
Tuition: free

Basic Fees: $2 per quarter
plus $5 per credit hour
Credit: yes

Appalachian State University
Cashier's Office
Administration Bldg.
Boon, NC 28608
704-262-2120
Minimum Age: 65
Tuition: free
Basic Fees: $117.50 for 3
credit hours; $235 for 6 credit
hours
Credit: yes

Beaufort County Community
College
P.O. Box 1069
Washington, NC 27889
919-946-6194
Minimum Age: 65
Tuition: free
Basic Fees: maximum $6
activity fee per semester
Credit: yes

Bladen Community College
P.O. Box 266
Dublin, NC 28332
919-862-2164
Minimum Age: 65
Tuition: free
Basic Fees: none
Credit: yes

Blue Ridge Community
College
Rt. 2, Box 133A
Flat Rock, NC 28731-9624
704-692-3572

Minimum Age: 65
Tuition: free
Basic Fees: $1.25 per quarter
Credit: yes

Brunswick Community College
P.O. Box 30
Supply, NC 28462
910-754-6900
Minimum Age: 65
Tuition: free
Basic Fees: $1.05 per quarter
Credit: yes

Cape Fear Community College
411 North Front St.
Wilmington, NC 28401-3993
910-343-0481
Minimum Age: 65
Tuition: free
Basic Fees: $1 ID fee per
semester, maximum $6 activity
fee per semester
Credit: yes

Carteret Community College
3505 Arendell St.
Morehead City, NC 28557
919-247-4142
Minimum Age: 65
Tuition: free
Basic Fees: $3.25 for 3 credit
hours
Credit: yes

Catawba Valley Community
College
2550 Highway 70, SE
Hickory, NC 28602
704-327-7009
Minimum Age: 65

Tuition: free
Basic Fees: $1.75 per quarter
Credit: yes

North Carolina University -
Raleigh
Adult Credit Program
Box 7401
Raleigh, NC 27695-7401
919-515-2434
Minimum Age: 65
Tuition: free
Basic Fees: none
Credit: yes

University of North Carolina -
Chapel Hill
CB# 2200, Jackson Hall
Chapel Hill, NC 27599
919-966-3621
Minimum Age: 65
Tuition: free
Basic Fees: $10 per semester
Credit: yes

North Dakota

North Dakota State University
P.O. Box 5454
Admissions
Fargo, ND 58105
701-237-8643
Minimum Age: 65
Tuition: free
Basic Fees: $20 per session
Credit: no

North Dakota State University:
Bottineau and Institute of
Forestry
First and Simrall Blvd.

Bottineau, ND 58318
Minimum Age: 65
701-228-2277
Minimum Age: 55
Tuition: free
Basic Fees: none
Credit: no

Standing Rock College
HCI Box 4
Fort Yates, ND 58538
701-854-3861
Tuition: free (tuition, books and
fees all waived if you don't
qualify for Pell Grant)
Basic Fees: none (see above)
Credit: yes

University of North Dakota:
Lake Region
1801 College Dr., North
Devils Lake, ND 58301-1598
701-662-1600
Minimum Age: 65
Tuition: free
Basic Fees: none
Credit: no

University of North Dakota:
Williston
1410 University Ave.
Williston, ND 58801
701-774-4210
Minimum Age: 65
Tuition: free
Basic Fees: $10/credit hour
Credit: no

Valley City State University
101 College St., SE
Valley City, ND 58072

701-845-7412
Minimum Age: 65
Tuition: free
Basic Fees: none
Credit: no

Ohio

Belmont Technical College
120 Fox Shannon Pl.
St. Clarisville, OH 43950
614-695-9500
Minimum Age: 60
Tuition: free
Basic Fees: none
Credit: yes

Bowling Green State University
Department of Continuing
Education
McFall Center
40 College Park
Bowling Green, OH 43403
419-372-2086
Minimum Age: 60
Tuition: free
Basic Fees: none
Credit: no

Bowling Green State University
- Firelands College
901 Rye Beach Rd.
Huron, OH 44839
419-433-5560
Minimum Age: 60
Tuition: free
Basic Fees: $5 per semester
Credit: no

Central Ohio Technical College
1179 University Dr.

Newark, OH 43055
614-366-9222
Minimum Age: 60
Tuition: free
Basic Fees: $5 per credit hour
Credit: no

Central State University
Registrar
1400 Brush Row Rd.
Wilberforce, OH 45384
513-376-6231
Minimum Age: 60
Tuition: free
Basic Fees: none
Credit: no

Cuyahoga Community College
District
Downtown Campus
Office of Admissions
2900 Community College Ave.
Cleveland, OH 44115
216-987-4200
Minimum Age: 60
Tuition: free
Basic Fees: none
Credit: yes

Kent State University
P.O. Box 5190
Kent, OH 44242-0001
216-672-2444
Minimum Age: 5O and retired
or 60
Tuition: free
Basic Fees: none
Credit: no

Ohio State University
Continuing Education

3rd Floor
Lincoln Tower
1800 Cannon Dr.
Columbus, OH 43210
614-292-8860
Minimum Age: 60
Tuition: free
Basic Fees: none
Credit: no

University of Akron
381 Buchtel Common
Akron, OH 44325-2001
216-972-7100
Minimum Age: 60
Tuition: free (3 course limit)
Basic Fees: none
Credit: no

University of Cincinnati
Office of Admission
1 Edward Center
Cincinnati, OH 45221-0091
513-556-1100
Minimum Age: 60
Tuition: free
Basic Fees: none
Credit: no

University of Toledo
Evening Session
University of Toledo
Toledo, OH 43606-3398
419-537-4137
Minimum Age: 60
Tuition: free (income limitation
of $50,000 annually)
Basic Fees: none
Credit: yes

Oklahoma

Cameron University
Business Office
2800 West Fore Blvd.
Lawton, OK 73505
405-581-2230
Minimum Age: 65
Tuition: free
Basic Fees: none
Credit: no

Carl Albert State College
P.O. Box 1507
South McLenna
Poteau, OK 74953-5208
918-647-1200
Minimum Age: 65
Tuition: free
Basic Fees: none
Credit: no

Connors State College
Business Office
Rt. 1, Box 1000
Warner, OK 74469
918-463-6250
Minimum Age: 65
Tuition: free
Basic Fees: none
Credit: no

Oklahoma Panhandle State
University
P.O. Box 430
Goodwell, OK 73939
405-349-2611
Minimum Age: 65
Tuition: free
Basic Fees: none
Credit: no

Oklahoma State University
104 Whitehurse
Stillwater, OK 74078
405-744-6858
Minimum Age: 65
Tuition: free
Basic Fees: none
Credit: no

University of Oklahoma
Office of Admissions
1000 Asp Ave., Room 127
Norman, OK 73019
405-325-2251
Minimum Age: 65
Tuition: free
Basic Fees: none
Credit: no

Oregon

Blue Mountain Community
College
Continuing Education
P.O. Box 100
Pendleton, OR 97801
503-276-1260
Minimum Age: 60
Tuition: $10 per credit hour
Basic Fees: none
Credit: yes

Central Oregon Community
College
Admissions
2600 Northwest College Way
Bend, OR 97701
503-382-6112
Minimum Age: 62
Tuition: 50% off (regular tuition
$32 per credit hour)

Basic Fees: $1.50 per credit
hour
Credit: yes

Chemeketa Community
College
Business Office
P.O. Box 14007
4000 Lancaster Dr., NE
Salem, OR 97305
503-399-5006
Minimum Age: 62
Tuition: 35% off (regular tuition
$32 per credit hour)
Basic Fees: none
Credit: yes

Clackamas Community
College
19600 South Molalla Ave.
Oregon City, OR 97045
503-657-6958
Minimum Age: 62
Tuition: free
Basic Fees: none
Credit: yes

Clatsop Community College
Extended Learning
1653 Jerome Ave.
Astoria, OR 97103
503-325-0910
Minimum Age: 62
Tuition: 50% off (another 10%
for early payment-regular
tuition $30 per credit hour
Basic Fees: none
Credit: yes

Lane Community College
Admissions

4000 East 30th Ave.
Eugene, OR 97405
503-726-2207
Minimum Age: 62
Tuition: 50% off (regular tuition
$30 per credit hour)
Basic Fees: none
Credit: yes

Linn-Benton Community
College
Registration
6500 Pacific Blvd., SW
Albany, OR 97321-3779
503-967-6105
Minimum Age: 62
Tuition: 50% off (regular tuition
$32 per credit hour)
Basic Fees: none
Credit: yes

Mount Hood Community
College
Business Office
26000 Southeast Stark St.
Gresham, OR 97030
503-667-6422
Minimum Age: 62
Tuition: free
Basic Fees: none (self-
enrichment classes are usually
$5 each plus materials)
Credit: yes

Oregon Institute of Technology
Registrar
3201 Campus Dr.
Klamath Falls, OR 97601-8801
503-885-1150
800-343-6653
Minimum Age: 65

Tuition: free
Basic Fees: none
Credit: no

Oregon State University
Corvallis, OR 97331
503-737-4411
Minimum Age: 65
Tuition: free
Basic Fees: none
Credit: no

Portland Community College
Admissions
P.O. Box 19000
Portland, OR 97280-0990
503-244-6111 ext. 4724
Minimum Age: 62
Tuition: 50% off (regular tuition
$30 per credit hour)
Basic Fees: $7 per quarter full-
time; $2 per quarter part-time
Credit: yes

Portland State University
Senior Adult Learning Center
P.O. Box 751
Portland, OR 97207-0751
503-725-3511
800-547-8887
Minimum Age: 65
Tuition: free
Basic Fees: none
Credit: no

Pennsylvania
Bloomsburg University of
Pennsylvania
Extended Learning
700 West Main St.

Bloomsburg, PA 17815
717-389-4420
Minimum Age: 60
Tuition: free
Basic Fees: $42.50 for 3 credit
hours; $304 for 12 credit hours
Credit: yes

Bucks County Community
College
Swamp Rd.
Newtown, PA 18940
215-968-8100
Minimum Age: 65
Tuition: free
Basic Fees: $48-$57 per
semester
Credit: yes

Butler County Community
College
Registrar
P.O. Box 1203
Butler, PA 16003-1203
412-287-8711
Minimum Age: 60
Tuition: free
Basic Fees: none
Credit: no

California University of
Pennsylvania
COPE Program
250 University Ave.
California, PA 15419
412-938-5930
Minimum Age: 60
Tuition: free
Basic Fees: $135 for 3 credit
hours; $408 for 12 credit hours
Credit: yes

Clarion University of
Pennsylvania
Admissions
B-16 Carrier Hall
Clarion, PA 16214
814-226-2306
Minimum Age: 65
Tuition: free
Basic Fees: none
Credit: no

Community College of Beaver
County
One Campus Dr.
Monaca, PA 15061
412-775-8561
Minimum Age: 65
Tuition: free
Basic Fees: $20 per session
Credit: yes

Pennsylvania State University
102 Wagner
University Park, PA 16802
814-865-6528
Minimum Age: 60
Tuition: free
Basic Fees: none
Credit: yes (evening classes)

University of Pennsylvania
3440 Market St.
Suite 100
Philadelphia, PA 19104
215-898-7326
Minimum Age: 65
Tuition: $50 donation for 1
class; $75 donation for 2
classes
Basic Fees: none
Credit: no

University of Pittsburgh
407 CL
Pittsburgh, PA 15260
412-624-7308
Minimum Age: 60
Tuition: $15 per class
Basic Fees: none
Credit: no

Rhode Island

Community College of Rhode
Island
Admissions
400 East Ave.
Warwick, RI 02886
401-825-2285
Minimum Age: 62
Tuition: free
Basic Fees: $15 per session
Credit: yes

Rhode Island College
Records Office
600 Mt. Pleasant Ave.
Providence, RI 02908
401-456-8234
Minimum Age: 65
Tuition: free
Basic Fees: $135 full-time per
semester
Credit: yes

University of Rhode Island
Financial Aid
Kingston, RI 02881-0806
401-792-2314
Minimum Age: 60
Tuition: free (income limitation)
Basic Fees: $96 for 3 credit
hours; $619 for 12 credit hours

plus $480 for insurance, which can be waived if they have comparable coverage
Credit: yes

South Carolina

Aiken Technical College
P.O. Drawer 696
Aiken, SC 29802-0696
803-593-9231
Minimum Age: 60
Tuition: free
Basic Fees: none
Credit: yes

Chesterfield-Marlboro
Technical College
Student Development
P.O. Drawer 1007
Cheraw, SC 29520
803-537-5286
Minimum Age: 60
Tuition: free
Basic Fees: $14.50 per
semester
Credit: yes

The Citadel
171 Moultri St.
Charleston, SC 29409
803-953-5000
Minimum Age: 60
Tuition: free
Basic Fees: $40 per semester
Credit: yes

Clemson University
Business Affairs
G-08 Sikes Hall
P.O. Box 345307

Clemson, SC 29634-5307
803-656-2287
Minimum Age: 65
Tuition: free
Basic Fees: none
Credit: yes

College of Charleston
Treasurers Office
66 George St.
Charleston, SC 29424
803-953-5592
Minimum Age: 60
Tuition: $25 per semester
Basic Fees: none
Credit: yes

Denmark Technical College
Business Office
P.O. Box 327
Solomon Blatt Blvd.
Denmark, SC 29042
803-793-3301
Minimum Age: 62
Tuition: free
Basic Fees: none
Credit: yes

Florence-Darlington Technical
College
Admissions
P.O. Box 100548
Florence, SC 29501-0548
803-661-8151
Minimum Age: 60
Tuition: free
Basic Fees: none
Credit: yes

Francis Marion College
Financial Aid

P.O. Box 100547
Florence, SC 29501-0547
803-661-1231
Minimum Age: 60
Tuition: free
Basic Fees: none
Credit: yes

Greenville Technical College
Admissions
P.O. Box 5616, Station B
Greenville, SC 29606-5616
803-250-8109
Minimum Age: 60
Tuition: free
Basic Fees: $23 per semester
Credit: yes

Horry-Georgetown Technical
College
Financial Aid
P.O. Box 1966
Conway, SC 29526
803-347-3186
Minimum Age: 60
Tuition: $10 per class; $45 for
computer classes
Basic Fees: $15 per session
Credit: yes

Lander College
Admissions
P.O. Box 6007
320 Stanley Ave.
Greenwood, SC 29649
803-229-8307
800-768-3600
Minimum Age: 60
Tuition: free
Basic Fees: none
Credit: yes

Midlands Technical College
Admissions
P.O. Box 2408
Columbia, SC 29202
803-738-7764
Minimum Age: 60
Tuition: free
Basic Fees: none
Credit: yes

South Dakota

Black Hills State University
Records and Admissions
USB 9502
Spearfish, SD 57799-9502
605-642-6343
800-255-2478
Minimum Age: 65
Tuition: $11.03 per credit hour
Basic Fees: none
Credit: yes

Dakota State University
Cashier
Heston Hall
Madison, SD 57042
605-256-5139
Minimum Age: 65
Tuition: $11.44 per credit hour
Basic Fees: $147.33 for 3
credit hours
Credit: yes

Northern State University
Finance Office
1200 South Jay St.
Aberdeen, SD 57401
605-626-2544
Minimum Age: 65
Tuition: 75% off (regular tuition

$45.78 per credit hour)
Basic Fees: $29.05 per credit
hour
Credit: yes

South Dakota School of Mines
and Technology
Registrars Office
501 East St. Joseph St.
Rapid City, SD 57701-3995
605-394-2400
Minimum Age: 65
Tuition: $11.36 per credit hour
Basic Fees: $15 per session
Credit: yes

University of South Dakota
Admissions
414 East Clark
Vermillion, SD 57069-2390
605-677-5434
Minimum Age: 65
Tuition: 75% off (regular tuition
$47.18 per credit hour)
Basic Fees: $15 per session
Credit: yes

Tennessee
Austin Peay State University
Admissions
P.O. Box 4548
Clarksville, TN 37044
615-648-7661
800-426-2604
Minimum Age: 65
Tuition: $33 per credit hour not
to exceed $75 per session
Basic Fees: none
Credit: yes

Chattanooga State Technical
Community College
Records Office
4501 Amnicola Hwy.
Chattanooga, TN 37406
615-697-4401
Minimum Age: 65 (60 to audit
free)
Tuition: 50% of not to exceed
$45 per session
Basic Fees: $12 per session
Credit: yes

Cleveland State Community
College
P.O. Box 3570
Cleveland, TN 37320
615-472-7141
Minimum Age: 65 (60 for audit)
Tuition: $16 per credit hour not
to exceed $45 per session;
audit free
Basic Fees: $5 per semester
Credit: yes

Columbia State Community
College
Admissions
P.O. Box 1315
Columbia, TN 38402-1315
615-540-2722
Minimum Age: 65 (60 for audit)
Tuition: $45 per session
Basic Fees: $5 one time
application fee and $5 per
session
Credit: yes

Dyersburg State Community
College
P.O. Box 648

Dyersburg, TN 38025-0648
901-286-3200
Minimum Age: 60
Tuition: 50% off not to exceed
$50 per session
Basic Fees: $10-$28/session
Credit: yes

East Tennessee State
University
Admissions
P.O. Box 70731
Johnson City, TN 37614
615-929-4213
Minimum Age: 65 (60 for audit)
Tuition: free
Basic Fees: $75 per semester
Credit: yes

Jackson State Community
College
Business Office
2046 North Pkwy.
Jackson, TN 38301
901-424-3520
Minimum Age: 65
Tuition: 50% off (regular tuition
$43 per credit hour)
Basic Fees: $5 per session
Credit: yes

Memphis State University
Admissions Office, Room 167
Memphis, TN 38152
901-678-2101
800-669-9678
Minimum Age: 65 (60 audit)
Tuition: $75 per semester;
audit free
Basic Fees: none
Credit: yes

Middle Tennessee State
University
Accounting and Records
Murfreesboro, TN 37132
615-898-2111
Minimum Age: 65
Tuition: 50% off (regular tuition
$72 per credit hour)
Basic Fees: $20 per session
Credit: yes

Motlow State Community
College
P.O. Box 88100
Tullahoma, TN 37388-8100
615-393-1500
Minimum Age: 65 (60 to audit)
Tuition: $21.50 per credit hour
not to exceed $45 per session
Basic Fees: $5 per session
Credit: yes

University of Tennessee
451 Communication Bldg.
Knoxville, TN 37996-0341
615-974-5361
Minimum Age: 65 (60 can
audit free)
Tuition: $7 per credit hour not
to exceed $75 per session
Basic Fees: $15 one time
application fee
Credit: yes

Texas
Alvin Community College
Records
3110 Mustang Rd.
Alvin, TX 77511-4898
713-388-4636

Minimum Age: 65
Tuition: free
Basic Fees: none
Credit: no

Amarillo College
Business Office
P.O. Box 447
Amarillo, TX 79176
806-371-5000
Minimum Age: 65 or belong to
senior citizen association
Tuition: free (some courses
excluded)
Basic Fees: $3 per semester
Credit: yes

Angelina College
P.O. Box 1768
Lufkin, TX 75902
409-639-1301
Minimum Age: 65
Tuition: free
Basic Fees: none
Credit: no

Bee County College
Business Office
3800 Charco Rd.
Beeville, TX 78102
512-358-3130
Minimum Age: 65
Tuition: free
Basic Fees: none
Credit: yes

Southwest Texas State
University
SWT General Accounting
601 University Dr.
San Marcos, TX 78666-4603

512-245-2541
Minimum Age: 65
Tuition: free
Basic Fees: none
Credit: no

University of Houston - Central
Campus
Bursars Office
Houston, TX 77204-2160
713-743-1096
Minimum Age: 65
Tuition: free
Basic Fees: none
Credit: no

University of North Texas
P.O. Box 13797
Denton, TX 76203
817-565-2681
Minimum Age: senior citizen
Tuition: free
Basic Fees: none
Credit: no

University of Texas - Austin
Office of the Registrar
Main Bldg., Room 1
Austin, TX 78712-1157
512-471-7701
Minimum Age: 65
Tuition: free
Basic Fees: none
Credit: no

Utah
Brigham Young University
BYU Evening Classes
120 Harman Bldg.
Provo, UT 84602

801-378-2872
Minimum Age: 55
Tuition: $10 per class
Basic Fees: none
Credit: no

College of Eastern Utah
451 East 400 North
Price, UT 84501
801-637-2120
Minimum Age: 65
Tuition: $10 per class
Basic Fees: none
Credit: no

Dixie College
The Office of the Registrar
225 South 700 East
St. George, UT 84770
801-673-4811 ext. 348
Minimum Age: 62
Tuition: $10 quarter (some
classes are excluded)
Basic Fees: none
Credit: no

Salt Lake Community College
Admissions
4600 South Redwood Rd.
Salt Lake City, UT 84130
801-957-4297
Minimum Age: 63
Tuition: $10 per class
Basic Fees: none
Credit: yes

Snow College
150 East College Ave.
Ephraim, UT 84627
801-283-4021
Minimum Age: 62

Tuition: $10 per quarter
Basic Fees: none
Credit: no

Southern Utah University
Cashiers Office
351 West Center
Cedar City, UT 84720
801-586-7740
Minimum Age: 62
Tuition: $10 per quarter
Basic Fees: none
Credit: yes

University of Utah
DCE
1185 Annex
Salt Lake City, UT 84112
801-581-8113
Minimum Age: 60
Tuition: $10 per quarter
Basic Fees: none
Credit: no

Utah State University
Registrar
Logan, UT 84322-1600
801-797-1107
800-662-3950
Minimum Age: 62
Tuition: $10 per class
Basic Fees: none
Credit: no

Utah Valley State College
Registrar
800 West 1200 South
Orem, UT 84058
801-222-8000
Minimum Age: 65
Tuition: $20 per class

Basic Fees: $20 one time
admission fee
Credit: no

Weber State University
3750 Harrison
Ogden, UT 84408-1015
801-626-6050
Minimum Age: 62
Tuition: $10 per quarter
Basic Fees: none
Credit: no

Vermont

Castleton State College
Admissions
Castleton, VT 05735
802-468-5611
Minimum Age: 62
Tuition: free
Basic Fees: $19/credit hour
Credit: yes

Community College of
Vermont
Registrar
P.O. Box 120
Waterbury, VT 05676
802-241-3535
Minimum Age: 62
Tuition: 50% off (regular tuition
$88 per credit hour)
Basic Fees: $42 per semester
Credit: yes

Johnson State College
Student Accounts
Stowe Rd.
Johnson, VT 05656
802-635-2356

800-635-2356
Minimum Age: 62
Tuition: 50% off (regular tuition
$138 per credit hour)
Basic Fees: $292 per
semester plus $125 in one
time fees
Credit: yes

Lyndon State College
Business Office
Lyndonville, VT 05851
802-626-9371, ext. 163
800-225-1998
Minimum Age: 60
Tuition: 50% off (regular tuition
$138 per credit hour)
Basic Fees: $58.50 for 3 credit
hours ($19.50 per credit hour)
Credit: yes

University of Vermont
194 South Prospect
Burlington, VT 05401
802-656-3170
Minimum Age: 62
Tuition: free
Basic Fees: none
Credit: yes

Virginia

In the State of Virginia the
following rule applies: If annual
federal taxable income is less
than $10,000 tuition and
application fees are waived
(audit only).

Blue Ridge Community
College

P.O. Box 80
Weyers Cave, VA 24486-9989
703-234-9261
Minimum Age: 60
Tuition: free
Basic Fees: none
Credit: yes

Central Virginia Community
College
Student Services
3506 Wards Rd.
Lynchburg, VA 24502
804-386-4500
Minimum Age: 60
Tuition: free
Basic Fees: none
Credit: yes

Clinch Valley College of the
University of Virginia
Admissions
College Ave.
Wise, VA 24293
703-328-0116
Minimum Age: 60
Tuition: free
Basic Fees: none
Credit: yes

College of William and Mary
Bursars Office
P.O. Box 8795
Williamsburg, VA 23187-8795
804-221-4000
Minimum Age: 60
Tuition: free
Basic Fees: none
Credit: yes

Dabney S. Lancaster
Community College
Continuing Education
P.O. Box 1000
Clifton Forge, VA 24422
703-862-4240
Minimum Age: 60
Tuition: free
Basic Fees: none
Credit: yes

Danville Community College
1008 S. Main St.
Danville, VA 24541
804-797-3553
Minimum Age: 60
Tuition: free
Basic Fees: none
Credit: yes

Eastern Shore Community
College
Student Services
Rt. 1, Box 6
Melfa, VA 23410-9755
804-787-5912
Minimum Age: 60
Tuition: free
Basic Fees: none
Credit: no

George Mason University
Office of Admissions
GMU
4400 University Dr.
Fairfax, VA 22030
703-993-2400
Minimum Age: 60
Tuition: free
Basic Fees: none
Credit: no

Germanna Community College
Admissions
P.O. Box 339
Locust Grove, VA 22508
703-423-1333
Minimum Age: 60
Tuition: free
Basic Fees: none
Credit: yes

James Madison University
Student Accounts
Harrisonburg, VA 22807
703-568-6147
Minimum Age: 60
Tuition: free
Basic Fees: none
Credit: yes

Northern Virginia Community
College
Admissions Office
8333 Little River Turnpike
Annandale, VA 22003
703-323-3400
Minimum Age: 60
Tuition: free
Basic Fees: none
Credit: no

University of Virginia
Charlottesville Regional
Programs
Div. of Continuing Education
P.O. Box 3697
Charlottesville, VA 22903
804-982-3200
Minimum Age: 60
Tuition: free
Basic Fees: none
Credit: no

Washington

Bellevue Community College
3000 Landerholm Circle, SE
Bellevue, WA 98007
206-641-2222
Minimum Age: 60
Tuition: free (2 class limit)
Basic Fees: $2.50 per class
Credit: yes

Big Bend Community College
7662 Chanute St.
Moses Lake, WA 98837
509-762-6226
Minimum Age: 60
Tuition: $10 per course (2
course limit)
Basic Fees: none
Credit: yes

Central Washington University
400 E. 8th Ave.
Ellensburg, WA 98926
509-963-1211
Minimum Age: 60
Tuition: $5 per credit hour up
to 6 credit hours
Basic Fees: $25 per session
Credit: no

Centralia College
600 West Locust
Centralia, WA 98531
206-736-9391
Minimum Age: 60
Tuition: $5 (2 class limit)
Basic Fees: none
Credit: no

Clark College
1800 East McLaughlin Blvd.

Vancouver, WA 98663
206-699-0213
Minimum Age: 60
Tuition: $2.50 per class (2 class limit)
Basic Fees: none
Credit: no

University of Washington
Access Program
Undergraduate Extension Office
5001 25th Ave., NE
Seattle, WA 98195
206-543-2320
Minimum Age: 60
Tuition: free
Basic Fees: $5 per session
Credit: no

West Virginia

Apparently, Legislature has been proposed several times to no avail. We were unable to find any schools who offered a discount to senior citizens.

Wisconsin

Chippewa Valley Technical College
620 West Clairmont Ave.
Eau Claire, WI 54701
715-833-6244
Minimum Age: 62
Tuition: free
Basic Fees: none
Credit: no

Madison Area Technical College
3350 Anderson St.
Madison, WI 53704-2599
608-246-6205
Minimum Age: 62
Tuition: varies ($3.50 and up non-credit only)
Basic Fees: varies
Credit: no

Mid-State Technical College
500 - 32nd St., North
Wisconsin Rapids, WI 54494
715-422-5500
Minimum Age: 62
Tuition: free
Basic Fees: none
Credit: no

Milwaukee Area Technical College
Downtown Campus
700 West State St.
Milwaukee, WI 53233
414 297-6600
Minimum Age: 62
Tuition: free
Basic Fees: none
Credit: no

Northcentral Technical College
Registrar
1000 W. Campus Dr.
Wausau, WI 54401
715-675-3331
Minimum Age: 62
Tuition: free
Basic Fees: none
Credit: no

Northeast Wisconsin Technical
College
Registrar's Office
P.O. Box 19043
Green Bay, WI 54307-9042
414-498-5703
800-272-2740
Minimum Age: 62
Tuition: up to 50% off (non-
credit only)
Basic Fees: none
Credit: no

Wyoming
Casper College
125 College Dr.
Casper, WY 82601
307-268-2110 ext. 2491
Minimum Age: 60
Tuition: free
Basic Fees: none
Credit: yes

Central Wyoming College
Continuing Education
2660 Peck Ave.
Riverton, WY 82501
307-856-9291 ext. 181
Minimum Age: 60
Tuition: free
Basic Fees: $11.50 per credit
hour
Credit: yes

Eastern Wyoming College
Records
3200 West C St.
Torrington, WY 82240

307-532-8334
800-658-3195
Minimum Age: 60
Tuition: free
Basic Fees: $9 per credit hour
Credit: yes

Laramie County Community
College
Admissions
1400 East College Dr.
Cheyenne, WY 82007
307-778-1212
Minimum Age: 65
Tuition: $5 per credit hour
Basic Fees: $10 one time
application fee
Credit: yes

University of Wyoming
Admissions
P.O. Box 3435
Laramie, WY 82071
307-766-5160
Minimum Age: 65
Tuition: free
Basic Fees: none
Credit: yes

Western Wyoming Community
College
P.O. Box 428
Rock Springs, WY 82901
307-382-1600
Minimum Age: 60
Tuition: free
Basic Fees: none
Credit: yes

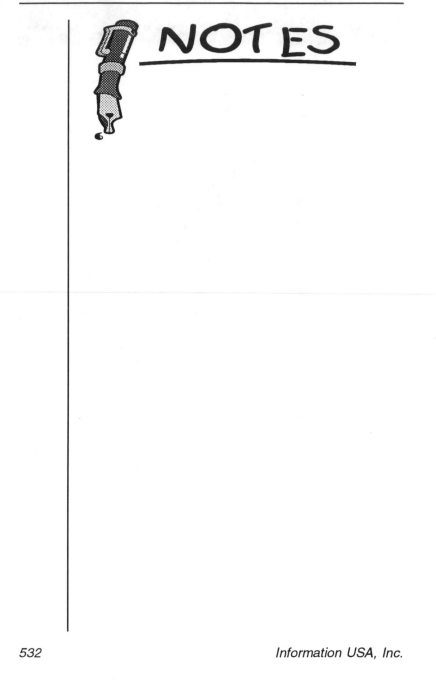

NOTES

Information USA, Inc.

No need to wonder where to turn for help, or even if help is out there. Uncle Sam realizes that the over 50 crowd is growing by leaps and bounds, and he's taking action to provide needed services for you.

You can find out about meal programs, home health assistance, insurance, and more with just a phone call. You can even learn what your own state is doing to help out those in your age group. Read on to find some good starting places you can try.

☆ ☆ ☆

Your Private Concierge

Need help finding out about local meals on wheels programs? Want to know about home health aides?

The Eldercare Locator provides access to an extensive network of organizations serving older people at state and local community levels. This service can connect you to information sources for a variety of services including: home delivered meals, transportation, legal assistance, housing options, recreation and social activities, adult daycare, senior center programs, home health services, elder abuse prevention, and nursing home ombudsman.

Contact Eldercare Locator, National Association of Area Agencies on Aging, 1112 16th St., NW, Washington, DC 20024; 800-677-1116 between 9 a.m. and 8 p.m. EST.

☆ ☆ ☆

Keep Current on Free Stuff

Ever wonder who is behind most of the programs serving the elderly? Probably not, but in case you did — it's the Administration on Aging (AoA). They're the ones who develop the government's aging programs and coordinate community services for older people.

Seniors can participate in AoA sponsored homemaker, nutrition, housing, employment, counseling, legal aid, transportation, and consumer affairs programs. You can also get your blood pressure checked and workout like Jane Fonda.

Most of these programs are handled through a national network of State

Agencies on Aging (see the Directory of State Information at the end of this book for your state office). You can locate services near you through the ElderCare Locator Hotline, National Association of Area Agencies on Aging, 112 16th St., NW, Washington, DC 20024; 800-677-1116.

AoA also publishes a quarterly subscription magazine titled *Aging*, covering a variety of topics of interest to seniors, and the free *Aging America: Trends and Projections*, a statistical compendium covering every aging issue.

For more information about AoA, contact Administration on Aging, 330 Independence Ave., SW, Washington, DC 20201; 202-619-0641.

☆ ☆ ☆

Stop Getting Taken

Starving kids in Bolivia? You've just won a bizillion dollars? Precious gem stones available only to you? These are just some of the common telephone scams con artists are using these days.

Tip-offs that you are dealing with less than honest people include using lines such as: "You have to act now or the offer won't be good"; or "You can't afford to miss this high profit, no risk offer"; or "Give me your credit card number and I'll send you all the information."

If you hear these or similar lines, just hang up the phone. You're not being rude; you're just being smart.

The Federal Trade Commission protects consumers from unfair or deceptive business practices. Programs focus on truth in advertising, fair packaging and labeling of products, warranty performance, fair credit reporting, direct mail advertising, door-to-door sales, and business practices of nursing homes. They have a listing of free publications which provide tips and information to help you with all your consumer issues.

To learn more, contact the State Attorney General's office listed in the Directory of State Information at the back of this book, or contact the Federal Trade Commission, Public Reference, Room 130, Washington, DC 20580; 202-326-2222.

Your Check Is (Ripped Off) In The Mail

For many elderly people living alone and on fixed incomes, shopping by mail is convenient. At the same time, older people are attractive targets for mail-order swindles.

Another mail-related crime that hits the elderly is the theft of benefit checks.

Seniors who find themselves victims of mail schemes or theft should contact their local Postmaster for an investigation. Remember also that many communities offer a Carrier Alert Program, where mail carriers watch post boxes for any unusual accumulation of mail that might indicate a need for help. They will also bring your mail to your door if your mail box is located some distance from your home.

The U.S. Postal Services have put together a booklet, *A Consumer's Guide to Postal Crime Prevention*, which offers tips on how to avoid being victimized by mail fraud and theft.

Contact your local post office for more information, or contact Public Affairs Branch, U.S. Postal Service, 475 L'Enfant Plaza, SW, Room 5541, Washington, DC 20260; 202-268-4293.

☆ ☆ ☆

Bennies For Vets

You have done your duty, and now it's time to take advantage of some of the great benefits available to you and your family. The Department of Veterans Affairs can answer all your questions about benefits for veterans and their families.

They can provide information and help you apply for programs such as education assistance, vocational rehabilitation, home loan programs, life insurance, comprehensive dental and medical care in outpatient clinics, medical centers, and nursing homes around the country.

They also provide burial services, including cemeteries, markers, and flags, to veterans and others who are eligible.

For more information on benefits and eligibility requirements, contact Department of Veterans Affairs, Office of Public Affairs, 810 Vermont Ave., NW, Washington, DC 20420; 800-827-1000.

☆ ☆ ☆

When You Don't Get No Respect

Some people missed the lesson about treating seniors with respect, and now prey on their elderly relatives (and maybe even their own spouses). Abuse of the elderly can be both physical and psychological, such as demanding their checks or not giving them their medications.

If you suspect someone is being abused, you should report it immediately to the proper authorities. The Clearinghouse on Family Violence can help refer you to state and local resources, as well as provide you with information on elder abuse.

Contact the Clearinghouse on Family Violence Information, P.O. Box 1182, Washington, DC 20013; 800-FYI-3366.

☆ ☆ ☆

Seniors Are Less Crime Prone...But

According to a special report published by the Bureau of Justice Statistics (BJS), people age 65 and older are the least likely of all age groups to be the victims of crime. For those seniors who are victims, they are more likely to be victimized at or near their home, and less likely to use measures of self-protection.

BJS can answer all your crime questions, and they publish statistics on crime, victims of crime, and criminal offenders. They have a free series of reports that describe some of the research they have available. Some of the titles include:

- *Violent Crime by Strangers and Nonstrangers*
- *The Crime of Rape*
- *The Risk of Violent Crime*
- *Crime Victims: Learning how to help them*

- *Lifetime Likelihood of Victimization*
- *Robbery Victims*
- *Elderly Victims*

Contact Justice Statistics Clearinghouse, Box 6000, Rockville, MD 20850; 800-732-3277.

☆ ☆ ☆

Send It Directly To Your Account

Rather than worry each month whether or not your check will arrive in time, many programs will directly deposit your check into a bank account. You can even have this done with your tax return in some places! It allows you to access your funds on the same day each month without the fear of your check being stolen or misplaced.

For those interested in having their Social Security checks directly deposited, contact your local Social Security office or call their hotline at 800-772-1213.

Elvis Presley Personally Delivered To You

Well, actually Elvis' face on a postage stamp. You do realize, of course, that the real Elvis stopped doing house calls in 1977. Anyone, especially homebound elderly, can order stamps and other

postal items that will be delivered right to their door. Request an order form from your mail carrier or local post office. Orders normally take 2 to 3 business days, with no extra charge.

Postal products can also be ordered by phone by calling the Postal Service's 24-hour toll-free number: 800-STAMP-24. To order over the phone a VISA or Master Card is needed, and there is a $3 service fee per order. Orders are normally delivered within 3 to 5 business days.

Where To Find People Like You

Did you know that during colonial times half the population was under age 16? Now less than 25% are under age 16. The number of people who are 100 or older numbered 35,808 in 1990, mostly females.

If you want to hang around with people your own age, head to California or Florida. California has the largest number of persons 65 and older (3.1 million), but Florida has the largest proportion of elderly at 18%. You can learn more interesting facts, such as the diversity of the elderly, the general health of the group, living arrangements and more.

These facts are all included in a series of reports published by the Bureau of the Census. You know, the guys who come knocking on your door every ten years, asking how many people live in your house, how many rooms do you have, etc.

They have published a series titled, *Profiles of America's Elderly*, which looks at growth of America's elderly, the racial and ethnic diversity, and living arrangements of this group.

For your copies or more information, contact Bureau of the Census, U.S. Department of Commerce, Washington, DC 20233; 301-457-4100.

☆ ☆ ☆

Discounts on Your Phone Bill

A house, a car, 2.3 kids, and a phone is the average American family. If you don't have a telephone because of the cost, and you're eligible for social service assistance programs, your local telephone company may offer you reduced connection and installation fees.

Under the Federal Communication Commission's Link-Up America program, low-income households seeking telephone service are given a 50% discount for connection charges, and may be able to pay installment payments on the remaining charge.

All states, the District of Columbia and Puerto Rico have federally approved connection assistance programs. If you are interested in signing up for this service, contact the consumer service representative at your local telephone company.

If you have trouble locating this service, contact Common Carrier, Federal Communications Commission, 1919 M St., NW, Washington, DC 20554; 202-418-0940.

☆ ☆ ☆

$7 Off Your Bill

Now that you've got the phone, here is some help with the monthly bill. The Federal Communication Commission's Federal Lifeline program helps low-income subscribers reduce their monthly telephone bill by waiving or reducing the line charge, up to approximately $7 per month.

To date, over 40 states and the District of Columbia have federally approved Lifeline programs. Eligibility varies from state to state, with some having income and/or age requirements. See the list below for more specifics.

For more information on Lifeline assistance, contact your local telephone company, or you can contact Common Carrier, Federal Communications Commission, 1919 M St., NW, Washington, DC 20554; 202-418-0940.

The following is a list of organizations which handle this program on the state level, along with a description of eligibility requirements for that state. The organizations listed for the state can be found by contacting the state government operator located in the state capital. If your state is not listed, contact the office of the Federal Communications Commission listed above.

Lifeline and Link-up State Eligibility Qualifications

Alabama
Entity: Public Service
Commission
Eligibility Criteria: Recipient of:
SSI, AFDC, or Food Stamps
Income Verification: Medicaid
or Food Stamp Card

Alaska
Entity: Anchorage Telephone
Eligibility Criteria: Recipient of:
SSI, AFDC, or Food Stamps
Income Verification: Alaska
Department of Health and
Human Services

Arizona
Entity: Corporation
Commission
Eligibility Criteria: Lifeline:
Income below 150% poverty
Link Up: Income at or below
poverty and participant in
Senior Telephone Discount
Program

Income Verification: Arizona
Department of Economic
Security

Arkansas
Entity: Public Service
Commission
Eligibility Criteria: Recipient of:
SSI, AFDC, HEAP, Food
Stamps, Medicaid, or
Subsidized housing
Income Verification: Dept. of
Human Services

California
Entity: Public Utilities
Commission
Eligibility Criteria: Income at or
below 150% poverty
Income Verification: Self
certified

Colorado
Entity: Public Utilities
Commission

Eligibility Criteria: Recipient of:
SSI, Old Age Pension, Aid to
the Blind, or Aid to the Needy
and Disabled
Income Verification:
Department of Social Services

Connecticut
Entity: Department of Public
Utility Control
Eligibility Criteria: Eligible for
any low-income assistance or
energy assistance program
administered by the
Connecticut Department of
Human Resources or
Connecticut Department of
Income Maintenance or SSI
Income Verification: Applicable
agency of those listed

District of Columbia
Entity: Public Service
Commission
Eligibility Criteria: LIHEAP
Eligible Over age 65 (Flat rate
$1.00); Head of Household
($3.00 measured + 6.5 cents
over 120 calls)
Income Verification: DC
Energy Office

Florida
Entity: Public Service
Commission
Eligibility Criteria: Recipient of:
Food Stamps or Medicaid
Income Verification:
Department of Health and
Rehabilitative Services

Georgia
Entity: Public Service
Commission
Eligibility Criteria: Recipient of
SSI, AFDC, and/or Food
Stamps
Income Verification:
Department of Human
Resources

Hawaii
Entity: Public Utilities
Commission
Eligibility Criteria: Age 60 or
older or handicapped with
annual household income
$10,000 or less
Income Verification: Hawaiian
Telephone Co.

Idaho
Entity: Public Utilities
Commission
Eligibility Criteria: Recipient of:
AFDC, Food Stamps, Aid to
the Aged, Blind and Disabled,
or Medical Assistance
Income Verification: Medical
Assistance or Food Stamp ID
card

Illinois
Entity: Illinois Commerce
Commission
Eligibility Criteria: Recipient of
public assistance in programs
administered by the Illinois
Department of Public Aid
Income Verification:
Department of Public Aid

Indiana
Entity: Utility Regulatory
Commission
Eligibility Criteria: Recipient of:
SSI, AFDC, HEAP, Medicaid,
or Food Stamps
Income Verification: Local
Exchange Companies

Iowa
Entity: State Utilities Board
Eligibility Criteria: Recipient of:
SSI, AFDC, LIHEAP, or Food
Stamps
Income Verification: Local
Exchange Companies

Kansas
Entity: Corporation
Commission
Eligibility Criteria: Recipient of:
SSI, AFDC, Food Stamps,
Medicaid, or General
Assistance
Income Verification: Local
Exchange Companies

Kentucky
Entity: Public Service
Commission
Eligibility Criteria: Recipient of:
SSI, AFDC, Food Stamps, or
Medical Assistance
Income Verification: Cabinet
for Human Resources

Louisiana
Entity: Public Service
Commission
Eligibility Criteria: Recipient of:
SSI, AFDC, or Food Stamps

Income Verification: Medicaid
or Food Stamp card

Maine
Entity: Public Utilities
Commission
Eligibility Criteria: Recipient of:
SSI, AFDC, HEAP, Medicaid,
or Food Stamps
Income Verification:
Department of Human
Services

Maryland
Entity: Public Service
Commission
Eligibility Criteria: Recipient of:
General Assistance
Income Verification: Dept. of
Human Resources

Massachusetts
Entity: Dept. of Public Utilities
Eligibility Criteria: Recipient of:
SSI, AFDC, General Public
Welfare, Food Stamps,
Medicaid, and Fuel Assistance
Income Verification: Dept. of
Public Welfare and/or Office of
Fuel Assistance

Michigan
Entity: Public Service
Commission
Eligibility Criteria: Income at or
below 130% poverty
Income Verification:
Department of Social Services
or Office of Services to the
Aging

Minnesota
Entity: Public Utilities Commission
Eligibility Criteria: Age 65 or older or income level which meets state poverty levels
Income Verification: Department of Human Services

Mississippi
Entity: Public Service Commission
Eligibility Criteria: Recipient of: SSI, AFDC, or Food Stamps
Income Verification: Medicaid or Food Stamp card

Missouri
Entity: Public Service Commission
Eligibility Criteria: Recipient of: Medicaid
Income Verification: Dept. of Social Services

Montana
Entity: Public Service Commission
Eligibility Criteria: Recipient of: SSI, AFDC, or Medicaid
Income Verification: Medicaid card and Social and Rehabilitation Services

Nebraska
Entity: Public Service Commission
Eligibility Criteria: Recipient of: SSI, AFDC, Energy Assistance, Food Stamps,
Medicaid, or Aid to the Aged, Blind or Disabled
Income Verification: Medicaid Agency or Department of Social Service or Food Stamp program

Nevada
Entity: Public Service Commission
Eligibility Criteria: Recipient of: SSI, AFDC, Energy Assistance, Food Stamps, Indian General Assist., Commodity Foods, or VA Improved Pension
Income Verification: Proof of enrollment in listed programs

New Hampshire
Entity: Public Utilities Commission
Eligibility Criteria: Recipient of: SSI, AFDC, Food Stamps, Fuel Assistance, Old Age Assistance, Weatherization Assist., Aid to Permanently/ Totally Disabled, Women, Infants and Children Feeding Program, Welfare, Title XX, or Subsidized Housing
Income Verification: Respective donor agency

New Jersey
Entity: Public Service Commission
Eligibility Criteria: Recipient of: SSI, AFDC, HEAP, Pharma- ceutical Assist. to the Aged, Welfare, or Lifeline Credit

Income Verification: Local
Exchange Companies

New Mexico
Entity: Mountain Bell
Telephone
Eligibility Criteria: Recipient of:
SSI, AFDC, or LITAP
Income Verification: Human
Services Department

Entity: Western NM Tel. Co.
Eligibility Criteria: Recipient of:
SSI, AFDC, or CCIC
Income Verification: Human
Services Department

New York
Entity: Public Service
Commission
Eligibility Criteria: Recipient of:
SSI, AFDC, Food Stamps,
Medicaid, or Home Relief
Income Verification:
Administering Agency

North Carolina
Entity: Utilities Commission
Eligibility Criteria: Recipient of:
SSI or AFDC
Income Verification: Dept. of
Human Resources

North Dakota
Entity: Public Service
Commission
Eligibility Criteria: Eligible for:
Food Stamps, Fuel Assist.,
AFDC, Medical Assist.
Income Verification: County
Social Service Board

Ohio
Entity: Public Utilities
Commission
Eligibility Criteria: Recipient of:
HEAP, E-Heap, Ohio Energy
Credits Program, SSI, AFDC
and Medicaid
Income Verification: Local
Exchange Companies

Oklahoma
Entity: Corporate Commission
Eligibility Criteria: Recipient of
aid from state low income
programs
Income Verification: Dept. of
Human Services

Oregon
Entity: Public Utilities
Commission
Eligibility Criteria: Eligible for:
Food Stamps and assistance
programs 135% of poverty
Income Verification: Dept. of
Human Resources

Pennsylvania
Entity: Public Utilities
Commission
Eligibility Criteria: Recipient of:
SSI, AFDC, Food Stamps,
General Assistance, or Blue
Card Medical Assist. Medically
Needy Only
Income Verification:
Department of Public Welfare

Puerto Rico
Entity: PR Tel. Co.
Eligibility Criteria: Recipient of:

Nutritional Assistance Program
Income Verification: Dept. of
Social Services

Rhode Island
Entity: Public Utilities
Commission
Eligibility Criteria: Recipient of:
SSI, AFDC, General
Assistance, or Medical
Assistance
Income Verification: Dept. of
Human Services

South Carolina
Entity: Public Utilities
Commission
Eligibility Criteria: Recipient of:
AFDC, Food Stamps,
Medicaid, or Temporary
Emergency Food Assistance
Income Verification: Local
Exchange Companies

South Dakota
Entity: Northwestern Bell
Eligibility Criteria: Recipient of:
HEAP or Food Stamps
Income Verification: Dept. of
Social Services

Tennessee
Entity: Public Service
Commission
Eligibility Criteria: Recipient of:
SSI, AFDC, Medicaid, or Food
Stamps
Income Verification: Medicaid
card or Food Stamp Notice of
Disposition

Texas
Entity: Public Utilities
Commission
Eligibility Criteria: Eligible for:
SSI, AFDC, LIHEAP, Food
Stamps, Medicaid, Medical
Assistance, or Maternal Health
Program
Income Verification: Local
Exchange Companies

Utah
Entity: Public Service
Commission
Eligibility Criteria: Eligible for:
SSI, AFDC, Food Stamps,
General Assistance, Home
Energy Assistance, Medical
Assistance, Refugee
Assistance, or Energy Work
Programs
Income Verification: Local
Exchange Companies

Vermont
Entity: Public Service Board
Eligibility Criteria: Recipient of:
SSI, AFDC, Food Stamps,
Medicaid, or Fuel Assistance
Income Verification:
Department of Social Welfare

Virginia
Entity: Corporation
Commission
Eligibility Criteria: Recipient of:
Virginia Universal Service Plan
Income Verification:
Department of Medical
Assistance Services

Washington
Entity: Utilities and
Transportation Commission
Eligibility Criteria: Recipient of:
SSI, AFDC, Food Stamps,
Refugee Assistance, Chore
Services, or Community
Options Program Entry System
Income Verification:
Department of Social and
Health Services

West Virginia
Entity: Public Service
Commission
Eligibility Criteria: Disabled or
age 60 or older and receives
SSI, AFDC, or Food Stamps or
is eligible for SSI
Income Verification:

Department of Human
Services

Wisconsin
Entity: Wisconsin Bell, GTE
Eligibility Criteria: Recipient of:
AFDC, SSI, Food Stamps,
Title 19 Medical and Energy
Programs
Income Verification:
Department of Health and
Social Services

Wyoming
Entity: Public Services
Commission United US West
Eligibility Criteria: Recipient of:
SSI, AFDC, LIHEAP, or Food
Stamps
Income Verification: Dept. of
Health and Social Services

☆ ☆ ☆

They Have The President's Ear

Mental health and aging, health care reform and long-term care, income security, housing and living arrangements, and even the problems faced by minority elders are just some of the topics that have been investigated by the Federal Council on Aging.

The Council is a special advisory group of a cross-section of rural and urban older Americans, national organizations with an interest in aging, business, labor, and the general public. The Council reviews and evaluates federal policies, programs, and activities that affect the lives of older Americans. The Council collects and distributes information on aging, as well as publishes an annual report to the President.

For more information on how to keep up to date on these issues, contact Federal Council on the Aging, Room 4280 HHS-N, 330 Independence Ave., SW, Washington, DC 20201; 202-619-2451.

☆ ☆ ☆

Find Out What the Government is Doing for You

You have your own special lobbying group to keep you up-to-date on what Congress is doing and you don't even have to take them golfing in Tahiti.

The U.S. Senate puts out a free report that outlines what each government agency is doing for seniors, from special arts programs at the National Endowment for the Arts to clinical trials on treatments for Alzheimer's at the National Institutes of Health.

Or you can get free copies of special reports on a variety of topics like prescription drug price increases or women's health issues.

For a current listing of all publications, or to obtain one of the free publications listed below, contact Special Committee on Aging, United States Senate, SD-G31, Washington, DC 20510; 202-224-5364.

Below is a partial listing of free publications:

- *Health Care Reform: The Time Has Come*, Serial No. 102-16
  February 10, Fort Smith, AR, *Long-Term Care and Prescription Drug Costs*
  February 11, 1992, Jonesboro, AR, *Skyrocketing Health Care Costs and the Impact on Individuals and Businesses*
  February 12, El Dorado, AR, *Answers to the Health Care Dilemma*

- *Continuing Long-Term Care Services* February 10, 1992, Lauderhill, FL, Serial No. 102-17*

- *Elderly Left Out in the Cold? The Effects of Housing and Fuel Assistance Cuts on Senior Citizens*, March 3, 1992, Washington, DC Serial No. 102-18

- *Medicare Balance Billing Limits: Has the Promise Been Fulfilled?* April 7, 1992, Washington, DC, Serial No. 102-19

- *Skyrocketing Prescription Drug Costs: Effects on Senior Citizens*, April 15, 1992, Lewiston, ME, Serial No. 102-20

- *The Effects of Escalating Drug Costs on the Elderly*, April 22, 1992, Macon and Atlanta, GA, Serial No. 102-21

- *Roundtable Discussion on Guardianship*, June 2, 1992, Washington, DC, Serial No. 102-22

- *Aging Artfully: Health Benefits of Art and Dance*, June 18, 1992, Washington, DC, Serial No. 102-23

- *Grandparents as Parents: Raising a Second Generation*, July 29, 1992, Serial No. 102-24

- *Consumer Fraud and the Elderly: Easy Prey?* September, 24, 1992, Washington, DC, Serial 102-25

- *Roundtable Discussion on Intergenerational Mentoring*, November 12, 1992, Washington, DC, Serial No. 102-26*

- *The Federal Government's Investment in New Drug Research and Development: Are We Getting Our Money's Worth?* February 24, 1993, Washington, DC, Serial No. 103-1

- *Prescription Drug Prices: Out-Pricing Older Americans*, April 14, 1993, Bangor, ME, Serial No. 103-2

- *Workshop on Innovative Approaches to Guardianship*, April 16, 1993, Washington, DC, Serial No. 103-3

- *Controlling Health Care Costs: The Long-Term Care Factor*, April 20, 1993, Washington, DC, Serial 103-4

- *Workshop on Cataract Surgery: Guidelines and Outcomes*, April 21, 1993, Washington, DC, Serial No. 103-5

- *Workshop on Rural Health and Health Reform*, May 3, 1993, Washington, DC, Serial No. 103-6*

- *Preventive Health: An Ounce of Prevention Saves a Pound of Cure*, May 6, 1993, Washington, DC, Serial No. 103-7

- *How Secure Is Your Retirement: Investments, Planning, and Fraud*, May 25, 1993, Washington, DC, Serial No. 103-8

- *The Aging Network: Linking Older Americans to Home and Community-Based Care*, June 8, 1993, Washington, DC, Serial No. 103-9

- *Mental Health and the Aging*, July 15, 1993, Washington, DC, Serial No. 103-10*

- *Health Care Fraud as It Affects the Aging*, August 13, 1993, Racine, WI, Serial No. 103-11

- *The Hearing Aid Marketplace: Is the Consumer Adequately Protected?* Washington, DC, September 15, 1993, Serial No. 103-12

- *Improving Income Security for Older Women in Retirement: Current Issues and Legislative Reform Proposals*, September 23, 1993, Washington, DC, Serial No. 103-13

- *Long-Term Care Provisions in the President's Health Care Reform Plan*, November 12, 1993, Madison, WI, Serial No. 103-14

- *Pharmaceutical Marketplace Reform: Is Competition the Right Prescription?* November 16, 1993, Washington, DC, Serial No. 103-15

- *Home Care and Community-Based Services: Overcoming Barriers to Access*, March 30, 1994, Kalispell, MT, Serial 103-16

- *Medicare Fraud: An Abuse*, April 11, 1994, Miami, FL, Serial No. 103-17

- *Health Care Reform: The Long-Term Care Factor*, Washington, DC, April 12, 1994, Serial No. 103-18

Information USA, Inc.

- *Elder Abuse and Violence Against Midlife and Older Women*, May 4, 1994, Washington, DC, Serial No. 103-19

- *Long-Term Care*, May 9, 1994, Milwaukee, WI, Serial No. 103-20
- *Health Care Reform: Implications for Seniors*, May 18, Lansing, MI, Serial No. 103-21

- *Fighting Family Violence: Response of the Health Care System*, June 20, 1994, Bangor, ME, Serial No. 103-22

- *Uninsured Bank Products: Risky Business for Seniors*, September 29, 1994, Washington, DC Serial No. 103-23

☆ ☆ ☆

We The American...Elderly

Did you know that in 1900, 1 in 25 Americans were elderly, and in 1990, 1 in 8 were? Just in sheer numbers, you will be a force to be reckoned with. But what is in store for you, and what is Washington thinking about the elderly?

To learn more, the Congressional Research Service (CRS) has written several easy to understand reports on the topic. The reports are free, but you must request them through your members of Congress. Some titles relating to the elderly include:

- *Economic Status Of the Elderly Population (87-101E)*
- *The Aged: A Profile (IP3A)*
- *Older Americans Act Amendments of 1992 (93-329EPW)*
- *The Aged: Bibliography In Brief (89-258L)*
- *Selected Legislation Affecting The Elderly (91-624EPW)*

These and other reports dealing with the elderly are available by contacting Your Representative or Senator, The Capitol, Washington, DC 20510; 202-224-3121.

Making Sure You Get Your Thirty-Two Cents Worth

Before you buy a long-term care insurance policy, you should look at what the government has learned about the policies in general. Even before you go under the laser for cataract surgery, you can discover data on the appropriateness and outcomes to that surgery and other procedures.

Pension plan violators, rental housing problems for seniors, and cataract surgery complications are just a few of the issues covered in the General Accounting Office (GAO) report titled *Aging Issues*. It lists all the subjects the GAO investigated, like long-term care insurance and lump sum retirements. Each listing also includes an abstract of the report or testimony.

All reports are free (except for the cost of a phone call or stamp) and can be requested by contacting U.S. General Accounting Office, P.O. Box 6015, Gaithersburg, MD 20884; 202-512-6000.

Consumer Power

Nine Ways To Lower Your Auto Insurance Costs. Medicare Pays For Flu Shots. Understanding Social Security. Food Facts For Older Adults. Estrogens — How To Take Your Medicine.

These are just a few of over 200 publications available for free or not much money from the Consumer Information Center.

Four times a year, the Center publishes the Consumer Information Catalog, which lists selected federal government publications of interest to consumers. Topics covered include automobiles, health, food, money management, nutrition, housing, employment, and education. Prices range from free to one dollar.

For your free catalog, write Consumer Information Center, P.O. Box 100, Pueblo, CO 81009.

"Help! I've Fallen And I Can't Get Up"

No need to spend a fortune on an emergency call button if you take some basic precautions.

The number one cause of accidents for the over 65 age group involves bathtubs, carpets, ladders, and other home furnishings and fixtures. The Consumer Product Safety Commission (CPSC) distributes the publication, *Home Safety Checklist for Older Consumers*, which can help you make your home a safer place. CPSC also answers questions and accepts complaints about consumer products, and can inform you of product recalls. They even maintain a clearinghouse which collects information about consumer product-related injuries.

For publications, a publications list, or other services, contact the Consumer Product Safety Commission, Office of Information and Public Affairs, 4330 East-West Hwy., Bethesda, MD 20207; 800-638-2772.

$150 A Month Just For Being Over 65

You get a special "Longevity Bonus" if you live in Alaska and make it to 65. The state of Alaska will pay you $150 a month just for the heck of it. Other states offer you a special state tax benefit to help you on your way to a possible refund.

Contact your State Department on Aging listed in the Directory of State Information at the end of this book to see if your state has any money for you.

☆ ☆ ☆

Your Own Television Station

Tired of those shoot and kill shows on T.V. every night? Now is your chance to turn the channel and find something that's just right for you. Arizona's Office of Aging produces a weekly cable television show which airs on their public access station, as does one in Ohio.

Interview topics have included employment and volunteer opportunities, as well as legislation of interest to senior adults.

Some cable stations even offer a discount rate to seniors who meet income and residency requirements.

To learn if your state provides similar programming, contact your local cable television company or your State Department on Aging listed in the Directory of State Information at the end of this book.

☆ ☆ ☆

No Car, No License, No Problem

Getting around town without a set of wheels is a big problem for many seniors. Fortunately, many transit systems offer free or reduced fares to those over 65. They even offer special pick-up services for those who have trouble making it to the nearest bus stop or who are in wheelchairs.

New Jersey offers the Senior Citizen and Disabled Resident Transportation Assistance Program which provides door-to-door service, fixed route service, local fare subsidies, and more to those over 60.

Contact your local transit authority to see what they offer, or your state Department on Aging from the Directory of State Information at the end of this book.

Free Deadbolt Locks

You can make breaking into your home a little harder by using a deadbolt lock. The Senior Lock Program provides locks and installation for Wilmington, Delaware homeowners, age 60 and over, whose income is under $10,000.

For more information, call the Wilmington Police Department Crime Prevention Unit, 300 N. Walnut St., Wilmington, DE 19801; 302-571-4470. For those outside of Delaware, contact your local police or fire department to learn what similar services they offer to seniors.

Free Fans

Fan Care is a great program sponsored by Virginia Power. If you are a resident of Virginia and 60 or older, you may be eligible for a free fan to help you make it safely through the hot summer.

To learn about eligibility requirements, contact Fan Care, Department for the Aging, 700 E Franklin St., 10th Floor, Richmond, VA 23219; 804-225-2271.

For those outside of Virginia, contact your state Department on Aging or your state utility commission, both listed in the Directory of State Information at the end of this book, to see what they have to offer.

☆ ☆ ☆

Free Phone Friends

Do what the telephone commercials tell you to do, and pick up the phone and call someone. Many seniors benefit from these telephone reassurance calls. They know people are calling to check on them on a regular basis, and it provides them needed contact with others. These phone calls don't require much of your time, but can offer a great deal in return.

To find out how you can become a volunteer phone friend, or to have a phone friend check on you, contact your state Department on Aging listed in the Directory of State Information at the end of this book.

☆ ☆ ☆

Turn 65, And Get A Discount

I bet you didn't realize that just by turning that magic number, you would actually be saving money left and right.

Golf courses, parks, beaches, fishing and hunting licenses, and even automobile tags are often provided to those over 65 at a great discount. All you need to do is ask.

You can:
- Save 1% on sales tax in South Carolina
- Save $100 on hearing aids in New Jersey
- Get free admission to state parks in many states

- Get free hunting and fishing licenses in most states
- Get a discount on cable television in New Jersey
- Save 15% on groceries in some stores in Ohio
- Get cheap tickets to the movies
- Go to the ballpark for half-price at many ballfields
- Get books of airplane tickets at cheap rates from most airlines
- Choose from lower-priced menus at many restaurants

Your state Department on Aging (see the Directory of State Information at the end of this book) can tell you about many of the state programs that provide these services to seniors, as well as many private enterprises.

Now the big question is, what are you going to do with all the money you save?

Help Close To Home

Did you know that Rhode Island will help pay for your hearing aid? Illinois will give you a reduced rate for your license tags. Ohio will give you a $50 tax credit against the amount of Ohio tax that you owe. Ohio also will provide you with a computerized printout of the special programs for which you qualify.

To learn more about programs which are specific to your state, contact your state Department on Aging. They can put you in contact with the right people to learn how you can save money on your utilities, medical bills, food, and even property taxes. Look in the Directory of State Information at the end of this book to locate your state Department on Aging.

Trouble With Utility Bills?

Can't afford to heat your house in the winter? Are you having trouble paying your electric or water bill because your income is so low?

Many utility offices offer special programs for seniors. Contact your local utility office to see if they have a program of discounts or reduced fees for seniors.

If the utility company is threatening to turn off your service because of unpaid bills, make sure to let them know you are a

Information USA, Inc.

senior citizen and need this service. In many cases, they will not cut off your service.

For more information, contact your local utility office. If you have trouble locating the office or need further assistance, contact your state Public Utilities Commission which is located in the Directory of State Information at the end of this book.

Sky High Bills?

Feel like your utility bill is high enough to heat your entire street? Think the meter reader needs his glasses checked?

If you are having trouble with your utility bills and have not gotten satisfaction from your local utility office, contact your State Public Utilities Commission office. This office regulates consumer services and rates for gas, electric, water, and telephone. They will help negotiate with your local office on your behalf.

To locate your state Public Utilities Commission office, look in the Directory of State Information at the end of this book.

Directory of
State Information

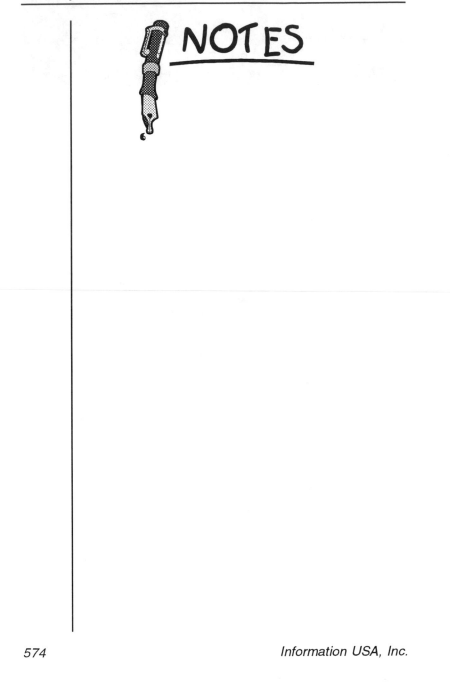

Alabama

*Federal Information
Center*
Birmingham, Mobile;
800-366-2998
All Other Locations;
301-722-9098

State Information Office
205-242-8000

*Cooperative Extension
Offices*
Dr. Ann Thompson,
Director
Alabama Cooperative
Extension Service
109 A Duncan Hall
Auburn University
Auburn, AL 36849-5612
205-844-4444

Chinelle Henderson,
Administrator
Alabama A&M University
Cooperative Extension
Service
P.O. Box 222
Normal, AL 35762
205-851-5710

Dr. Moore, Director
Cooperative Extension
Program
U.S. Department of

Agriculture
Tuskegee University
207 N. Main St., Suite 400
Tuskegee, AL 36083-1731
205-727-8806

Attorney Grievances
Alabama State Bar
Center for Professional
Responsibility
P.O. 671
Montgomery, AL 36101
205-269-1515

*Client Security Trust
Fund & Fee Arbitration*
Alabama State Bar
P.O. Box 671
Montgomery, AL 36101
205-269-1515

*State Consumer
Protection Office*
Consumer Protection
Division
Office of Attorney General
11 S. Union St.
Montgomery, AL 36130
205-242-7334
800-392-5658

HUD Field Office
600 Beacon Pkwy, West
Suite 300

Information USA, Inc.

Birmingham, AL 35209
205-290-7617

State Insurance Commissioner
Insurance Commissioner
135 S. Union St. #181
P.O. Box 303351
Montgomery, AL
36130-3351
205-269-3550

Nursing Home Ombudsmen
Commission on Aging
7070 Washington Ave.
R.F.A. Plaza, #470
Montgomery, AL 36130
205-242-5743
800-243-5463

State Government Banking Commissioner
Superintendent of Banks
101 S. Union St.
Montgomery, AL 36130
205-242-3452

State Office on Aging
Aging Commission
770 Washington Ave.
Suite 470
Montgomery, AL 36130
205-242-5743

State Utility Commission
Public Service Commission
P.O. Box 991
Montgomery, AL 36101
334-242-5207
800-392-8050 (AL only)

Alaska

Federal Information Center
Anchorage; 800-729-8003
All Other Locations;
301-722-9098

State Information Office
907-465-2111

Cooperative Extension Office
Hollis D. Hall, Director
Alaska Cooperative
Extension
University of Alaska
Fairbanks
P.O. Box 756180
Fairbanks, AK 99775-6180
907-474-7246

Attorney Grievances, Client Security Trust Fund, & Fee Arbitration
Alaska Bar Association
P.O. Box 100279
510 L. St., Suite 602
Anchorage, AK 99501
907-272-7469

State Consumer Protection Office
Attorney General
1031 W. Fourth Ave.
Suite 200
Anchorage, AK 99501
907-269-5100

HUD Field Office
Federal Bldg.
222 W. 8th Ave., #64
Anchorage, AK 99513
907-271-4170

State Insurance Commissioner
Director of Insurance
P.O. Box 110805
Juneau, AK 99811-0805
907-465-2515

Nursing Home Ombudsmen
Office of the Older
Alaskans Ombudsman
3601 C St.
Suite 260
Anchorage, AK 99503-5209
907-279-2232
800-478-9996 (long term care)

State Government Banking Commissioner
Director of Banking
Securities and Corporations
P.O. Box 110807
Juneau, AK 99811-0807
907-465-2521

State Office on Aging
Division of Senior Services
Commission on Aging
P.O. Box 110209
Juneau, AK 99811-0209
907-465-3250

State Utility Commission
Public Utilities Commission
1016 W. 6th Ave.
Suite 400
Anchorage, AK 99501
907-276-6222

Information USA, Inc.

Arizona

Federal Information Center
Phoenix; 800-359-3997
All Other Locations;
301-722-9098

State Information Office
602-542-4900

Cooperative Extension Office
Jim Christenson, Director
Cooperative Extension
Office
University of Arizona
Forbes 301
Tucson, AZ 85721
602-621-7205

Attorney Grievances, Client Security Trust Fund, & Fee Arbitration
Chief Bar Counsel
State Bar of Arizona
111 West Monroe
Suite 1800
Phoenix, AZ 85003-1742
602-252-4804

State Consumer Protection Office
Consumer Protection
Division
Office of Attorney General

1275 W. Washington St.
Room 259
Phoenix, AZ 85007
602-542-3702
800-352-8431 (AZ only)

HUD Field Office
400 N. 5th St.
Suite 1600
2 Arizona Center
Phoenix, AZ 85004
602-379-4434

State Insurance Commissioner
Director of Insurance
2910 N. 44th St., Suite 210
Phoenix, AZ 85018
602-912-8400

Nursing Home Ombudsmen
Aging and Adult
Administration
1789 W. Jefferson
Phoenix, AZ 85007
602-542-4446

State Government Banking Commissioner
Superintendent of Banks
2910 N. 44th St.
Suite 310
Phoenix, AZ 85018

602-255-4421
800-544-0708

Phoenix, AZ 85005
602-542-4446

State Office on Aging
Aging and Adult
Administration
Economic Security
Department
P.O. Box 6123

State Utility Commission
Corporation Commission
1200 W. Washington St.
Phoenix, AZ 85007
602-542-3935
800-222-7000 (AZ only)

Arkansas

Federal Information Center
Little Rock; 800-366-2998
All Other Locations;
301-722-9098

State Information Office
501-682-3000

Cooperative Extension Offices
David Foster, Director
Cooperative Extension
Service
P.O. Box 391
Little Rock, AR 72203
501-671-2000

Dr. Mazo Price, Director
Cooperative Extension
Service
1200 N. University
Box 4005
University of Arkansas at
Pine Bluff
Pine Bluff, AR 71601
501-543-8131

Attorney Grievances
Committee on Professional
Conduct
625 Marshall St., 2nd Floor
Little Rock, AR 72207
501-376-0313

Client Security Trust Fund
Clerk
Clerk Office
625 Marshall St.
Little Rock, AR 72201
501-682-6849

State Consumer Protection Office
Consumer Protection
Division
Office of Attorney General
200 Tower Building
323 Center St.
Little Rock, AR 72201
501-682-2341
800-482-8982 (AR only)

HUD Field Office
Lafayette Bldg.
Suite 200
523 Louisiana
Little Rock, AR 72201
501-324-5931

State Insurance Commissioner
Insurance Commissioner
1123 S. University
Suite 400
Little Rock, AR 72204
501-686-2900

Nursing Home Ombudsmen

Division of Aging and Adult
Services
1417 Donaghey Plaza
South
P.O. Box 1437
Little Rock, AR 72203-1437
501-682-2441

State Government Banking Commissioner

Bank Commissioner
Tower Bldg.
323 Center St., Suite 500
Little Rock, AR 72201
501-324-9019

State Office on Aging

Aging and Adult Services
Division
Human Services
Department
P.O. Box 1437
Little Rock, AR 72203
501-682-8491

State Utility Commission

Public Service Commission
1000 Center St.
P.O. Box 400
Little Rock, AR 72203-0400
501-682-1453
800-482-1164 (AR only)

California

Federal Information Center
Los Angeles, San Diego,
San Francisco, Santa Ana;
800-726-4995
Sacramento; 916-973-1695
All Other Locations;
301-722-9098

State Information Office
916-322-9900

Cooperative Extension Office
Kenneth Farrell, Vice
President
University of California
Division of Agriculture and
Natural Resources
300 Lakeside Dr., 6th Floor
Oakland, CA 94612-3560
510-987-0060

Attorney Grievances
Southern California
Chief Trial Counsel
State Bar of California
1149 South St., 4th Floor
Los Angeles, CA 90015
213-765-1000
800-843-9053 (CA only)

Northern California
Chief Trial Counsel

State Bar of California
100 Van Ness Ave.
28th Floor
San Francisco, CA 94102
415-561-8200
800-843-9053 (CA only)

Client Security Trust Fund
Southern California
Grievance Committee
State Bar of California
1149 S. Hill St., 9th Floor
Los Angeles, CA 90017
213-765-1140

Fee Arbitration
Chief Trial Counsel
State Bar of California
100 Van Ness Ave.
28th Floor
San Francisco, CA 94102
415-241-2020
800-843-9053 (CA only)

State Consumer Protection Offices
Public Inquiry Unit
Office of Attorney General
1515 K St., Suite 511
P.O. Box 944255
Sacramento, CA 94244
916-322-3360
800-952-5225 (CA only)

California Department of
Consumer Affairs
400 R St.
Sacramento, CA 95814
916-445-0660
800-344-4410 (CA only)

Bureau of Automotive
Repair
California Department of
Consumer Affairs
400 R St.
Sacramento, CA 95827
916-366-5100
800-952-5210 (CA only-
auto repair only)

HUD Field Offices
1615 W. Olympic Blvd.
Los Angeles, CA 90015
213-251-7122

450 Golden Gates Ave.
P.O. Box 36003
San Francisco, CA 94102
415-556-4752

777 12th St., Suite 200
Sacramento, CA 95814
916-551-1351

**State Insurance
Commissioner**
Commissioner of Insurance
300 S. Spring St.

Los Angeles, CA 90013
916-322-3555 (Santa
Monica)
213-346-6400 (Los
Angeles)
800-927-HELP (complaints)

**Nursing Home
Ombudsmen**
Department of Aging
1600 K St.
Sacramento, CA 95814
916-323-6681
or toll free in state:
800-231-4024

**State Government
Banking Commissioner**
Superintendent of Banks
111 Pine St., Suite 1100
San Francisco, CA 94111
415-557-3535
800-622-0620

State Office on Aging
Aging Commission
1020 9th St., Room 260
Sacramento, CA 95814
916-322-5630

State Utility Commission
Public Utilities Commission
505 Van Ness Ave.
San Francisco, CA 94102
415-703-1282

Colorado

Federal Information Center
Colorado Springs, Denver,
Pueblo; 800-359-3997
All Other Locations;
301-722-9098

State Information Office
303-866-5000

Cooperative Extension Office
Milan Rewets, Director
Colorado State University
Cooperative Extension
1 Administrative Building
Fort Collins, CO 80523
303-491-6281

Attorney Grievances S.C.D.C
Disciplinary Counsel
Supreme Court of Colorado
Dominion Plaza Bldg.
600 17th St.
Suite 510 S.
Denver, CO 80202
303-893-8121

Client Security Trust Fund
Colorado Bar Association
1900 Grant St., Suite 950
Denver, CO 80203-4309

303-863-7221
800-332-6736 (CO only)

Fee Arbitration
Legal Fee Arbitration
Committee
Colorado Bar Association
1900 Grant St., Suite 950
Denver, CO 80203-4309
303-860-1112
800-332-6736 (CO only)

State Consumer Protection Office
Consumer Protection Unit
Office of Attorney General
1525 Sherman St.
5th Floor
Denver, CO 80203
303-866-5189
800-332-2071 (CO only)

HUD Field Office
Executive Tower Bldg.
1405 Curtis St.
Denver, CO 80202
303-844-4513

State Insurance Commissioner
Commissioner of Insurance
1560 Broadway, Suite 850
Denver, CO 80202
303-894-7490

Nursing Home Ombudsmen
The Legal Center
455 Sherman St., Suite 130
Denver, CO 80203
303-722-0300
or toll free in-state:
800-288-1376

State Government Banking Commissioner
State Bank Commissioner
Division of Banking
1560 Broadway, Suite 1175
Denver, CO 80202
303-894-7575

State Office on Aging
Commission For Aging and
Adult Services
Social Services Dept.
110 16th St., Suite 200
Denver, CO 80202
303-620-4146

State Utility Commission
Public Utilities Commission
1580 Logan St.
Logan Tower
Office Level 2
Denver, CO 80203
303-894-2000
800-888-0170 (CO only)

Connecticut

**Federal Information
Center**
Hartford, New Haven;
800-347-1997
All Other Locations;
301-722-9098

State Information Office
203-240-0222

**Cooperative Extension
Office**
Associate Director
Cooperative Extension
System
University of Connecticut
1376 Storrs Rd.
Storrs, CT 06269-4036
203-486-4125

Attorney Grievances
Statewide Grievance
Committee
P.O. Box 260888
287 Main St.
2nd Floor, Suite 3
East Hartford, CT 06118
203-568-5157

**Client Security Trust
Fund**
George Buckley, Jr.
State Bar Association
101 Corporate Place

Rocky Hill, CT 06067-1894
203-721-0025

**Committee on Arbitration
of Fee Disputes**
State Bar Association
101 Corporate Place
Rocky Hill, CT 06067-1894
203-721-0025

**State Consumer
Protection Office**
Department of Consumer
Protection
State Office Building
165 Capitol Ave.
Hartford, CT 06106
203-566-4999
800-538-CARS(2277)
800-842-2649 (complaints
line) government
information (CT only)

HUD Field Office
330 Main St., 1st Floor
Hartford, CT 06106
203-240-4522

**State Insurance
Commissioner**
Insurance Commissioner
P.O. Box 816
Hartford, CT 06142-0816
203-297-3800

Information USA, Inc.

**Nursing Home
Ombudsmen**
Department of Social
Services
Elderly Services Division
25 Sigourney St.
Hartford, CT 06106
203-424-5242

**State Government
Banking Commissioner**
Banking Commissioner
44 Capitol Ave.
Hartford, CT 06106
203-566-4560

State Office on Aging
Elderly Services
Division of Social Services
25 Sigourney St.
Hartford, CT 06106
203-424-5025

State Utility Commission
Department of Public Utility
Control
One Central Park Plaza
New Britain, CT 06051
203-827-1553
800-382-4586 (CT only)

Delaware

Federal Information Center
All Locations; 301-722-9098

State Information Office
302-739-4000

Cooperative Extension Offices
Dr. Richard E. Fowler,
Director
Cooperative Extension
131 Townsend Hall
University of Delaware
Newark, DE 19717-1303
302-831-2504

Dr. Starlene Taylor
Assistant Administrator
Delaware State College
Cooperative Extension
Service
1200 N. DuPont Hwy.
Dover, DE 19901
302-739-5157

Attorney Grievances
Office of Disciplinary
Counsel
P.O. Box 472
Wilmington, DE 19899
302-571-8703

Lawyer's Fund for Client Protection
200 West 9th St.
Suite 300B
Wilmington, DE 19899
302-652-2117

State Consumer Protection Office
Justice Dept.
Attorney General
Consumer Protection Unit
820 N. French St.
4th Floor
Wilmington, DE 19801
302-577-3250

HUD Field Office
Liberty Square Bldg.
105 S. 7th St.
Philadelphia, PA 19106-
3392
215-597-2560

State Insurance Commissioner
Insurance Commissioner
841 Silver Lake Blvd.
Dover, DE 19901
302-739-4251
800-282-8611

Nursing Home Ombudsmen
Division of Aging
11-13 N. Church Ave.
Milford, DE 19963
302-422-1386
or toll free in-state:
800-292-1515

State Government Banking Commissioner
State Bank Commissioner
555 E. Lockerman St.
Suite 210
Dover, DE 19901
302-739-4235

State Office on Aging
Aging Division
Health and Social Services
Department
1901 N. Dupont Hwy.
New Castle, DE 19720
302-577-4660

State Utility Commission
Public Service Commission
1560 South DuPont
Highway
P.O. Box 457
Dover, DE 19903
302-739-4247
800-282-8574 (DE only)

Information USA, Inc.

District of Columbia

Cooperative Extension Office
Reginald Taylor, Acting
Director
Cooperative Extension
Service
University of the District of
Columbia
901 Newton St., NE
Washington, DC 20017
202-576-6993

Attorney Grievances
Office of Bar Counsel
515 5th St., NW
Building A, Room 127
Washington, DC 20001
202-638-1501

Client Security Trust Fund
District of Columbia Bar
11250 H St., NW
6th Floor
Washington, DC 20005
202-737-4700 x237

Fee Arbitration
Attorney-Client Arbitration
Board
District of Columbia Bar
1250 H St., NW, 6th Floor
Washington, DC 20005
202-737-4700 x238

State Consumer Protection Office
Department of Consumer
and Regulatory Affairs
614 H St., NW
Washington, DC 20001
202-727-7000

HUD Field Office
820 First St., NE
Washington, DC 20002
202-275-9200

State Insurance Commissioner
Commissioner of Insurance
441 4th St., NW
8th Floor N.
Washington, DC 20001
202-727-7424

Nursing Home Ombudsmen
Legal Counsel for the
Elderly
601 E. St., NW
Building A, 4th Floor
Washington, DC 20049
202-662-4933

State Government Banking Commissioner
Superintendent of Banking
and Financial Institutions

717 14th St., NW
11th Floor
Washington, DC 20006
202-727-1563

State Office on Aging
Aging Office
441 4th St., NW, Suite 900

Washington, DC 20001
202-724-5622

State Utility Commission
Public Service Commission
450 5th St., NW
Washington, DC 20001
202-626-5110

Florida

Federal Information Center
Ft. Lauderdale,
Jacksonville, Miami,
Orlando, St. Petersburg,
Tampa, West Palm Beach;
800-347-1997
All Other Locations;
301-722-9098

State Information Office
904-488-1234

Cooperative Extension Offices
John T. Woeste, Director
Florida Cooperative
Extension Service
P.O. Box 110210
University of Florida
Gainesville, FL 32611-0210

Lawrence Carter, Director
Cooperative Extension
Service
215 Perry Paige Building
Florida A&M University
Tallahassee, FL 32307
904-599-3546

Attorney Grievances, Client Security Trust Fund, & Fee Arbitration
Staff Counsel

Florida Bar
650 Apalachee Parkway
Tallahassee, FL 32399-2300
904-561-5839
800-342-8060 (FL only)

State Consumer Protection Office
Division of Consumer
Services
Mayo Building
Tallahassee, FL 32399-0800
904-488-2221
800-HELP-FLA (FL only)

HUD Field Office
301 W. Bay St. Suite 220
Jacksonville, FL 32202
904-232-2626

State Insurance Commissioner
Insurance Commissioner
200 E. Gaines St.
Tallahassee, FL
32399-0300
904-922-3100
800-342-2762

State Government Banking Commissioner
State Comptroller

Division of Banking
State Capitol Bldg.
Tallahassee, FL 32399
904-488-0286

State Office on Aging
Aging and Adult Services
Office
Health and Rehabilitative
Services Division
1317 Winewood Blvd.

Tallahassee, FL 32399-
0700
904-488-2881

State Utility Commission
Public Service Commission
101 E. Gaines St.
Tallahassee, FL 32399-
0850
904-488-5573
800-342-3552 (FL only)

Georgia

Federal Information Center
Atlanta;
800-347-1997
All Other Locations;
301-722-9098

State Information Office
404-656-2000

Cooperative Extension Offices
Wayne Jordon, Director
Cooperative Extension
Service
University of Georgia
1111 Conner Hall
Athens, GA 30602
706-542-3824

Dr. Fred Harrison, Jr.,
Director
Cooperative Extension
Service
P.O. Box 4061
Fort Valley State College
Fort Valley, GA 31030
912-825-6269

Attorney Grievances & Committee on Arbitration of Fee Disputes
State Bar of Georgia
Office of General Counsel

800 Hurt Bldg.
50 Hurt Plaza
Atlanta, GA 30303
404-527-8720
404-527-8752 for fee
arbitration
404-527-8771 for client
security trust fund

State Consumer Protection Office
Office of Consumer Affairs
2 Martin Luther King, Jr. Dr.
Suite 356
Plaza Level
East Tower
Atlanta, GA 30334
404-656-3790
800-869-1123 (GA only)

HUD Field Office
Richard B. Russell Federal
Bldg.
75 Spring St., SW
Atlanta, GA 30303
404-331-5136

State Insurance Commissioner
Insurance Commissioner
2 Martin Luther King, Jr. Dr.
Atlanta, GA 30334
404-656-2056

Nursing Home Ombudsmen
Office of Aging
Department of Human Resources
2 Peachtree St., NW
18th Floor
Atlanta, GA 30303
404-894-5336

State Government Banking Commissioner
Commissioner of Banking and Finance
2990 Brandywine Rd.
Suite 200

Atlanta, GA 30341
404-986-1633

State Office on Aging
Aging Services Office
2 Peachtree St., NW
Atlanta, GA 30303
404-657-5258

State Utility Commission
Public Service Commission
244 Washington St., SW
Atlanta, GA 30334
404-656-4501
800-282-5813 (GA only)

Hawaii

Federal Information Center
Honolulu; 800-733-5996
All Other Locations;
301-722-9098

State Information Office
808-548-6222

Cooperative Extension Office
Dr. Po'Yung Lai, Assistant
Director
Cooperative Extension
Service
3050 Maile Way
Honolulu, HI 96822
808-956-8397

Attorney Grievances
Office of Disciplinary
Counsel
Supreme Court of the State
of Hawaii
1164 Bishop St., Suite 600
Honolulu, HI 96813
808-521-4591

Lawyers Fund for Client Protection of the Bar of Hawaii
1164 Bishop St., Suite 600
Honolulu, HI 96813
808-599-2483

Fee Arbitration
Attorney-Client
Coordination Committee
Hawaii State Bar
Association
P.O. Box 26
Honolulu, HI 96810
808-537-1868

State Consumer Protection Office
Office of Consumer
Protection
Department of Commerce
and Consumer Affairs
828 Fort Street Mall
Suite 600B
P.O. Box 3767
Honolulu, HI 96813-3767
808-587-3222

HUD Field Office
7 Waterfront Plaza
Suite 500
500 Ala Moana Blvd.
Honolulu, HI 96813-4918
808-541-1323

State Insurance Commissioner
Insurance Commissioner
P.O. Box 3614
Honolulu, HI 96811
808-586-2790

Nursing Home Ombudsmen
Executive Office on Aging
335 Merchant St.
Room 241
Honolulu, HI 96813
808-586-0100

State Government Banking Commissioner
Commissioner
Financial Institutions
P.O. Box 2054
Honolulu, HI 96805
808-586-2820

State Office on Aging
Aging Office
335 Merchant St.
Room 241
Honolulu, HI 96813
808-586-0100

State Utility Commission
Public Utilities Commission
465 S. King St.
Room 103
Honolulu, HI 96813
808-586-2020

Idaho

Federal Information Center
All Locations;
301-722-9098

State Information Office
208-334-2411

Cooperative Extension Office
Dr. LeRoy D. Luft,
Director
Cooperative Extension
System
College of Agriculture
University of Idaho
Moscow, ID 83844-2338
208-885-6639

Attorney Grievances, Client Security Trust Fund, & Fee Arbitration
Bar Counsel
Idaho State Bar
P.O. Box 895
Boise, ID 83701
208-334-4500

HUD Field Office
520 SW 6th Ave.
Portland, OR 97204
503-326-2561

State Insurance Commissioner
Director of Insurance
700 W. State St.
Boise, ID 83720
208-334-2250

Nursing Home Ombudsmen
Office on Aging
State House, Room 108
700 W. Jefferson
P.O. Box 83720
Boise, ID 83720-0007
208-334-3833

State Government Banking Commissioner
Department of Finance
P.O. Box 83720
Boise, ID 83720-0031
208-334-3319

State Office on Aging
Aging Office
P.O. Box 83720
Boise, ID 83720-0007
208-334-3833

State Utility Commission
Public Utilities Commission
P.O. Box 83720
Boise, ID 83720-0074
208-334-3427

Illinois

Federal Information Center
Chicago; 800-366-2998
All Other Locations;
301-722-9098

State Information Office
217-782-2000

Cooperative Extension Office
Donald Uchtmann, Director
University of Illinois
Cooperative Extension Svc.
122 Mumford Hall
1301 W. Gregory Dr.
Urbana, IL 61801
217-333-2660

Attorney Grievances
Attorney Registration and
Disciplinary Commission of
the Supreme Court of
Illinois
One N. Old Capitol Plaza
Suite 345
Springfield, IL 62701-1507
217-522-6838
800-252-8048 (IL only)

Client Protection Program
1 Prudential Plaza
130 E. Randolph Dr.

Suite 1500
Chicago, IL 60601
312-565-2600

Illinois State Bar
Association
424 S. Second St.
Springfield, IL 62701
217-525-1760

State Consumer Protection Office
Consumer Division
Attorney General's Office
500 S. Second St.
Springfield, IL 62706
217-217-782-9011
217-782-9012
800-252-8666 (IL only)

HUD Field Office
77 W. Jackson Blvd.
26th Floor
Chicago, IL 60604-3507
312-353-5680

State Insurance Commissioner
Director of Insurance
320 W. Washington St.
Springfield, IL 62767
217-782-4515

Nursing Home
Ombudsmen
Department on Aging
421 East Capitol Ave
Springfield, IL 62701
217-785-3140
or toll free:
800-252-8966

217-782-7966
800-634-5452

State Office on Aging
Aging Department
421 E. Capitol Ave. #100
Springfield, IL 62701-1789
217-385-2870

State Government
Banking Commissioner
Commissioner of Banks
and Trust Companies
500 E. Monroe St.
Springfield, IL 62701

State Utility Commission
Commerce Commission
527 E. Capitol Ave.
P.O. Box 19280
Springfield, IL 62794-9280
217-782-7295

Indiana

Federal Information Center
Gary; 800-366-2998
Indianapolis; 800-347-1997
All Other Locations;
301-722-9098

State Information Office
317-232-1000

Cooperative Extension Office
Dr. Wadsworth, Director
1140 AGAD
CES Administration
Purdue University
West Lafayette, IN
47907-1140
317-494-8489

Attorney Grievances
Disciplinary Commission of
the Supreme Court of
Indiana
150 W. Washington St.
South Tower, Suite 1060
Indianapolis, IN 46204
317-232-1807

Clients' Financial Assistance Fund
Attn: Tom Pyrz
Indiana State Bar
Association

230 E. Ohio St., 4th Floor
Indianapolis, IN 46204
317-639-5465

Fee Arbitration
Contact Clients' Financial
Assistance Fund for referral
to local programs.

State Consumer Protection Office
Consumer Protection
Division
Office of Attorney General
219 State House
402 W. Washington
5th Floor
Indianapolis, IN 46204
317-232-6330
800-382-5516 (IN only)

HUD Field Office
151 N. Delaware St.
Indianapolis, IN 46204
317-226-6303

State Insurance Commissioner
Commissioner of Insurance
311 W. Washington St.
Suite 300
Indianapolis, IN 46204
317-232-2385
800-622-4461

Nursing Home Ombudsmen
Aging Division
Department of Human Services
P.O. Box 7083
Indianapolis, IN 46207-7083
317-232-7020
or toll free in-state:
800-622-4484

State Government Banking Commissioner
Department of Financial Institutions
402 W. High St.
Room W066
Indianapolis, IN 46204-2751

317-232-3955
800-382-4880

State Office on Aging
Aging and Rehabilitative Services Division
Family and Social Services Administration
402 W. Washington St.
Room N451
Indianapolis, IN 46207
317-232-1147

State Utility Commission
Utility Regulatory Commission
302 W. Washington St.
Suite E306
Indianapolis, IN 46204
317-232-2701

Iowa

Federal Information Center
All Locations; 800-735-8004

State Information Office
515-281-5011

Cooperative Extension Office
Dr. Robert Anderson,
Director
Cooperative Extension
Service
315 Boardshear
Iowa State University
Ames, IA 50011
515-294-9434

Attorney Grievances and Fee Arbitration
Iowa State Bar Association
521 E. Locust
Des Moines, IA 50309
515-243-3179

Client Security Trust Fund
Client Security Trust Fund
Commission
Iowa Supreme Court
Iowa State House
State Capitol
Des Moines, IA 50319
515-246-8076

State Consumer Protection Office
Iowa Citizens' Aide
Ombudsman
215 E. 7th St.
Capitol Complex
Des Moines, IA 50319
515-281-3592
800-358-5510 (IA only)

HUD Field Office
Federal Bldg.
210 Walnut St.
Room 239
Des Moines, IA 50309
515-284-4512

State Insurance Commissioner
Insurance Commissioner
Lucas State Office Bldg.
6th Floor
Des Moines, IA 50319
515-281-5705

Nursing Home Ombudsmen
Department of Elder Affairs
914 Grand Ave.
Suite 236
Des Moines, IA 50309-2801
515-281-5187
or toll free in-state:
800-532-3213

State Government
Banking Commissioner
Superintendent of Banking
200 E. Grand, Suite 300
Des Moines, IA 50309
515-281-4014

State Office on Aging
Elder Affairs Department
236 Jewett Bldg.

914 Grand Ave.
Des Moines, IA 50309
515-281-5188

State Utility Commission
Iowa Utilities Board
Lucas State Office Building
5th Floor
Des Moines, IA 50319
515-281-5979

Kansas

Federal Information Center
All Locations; 800-735-8004

State Information Office
913-296-0111

Cooperative Extension Office
Mark Johnson, Interim
Director
Cooperative Extension
Service
Kansas State University
123 Umberger Hall
Manhattan, KS 66506
913-532-5820

Attorney Grievances, Client Security Trust Fund & Fee Arbitration
Disciplinary Administrator,
Supreme Court of Kansas
3706 S. Topeka Ave.
Suite 100
Topeka, KS 66609
913-296-2486

State Consumer Protection Office
Consumer Protection Div.
Office of Attorney General
Kansas Judicial Center
301 West 10th St.

Topeka, KS 66612
913-296-3751
800-432-2310 (KS only)

HUD Field Office
Gateway Towers 2
400 State Ave.
Kansas City, KS 66101
913-236-2162

State Insurance Commissioner
Commissioner of Insurance
420 SW 9th St.
Topeka, KS 66612
913-296-7801
800-432-2484

Nursing Home Ombudsmen
Department on Aging
Docking State Office
Building 150 South
915 Southwest Harrison St.
Topeka, KS 66612-4986
913-296-4986
or toll free in-state:
800-432-3535

State Government Banking Commissioner
State Bank Commissioner
700 SW Jackson St.
Suite 300

Topeka, KS 66603
913-296-2266

State Office on Aging
Aging Department
915 SW Harrison St.
Room 150
Topeka, KS 66612-1500
913-296-4986

State Utility Commission
State Corporation
Commission
1500 SW Arrowhead Rd.
Topeka, KS 66604-4027
913-271-3100
800-662-0027 (KS only)

Kentucky

Federal Information Center
Louisville; 800-347-1997
All Other Locations;
301-722-9098

State Information Office
502-564-3130

Cooperative Extension Offices
Dr. Absher, Director
Cooperative Extension
Service
310 W.P. Garrigus Building
University of Kentucky
Lexington, KY 40546
606-257-1846

Dr. Harold Benson, Director
Kentucky State University
Cooperative Extension
Program
Frankfort, KY 40601
502-227-5905

Attorney Grievances, Client Security Trust Fund, Fee Arbitration
Kentucky Bar Association
514 W. Main
Frankfort, KY 40601-1883
502-564-3795

State Consumer Protection Office
Consumer Protection
Division
Office of Attorney General
209 St. Clair St.
Frankfort, KY 40601
502-573-2200
800-432-9257 (KY only)

HUD Field Office
P.O. Box 1044
601 W. Broadway
Louisville, KY 40201
502-582-5251

State Insurance Commissioner
Insurance Commissioner
215 W. Main St.
P.O. Box 517
Frankfort, KY 40602
502-564-3630

Nursing Home Ombudsmen
Division for Aging Services
Dept. for Social Services
275 East Main St.
5th Floor West
Frankfort, KY 40621
502-564-6930
or toll free in-state:
800-372-2991

State Government
Banking Commissioner
Commissioner, Department
of Financial Institutions
477 Versailles Rd.
Frankfort, KY 40601
502-573-3390

State Office on Aging
Aging Services Division
Social Services Department

275 E. Main St., 5th Floor
Frankfort, KY 40621
502-564-6930

State Utility Commission
Public Service Commission
730 Schenkel Lane
P.O. Box 615
Frankfort, KY 40602
502-564-3940
800-772-4636

Louisiana

Federal Information Center
New Orleans;
800-366-2998
All Other Locations;
301-722-9098

State Information Office
504-342-6600

Cooperative Extension Offices
Bruce Flint, Director
Cooperative Extension
Service
Louisiana State University
P.O. Box 25100
Baton Rouge, LA
70894-5100
504-388-4141

Dr. Adell Brown, Assistant
Administrator
Cooperative Extension
Program
Southern University and
A&M College
P.O. Box 10010
Baton Rouge, LA 70813
504-771-2242

Grievances Fund
Office of Disciplinary
Counsel
601 St. Charles Ave.
4th Floor
New Orleans, LA 70130
504-523-1414

Client Security Trust Fund
Executive Counsel
Louisiana State Bar
Association
601 St. Charles Ave.
New Orleans, LA 70130
504-566-1600
800-421-5722 (toll free)

State Consumer Protection Office
Consumer Protection
Section
Office of Attorney General
State Capitol Building
P.O. Box 94005
Baton Rouge, LA 70804
504-342-9638

HUD Field Office
Fisk Federal Bldg.
1661 Canal St.
New Orleans, LA 70112
504-589-7200

State Insurance Commissioner
Commissioner of Insurance

P.O. Box 94214
Baton Rouge, LA
70804-9214
504-342-5900

Nursing Home
Ombudsmen
Governors Office of Elderly
Affairs
4550 North Blvd, 2nd Floor
Baton Rouge, LA 70806
504-925-1700
800-259-4990

State Government
Banking Commissioner
Commissioner
Financial Institutions
P.O. Box 94095

Baton Rouge, LA
70804-9095
504-925-4660

State Office on Aging
Elderly Affairs
P.O. Box 80374
Baton Rouge, LA 70898-
0374
504-925-1700

State Utility Commission
Public Service Commission
One American Place
Suite 1630
P.O. Box 9115H
Baton Rouge, LA 70825
504-342-4404
800-228-9368 (LA only)

Maine

Federal Information Center
All Locations; 301-722-9098

State Information Office
207-582-9500

Cooperative Extension Office
Vaughn Holyoke, Director
Cooperative Extension Svc.
University of Maine
5741 Libby Hall, Room 102
Orono, ME 04469-5741
207-581-3188

Attorney Grievances and Fee Arbitration
Maine Board of Overseers
of the Bar
P.O. Box 1820
Augusta, ME 04332-1820
207-623-1121

State Consumer Protection Office
Consumer Assistance Svcs.
Office of Attorney General
State House Station No. 6
Augusta, ME 04333
207-626-8849

HUD Field Office
Norris Cotton Federal Bldg

275 Chestnut St.
Manchester, NH 03101
603-666-7681

State Insurance Commissioner
Superintendent of
Insurance
State House Station 34
Augusta, ME 04333
207-582-8707

State Government Banking Commissioner
Superintendent of Banking
State House Station #36
Augusta, ME 04333-0036
207-582-8713

State Office on Aging
Elder and Adult Services
Human Services Dept.
State House Station #11
35 Anthony Ave.
Augusta, ME 04333
207-624-5335

State Utility Commission
Public Utilities Commission
State House Station 18
Augusta, ME 04333-0018
207-287-3831
800-452-4699 (ME only)

Maryland

Federal Information Center
Baltimore; 800-347-1997
All Other Locations;
301-722-9098

State Information Office
410-974-2000

Cooperative Extension Offices
Dr. Nan Booth
Regional Directors Office
Cooperative Extension
Service
Room 2120, Simons Hall
University of Maryland
College Park, MD 20742
301-405-2907

Dr. Henry Brookes,
Administrator
Cooperative Extension
Service, UMES
Princess Anne, MD 21853
410-651-6206

Attorney Grievance Commission and the Committee on Resolution of Fee Disputes
100 Community Place
Suite 3301
Crownsville, MD 21032

410-514-7051
800-492-1660 (MD only)

Client Security Trust Fund
100 Community Place
Suite 3301
Crownsville, MD 21032
410-987-9478

State Consumer Protection Office
Consumer Protection Div.
Office of Attorney General
200 St. Paul Pl.
Baltimore, MD 21202
410-528-8662
202-727-7000 in the
Washington, DC metro area

HUD Field Office
Equitable Bldg., 3rd Floor
10 N. Calvert St.
Baltimore, MD 21202
301-962-2520

State Insurance Commissioner
Insurance Commissioner
501 St. Paul Place
7th Floor S.
Baltimore, MD 21202
410-333-6300
800-492-6116

Nursing Home Ombudsmen
Office on Aging
301 West Preston St.
10th Floor
Baltimore, MD 21201
410-225-1100

State Government Banking Commissioner
Bank Commissioner
501 St. Paul Place
13th Floor
Baltimore, MD 21202
410-333-6330

State Office on Aging
Aging Office
301 W. Preston St.
Room 1004
Baltimore, MD 21201-2374
410-225-1102

State Utility Commission
Public Service Commission
6 St. Paul St.
Baltimore, MD 21202
410-767-8000
800-492-0474 (MD only)

Massachusetts

Federal Information Center
Boston;
800-347-1997
All Other Locations;
301-722-9098

State Information Office
617-722-2000

Cooperative Extension Office
Dr. John Gerber,
Associate Director
210C Stockbridge Hall
University of Massachusetts
Amherst, MA 01003
413-545-4800

Attorney Grievances and Client Security Trust Fund
Massachusetts Board of
Bar Overseers
75 Federal St.
Boston, MA 02110
617-357-1860

Fee Arbitration
Massachusetts Bar
Association
Fee Arbitration Board
Attn: Stacy Shunk
20 West St.

Boston, MA 02111-1218
617-542-3602

State Consumer Protection Office
Consumer Protection
Division
Department of Attorney
General
131 Tremont St.
Boston, MA 02111
617-727-8400

HUD Field Office
Thomas P. O'Neill Jr.,
Federal Bldg.
10 Cassoway St.
Room 375
Boston, MA 02222
617-565-5234

State Insurance Commissioner
Commissioner of Insurance
470 Atlantic Ave.
6th Floor
Boston, MA 02210
617-521-7777

Nursing Home Ombudsmen
Executive Office of Elder
Affairs
1 Ashburton Place

Boston, MA 02101
617-727-7750
or toll free in-state:
800-882-2003

**State Government
Banking Commissioner**
Commissioner of Banks
100 Cambridge St.
Boston, MA 02202
617-727-3120

State Office on Aging
Elder Affairs Department
1 Ashburton Place
5th Floor, Room 517
Boston, MA 02108
617-727-7750

State Utility Commission
Dept. of Public Utilities
100 Cambridge St., 12th Fl.
Boston, MA 02202
617-727-3500

Michigan

Federal Information Center
Detroit, Grand Rapids;
800-347-1997
All Other Locations;
301-722-9098

State Information Office
517-373-1837

Cooperative Extension Office
Gail Emig, Director
Michigan State University
Extension
Room 108, Agriculture Hall
Michigan State University
East Lansing, MI 48824
517-355-2308

Attorney Grievances
Michigan Attorney
Grievance Commission
243 W. Congress
Marquette Bldg., Suite 256
Detroit, MI 48226
313-961-6585

Client Protection Fund and Fee Arbitration
State Bar of Michigan
306 Townsend St.
Lansing, MI 48933-2083
517-372-9030

State Consumer Protection Office
Consumer Protection
Division
Office of Attorney General
P.O. Box 30213
Lansing, MI 48909
517-373-1140

HUD Field Offices
Patrick V. McNamara
Federal Bldg.
477 Michigan Ave
Detroit, MI 48226
313-226-7900

2922 Fuller Ave., NE
Grand Rapids, MI 49505
616-456-2100

State Insurance Commissioner
Commissioner of Insurance
Insurance Bureau
P.O. Box 30220
Lansing, MI 48909-7720
517-373-9273

Nursing Home Ombudsmen
Citizens for Better Care
416 N. Homer, Suite 101
Lansing, MI 48912-4700
517-336-6753

or toll free in-state:
800-292-7852

State Government
Banking Commissioner
Commissioner
Financial Institutions
Bureau
P.O. Box 48909
Lansing, MI 48933
517-373-3460

State Office on Aging
Aging Office
P.O. Box 30026
Lansing, MI 48909
517-373-8230

State Utility Commission
Public Service Commission
6545 Mercantile Way
P.O. Box 30221
Lansing, MI 48909
517-334-6445
800-292-9555 (MI only)

Minnesota

Federal Information
Center
Minneapolis; 800-366-2998
All Other Locations;
301-722-9098

State Information Office
612-296-6013

Cooperative Extension
Office
Patrick Borich
Minnesota Extension
Service
University of Minnesota
240 Coffey Hall
1420 Eckles Ave.
St. Paul, MN 55108
612-625-3797

Attorney Grievances and
Client Security Trust
Fund
Office of Lawyers'
Professional Responsibility
25 Constitution Ave.
Suite 101
St. Paul, MN 55155-4196
612-296-3952
800-657-3601 (MN only)

Fee Arbitration
Minnesota Bar Association
514 Nicollet Mall

Suite 300
Minneapolis, MN 55402
612-333-1183
800-882-MSBA (MN only)

State Consumer
Protection Office
Office of Consumer
Services
Office of Attorney General
1400 N.C.L. Tower
445 Minnesota St.
St. Paul, MN 55101
612-296-3353

HUD Field Office
220 2nd St., South
Minneapolis, MN 55401
612-370-3000

State Insurance
Commissioner
Commissioner of
Commerce
133 E. 7th St.
St. Paul, MN 55101
612-296-2594

Nursing Home
Ombudsmen
Board on Aging
Office of Ombudsman for
Older Minnesotans
444 Lafayette Rd.

St. Paul, MN 55155-3843
612-296-2770
800-657-3591

State Government
Banking Commissioner
Deputy Commissioner of
Commerce
133 E. 7th St.
St. Paul, MN 55101
612-296-2135

State Office on Aging
Aging Program Division
Social Services Department
444 LaFayette Rd.
St. Paul, MN 55155-3843
612-296-2544

State Utility Commission
Public Utilities Commission
121 7th Place East
St. Paul, MN 55501-2147
612-296-7124
800-657-3782 (MN only)

Mississippi

Federal Information
Center
All Locations; 301-722-9098

State Information Office
601-359-1000

Cooperative Extension
Offices
Danny Cheatham, Director
Cooperative Extension
Service
Mississippi State University
P.O. Box 9601
Mississippi State, MS
39762
601-325-3034

LeRoy Davis, Dean
P.O. Box 690
Alcorn Cooperative
Extension Program
Lorman, MS 39096
601-877-6128

Attorney Grievances,
Client Security Trust
Fund, & Fee Arbitration
Mississippi State Bar
P.O. Box 2168
Jackson, MS 39225-2168
601-948-4471
800-682-6423 (MS only)

State Consumer
Protection Office
Consumer Protection Div.
Office of Attorney General
P.O. Box 22947
Jackson, MS 39225
601-359-4230

HUD Field Office
Dr. A.H. McCoy Federal
Bldg.
100 W. Capitol St.
Room 910
Jackson, MS 39269
601-965-5308

State Insurance
Commissioner
Commissioner of Insurance
1804 Walter Sillers Bldg.
P.O. Box 79
Jackson, MS 39201-0079
601-359-3569
800-562-2957

Nursing Home
Ombudsmen
Division of Aging and Adult
Services
750 N. State St.
Jackson, MS 39202
601-359-4927
or toll free in-state:
800-948-3090

State Government
Banking Commissioner
Commissioner
Department of Banking and
Consumer Finance
P.O. Box 23729
Jackson, MS 39225-3729
601-359-1031
800-844-2499

State Office on Aging
Aging and Adult Services

Division
Human Services
Department
P.O. Box 352
Jackson, MS 39205-0352
601-359-4929

State Utility Commission
Public Service Commission
P.O. Box 1174
Jackson, MS 39215
601-961-5400

Information USA, Inc.

Missouri

Federal Information Center
St. Louis; 800-366-2998
All Other Locations;
800-735-8004

State Information Office
314-751-2000

Cooperative Extension Offices
Ronald J. Turner, Interim
Director
Cooperative Extension
Service
University of Missouri
309 University Hall
Columbia, MO 65211
314-882-7754

George Enlaw, Director
Cooperative Extension
Service
Lincoln University
110A Allen Hall
P.O. Box 29
Jefferson City, MO
65102-0029
314-681-5550

Attorney Grievances
Office of Chief Disciplinary
Council
3335 American Ave.

Jefferson City, MO 65109
314-635-7400

Client Security Trust Fund & Fee Arbitration
Missouri Bar Association
P.O. Box 119
Jefferson City, MO 65102
314-635-4128

State Consumer Protection Office
Public Protection Division
Office of Attorney General
P.O. Box 899
Jefferson City, MO 65102
314-751-3321
800-392-8222 (MO only)

HUD Field Offices
(Eastern)
1222 Spruce St.
St. Louis, MO 63103
314-539-6560

(Western)
Gateway Towers 2
400 State Ave.
Kansas City, KS 66101
913-236-2162

State Insurance Commissioner
Director of Insurance

301 W. High St.
Room 630
P.O. Box 690
Jefferson City, MO 65102
314-751-4126

Nursing Home Ombudsmen
Division of Aging
P.O. Box 1337
Jefferson City, MO 65102
314-751-3082

State Government Banking Commissioner
Commissioner of Finance
P.O. Box 716

Jefferson City, MO 65102
314-751-3242

State Office on Aging
Aging Division
P.O. Box 1337
Jefferson City, MO 65102
314-751-8535

State Utility Commission
Public Service Commission
P.O. Box 360
Jefferson City, MO 65102
314-751-3234
800-392-4211 (MO only)

Montana

Federal Information Center
All Locations; 301-722-9098

State Information Office
406-444-2511

Cooperative Extension Office
Andrea Pagenkopf
Vice Provost for Outreach
and Director of Extension
212 Montana Hall
Montana State University
Bozeman, MT 59717
406-994-4371

Attorney Grievances
Commission on Practice of
the Supreme Court of
Montana
Justice Bldg.
Room 315
215 N. Sanders
Helena, MT 59620-3002
406-444-2634

Client Security Trust Fund & Fee Arbitration
State Bar of Montana
P.O. Box 577
Helena, MT 59624
406-442-7660

State Consumer Protection Office
Office of Consumer Affairs
Department of Commerce
1424 9th Ave.
Helena, MT 59620
406-444-4312

HUD Field Office
Executive Tower Bldg.
1405 Curtis St.
Denver, CO 80202
303-844-4513

State Insurance Commissioner
Commissioner of Insurance
P.O. Box 4009
Helena, MT 59604-4009
406-444-2040
800-332-6148

Nursing Home Ombudsmen
Governor's Office on Aging
Family Services
P.O. Box 8005
Helena, MT 59604-8005
406-444-4676

State Government Banking Commissioner
Commissioner
Division of Banking and

Financial Institutions
1520 E. Sixth Ave.
Room 50
Helena, MT 59620
406-444-2091

State Office on Aging
Aging Services Coordinator
Family Services Dept.

Box 8005
Helena, MT 59604
406-444-5900

State Utility Commission
Public Service Commission
1701 Prospect Ave.
P.O. Box 202601
Helena, MT 59620-2601
406-444-6199

Nebraska

Federal Information Center
Omaha; 800-366-2998
All Other Locations;
800-735-8004

State Information Office
402-471-2311

Cooperative Extension Office
Lloyd Young, Director
University of Nebraska
S.E. Research and
Extension Center
211 Mussehl Hall
East Campus
Lincoln, NE 68583
402-472-3674

Attorney Grievances & Client Security Fund
Counsel for Discipline
Nebraska State Bar
Association
635 S. 14th St.
Lincoln, NE 68501-1809
402-475-7091

State Consumer Protection Office
Consumer Protection
Division
Office of Attorney General

2115 State Capitol
Room 2115
Lincoln, NE 68509
402-471-2682

HUD Field Office
10909 Mill Valley Rd.
Omaha, NE 68154
402-492-3100

State Insurance Commissioner
Director of Insurance
941 O St., Suite 400
Lincoln, NE 68508
402-471-2201

Nursing Home Ombudsmen
Department on Aging
State Office Building
P.O. Box 95044
Lincoln, NE 68509
402-471-2306
402-471-2307
800-942-7830

State Government Banking Commissioner
Director of Banking and
Finance
P.O. Box 95006
Lincoln, NE 68509
402-471-2171

State Office on Aging
Aging Department
P.O. Box 95044
Lincoln, NE 68509-5044
402-471-2308

State Utility Commission
Public Service Commission
300 The Atrium
1200 N St.
P.O. Box 94927
Lincoln, NE 68509
402-471-3101

Nevada

**Federal Information
Center**
All Locations; 301-722-9098

State Information Office
702-687-5000

**Cooperative Extension
Office**
Bernard M. Jones, Director
Nevada Cooperative
Extension
University of Nevada, Reno
Mail Stop 189
Reno, NV 89557-0106
702-784-1614

**Attorney Grievances,
Client Security Trust
Fund, & Fee Arbitration**
State Bar of Nevada
201 Las Vegas Blvd., South
Suite 200
Las Vegas, NV 89101
702-382-0502

**State Consumer
Protection Office**
Consumer Affairs Division
Department of Commerce
4600 Kietezke Lane
Building B
Suite 113
Reno, NV 89502

702-688-1800
800-992-0900 (NV only)

HUD Field Office
(Las Vegas, Clark Co)
400 N. 5th St., Suite 1600
2 Arizona Center
Phoenix, AZ 85004
602-379-4434

(Remainder of State)
450 Golden Gate Ave.
P.O. Box 36003
San Francisco, CA 94102
415-556-4752

**State Insurance
Commissioner**
Commissioner of Insurance
1665 Hot Springs Rd.
Capitol Complex 152
Carson City, NV 89706
702-687-4270
800-992-0900

**Nursing Home
Ombudsmen**
Division for Aging Services
Department of Human
Resources
340 N. 11th St.
Suite 203
Las Vegas, NV 89101
702-486-3545

State Government
Banking Commissioner
Commissioner
Financial Institutions
406 E. Second St.
Carson City, NV 89710
702-687-4260

State Office on Aging
Aging Services Division
Human Resources Dept.

340 N. 11th St.
Howard Cannon Center
Las Vegas, NV 89101
702-786-3545

State Utility Commission
Public Service Commission
727 Fairview Dr.
Carson City, NV 89710
702-687-6000

New Hampshire

**Federal Information
Center**
All Locations; 301-722-9098

State Information Office
603-271-1110

**Cooperative Extension
Office**
Peter J. Horne
Dean and Director
UNH Cooperative
Extension
59 College Rd.
Taylor Hall
Durham, NH 03824
603-862-1520

Attorney Grievances
New Hampshire Supreme
Court
Professional Conduct
Committee
4 Park St.
Suite 304
Concord, NH 03301
603-224-5828

**Clients' Indemnity Fund &
Fee Resolution
Committee**
New Hampshire Bar
Association
112 Pleasant St.

Concord, NH 03301
603-224-6942

**State Consumer
Protection Office**
Consumer Protection and
Antitrust Bureau
Office of Attorney General
33 Capitol St.
Concord, NH 03301-0397
603-271-3641

HUD Field Office
Norris Cotton Federal Bldg.
275 Chestnut St.
Manchester, NH 03101
603-666-7681

**State Insurance
Commissioner**
Insurance Commissioner
169 Manchester St.
Concord, NH 03301
603-271-2261
800-852-3416

**Nursing Home
Ombudsmen**
Division of Elderly and
Adult Services
State Office Park South
Annex One
115 Pleasant St.
Concord, NH 03301-3843

603-271-4375
or toll free in-state:
800-442-5640

**State Government
Banking Commissioner**
Bank Commissioner
169 Manchester St.
Concord, NH 03301
603-271-3561

State Office on Aging
Elderly and Adult Services
Division

State Office Park South
115 Pleasant St.
Annex Bldg. 1
Concord, NH 03301-3843
603-271-4384

State Utility Commission
Public Utilities Commission
8 Old Suncook Rd.
Building #1
Concord, NH 03301
603-271-2431
800-852-3793 (NH only)

Information USA, Inc.

New Jersey

Federal Information Center
Newark, Trenton;
800-347-1997
All Other Locations;
301-722-9098

State Information Office
609-292-2121

Cooperative Extension Office
Mr. Helsel, Director
Rutgers Cooperative
Extension
P.O. Box 231
New Brunswick, NJ 08903
908-932-9306

Attorney Grievances & Fee Arbitration
Supreme Court of New
Jersey
Richard J. Hughes Justice
Complex, CN-963
Trenton, NJ 08625
609-292-8750

Client Protection Trust Fund
Supreme Court of New
Jersey
Richard J. Hughes Justice
Complex, CN-961

Trenton, NJ 08625
609-984-7179

State Consumer Protection Office
Division of Consumer
Affairs
P.O. Box 45025
Newark, NJ 07101
201-504-6200

HUD Field Office
Military Park Bldg.
60 Park Pl.
Newark, NJ 07102
201-877-1662

State Insurance Commissioner
Commissioner
Department of Insurance
20 W. State St.
CN-329
Trenton, NJ 08625
609-292-5363

State Government Banking Commissioner
Commissioner of Banking
20 W. State St.
CN-040
Trenton, NJ 08625
609-292-3421

State Office on Aging
Aging Division
Community Affairs
Department
101 S. Broad St., CN807
Trenton, NJ 08625
609-292-4833

State Utility Commission
Board of Public Utilities
Two Gateway Center
Newark, NJ 07102
201-648-2027
800-624-0241 (NJ only)

New Mexico

Federal Information Center
Albuquerque; 800-359-3997
All Other Locations;
301-722-9098

State Information Office
505-827-4011

Cooperative Extension Office
Dr. Jerry Schickenanz
New Mexico State
University
Box 3AE
Las Cruces, NM 88003
505-646-3016

Attorney Grievances
Disciplinary Board of the
Supreme Court of New
Mexico
400 Gold SW, Suite 800
Albuquerque, NM 87102
505-842-5781

Fee Arbitration
State Bar of New Mexico
Fee Arbitration Committee
P.O. Box 25883
Albuquerque, NM 87125
505-842-6132
800-876-6227 (NM only)

State Consumer Protection Office
Consumer Protection
Division
Office of Attorney General
P.O. Drawer 1508
Santa Fe, NM 87504
505-827-6060
800-678-1508 (NM only)

HUD Field Office
625 Truman St., NE
Albuquerque, NM 87110
505-262-6463

State Insurance Commissioner
Superintendent of
Insurance
P.O. Drawer 1269
Santa Fe, NM 87504-1269
505-827-4500

Nursing Home Ombudsmen
Agency on Aging
228 East Palace Ave.
Ground Floor
Santa Fe, NM 87501
505-827-7640
or toll free in-state:
800-432-2080

State Government
Banking Commissioner
Director, Financial
Institutions Division
P.O. Box 25101
Santa Fe, NM 87504
505-827-7100

State Office on Aging
State Agency on Aging

228 E. Palance Ave.
Santa Fe, NM 87501
505-827-7640

State Utility Commission
Public Service Commission
224 E. Palace Ave.
Santa Fe, NM 87501-2013
505-827-6940

New York

Federal Information Center
Albany, Buffalo, New York,
Rochester, Syracuse;
800-347-1997
All Other Locations;
301-722-9098

State Information Office
518-474-2121

Cooperative Extension Office
Lucinda Noble, Director
Cornell Cooperative
Extension
276 Roberts Hall
Ithaca, NY 14853
607-255-2237

Attorney Grievances
Departmental Disciplinary
Committee for the First
Judicial Department
41 Madison Ave., 39th Fl.
New York, NY 10010
212-685-1000

New York State Grievance
Committee for the 2nd and
11th Judicial Districts
210 Joralemon St.
Municipal Bldg.
Room 1200

Brooklyn, NY 11201
718-624-7851

Grievance Committee for
the 9th Judicial District
Crosswest Office Center
399 Knollwood Rd., #200
White Plains, NY 10603
914-949-4540

New York State Grievance
Committee for the 10th
Judicial District
900 Ellison Ave., Suite 304
Westbury, NY 11590
516-364-7344

3rd Department Committee
on Professional Standards
Alfred E. Smith Bldg.
22nd Floor
P.O. Box 7013
Capitol Station Annex
Albany, NY 12225-0013
518-474-8816

Appellate Division
Supreme Court
4th Judicial Department
Office of Grievance
Committee
1036 Ellicott Square Bldg.
Buffalo, NY 14203
716-858-1190

Lawyers' Fund for Client Protection
55 Elk St.
Albany, NY 12210
518-474-8438
800-442-3863 (NY only)

State Consumer Protection Offices
Bureau of Consumer
Frauds and Protection
NY State Dept. of Law
The Capitol
Albany, NY 12224
518-474-5481

Bureau of Consumer
Frauds and Protection
Office of Attorney General
120 Broadway
New York, NY 10271
212-416-8345

HUD Field Offices
(Upstate)
Lafayette Ct., 465 Main St.
Buffalo, NY 14203
716-846-5755

(Downstate)
26 Federal Plaza
New York, NY 10278
212-264-6500

State Insurance Commissioner
Superintendent of

Insurance
160 W. Broadway
New York, NY 10013-3393
212-602-0249
800-342-3736

Nursing Home Ombudsmen
Office for the Aging
Agency Building A
Empire State Plaza
Albany, NY 12223
518-474-5731
or toll free in-state:
800-342-9871 (NY only)

State Government Banking Commissioner
Superintendent of Banks
Two Rector St.
New York, NY 10006
212-618-6642
800-522-3330

State Office on Aging
Aging Office
Bldg. 2
Empire State Plaza
Albany, NY 12223-001
518-474-4425

State Utility Commission
Public Service Commission
3 Empire State Plaza
Albany, NY 12223
518-474-7080
800-342-3377 (NY only)

North Carolina

Federal Information Center
Charlotte; 800-347-1997
All Other Locations;
301-722-9098

State Information Office
919-733-1110

Cooperative Extension Offices
Dr. Robert C. Wells,
Director
Cooperative Extension Svc.
North Carolina State
University
Box 7602
Raleigh, NC 27695
919-515-2811

Dr. Daniel Godfrey, Director
Cooperative Extension
Program
North Carolina A&T State
University
P.O. Box 21928
Greensboro, NC
27420-1928
910-334-7956

Attorney Grievances, Client Security Trust Fund, & Fee Arbitration
North Carolina State Bar

P.O. Box 25908
Raleigh, NC 27611
919-828-4620

State Consumer Protection Office
Consumer Protection
Division
Office of Attorney General
P.O. Box 629
Raleigh, NC 27602
919-733-7741

HUD Field Office
2306 W. Meadowview Rd.
Greensboro, NC 27407
919-547-4000

State Insurance Commissioner
Commissioner of Insurance
Dobbs Bldg.
P.O. Box 26387
Raleigh, NC 27611
919-733-7343
800-662-7777

Nursing Home Ombudsmen
Division of Aging
Department of Human
Resources
693 Palmer Dr.
Raleigh, NC 27626-0531

919-733-3983
or toll free in-state:
800-662-7030

State Government
Banking Commissioner
Commissioner of Banks
P.O. Box 29512
Raleigh, NC 27626
919-733-3016

State Office on Aging
Aging Division
Human Resources Dept.
693 Palmer Dr.
Raleigh, NC 27603
919-733-3983

State Utility Commission
Utilities Commission
P.O. Box 29510
Raleigh, NC 27626-0510
919-733-4249

North Dakota

Federal Information Center
All Locations; 301-722-9098

State Information Office
701-224-2000

Cooperative Extension Office
Bob Cristman, Director
Cooperative Extension
Service
North Dakota State
University
Morrill Hall, Room 311
Box 5437
Fargo, ND 58105
701-237-8944

Attorney Grievances
Disciplinary Board of the
Supreme Court
P.O. Box 2297
Bismarck, ND 58502
701-328-3925

Client Security Trust Fund & Fee Arbitration
State Bar Association of
North Dakota
P.O. Box 2136
Bismarck, ND 58502
701-255-1404
800-472-2685 (ND only)

State Consumer Protection Office
Consumer Fraud Division
Office of Attorney General
600 E. Blvd.
Bismarck, ND 58505
701-328-3404
800-472-2600 (ND only)

HUD Field Office
Executive Tower Bldg.
1405 Curtis St.
Denver, CO 80202
303-844-4513

State Insurance Commissioner
Commissioner of Insurance
Capitol Bldg., 5th Floor
600 E. Boulevard Ave.
Bismarck, ND 58505
701-224-2440
800-247-0560

Nursing Home Ombudsmen
Aging Services
Department of Human
Services
1929 N. Washington St.
Bismarck, ND 58505
701-224-2310
or toll free in-state:
800-472-2622

State Government
Banking Commissioner
Commissioner of Banking
and Financial Institutions
600 E. Boulevard
13th Floor
Bismarck, ND 58501
701-224-2256

State Office on Aging
Aging Services Division

Human Services Dept.
1929 N. Washington
P.O. Box 7070
Bismarck, ND 58507-7070
701-328-2577

State Utility Commission
Public Service Commission
State Capitol Building
Bismarck, ND 58505
701-328-2400

Ohio

Federal Information Center
Akron, Cincinnati,
Cleveland, Columbus,
Dayton, Toledo;
800-347-1997
All Other Locations;
301-722-9098

State Information Office
614-466-2000

Cooperative Extension Office
Keith Smith, Director
OSU Extension
2120 Fiffe Rd.
Agriculture Administration
Building
Columbus, OH 43210
614-292-6181

Attorney Grievances
Office of Disciplinary
Counsel of the Supreme
Court of Ohio
175 S. 3rd St., Suite 280
Columbus, OH 43215
614-461-0256

Clients' Security Fund
175 S. 3rd St.
Suite 285
Columbus, OH 43215

614-221-0562
800-231-1680 (OH only)

Fee Arbitration
Ohio State Bar Association
1700 Lake Shore Dr.
P.O. Box 16562
Columbus, OH 43216-6562
614-487-2050
800-282-6556 (OH only)

State Consumer Protection Office
Consumer Protection
Division
Office of Attorney General
30 E. Broad St.
State Office Tower
25th Floor
Columbus, OH 43266-0410
614-466-4986
800-282-0515 (OH only)

HUD Field Offices
Federal Office Bldg.
550 Main St., Room 9002
Cincinnati, OH 45202
513-684-2884

One Playhouse Sq.
1375 Euclid Ave.
Room 420
Cleveland, OH 44114
216-522-4058

200 N. High St.
Columbus, OH 43215
614-469-5737

State Insurance Commissioner
Director of Insurance
2100 Stella Court
Columbus, OH 43266-0566
614-644-2651
800-686-1526 (consumer)
800-686-1527 (fraud)

Nursing Home Ombudsmen
Department of Aging
50 West Broad St.
9th Floor
Columbus, OH 43266-0501
614-466-5500
toll free in-state:
800-282-1206

State Government Banking Commissioner
Superintendent of Banks
77 S. High St.
21st Floor
Columbus, OH 43266-0549
614-466-2932

State Office on Aging
Aging Department
50 W. Broad St.
8th Floor
Columbus, OH 43215-5928
614-466-7246

State Utility Commission
Public Utilities Commission
180 E. Broad St.
Columbus, OH 43215-3793
614-466-3016
800-686-7826 (OH only)

Oklahoma

Federal Information Center
Oklahoma City, Tulsa;
800-366-2998
All Other Locations;
301-722-9098

State Information Office
405-521-2011

Cooperative Extension Offices
Dr. Ray Campbell
Interim Associate Director
Oklahoma Cooperative
Extension Service
Oklahoma State University
139 Agriculture Hall
Stillwater, OK 74078
405-744-5398

Dr. Ocleris Simpston,
Director
Cooperative Research and
Extension
P.O. Box 730
Langston University
Langston, OK 73050
405-466-3836

Attorney Grievances, Client Security Trust Fund, & Fee Arbitration
General Counsel

Oklahoma Bar Center
1901 N. Lincoln Blvd.
P.O. Box 53036
Oklahoma City, OK 73152
405-524-2365

State Consumer Protection Office
Consumer Protection Unit
Office of Attorney General
2300 N. Lincoln
Room 112
Oklahoma City, OK 73105-4894
405-521-4274

HUD Field Office
Murrah Federal Bldg.
200 NW 5th St.
Oklahoma City, OK 73102
405-231-4181

State Insurance Commissioner
Insurance Commissioner
P.O. Box 53408
Oklahoma City, OK 73152
405-521-2828
800-522-0071

Nursing Home Ombudsmen
Special Unit on Aging
P.O. Box 25352

Oklahoma City, OK 73125
405-521-2281

**State Government
Banking Commissioner**
Bank Commissioner
4545 N. Lincoln Blvd.
Suite 16
Oklahoma City, OK 73105
405-521-2783

State Office on Aging
Aging Services Division

Human Services Dept.
P.O. Box 25352
Oklahoma City, OK 73125
405-521-2327

State Utility Commission
Corporation Commission
Jim Thorpe Office Building
P.O. Box 52000-2000
Oklahoma City, OK 73152-2000
405-521-2264

Oregon

Federal Information Center
Portland; 800-726-4995
All Other Locations;
301-722-9098

State Information Office
503-378-3111

Cooperative Extension Office
O.E. Smith, Director
Oregon State Extension
Service Administration
Oregon State University
Ballard Extension Hall #101
Corvallis, OR 97331-3606
503-737-2711

Attorney Grievances & Client Security Trust Fund
Oregon State Bar
P.O. Box 1689
Lake Oswego, OR 97035
503-620-0222

State Consumer Protection Office
Financial Fraud Section
Consumer Complaints
1162 Court St., NE
Department of Justice
Justice Building
Salem, OR 97310
503-378-4320

HUD Field Office
520 SW 6th Ave.
Portland, OR 97204
503-326-2561

State Insurance Commissioner
Insurance Commissioner
440 Labor & Industries
Bldg.
Salem, OR 97310
503-378-4271

Nursing Home Ombudsmen
Office of LTC Ombudsman
2475 Lancaster Dr.
Bldg. B, #9
Salem, OR 97310
503-378-6533
or toll free in-state:
800-522-2602

State Government Banking Commissioner
Administrator
Division of Finance and
Corporate Securities
21 Labor & Industries Bldg.
Salem, OR 97310
503-378-4140

State Office on Aging
Senior and Disabled
Services
500 Summer St., NE
Salem, OR 97310-1015
503-945-5811

State Utility Commission
Public Utility Commission
550 Capital St., NE
Salem, OR 97310
503-378-6611
800-522-2404 (OR only)

Pennsylvania

Federal Information Center
Philadelphia, Pittsburgh;
800-347-1997
All Other Locations;
301-722-9098

State Information Office
717-787-2121

Cooperative Extension Office
Dean Hood, Director
Pennsylvania State
University
Room 217, A.G.
Administration
University Park, PA 16802
814-863-0331

Attorney Grievances & Fee Arbitration
District 1:
Office of the Disciplinary
Counsel
121 S. Broad St.
Suite 2100
N. American Building
Philadelphia, PA 19107
215-560-6296

District 2:
Office of the Disciplinary
Counsel

One Montgomery Plaza
Suite 411
Norristown, PA 19401
610-270-1896

District 3:
Office of the Disciplinary
Counsel
2 Lemoyne Dr.
2nd Floor
Lemoyne, PA 17043
717-731-7073

District 4:
Office of the Disciplinary
Counsel
Suite 400
Union Trust Building
501 Grant St.
Pittsburgh, PA 15219
412-565-3173

Pennsylvania Client Security Fund
1515 Market St.
Suite 1420
Philadelphia, PA 19102
215-560-6335

State Consumer Protection Office
Bureau of Consumer
Protection
Office of Attorney General

Strawberry Square
14th Floor
Harrisburg, PA 17120
717-787-9707
800-441-2555 (PA only)

HUD Field Offices
(Western)
412 Old Post Office &
Courthouse Bldg.
700 Grant St.
Pittsburgh, PA 15219
412-644-6428

(Eastern)
Liberty Square Bldg.
105 S. 7th St.
Philadelphia, PA 19106-
3392
215-597-2560

**State Insurance
Commissioner**
Insurance Commissioner
1326 Strawberry Square
Harrisburg, PA 17120
717-787-5173

**Nursing Home
Ombudsmen**
Department of Aging
400 Market Sq.
State Office Bldg
4th Floor
Harrisburg, PA 17101-2301
717-783-3126

**State Government
Banking Commissioner**
Secretary of Banking
333 Market St., 16th Floor
Harrisburg, PA 17101-2290
717-787-6991
800-PA-BANKS

State Office on Aging
Aging Department
400 Market St.
State Office Bldg., 6th Floor
Harrisburg, PA 17101-2301
717-783-1550

State Utility Commission
Public Utility Commission
P.O. Box 3265
Harrisburg, PA 17120
717-783-1740
800-782-1110 (PA only)

Rhode Island

Federal Information Center
Providence; 800-347-1997
All Other Locations;
301-722-9098

State Information Office
401-277-2000

Cooperative Extension Office
Kathleen Mallon, Director
Cooperative Extension
Education Center
University of Rhode Island
East Alumni Ave.
Kingston, RI 02881-0804
401-792-2900

Attorney Grievances & Fee Arbitration
Disciplinary Board of the
Supreme Court of Rhode
Island
D.B. of the S.C.
John E. Fogarty Judicial
Annex
24 Weybuffet St., 2nd Floor
Providence, RI 02903
401-277-3270

Client Security Trust Fund
Rhode Island Bar

Association
115 Cedar St.
Providence, RI 02903
401-421-5740

State Consumer Protection Office
Consumer Protection
Division
Dept. of Attorney General
72 Pine St.
Providence, RI 02903
401-274-4400
800-852-7776

HUD Field Office
330 John O. Pastore
Federal Bldg. and
U.S. Post Office
Kennedy Plaza
Providence, RI 02903
401-528-5351

State Insurance Commissioner
Insurance Commissioner
233 Richmond St.
Providence, RI 02903
401-277-2246

Nursing Home Ombudsmen
Department of Elderly
Affairs

160 Pine St.
Providence, RI 02903-3708
401-277-2880
or toll free in-state:
800-322-2880

**State Government
Banking Commissioner**
Director and
Superintendent of Banking
and Securities
233 Richmond St.
Suite 231
Providence, RI 02903-4231
401-277-2405

State Office on Aging
Elderly Affairs Department
160 Pine St.
Providence, RI 02903
401-277-2858

State Utility Commission
Public Utilities Commission
100 Orange St.
Providence, RI 02903
401-277-3500
800-341-1000 (RI only)

South Carolina

Federal Information Center
All Locations; 301-722-9098

State Information Office
803-734-1000

Cooperative Extension Offices
E.V. Jones, Director
Clemson University
Cooperative Extension
Service
P.O. Box 995
Pickens, SC 29671
803-868-2810

Director
Cooperative Extension
Service
P.O. Box 7265
South Carolina State
University
Orangeburg, SC 29117
803-536-8928

Attorney Grievances
Grievance Commission
South Carolina Supreme
Court
P.O. Box 11330
Columbia, SC 29211
803-734-2038

Client Security Trust Fund & Fee Arbitration
South Carolina Bar
P.O. Box 608
Columbia, SC 29202-0608
803-799-6653

State Consumer Protection Office
Department of Consumer
Affairs
P.O. Box 5757
Columbia, SC 29250
803-734-9452
800-922-1594 (SC only)

HUD Field Office
Strom Thurmond Federal
Bldg.
1835 Assembly St.
Columbia, SC 29201
803-765-5592

State Insurance Commissioner
Chief Insurance
Commissioner
P.O. Box 100105
Columbia, SC 29202-3105
803-737-6117
800-768-3467

Nursing Home Ombudsmen
Office of the Governor
Division of Ombudsman
and Citizens' Service
1205 Pendleton St.
Suite 308
Columbia, SC 29201
803-734-0457

State Government Banking Commissioner
Commissioner of Banking
1015 Sumter St.
Room 309
Columbia, SC 20201
803-734-2001

State Office on Aging
Aging Division
Executive Policy and
Programs Office
202 Arbor Lake Dr.
Suite 301
Columbia, SC 29223
803-737-7500

State Utility Commission
Public Service Commission
P.O. Drawer 11649
Columbia, SC 29211
803-737-5100
800-922-1531 (SC only)

South Dakota

Federal Information Center
All Locations; 301-722-9098

State Information Office
605-773-3011

Cooperative Extension Office
Mylo Hellickson, Director
SDSU
Box 2270D
AG Hall 154
Brookings, SD 57007
605-688-4792

Attorney Grievances
State Bar of South Dakota
Attn: Tom Barnett
222 East Capitol
Pierre, SD 57501
605-224-7554

Client Security Trust Fund
State Bar of South Dakota
222 E. Capitol
Pierre, SD 57501
605-224-7554
800-952-2333 (SD only)

State Consumer Protection Office
Div. of Consumer Affairs

Office of Attorney General
500 East Capitol
Capitol Building
Pierre, SD 57501
605-773-4400
800-300-1986 (SD only)

HUD Field Office
Executive Towers Bldg.
1405 Curtis St.
Denver, CO 80202
303-844-4513

State Insurance Commissioner
Director of Insurance
Insurance Bldg.
500 E. Capitol St.
Pierre, SD 57501
605-773-3563

Nursing Home Ombudsmen
Office of Adult Services and Aging
700 Governor Dr.
Pierre, SD 57501
605-773-3656

State Government Banking Commissioner
Director of Banking
State Capitol Bldg.
500 E. Capitol Ave.

Pierre, SD 57501-5070
605-773-3421

Pierre, SD 57501
605-773-3656

State Office on Aging
Adult Services on Aging
Office
Social Services Department
700 Governors Dr.

State Utility Commission
Public Utilities Commission
500 E. Capitol Ave.
Pierre, SD 57501
605-773-3201

Tennessee

Federal Information Center
Chattanooga; 800-347-1997
Memphis, Nashville;
800-366-2998

State Information Office
615-741-3011

Cooperative Extension Offices
Billy G. Hicks, Dean
Agricultural Extension
Service
University of Tennessee
P.O. Box 1071
Knoxville, TN 37901-1071
615-974-7114

Cherry Lane Zon
Schmittou, Extension
Leader
Davidson County
Agricultural Service
Tennessee State University
800 Second Ave. N.
Suite 3
Nashville, TN 37201-1084
615-254-8734

Attorney Grievances & Fee Arbitration
Board of Professional
Responsibility of the

Supreme Court of
Tennessee
1101 Kermit Dr., Suite 730
Nashville, TN 37217
615-361-7500

State Consumer Protection Office
Division of Consumer
Affairs
500 James Robertson
Parkway, 5th Floor
Nashville, TN 37243-0600
615-741-4737
800-342-8385 (TN only)

HUD Field Offices
710 Locust St., 3rd Floor
Knoxville, TN 37902
615-549-4384

251 Cumberland Bend Dr.
Suite 200
Nashville, TN 37228
615-763-5213

State Insurance Commissioner
Commissioner of Insurance
500 James Robertson
Parkway
Nashville, TN 37243-0565
615-741-2241
800-342-4029

**Nursing Home
Ombudsmen**
Commission on Aging
500 Deaderick St.
9th Floor
Nashville, TN 37243-0860
615-741-2056

**State Government
Banking Commissioner**
Commissioner
Financial Institutions
John Sevier Bldg.
500 Charlotte Ave.
4th Floor
Nashville, TN 37243
615-741-2236

State Office on Aging
Aging Commission
500 Deaderick St.
Andrew Jackson Bldg.
9th Floor
Nashville, TN 37243-0860
615-741-2056

State Utility Commission
Public Service Commission
460 James Robertson
Parkway
Nashville, TN 37243
615-741-2904
800-342-8359 (TN only)

Texas

Federal Information Center
Austin, Dallas, Fort Worth, Houston, San Antonio;
800-366-2998
All Other Locations;
301-722-9098

State Information Office
512-463-4630

Cooperative Extension Offices
Dr. Zerle Carpenter, Director
Texas Agricultural Extension Service
Texas A&M University
College Station, TX 77843
409-845-7967

Hoover Carden, Director
Cooperative Extension Program
P.O. Box Drawer-B
Prairie View, TX
77446-2867
409-857-2023

Attorney Grievances, Client Security Trust Fund, & Fee Arbitration
State Bar of Texas
P.O. Box 12487

Capitol Station
Austin, TX 78711-1648
512-463-1463

State Consumer Protection Office
Consumer Protection Div.
Office of Attorney General
Capitol Station
P.O. Box 12548
Austin, TX 78711
512-463-2070
800-621-0508 (TX only)

HUD Field Offices
1600 Throckmorton
P.O. Box 2905
Fort Worth, TX 76113
817-885-5401

Norfolk Tower
2211 Norfolk
Suite 200
Houston, TX 77098
713-963-3274

Washington Square
800 Dolorosa
San Antonio, TX 78207
512-229-6800

State Insurance Commissioner
Director

Claims and Compliance
Division
State Board of Insurance
P.O. Box 149091
Austin, TX 78714-9091
512-463-6515
800-252-3439

Nursing Home
Ombudsmen
Department on Aging
P.O. Box 12786
Capitol Station
Austin, TX 78711
512-444-2727
or toll free in-state:
800-252-2412

State Government
Banking Commissioner
Banking Commissioner
2601 N. Lamar Blvd.
Austin, TX 78705-4207
512-479-1200

State Office on Aging
Aging Department
Box 12786
Austin, TX 78711
512-444-2727

State Utility Commission
Public Utility Commission
7800 Shoal Creek Blvd.
Austin, TX 78757
512-458-0100

Utah

Federal Information Center
Salt Lake City;
800-359-3997
All Other Locations;
301-722-9098

State Information Office
801-538-3000

Cooperative Extension Office
Dr. Robert Gilliland
Vice President for
Extension and Continuing
Education
Utah State University
Logan, UT 84322-4900
801-750-2200

Attorney Grievances & Fee Arbitration
Bar Counsel
Utah State Bar
645 S. 200 East
Salt Lake City, UT 84111-3834
801-531-9110

Client Security Trust Fund
Bar Counsel
Utah State Bar
645 S. 200 East

Salt Lake City, UT 84111-3834
801-531-9077

State Consumer Protection Office
Division of Consumer
Protection
Department of Commerce
160 E. 3rd South
P.O. Box 45804
Salt Lake City, UT 84145
801-530-6601

HUD Field Office
Executive Tower Bldg.
1405 Curtis St.
Denver, CO 80202
303-844-4513

State Insurance Commissioner
Commissioner of Insurance
3110 State Office Bldg.
Salt Lake City, UT 84114
801-538-3800

Nursing Home Ombudsmen
Division of Aging and Adult
Services
P.O. Box 45500
Salt Lake City, UT 84145
801-538-3920

State Government
Banking Commissioner
Commissioner
Financial Institutions
P.O. Box 89
Salt Lake City, UT
84110-0089
801-538-8830

State Office on Aging
Aging and Adult Services
Division

Human Services Dept.
P.O. Box 65729
Salt Lake City, UT 84165-
0729
801-487-3465

State Utility Commission
Public Service Commission
160 E. 300 South
P.O. Box 45585
Salt Lake City, UT 84145
801-530-6716

Vermont

Federal Information Center
All Locations; 301-722-9098

State Information Office
802-828-1110

Cooperative Extension Office
Larry Forchier, Dean
Division of Agriculture,
Natural Resources, and
Extension
University of Vermont
601 Main
Burlington, VT 05401-3439
802-656-2990

Attorney Grievances
Professional Conduct Board
C/O Bar Counsel
59 Elm St.
Montpelier, VT 05602
802-828-3368

Client Security Trust Fund & Fee Arbitration
Vermont Bar Association
P.O. Box 100
Montpelier, VT 05601
802-223-2020

State Consumer Protection Office
Public Protection Division
Office of Attorney General
109 State St.
Montpelier, VT 05609
802-828-3171

HUD Field Office
Norris Cotton Federal Bldg.
275 Chestnut St.
Manchester, NH 03101
603-666-7681

State Insurance Commissioner
Commissioner of Banking
and Insurance
89 Main St., Drawer 20
Montpelier, VT 05620
802-828-3301

Nursing Home Ombudsmen
Vermont Legal Aid
18 Main St.
St. Johnsbury, VT 05819
802-748-8721

State Government Banking Commissioner
Commissioner
Banking and Insurance

89 Main St.
Drawer 20
Montpelier, VT 05620-3101
802-828-3301

State Office on Aging
Central Vermont Council on
Aging
18 S. Main St.

Barre, VT 05641-4897
802-479-0531

State Utility Commission
Public Service Board
112 State St.
State Office Building
Montpelier, VT 05620
802-828-2358
800-622-4496 (VT only)

Virginia

Federal Information Center
Norfolk, Richmond,
Roanoke; 800-347-1997
All Other Locations;
301-722-9098

State Information Office
804-786-0000

Cooperative Extension Offices
Dr. William Allen, Interim
Director
Virginia Cooperative
Extension
Virginia Tech
Blacksburg, VA 24061-0402
703-231-5299

Lorenza Lyons, Director
Cooperative Extension
Virginia State University
Petersburg, VA 23806
804-524-5961

Attorney Grievances
Virginia State Bar
707 E. Main St.
Suite 1500
Attn: June Fletcher, Esquire
Richmond, VA 23219-2900
804-775-0500

Client Security Trust Fund
Virginia State Bar
707 E. Main St., Suite 1500
Attn: Susan Busch
Richmond, VA 23219-2900
804-775-0500

State Consumer Protection Office
Div. of Consumer Affairs
P.O. Box 1163
Richmond, VA 23209
804-786-2042
800-552-9963 (VA only)

HUD Field Office
3600 West Broad St.
P.O. Box 90331
Richmond, VA 23230
804-278-4559

State Insurance Commissioner
Commissioner of Insurance
700 Jefferson Bldg.
P.O. Box 1157
Richmond, VA 23209
804-371-9741
800-552-7945

Nursing Home Ombudsmen
Department for the Aging

700 East Franklin St.
10th Floor
Richmond, VA 23219
804-225-2271
toll free in-state:
800-552-3402

**State Government
Banking Commissioner**
Commissioner
Financial Institutions
P.O. Box 640
Richmond, VA 23205-0640
804-371-9704
800-552-7945

State Office on Aging
Aging Department
700 E. Franklin St.
10th Floor
Richmond, VA 23219-2327
804-225-2271

State Utility Commission
State Corporation
Commission
P.O. Box 1197
Richmond, VA 23209
804-371-9967
800-552-7945 (VA only)

Washington

Federal Information Center
Seattle, Tacoma;
800-726-4995
All Other Locations;
301-722-9098

State Information Office
206-753-5000

Cooperative Extension Office
Harry Burcalow, Interim
Director
Cooperative Extension
411 Hulbert
Washington State
University
Pullman, WA 99164-6230
509-335-2811

Attorney Grievances, Client Security Program, & Fee Arbitration
Washington State Bar
Association
500 Westin Bldg.
2001 6th Ave.
Seattle, WA 98121-2599
206-727-8200

State Consumer Protection Office
Consumer and Business

Fair Practice Division
Office of Attorney General
900 4th Ave.
Suite 2000
Seattle, WA 98164
206-464-6684
800-551-4636 (WA only)

HUD Field Office
Arcade Plaza Bldg
1321 2nd Ave.
Seattle, WA 98101
206-553-5414

State Insurance Commissioner
Insurance Commissioner
Insurance Bldg. AQ21
P.O. Box 40255
Olympia, WA 98504-0255
206-753-7301
800-562-6900

Nursing Home Ombudsmen
South King County Multi-
Service Center
1200 South 336 St.
P.O. Box 23699
Federal Way, WA 98903-
0699
206-838-6810
800-422-1384

State Government
Banking Commissioner
Supervisor of Banking
P.O. Box 41200
Olympia, WA 98504
206-753-6520

State Office on Aging
Aging and Adult Services
P.O. Box 45600

Olympia, WA 98504
206-493-2500

State Utility Commission
Utilities and Transportation
Commission
1300 Evergreen Park Dr.,
South
Olympia, WA 98504
206-753-6423
800-562-6150 (WA only)

West Virginia

**Federal Information
Center**
All Locations; 301-722-9098

State Information Office
304-558-3456

**Cooperative Extension
Office**
Rachael Tompkins, Director
Cooperative Extension
305 Stewart Hall
P.O. Box 6201
West Virginia University
Morgantown, WV 26506-
6201
304-293-3408

**Attorney Grievances and
Client Security Trust
Fund**
West Virginia State Bar
2006 Kanawha Blvd. East
Charleston, WV 25311
304-558-2456

**State Consumer
Protection Office**
Consumer Protection
Division
Office of Attorney General
812 Quarrier St.
6th Floor
Charleston, WV 25301

304-558-8986
800-368-8808 (WV only)

HUD Field Office
405 Capitol St.
Suite 708
Charleston, WV 25301
304-347-7000

**State Insurance
Commissioner**
Insurance Commissioner
2019 Washington St., E.
Charleston, WV 25305
304-558-3394
800-642-9004

**Nursing Home
Ombudsmen**
Commission on Aging
State Capitol
1900 Kanola Blvd
East, Holly Grove
Charleston, WV 25305
304-558-3317

**State Government
Banking Commissioner**
Commissioner of Banking
State Capitol Complex
Bldg. 3, Room 311
Charleston, WV 25305
304-558-2294
800-642-9056

State Office on Aging
Aging Commission
State Capitol, Holly Grove
Charleston, WV 25305
304-558-3317

State Utility Commission
Public Service Commission
P.O. Box 812
Charleston, WV 25323-0812
304-340-0300
800-344-5113 (WV only)

Wisconsin

Federal Information Center
Milwaukee; 800-366-2998
All Other Locations;
301-722-9098

State Information Office
608-266-2211

Cooperative Extension Office
Aeyse Somersan, Director
432 N. Lake St., Room 601
Madison, WI 53706
608-262-7966

Attorney Grievances
Board of Attorneys
Professional Responsibility
Tenney Bldg.
110 E. Main St., Room 410
Madison, WI 53703
608-267-7274

Client Security Trust Fund and Fee Arbitration
State Bar of Wisconsin
P.O. Box 7158
Madison, WI 53707
608-257-3838

State Consumer Protection Office
Office of Consumer

Protection and Citizen
Advocacy
Department of Justice
P.O. Box 7856
Madison, WI 53707-7856
608-266-1852
800-362-8189 (WI only)

HUD Field Office
Henry Rouss Federal Plaza
310 W. Wisconsin Ave.
Milwaukee, WI 53203
414-297-3214

State Insurance Commissioner
Commissioner of Insurance
P.O. Box 7873
Madison, WI 53707-7873
608-266-3585
800-236-8517

Nursing Home Ombudsmen
Board on Aging and Long
Term Care
214 N. Hamilton St.
Madison, WI 53703
608-266-8944

State Government Banking Commissioner
Commissioner of Banking
131 W. Wilson

8th Floor
P.O. Box 7876
Madison, WI 53707-7876
608-266-1621

State Office on Aging
Aging and Long Term Care
Board
217 S. Hamilton St.

Madison, WI 53703
608-266-2536

State Utility Commission
Public Service Commission
4802 Sheboygan Ave.
Madison, WI 53707
608-266-2001

Wyoming

Federal Information Center
All Locations; 301-722-9098

State Information Office
307-777-7011

Cooperative Extension Office
Jim Debree, Director
CES
University of Wyoming
Box 3354
Laramie, WY 82071
307-766-3567

Attorney Grievances, Client Security Trust Fund, & Fee Arbitration
Wyoming State Bar
P.O. Box 109
Cheyenne, WY 82003-0109
307-632-9061

State Consumer Protection Office
Consumer Affairs
Office of Attorney General
123 State Capitol Bldg.
Cheyenne, WY 82002
307-777-7841

HUD Field Office
Executive Tower Bldg.

1405 Curtis St.
Denver, CO 80202
303-844-4513

State Insurance Commissioner
Commissioner of Insurance
Herschler Bldg.
122 W. 25th St
Cheyenne, WY 82002
307-777-7401
800-438-5768

Nursing Home Ombudsmen
Long Term Care
Ombudsman
900 9th St.
Wheatland, WY 82201
307-322-5553

State Government Banking Commissioner
Manager, Div. of Banking
Herschler Bldg.
3rd Floor E.
Cheyenne, WY 82002
307-777-6600

State Utility Commission
Public Service Commission
700 W. 21st St.
Cheyenne, WY 82002
307-777-7427

Index

- A -

- B -

      Information USA, Inc.

- C -

Information USA, Inc.

- D -

- E -

- F -

- G -

- I -

- K -

- L -

- M -

- N -

- O -

- P -

         Information USA, Inc.

- Q -

- R -

- S -

- T -

- U -

- V -

- W -

Information USA, Inc.